Outline
(See everything you are going to learn)

Defined
(Learn what the concept is)

Explained
(Understand the concept)

Applied
(See how it is used and why you should care)

Example
(See the concept in action)

Visual Summary
(Tie everything back together with a visual summary)

To my wife, Denise, and daughters, Colette and Elyse

—**Michael Levens**

Marketing: Defined, Explained, Applied

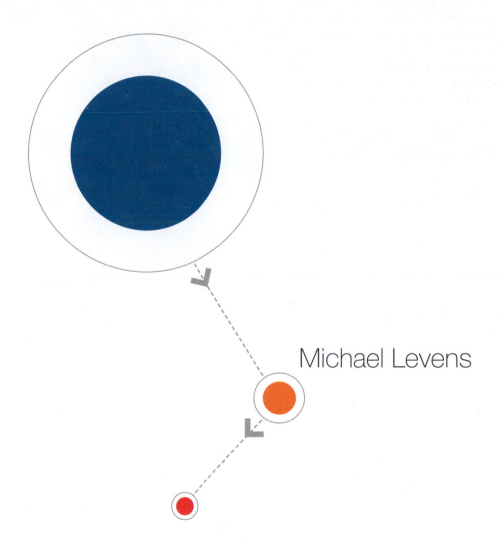

Michael Levens

Marketing: Defined, Explained, Applied

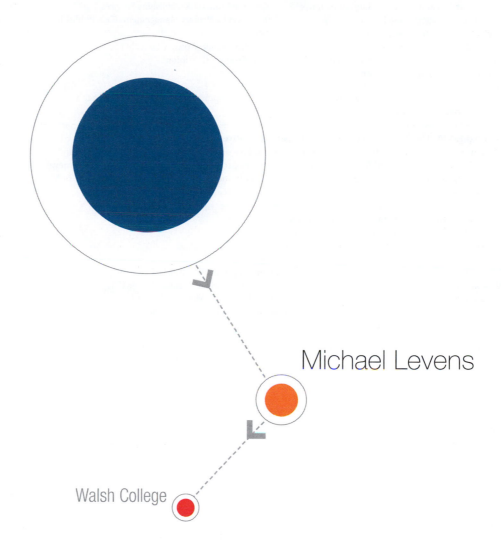

Michael Levens

Walsh College

Prentice Hall

Upper Saddle River, New Jersey

Library of Congress Cataloging-in-Publication information is on file.

Executive Editor: Melissa Sabella
Editorial Director: Sally Yagan
Editor in Chief: Eric Svendsen
Development Editor: Laura Town
Product Development Manager: Ashley Santora
Editorial Assistant: Karin Williams
Director of Marketing: Patrice Lumumba Jones
Marketing Manager: Anne Fahlgren
Marketing Assistant: Susan Osterlitz
Senior Managing Editor: Judy Leale
Senior Operations Specialist: Arnold Vila
Operations Specialist: Ben Smith

Art Director: Blair Brown
Designer: Blair Brown
Cover Designer: Blair Brown
Manager, Rights and Permissions: Zina Arabia
Manager, Visual Research: Beth Brenzel
Image Permission Coordinator: Angelique Sharps
Composition: GEX Publishing Services
Full-Service Project Management: GEX Publishing Services
Printer/Binder: Courier/Kendallville
Typeface: 10/12 Minion

Credits and acknowledgments borrowed from other sources and reproduced, with permission, in this textbook appear on appropriate page within text.

Pearson Prentice Hall™ is a trademark of Pearson Education, Inc.
Pearson® is a registered trademark of Pearson plc
Prentice Hall® is a registered trademark of Pearson Education, Inc.

Pearson Education Ltd., London
Pearson Education Singapore, Pte. Ltd
Pearson Education, Canada, Inc.
Pearson Education–Japan
Pearson Education Australia PTY, Limited

Pearson Education North Asia, Ltd., Hong Kong
Pearson Educación de Mexico, S.A. de C.V.
Pearson Education Malaysia, Pte. Ltd
Pearson Education Upper Saddle River, New Jersey

10 9 8 7 6 5 4 3 2 1

Prentice Hall
is an imprint of

www.pearsonhighered.com

ISBN-13: 978-0-13-607569-1
ISBN-10: 0-13-607569-X

Brief **Contents**

Contents

● About the Author

Michael Levens is Chair of Business Administration and Marketing and Director of the Business Leadership Institute at Walsh College. Dr. Levens has previously served as the Head of Consumer Research at OnStar, Brand Manager at SAAB, and has held a variety of marketing leadership positions at General Motors. Dr. Levens also has business start-up experience, receiving Global 1st Runner-up recognition in the 1996 International Entrepreneurial Challenge (MOOT CORP®).

Educated in the United States and Australia, Dr. Levens received his B.S. in Management Systems (Marketing) from Kettering University, M.B.A. from Bond University, and Ph.D. in Organization and Management (Marketing) from Capella University. His research is focused on luxury brand management, affluent consumer behavior, and mixed-methodology marketing research techniques. Dr. Levens has served as a featured speaker at conferences hosted by the American Marketing Association, Advertising Research Foundation, Association of Marketing Theory and Practice, Automotive Market Research Council, and the Canadian Marketing Association. He regularly provides consulting services to *Fortune* 100 companies and consults pro bono for major not-for-profits. In addition to being active in MENSA and the American Marketing Association, Dr. Levens serves on the board of directors of the Eisenhower Dance Ensemble.

Marketing: Defined, Explained, Applied

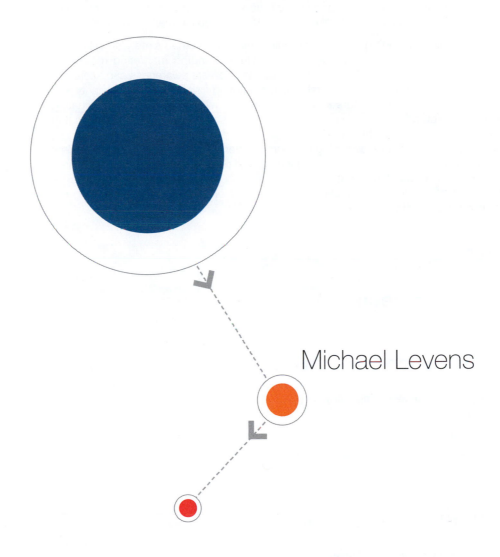

Michael Levens

chapter **1**

The Meaning of **Marketing**

Chapter Overview Everyone has some experience with marketing. Whether or not you have worked in a marketing position in an organization, you have certainly been exposed to advertising, evaluated sales offers, made purchase decisions, and promoted yourself in some capacity, such as applying to a college or university. These, and many other aspects of everyday life, place you in marketing situations.

Of course, understanding marketing requires much more than simply recalling and becoming aware of everyday experiences. Understanding marketing requires a familiarity with the strategies that businesses use to create awareness and interest in their products and services. Understanding marketing also requires a familiarity with the processes that consumers knowingly and unknowingly follow when evaluating and making purchase decisions. In addition, understanding marketing requires that you have knowledge of the various activities that marketing comprises, for example, exchange, physical, and facilitating functions. Understanding marketing also requires familiarity with disciplines, such as economics and psychology, that have contributed by providing context to what is currently known as marketing. This chapter is designed to provide a foundation for your study of marketing by explaining the meaning of marketing.

▼ Chapter **Outline**

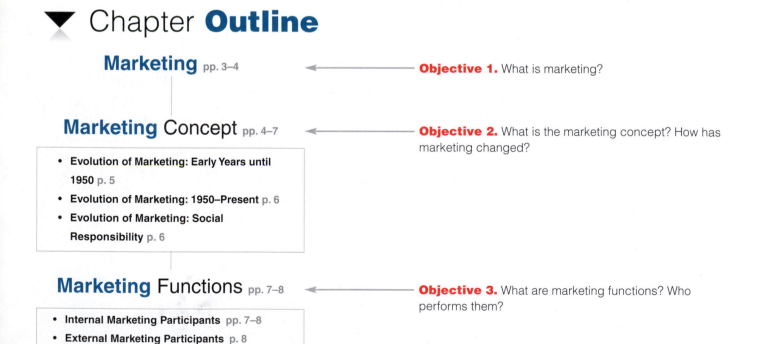

Marketing pp. 3–4 ← **Objective 1.** What is marketing?

Marketing Concept pp. 4–7 ← **Objective 2.** What is the marketing concept? How has marketing changed?

- **Evolution of Marketing: Early Years until 1950** p. 5
- **Evolution of Marketing: 1950–Present** p. 6
- **Evolution of Marketing: Social Responsibility** p. 6

Marketing Functions pp. 7–8 ← **Objective 3.** What are marketing functions? Who performs them?

- **Internal Marketing Participants** pp. 7–8
- **External Marketing Participants** p. 8

MARKETING (pp. 3–4)

> ▼ DEFINED **Marketing** *is an organizational function and a collection of processes designed to plan for, create, communicate, and deliver value to customers and to build effective customer relationships in ways that benefit the organization and its stakeholders.*[1]

▼ EXPLAINED

Marketing

Marketing is a distinct activity within an organization, as well as certain tasks, such as assembling, pricing, and promoting, that result in products, services, ideas, and other tangible and intangible items. Those items, in turn, produce profits or achieve some other stated goals for an organization and its stakeholders, including shareholders, employees, or donors. Profits or other organizational goals are achieved by creating value for consumers. The creation of **value** is the realization of benefits that exceed the cost of products, services, or other items.

Marketing has grown from roots in economics, psychology, sociology, and statistics. One important concept that marketing has borrowed from the study of economics is the idea of utility. **Utility** is the satisfaction received from owning or consuming a product or service. Utility, in a marketing sense, is the value that marketers intend consumers to attach to that marketer's products or services. Supply and demand for products and services influence price, production costs influence supply, and utility influences demand. The utility that consumers attached to the Toyota Prius is what increased demand and what has caused Toyota to add U.S.-based production of the Prius beginning in 2010. Consumers are the ultimate adjudicators of utility. If consumers perceive that a particular product or service has utility, then they are inclined to consider purchasing that product or service.

A **need** is a necessity to meet an urgent requirement. A **want** is a desire for something that is not essential. For instance, a person has a need for food, but a person simply wants ice cream. There are strict definitions for wants and needs. However, businesses often use marketing to transform a want into a *perceived* need for a particular product or service. Businesses can increase **demand**, the financial capacity to buy what a person wants, for that business's brand of products or services through marketing activities such as advertising. A **brand** is a promise to deliver to consumers specific benefits associated with products or services. The brand can contrast the products or services of one company with the products or services of another company, and, through effective marketing, command a perception of greater value that can lead to higher sales revenue and profits.

▼ APPLIED

Marketing

In practice, marketing is much more than simply selling or advertising. Marketing influences you as a consumer through your current and future career choices, and through the economy. Businesses create value through their offerings, communicate that value to consumers, and then deliver value in exchange for money from consumers. Marketing applies to more than just products or services, however. Marketing extends to a variety of tangible and intangible items, including the following:

- Products
- Services
- People
- Places
- Causes
- Events
- Ideas

Facebook is a social networking utility created in 2004 at Harvard. Currently, Facebook has about 125 million users around the world and allows contacts with friends and colleagues to communicate and share photos, videos, and other links. People register with an e-mail address and join one or more networks based on companies, schools, or regions. In addition to allowing people to connect with each other, the site also has evolved as a marketing tool for individuals and businesses. The Facebook platform allows the hosting of events, such as the 2008 Presidential debates in partnership with ABC News, and also allows advertisements to be placed on networks. Target enjoyed considerable success through its involvement with Facebook. Target took its hip image to Facebook in 2007 by sponsoring a page identified as the "Dorm Survival Guide." Target made considerable preparation for the page, including an effort to understand how users interact on Facebook. Based on that insight, discussion groups, decorating tips, and pictures of dorm rooms complemented the product information. Target's overall fall 2007 campaign helped increase sales over 6% from the previous year.[2]
PHOTO: AP Photo/Paul Sakuma

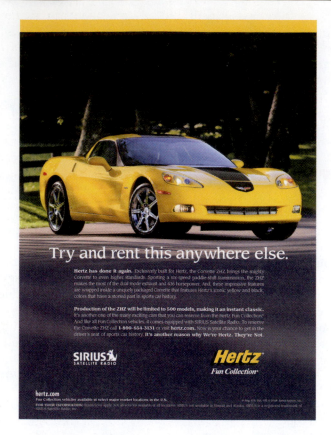

Try and rent this anywhere else.

The Corvette ZHZ, offered exclusively by Hertz as part of their "Fun Collection" portfolio in the United States, has both product and service characteristics. The vehicle is a product, but the rental is a service. The Hertz Corporation, the world's largest general-use car rental brand with 8,100 locations in 147 countries, creates value for their customers in a variety of ways. Some of those methods include working with General Motors, manufacturer of the Chevrolet Corvette, to offer a product that Hertz's competitors do not. Few people might rent the Corvette ZHZ, but the Hertz portfolio also includes subcompacts to minivans to luxury cars, and those choices are presented to consumers as innovative and contemporary.[3]

PHOTO: © 2010 Hertz System, Inc. Hertz is a registered service mark and trademark of Hertz System, inc.

>> END EXAMPLE

Products include items often used or consumed for personal use, such as shavers or ice cream, and items that are consumed by businesses or used to produce items that are resold, such as raw materials or components. Services include items that are used and not retained by the consumer, for example, a massage or a haircut, and items that are used and not retained by businesses, such as repair or maintenance services.

Beyond products and services, many other items can also be marketed. People such as celebrities, athletes, and politicians are engaged in marketing themselves and building their own brands. Similarly, as you build your career, you will constantly be marketing yourself to others. Places, from Paris to New York, can also be marketed. Place marketing can be

designed to accomplish one of a wide variety of objectives, such as introducing potential visitors to a place with which they may not be familiar, reinventing a location to stand for something different from what it is currently known, or encouraging more frequent visits. Causes, including many not-for-profit organizations such as the Humane Society, museums, and art institutes, are also marketed to potential donors and to those who may use the services of the not-for-profit. Events, such as the Olympics, the Super Bowl, and the World Cup, market themselves, but also serve as marketing platforms for other businesses. Ideas, such as antilittering campaigns and political views, as well as concepts and messages, are also marketed.

Marketing Concept (pp. 4–7)

 DEFINED *The* **marketing concept** *is an organizational philosophy dedicated to understanding and fulfilling consumer needs through the creation of value.*

▼ **EXPLAINED**
Marketing Concept

Marketing, as stated earlier, involves the creation of value that results in effective customer relationships. **Customer relationships** are created when businesses and consumers interact through a sales transaction of a product or service and continue that relationship based on ongoing interaction between the business and the customer. The management of customer relationships, commonly referred to as **customer relationship management (CRM)**, involves those elements of business strategy that enable meaningful, personalized communication between businesses and customers. By implementing CRM, a business is committing to understanding customer lifetime value. **Customer lifetime value** includes the projected sales revenue and profitability that a customer could provide to a firm. If customer relationships serve as the foundation for marketing activities, then a business is practicing the marketing concept.

▼ **APPLIED**
Marketing Concept

While generally considered a contemporary idea, the marketing concept has been used for many years, in practice, if not in name, by businesses trying to distinguish themselves from their competition by focusing on the customer. L.L.Bean founded its business in 1912 by referring to the customer as "...the most important person ever in this office—in person or by mail." L.L.Bean developed a marketing philosophy based on customer service and marketed a guarantee to provide "...perfect satisfaction in every way."[4] Currently, many businesses, as well as churches, schools, and state and local tourism entities, practice the marketing concept by focusing on the expectations of their customers.

EXAMPLE   MARKETING CONCEPT

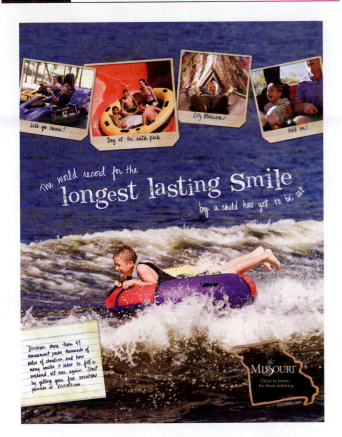

Missouri recently began an advertising campaign with its central message: "Close to home. Far from ordinary." This message is designed to attract visitors from nearby states. It is hoped those visitors will drive to Missouri and experience the wide

range of activities available. The message concentrates on the actual experience of travel, and not simply the destination. Practicing the marketing concept, this advertising has targeted specific groups of individuals, including families, young women, and baby boomers. By targeting certain groups, Missouri can create tailored messages that in turn create additional value that surpasses the value that might be obtained by communicating a broader message to the entire population.

Contrast Missouri's advertising campaign to the Las Vegas advertising campaign. Look at the two ads, and you can see that they appeal to different groups. After Las Vegas moved away from previous advertising as a family destination, the "what happens here, stays here" advertising campaign clearly establishes Las Vegas as an adults-only playground. The campaign focuses on the core benefit of a wide range of adult activities and targets those who place value on those activities. Las Vegas's advertising campaign even inspired the 2008 movie *What Happens in Vegas*.[5]

PHOTO: Courtesy of Missouri Dept. of Economic Development

>> END EXAMPLE

Evolution of Marketing: Early Years until 1950

Sales and marketing activities have existed in varying forms throughout time, from ancient civilizations through the modern era. Traditionally, the marketing emphasis was placed on the production of crafts, agricultural products, and other goods for sale through local markets. Over time, distinctive marks and designs such as cattle brands were associated with these products to distinguish one seller from another.

The early years of American marketing included advertisements that were placed in newly created media, such as newspapers and magazines, as well as the formation of the first advertising agency in the United States. In 1704, the *Boston News-Letter* published the first newspaper advertisement offering items for sale. The advertisement was for real estate on Oyster Bay, Long Island.[6] The first American magazine ads were published in Benjamin Franklin's *General Magazine* in 1742.[7] The first advertising agency was opened in Philadelphia in 1843.[8]

Sales opportunities in the United States expanded rapidly after the Revolutionary War as individuals moved across the country selling products such as clocks and books.[9] These sales roles evolved to salespeople managing orders for newly formed manufacturing companies of the nineteenth century.[10]

Through the early part of the twentieth century, both marketing and sales activities were designed to support production. Products were often created, and then customers were sought. The **production orientation** reflects a business focus on efficient production and distribution with little emphasis on any marketing strategy. This period existed roughly from the mid-1800s until the 1920s. With the advent of the Great Depression in the late 1920s and early 1930s, and the resulting increase in product inventory, the sales function became a primary activity and was considered synonymous with marketing. A **sales orientation** reflects a business focus on advertising and personal selling to create demand and move product inventory. This period lasted from the 1930s into the 1950s.

Evolution of Marketing: 1950–Present

From the 1950s into the 1980s, companies generally focused on the needs and wants of consumers more than they did in prior years. A **consumer orientation** reflects a business focus on satisfying unmet consumer needs and wants. Also in the 1980s, businesses began to consider not only consumers but also suppliers as sources of value-based relationships. A **relationship orientation** reflects a business focus on creating value-added relationships with both suppliers and consumers. A value-added relationship is much more than buying and selling. The idea of value-added relationships involves business practices that support long-term relationships. These relationships may incur short-term costs, such as additional customer support and enhanced after-sales service, but are intended to reinforce the value of the product or service, relative to the competition.

EXAMPLE   **EVOLUTION OF MARKETING: 1950–PRESENT**

Kelly Services, operating in 37 countries and territories and providing employment to over 750,000 employees annually, provides business services, such as temporary staffing services and outsourcing solutions, and consumer services, such as temporary and full-time job placement. Kelly's marketing efforts are targeted both to employers and to workers who are

unemployed or looking to change careers. Kelly's "work to live, not live to work" advertising is targeted primarily toward workers and creates value for them by identifying with an individual's desire to balance work and home life. Kelly's communication to employers is designed to address specific needs in automotive, contact center, education, electronic assembly, engineering, finance and accounting, health care, information technology, legal, light industrial, marketing, office, scientific, and security clearance. Kelly's consulting and outsourcing activity uses the advertising message "If it's outside your scope, it's probably within ours." Value is created for business clients by offering expertise in specific employment fields.

PHOTO: © 2008 Kelly Services, Inc.

>> END EXAMPLE

Evolution of Marketing: Social Responsibility

During the last decade, there has been an increased focus on social responsibility, ethics, and accountability in business. The overriding idea is that a person (or business) can make money by focusing on socially responsible marketing activities and abiding by high ethical standards. Social responsibility is the idea that businesses consider society as a whole as one of their stakeholders and that businesses make decisions that take into account the well-being of society. For example, organizations such as the American Marketing Association (AMA) developed standards of ethical behavior for marketers.

A major issue that organizations must consider when practicing socially responsible marketing involves how products affect the global environment. Everything from the pollution generated by producing the products, forms of packaging used and their potential for recycling, and the amount of energy used to consume products must be considered. Some organizations adopt operating standards that govern their socially responsible marketing practices, while others choose to financially support causes that benefit society. Many accomplish both by developing green marketing products and supporting cause-marketing activities. Socially responsible marketing can be both altruistic and profitable. A recent study by Cone LLC found that two-thirds of Americans claim that a company's business practices are considered when making purchase decisions.[11] Social responsibility and related concepts are discussed in greater detail in Chapter 4.

EXAMPLE   **EVOLUTION OF MARKETING: SOCIAL RESPONSIBILITY**

Many for-profit companies advertise their support for not-for-profit organizations through cause marketing. The Susan B. Komen Breast Cancer Foundation is involved in several cause-marketing events with many different businesses. The BMW Ultimate Drive®, since its inception in 1997, has raised over $11 million dollars for breast cancer research, education, screening, and treatment programs. The program involves BMW donating $1 to the Susan B. Komen Breast Cancer Foundation

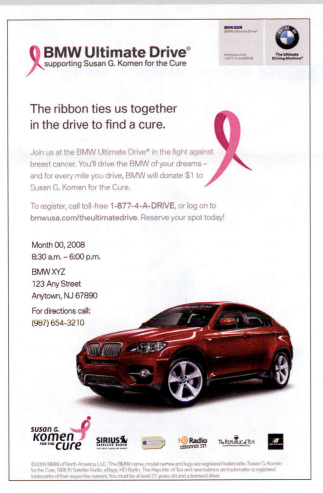

for each mile that consumers test-drive a special fleet of BMW models. Besides good philanthropic practices, cause marketing connects the positive emotions toward the sponsored event with the sponsoring company. The sponsored event benefits from the financial support and promotion of the event.

PHOTO: Courtesy of BMW of North America, LLC and Susan G. Komen for the Cure®

>> END EXAMPLE

Marketing
Functions (pp. 7–8)

 DEFINED **Marketing functions** *are activities performed within organizations that create value for specific products or services.*

 **EXPLAINED**
Marketing Functions

Noted management guru Peter Drucker identified the critical role that marketing performs for business: "Because the purpose of business is to create a customer, the business enterprise has two—and only two—basic functions: marketing and innovation.

Marketing and innovation produce results; all the rest are costs. Marketing is the distinguishing, unique function of the business."[12] The process of creating value through uniqueness occurs well before and well after the selling process. Marketing functions can be grouped into three general categories with functions from each category occurring throughout the marketing process. The three categories are the following:

- Exchange functions
- Physical functions
- Facilitating functions

Exchange functions are activities that promote and enable transfer of ownership. Examples of exchange functions include buying, selling, and pricing, as well as advertising, sales promotion, and public relations. **Physical functions** are activities that enable the flow of goods from manufacturer to consumer. Examples of physical functions include assembling, transporting and handling, warehousing, processing and packaging, standardizing, and grading. **Facilitating functions** are activities that assist in the execution of exchange and physical functions. Examples of facilitating functions include financing and risk-taking, marketing information and research, as well as the promise of servicing.

▼ **APPLIED**
Marketing Functions

In practice, some businesses view marketing from a limited perspective by considering it synonymous to sales or advertising. Other businesses understand that marketing performs a broad range of functions, ranging from securing products to servicing products after a sale, and that the marketing activity is connected to all other business functions. Successful businesses generally consider marketing departments as the link between customers and businesses. Marketing departments are in a unique position to identify and communicate customer requirements to other departments within an organization, such as finance, accounting, manufacturing and business planning.

Internal Marketing Participants

There are many different marketing stakeholders. Those stakeholders within a business or with direct oversight include the following:

- Marketing department
- Other business departments
- Business leadership/board of directors

The marketing department performs a primary role in managing marketing functions, including activities such as establishing a product or service portfolio, determining pricing, establishing distribution channels, and creating promotions. These elements compose the most common representation of the marketing mix, referred to as the **4 Ps** (Product, Price, Place, and Promotion). The marketing mix is a collection of marketing variables that are managed to achieve the desired sales performance in a target market. In addition, functions such as defining the brand and creating a CRM process are all activities performed by the marketing department.

Other business departments, such as finance, use marketing information and contribute to marketing activities in a variety of ways, including securing financing for expanded manufacturing or by providing cost information to marketing to assist in understanding the profitability of marketing decisions. Persons in positions of business leadership, such as the President or Chief Operating Officer, and the Board of Directors, also consume marketing information and make decisions to support or limit marketing activities through resource allocation.

External Marketing Participants

There are a number of marketing stakeholders that operate outside a business, yet have tremendous influence on marketing activities. They include the following:

- Investors
- Consumers/customers
- Advertising/PR agency
- Information providers/marketing research companies
- Government
- Partners
- Competitors

Investors can influence marketing ideas through letters to management and through attending shareholder meetings. Recent investor actions have included proposals to practice more socially responsible marketing.

Consumers and customers influence marketing through purchase decisions and feedback on survey questions. Advertising and public relations companies assist businesses in understanding consumers and customers, as well as in presenting products and services in the most favorable perspective through the creation of media content. Information providers and marketing research companies collect a wide range of consumer and market information for marketing departments. Whether studying the success of advertising or the product desires of consumers, the collection of information is critical to marketing decisions.

The government primarily influences marketing through legislation or regulation. Partners, other businesses or organizations that already work with or may work with a particular business, influence marketing choices by presenting opportunities to reach more consumers or to share in the cost of marketing activities. Competitors also influence marketing actions by their advertising investment and product launches. Thus, there are many marketing stakeholders, and

their collective efforts will ultimately define the level of success a business will realize in their marketing practices.

EXAMPLE   **EXTERNAL MARKETING PARTICIPANTS**

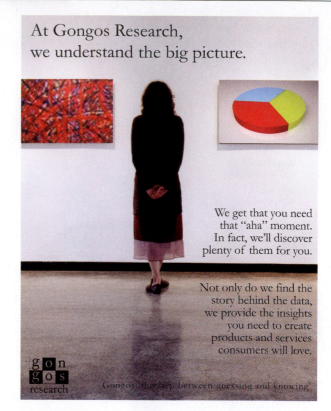

When people think of marketing research, they tend to think of receiving phone calls during dinner and being stopped at shopping malls to complete surveys. In fact, the marketing research field is far more complex. Gongos Research is a custom marketing research company that has enjoyed rapid growth through the use of technology and innovation such as i°Communities and metaCommunities. These are private online communities of individuals who have chosen to become active in the communities' social aspects (such as creating their own discussion groups) and business aspects (such as completeing surveys), and are compensated for their involvement. Gongos Research assists a wide range of businesses in many different business sectors, including financial services, automotive, powersports, and consumer products.

PHOTO: Courtesy of Gongos Research, Inc.

>> END EXAMPLE

▼Visual Summary

Chapter 1 Summary

Building on the idea that everyone has some experience with marketing, the concept of marketing and marketing functions was developed and expanded. Marketing involves the creation of value that results in effective customer relationships. Marketing is used for a variety of tangible and intangible items, including the following:

- Products
- Services
- People
- Places
- Causes
- Events
- Ideas

Marketing functions are the tasks that are applied to the various items that can be marketed. Marketing functions can be grouped into three general categories:

- Exchange functions
- Physical functions
- Facilitating functions

A variety of marketing stakeholders either utilize or contribute to marketing activities:

- Marketing department
- Other business departments
- Business Leadership/Board of Directors
- Investors
- Consumers/Customers
- Advertising/PR agency
- Information providers/Marketing Research companies
- Government
- Partners
- Competitors

Marketing pp. 3–4

satisfying

Marketing is simply the identification and satisfaction of customers' needs and wants.

The **Marketing Concept** pp. 4–7

profit

The marketing concept states that companies and organizations should strive to satisfy customer needs and wants at a profit. The expanded marketing concept says that marketers should strive to "wow" the customers while generating profits.

Marketing Functions pp. 7–8

value

Marketing Functions include the processes of developing exchange functions, physical functions, and facilitating functions. The concept of these marketing functions is to create value for the customer and organization.

Capstone **Exercise** p. 11

▼Chapter Key Terms

Marketing (pp. 3–4)

Marketing *is an organizational function and a collection of processes designed to plan for, create, communicate, and deliver value to customers and to build effective customer relationships in ways that benefit the organization and its stakeholders.* (p. 3)
Example: Marketing (p. 4) Opening Example (p. 3)

Key Terms (p. 3)

Brand is a promise to deliver specific benefits associated with products or services to consumers. **(p. 3)**

Demand is the financial capacity to buy what one wants. **(p. 3)**

Need is a necessity to meet an urgent requirement. **(p. 3)**

Utility is the satisfaction received from owning or consuming a product or service. **(p. 3)**

Value is the benefits that exceed the cost of products, services, or other items. **(p. 3)**

Want is a desire for something that is not essential. **(p. 3)**

Marketing Concept (pp. 4–7)

Marketing concept *is an organizational philosophy dedicated to understanding and fulfilling consumer needs through the creation of value.* (p. 4) **Example: Marketing Concept (p. 5)**
Example: Evolution of Marketing: 1950–Present (p. 6)

Key Terms (pp. 4–6)

Customer lifetime value is the present value of all profits expected to be earned from a customer over the lifetime of their relationship with a company. **(p. 4)**

Customer relationship management (CRM) is the activities that are used to establish, develop, and maintain customer relationships. **(p. 4)**

Customer relationships are created when businesses and consumers interact through a sales transaction of a product or service and continue based on ongoing interaction between the business and the consumer. **(p. 4)**

Consumer orientation reflects a business focus on satisfying unmet consumer needs and wants. **(p. 6) Example: Marketing (p. 4)**

Production orientation reflects a business focus on efficient production and distribution with little emphasis on any marketing strategy. **(p. 5)**

Relationship orientation reflects a business focus on creating value-added relationships with suppliers and consumers. **(p. 6) Example: Evolution of Marketing 1950–Present (p. 6)**

Sales orientation reflects a business focus on advertising and personal selling to create demand and move product inventory. **(p. 5)**

Marketing Functions (pp. 7–8)

Marketing functions *are activities performed both by consumers and by businesses involved in value creation for specific products or services.* (p. 7) **Example: External Market Participants (p. 8)**

Key Terms (p. 7)

4 Ps are the most common classification of a marketing mix and consist of product, price, place, and promotion. **(p. 7)**

Exchange functions are activities that promote and enable transfer of ownership. **(p. 7)**

Facilitating functions are activities that assist in the execution of exchange and physical functions. **(p. 7)**

Physical functions are activities that enable the flow of goods from manufacturer to consumer. **(p. 7)**

▼Capstone Exercise

One aspect of marketing is the art of making people want something that they may not need. Of course, as a socially responsible marketer, we are not advocating that you mislead people with your promotions or advertising.

The key is to understand what people want versus what they need. Your personal wants and needs change, depending on your economic position, your age, your gender, and where you live.

1. Write one sentence describing a need, and write one sentence describing a want.

2. Make a list of 10 items that you want and 10 items that you need.

3. Compare your list with the list of someone of the opposite gender. Can you explain the differences?

4. Ask someone who is at least 10 years older or younger than you to make the same list, and then compare the two lists. What are the differences? What are the reasons for those differences? If you had more or less money, would your list change?

5. Think about what would be on your list if you lived in another country. What about if you lived in the Sudan in Africa, versus if you lived in France in Europe?

6. The key to this exercise is try to understand why some of the things you think you need are really things you want. Why are things that are really wants on your needs list?

▼Application Exercises

Complete the following exercises:

1. Write a paragraph describing what marketing means to you.

2. Discuss the three marketing functions, and provide examples of each.

3. Since its launch in 1934, MONOPOLY has become the best-selling board game in the world, with over 250 million games sold worldwide. The MONOPOLY game is licensed in 103 countries and has been published in 37 languages. MONOPOLY is published by Parker Brothers, a division of Hasbro Inc., which is a worldwide leader in children's and family leisure-time entertainment products and services.

With its roots in the Great Depression, MONOPOLY contains tokens such as a shoe, thimble, top hat, and battleship. The game is based on the economic concept of a monopoly, which, in the case of this game, means controlling the game board. In 2006, Hasbro released an updated version known as MONOPOLY *Here & Now*. The tokens were updated and some were branded, such as McDonald's® French Fries and a Toyota Prius hybrid vehicle. Large airports replaced the four traditional railroads. Hasbro does not want to alienate customers who prefer the traditional product, so the company continues to sell the classic version of MONOPOLY along with the newer versions. Discuss how MONOPOLY creates value for its customers.

The **Market in Marketing**

Chapter Overview In the previous chapter the concepts of marketing and marketing functions were presented and developed, based on the idea that everyone has at least some experience with marketing. This chapter expands those comments by considering the elements of the marketing environment. In addition, consumer markets are discussed as well as business markets.

▼ Chapter **Outline**

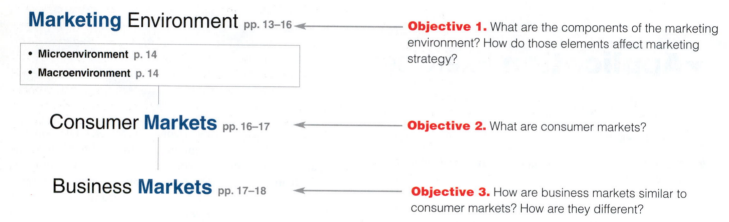

Marketing Environment pp. 13–16 ⟵ **Objective 1.** What are the components of the marketing environment? How do those elements affect marketing strategy?

- **Microenvironment** p. 14
- **Macroenvironment** p. 14

Consumer **Markets** pp. 16–17 ⟵ **Objective 2.** What are consumer markets?

Business **Markets** pp. 17–18 ⟵ **Objective 3.** How are business markets similar to consumer markets? How are they different?

MARKETING ENVIRONMENT (pp. 13–16)

> ▼ **DEFINED** *The **marketing environment** is a set of forces, some controllable and some uncontrollable, that influence the ability of a business to create value and attract and serve customers.*

▼ **EXPLAINED**

Marketing Environment

Businesses strive to create value that leads to productive customer relationships. Many factors influence value creation and the nature of customer relationships, including factors that are internal to the business and factors that are external to the business. The **internal environment** of a business involves all those activities, including marketing, that occur within the organizational functions in a business. **Internal marketing** is the implementation of marketing practices within an organization to communicate organizational policies and practices to employees and internal stakeholders. The topics of internal marketing efforts are the business's resources, including human and financial capital, as well as intangible assets, such as brands or patents. These factors represent many of the elements that can influence changes within a business.

The **external environment** of a business involves all activities, such as supplier and customer actions, that occur outside the organizational functions of a business. **External marketing** is the implementation of marketing practices directed outside the business to create value and to form productive customer relationships. External marketing influences the external environment in distinct areas, including the microenvironment and the macroenvironment.

▼ **APPLIED**

Marketing Environment

In practice, businesses typically concentrate their efforts on developing strategies that assist in managing the microenvironment. The increasing sophistication of methods to gather marketing research information, from checkout scanner data and from purchase transaction databases, allows for quicker responses to changes in the microenvironment. More companies are realizing the importance of internal marketing to employees and internal stakeholders. Such internal marketing communicates the values and expectations of the business and creates business proponents in the marketplace when the employees interact with others. Many companies are also engaged in lobbying the U.S. government and governments of other countries to influence the macroenvironment. Businesses, however, typically do not directly influence the macroenvironment.

California's decision to ban trans fats, products that are used to provide enhanced taste to food products but that are also linked to coronary heart disease, from its restaurants by 2010 changed the marketing environment for many restaurants. Debate about the ban has pitted politicians against one another as well as against restaurant associations, children's advocates, and a wide range of advocacy groups. Following trans fat bans in cities such as New York, California became the first state to ban the products. Some restaurants had argued that ingredients should be determined by customer desires as opposed to government regulation, that certain ethnic dishes would be difficult to prepare, and that costs would increase to use alternatives to trans fats. Some restaurants had anticipated the changes in trans fat legislation and had already taken action. Wendy's adopted a soy-corn cooking oil for its restaurants in the United States and Canada in 2006. Other restaurant chains that have fully or partly eliminated trans fat, or previously committed to doing so, include Applebee's, Burger King, Denny's, IHOP, KFC, Olive Garden, Panera Bread, Red Lobster, Starbucks, Subway, and Taco Bell. Responses to these changes in the marketing environment could include advertising the elimination of trans fats to consumers to create additional product interest.¹

PHOTO: Jonathan Vasata

Microenvironment

The **microenvironment** includes those forces close to a company, yet outside its internal environment, that influence the ability of a business to serve its customers.[2] The microenvironment comprises entities such as customers, suppliers, competitors, and other businesses that assist or influence a business's ability to sell, distribution, promote, and develop products or services.

A tool that helps determine where power exists in the microenvironment of a business is Porter's Five Forces of Competitive Position Model.[3] The Porter analysis can assist a business with understanding the potential for new product development, the attractiveness of a particular market segment, or the potential to reduce costs of supply or distribution, among many other applications.

| FIGURE 2.1 | Five Forces of Competitive Position |

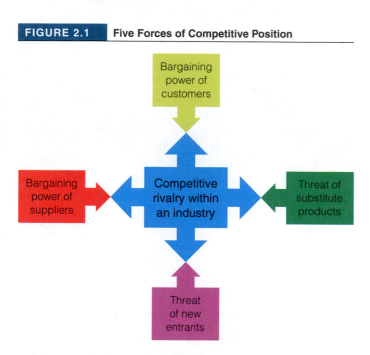

The central concept of the Five Forces of Competitive Position Model (Figure 2.1) is that five forces determine the power in a business's microenvironment. Those forces are the following:

- Threat of new entrants
- Bargaining power of suppliers
- Bargaining power of customers
- Threat of substitute products
- Competitive rivalry within an industry

The threat of new entrants can influence a business's level of power in an industry by the existing barriers to entry. Strong barriers to entry, such as intellectual property or economies of scale, provide a company power to resist new entrants.

Suppliers can assert power if they are the only one or one of a few businesses that can provide a particular product or service. Buyers (or customers) can also exert power on a business through the number and nature of buyers. The more buyers that are available, the less important an individual buyer is to a business. The fewer buyers that are available, the more power they can project. In some cases, one buyer, such as Wal-Mart, is so large that they constitute a significant percentage of total purchases from a business.

The threat of substitutes can reduce the power of a business if many substitutes exist for a particular product or service. If a product exists that is tied to another product, such as certain technical computer software, there is less threat from substitutes.

The nature of the rivalry among existing industry competitors influences the balance of power in the industry. Any change in status, whether it be the quantity and size of competing businesses, their portfolio, or financial position, will influence the power any one business can exert on the industry.

Macroenvironment

The **macroenvironment** includes societal forces that are essentially uncontrollable and influence the microenvironment of a business. The macroenvironment contains the following variety of sub-environments:

- Economic
- Social and cultural
- Competitive
- Legal
- Political
- Technological

| EXAMPLE | MACROENVIRONMENT |

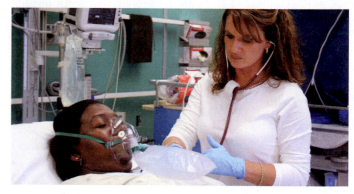

A legislative change can create challenges for some businesses, and opportunities for others. Medicare's 2007 announcement that they would not reimburse hospitals for many hospital-acquired infections was problematic for hospitals and medical providers, but created opportunities for products to mitigate hospital infections. Businesses in the paint and coatings industries have opportunities to market and sell antimicrobial coatings that can be used on floors and walls throughout hospitals. An example is Orion Industries' FluoroPlate® AM and FluoroMed® AM coatings, which use silver to resist a wide range of bacteria, including the difficult-to-treat MRSA (methicillin resistant *Staphylococcus aureus*, *S. aureus*, bacteria).[4]

PHOTO: Andrew Gentry

>> END EXAMPLE

Economic Environment

As mentioned, one of the components of the macroenvironment is the economic environment. The **economic environment** includes factors that influence consumer purchase ability and buying behavior. Inflation rates, income levels, and unemployment levels all contribute the economic environment. **Inflation** is an increase in the price of a collection of goods that represent the overall economy. As inflation increases, prices of items such as gasoline, food, and health services generally rise, and, if average income does not keep pace, products and services can become too expensive for consumers. The result is that demand generally decreases either voluntarily or involuntarily. **Income levels** are average consumer earnings used to approximate national earnings. Changes in income inversely relate to changes in demand. **Unemployment levels** are the number of unemployed persons divided by the aggregate labor force. Increases in unemployment reduce the ability of individuals to purchase products and services.

Social and Cultural Environment

The **social and cultural environment** includes factors that relate marketing to the needs and wants of society and culture. Changes in various types of demographics contribute to the social and cultural environment. **Demographics** are characteristics of human population that are used to identify markets. These characteristics include elements such as age, race, and household structure. As consumers age, levels of income generally increase and life stages change. The result is differing product and service demands. Businesses must carefully track changes such as age to make sure their portfolio continues to provide value to a market of relevant size. The United States is becoming an increasingly diverse market. As population segments such as Hispanics, Asian Americans, and African Americans increase, product and service requirements and different advertising methods change to reach diverse audiences. Household structure is also changing. There are more single-family households because people wait to marry later in life or not at all. Quantities and types of products and services need to consider these realities.

Competitive Environment

The **competitive environment** includes factors that relate to the nature, quantity, and potential actions of competitors. Changes in the context of competitors contribute to the competitive environment. If a business operates with a small number of competitors, there are fewer requirements to react to a competitive action and more time to make strategic decisions. In a competitive market, however, many more factors can impede a business from taking the actions that they want to take. For example, if maintaining margins on products is important to generate money to fund important new product development, then a competitor's aggressive move to reduce price could hurt that business strategy. Maintaining margins would take second place to a need to respond to maintain market position.

EXAMPLE COMPETITIVE ENVIRONMENT

The 1972 launch of Pong, a video game that looked like video table tennis, is credited as greatly expanding the video game market. Pong first appeared in arcades, but Atari launched a home version in 1974. Atari's home version was a console-based game system that used cartridges and was wildly successful. In the early 1980s, competition from PC manufacturers and other video-game manufacturers began eroding Atari's market share. A lack of product investment and oversupply of inventory, among other factors, caused a dramatic decline in Atari's fortunes. Atari struggles to this day.

In contrast, Nintendo entered the U.S. market in the early 1980s with its proprietary console, the Nintendo Entertainment System. Nintendo had to convince resellers to stock its product in light of Atari's problems. Nintendo reduced the risks of resellers by agreeing to take back products that did not sell. Nintendo carefully controlled its inventory and focused on building quality products. It built a strong market presence and used that presence to influence resellers to stock a higher share of its products than those of competitors. Nintendo enjoyed great success with this strategy and continues that success today with its Wii system, among other products.

PHOTO: Diego Cervo

>> END EXAMPLE

Legal Environment

The **legal environment** includes factors that provide rules and penalties for violations, and is designed to protect society and consumers from unfair business practices and to protect businesses from unfair competitive practices. Changes in legislation and regulations contribute to the legal environment. There are many different categories of legislation, including trade practices (fair trade), business competition, product safety, environmental protection, consumer privacy, fair pricing, packaging, and advertising disclosure and restrictions. Regulatory agencies include the Federal Communications Commission (FCC), an agency responsible for regulating interstate and international communications by television, satellite, cable, radio, and wire; the U.S. Consumer Product Safety Commission (USCPSC), an agency responsible for protecting consumers from unreasonable risks of serious injury from over 15,000 types of consumer products; and the Food and Drug Administration (FDA), an agency within the Department of Health and Human Services that has nine different centers, ranging from radiological health to food safety. In addition to national governmental legislation and regulations, there are also state and local legal requirements. The legal environment can become even more complicated as businesses increase global activities and must deal with foreign governments' legal environments that are different from those within the United States.

EXAMPLE | **LEGAL ENVIRONMENT**

In 2004, California vehicle emissions requirements prohibited the sale of turbo direct injection diesel (TDI) versions of Volkswagen's Golf, Passat, Jetta, and Touareg. California emission requirements influence vehicle sales not only in California, but also in several Northeastern states, including Maine, which have adopted California standards. Despite offering significantly improved fuel economy over nondiesel models, the Volkswagen TDI engine did not meet California requirements designed to improve air quality. TDI vehicles were restricted in some states, but they were available for sale in most others. Volkswagen addressed this challenge in the regulatory environment by developing a new clean diesel engine for 2009 models that met California requirements.[5]

PHOTO: Max Earey

>> END EXAMPLE

Political Environment

The **political environment** includes factors that select national leadership, create laws, and provide a process for discourse on a wide range of issues. Changes in form of government and scope and type of social movements contribute to the political environment. A Federal system of government, where a central government performs specific duties, such as national defense, and state and local governments have limited autonomy, is practiced in the United States. However, some countries are dictatorships. Everything in those countries, such as North Korea, including commercial practices, is controlled by the government. The implications for businesses are significant, because investment may be restricted when high levels of risk exist. Social movements, either a new political party or cause, can also create trends such as interest in "green" or "fair trade" products. Whether protesting in cities or funding advocacy advertisements, these causes can have tremendous influence on consumer attitudes and interest in products or services.

Technological Environment

The **technological environment** includes factors that influence marketing based on scientific actions and innovation. Changes in consumer perspectives on scientific activities and new discoveries contribute to the technological environment. Policies on cloning, stem cell research, or other controversial topics influence marketing opportunities. Funding is either made available or is restricted based on consumer perspectives that are often translated into legal framework. New discoveries, such as fiber-optic cable and hybrid vehicle propulsion systems, create marketing opportunities where businesses can take advantage of creating value in a way that competitors cannot. Consumption patterns could change based on the significance of the product or service.

Consumer **Markets** (pp. 16–17)

> **DEFINED** **Consumer markets** *are the end user of the product or service and include individuals and households that are potential or actual buyers of products and services.*[6]

▼ EXPLAINED

Consumer Markets

Both macroenvironments and microenvironements influence, through factors such as demand and supply, consumers and businesses as they make purchase decisions. U.S. consumer buying power exceeded $10 trillion in 2007, up from $4.2 trillion in 1990.[7] Over one-third of that buying power came from California, Texas, New York, and Florida consumer markets.[8] Consumer markets exist with respect to the product or service being marketed and can be considered as broad as the population of an entire country for certain food products, or as small as the limited number of people who can afford to be space tourists. **Consumer products** are products that directly fulfill the desires of consumers and are not intended to assist in the manufacture of other products.[9] Consumers make purchase decisions in consumer markets by assessing the utility of the products and services offered. A **consumer's surplus** occurs when a consumer purchases a product or service at a price less than the utility of the product or service.[10] This surplus reflects a marketer's missed opportunity to charge more for products or services and reflects an advantage to consumers. However, a significant disparity between purchase price and perceived utility may cause consumers to question what might be wrong with the product or service to warrant such a discount. Ultimately, marketing links production and consumption in the consumer market.

▼ APPLIED

Consumer Markets

In practice, purchase decisions in consumer markets are influenced heavily by the marketing and promotion of brands. Brands are used to convey value to consumers and conveying this value is accomplished through a wide range of marketing activities, including advertising and sales promotion. Marketing can be used to influence perceptions of utility and present one brand of product or service as different from another. Certain consumer markets, such as the market for shampoo and other personal care products, are saturated with brands, while others, such as the market for ultra luxury yachts, are served by few brands. Regardless of the number of competitors, each brand strives to be unique, as opposed to its competition, while remaining relevant to its consumer market.

Business **Markets** (pp. 17–18)

 DEFINED **Business markets** *include individuals and organizations that are potential or actual buyers of goods and services that are used in, or in support of, the production of other products or services that are supplied to others.*[11]

 EXPLAINED

Business Markets

Similar to consumers, businesses purchase many products and services to fulfill needs. Products and services are used to create other products and services. Products and services also are consumed by the business through the course of its normal operations. Participants in the business market include manufacturers, some of which may also sell directly to consumers, intermediaries, and entities that wholesale products. Participants also include business customers, for example, other businesses, institutions such as churches and universities, and governments, both United States and foreign. Businesses can be classified by several systems, including the **North American Industrial Classification System (NAICS)**, which classifies businesses operating in the United States, Canada, and Mexico into groups based on their activities. For example, paging services are classified as 513321. The first two numbers represent the sector, in this case information. The third digit represents the subsector of broadcasting and telecommunciations. The fourth digit represents the industry group of telecommunications. The fifth digit represents the industry of wireless communciation carriers, except satellite, and the sixth digit represents the U.S. paging industry.

Business-to-business, also referred to as **B2B**, involves the sale of products and services from one business to another. Businesses involved in B2B sales range in size from one-person small businesses to large multinational companies. Although different in size, firms operating in business markets face market characteristics that are similar to those businesses that operate in consumer markets. Compared to consumer markets, business markets generally are organized by similar geographic locations, such as automotive parts manufacturers clustering in southeastern Michigan, are influenced by consumer market demand, exist in fewer numbers, involve more individuals in the buying process, and are subject to a formal buying process.

Demand for business products and services can be created from a variety of circumstances, including the demand for a complementary product or service, shortages in inventory stock for manufacturing, or dramatic changes in market economic conditions. Just as with consumer products, demand for business products can be responsive to price changes or will experience few effects from price changes, based on the nature of the product, such as price range and number of competitors. Demand

can also be influenced by the circumstances of the buying situation. There are three major classifications, or **buyclasses**, of business buying situations.[12] These include the following:

- **New tasks**—A first-time or unique purchase decision that requires extensive effort. An example of this is when ACME publishing company buys a printing press to print its own books rather than working through its vendor.
- **Modified rebuy**—A buyer decides to consider alternative sources for the company's purchasing requirements. For example, ACME publishing company asks for bids from other print vendors rather than staying with its current vendor.
- **Straight rebuy**—A buyer decides to continue the existing procurement relationship and does not see any reason to search for additional information to assist in the purchase process. For example, ACME publishing company continues to print its books with the same vendor that it has used for the past five years.

Depending on the type of buying situation, some or all of the steps in the buyer purchase process are conducted. There are eight distinct steps, or phases, in the buyer purchase process.[13]

FIGURE 2.2   Steps in the Buyer Purchase Process

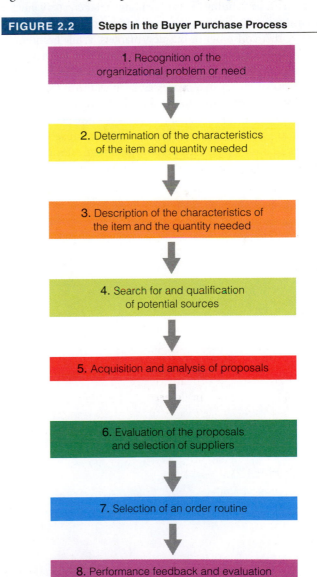

1. Recognition of the organizational problem or need
2. Determination of the characteristics of the item and quantity needed
3. Description of the characteristics of the item and the quantity needed
4. Search for and qualification of potential sources
5. Acquisition and analysis of proposals
6. Evaluation of the proposals and selection of suppliers
7. Selection of an order routine
8. Performance feedback and evaluation

A decision a business must make when determining how to fulfill a purchasing need is whether to make the product, buy the product, or lease the product. A business may choose to produce a product if the company has the capability and capacity to do so. There may also be a strategic reason to manufacture certain items instead of externally sourcing them. Examples could include a government not wanting to externally source critical military components for security reasons or an automaker not wanting to externally source its powertrain components so as to retain a competitive uniqueness. A business may also decide to purchase the product from a supplier. Reasons for sourcing a product from a supplier could include cost advantages or a lack of technical expertise for that specific product. A business could also lease a product. If a particular product is exposed to rapid technological change or requires regular servicing or other support, a leasing option might be most appropriate.

 APPLIED

Business Markets

Successful marketing to either business or consumer markets requires an understanding of customers and what creates value for those customers. Business uniqueness is important for businesses selling to either consumer or business markets. While branding is important in both business and consumer markets, the nature of the purchasing process in B2B requires particular attention to the buying process. Structured processes, such as those required to secure government or institutional business, require a level of sophistication in the processes of particular entities. Personal relationships are another critical factor in B2B because far fewer customers account for a greater percentage of total sales. Most personal relationships would be cost prohibitive in B2C.

Some businesses, such as private equity groups, are purchasing a wide range of related businesses, including suppliers and manufacturers. Different elements of the operations of these businesses are being combined and managed to extract greater profitability from the value chain. Other businesses are forming partnerships with their suppliers to manage cost exposure and to keep suppliers financially viable. This is because many companies have single sources of supply due to economies of scale and business conditions could dramatically change, which would cause incredible financial pressure on suppliers and their customers.

EXAMPLE   **BUSINESS MARKETS**

NeoPath Health provides customized employee health solutions, for example, placing a medical doctor at a work site, to midsize companies that have from 250–300 employees. Founded in 2007, NeoPath Health offers a health-management system, which includes an onsite clinic staffed with medical professionals, health assessments, patient education, and data collection and analysis that lead to early detection of chronic conditions. NeoPath Health creates value for businesses through lowering medical expenses, increasing productivity, reducing absenteeism, and adding a highly valued employee benefit.[14]

PHOTO: Shutterstock

>> END EXAMPLE

▼Visual Summary

Chapter 2 Summary

Building on the concept of marketing and the marketing function, the marketing environment was introduced, as were consumer and business markets. The marketing environment is a set of forces, some controllable and some uncontrollable, that influence a business's ability to create value and attract and serve customers. Many factors influence value creation and the nature of customer relationships in the marketing environment. Some of those influential factors are internal to the business, while others are external to the business. The internal environment of a business involves all activities, including marketing, that occur within the organizational functions in a business. The external environment of a business involves all activities that occur outside the organizational functions of a business. The external environment can be divided into the microenvironment and the macroenvironment. The central concept of the Five Forces of Competitive Position Model is that five forces determine the power in a business's microenvironment. The macroenvironment includes societal forces that are essentially uncontrollable and influence the microenvironment of a business.

Consumer markets include individuals and households that are potential or actual buyers of products and services that assist in further production only indirectly or incidentally, if at all. Business markets include individuals or organizations that are potential or actual buyers of goods and services that are used in, or in support of, the production of other products or services that are supplied to others. Business markets generally are organized by similar geographic locations, are influenced by consumer market demand, exist in fewer numbers, involve more individuals in the buying process, and are subject to a more formal buying process than are consumer markets.

Marketing Environment pp. 13–16

variables

The marketing environment includes controllable and uncontrollable variables that affect the way a marketer can reach customers.

Consumer Markets pp. 16–17

Customer markets are those customers that make up a company's end-user base. This market includes actual product users.

end user

Business Markets pp. 17–18

Business markets include those customers who buy products to use in their day-to-day business operations, or who buy products for resale.

operations

Capstone **Exercise** p. 21

▼**Chapter** Key Terms

Marketing Environment (pp. 13–16)

Marketing environment *is a set of forces, some controllable and some uncontrollable, that influence the ability of a business to create value and attract and serve customers. (p. 13)* **Opening Example (p. 13) Example: Macroenvironment (p. 14) Example: Competitive Environment (p. 15) Example: Legal Environment (p. 16)**

Key Terms (pp. 13–16)

Competitive environment includes those factors that relate to the nature, quantity, and potential actions of competitors. **(p. 15) Example: Competitive Environment (p. 15)**

Demographics are characteristics of human population used to identify markets. **(p. 15)**

Economic environment includes those factors that influence consumer purchase ability and buying behavior. **(p. 15)**

External environment of a business involves all those activities that occur outside the organizational functions of a business. **(p. 13)**

External marketing is the implementation of marketing practices directed outside the business to create value and to form productive customer relationships. **(p. 13)**

Income levels are average consumer earnings used to approximate national earnings. **(p. 15)**

Inflation is an increase in the price of a collection of goods that represent the overall economy. **(p. 15)**

Internal environment of a business involves all those activities that occur within the organizational functions in a business. **(p. 13)**

Internal marketing is the implementation of marketing practices within an organization to communicate organizational policies and practices to employees and internal stakeholders. **(p. 13)**

Legal environment includes those factors that provide rules, and penalties for violations, designed to protect society and consumers from unfair business practices and to protect businesses from unfair competitive practices. **(p. 15) Example: Legal Environment (p. 16)**

Macroenvironment includes societal forces that are essentially uncontrollable and influence the microenvironment of a business. **(p. 14) Example: Macroenvironment (p. 14)**

Microenvironment includes those forces close to a company, yet outside its internal environment, that influence the ability of a business to serve its customers. **(p. 14) Example: Business Markets (p. 18)**

Political environment includes factors that select national leadership, create laws, and provide a process for discourse on a wide range of issues. **(p. 16) Opening Example; Example: Legal Environment (p. 16)**

Social and cultural environment includes factors that relate marketing to the needs and wants of society and culture. **(p. 15)**

Technological environment includes factors that influence marketing, based on scientific actions and innovation. **(p. 16)**

Unemployment levels are the number of unemployed persons divided by the aggregate labor force. **(p. 15)**

Consumer Markets (pp. 16–17)

Consumer markets *include individuals and households that are potential or actual buyers of goods and services that assist in further production only indirectly or incidentally, if at all. (p. 16)*

Key Terms (pp. 16)

Consumer products are products that directly fulfill the desires of consumers and are not intended to assist in the manufacture of other products. **(p. 16)**

Consumer's surplus occurs when a consumer purchases a product or service at a price less than the utility of the product or service. **(p. 16)**

Business Markets (pp. 17–18)

Business markets *include individuals and organizations that are potential or actual buyers of goods and services that are used in, or in support of, the production of other products or services that are supplied to others. (p. 18)* **Example: Business Markets (p. 18)**

Key Terms (pp. 17–18)

Business-to-business, also referred to as **B2B**, involves the sales of products and services from one business to another. **(p. 17) Example: Business Markets (p. 18)**

Buyclasses are major classifications of business buying situations. **(p. 17)**

North American Industrial Classification System (NAICS) classifies businesses operating in the United States, Canada, and Mexico into groups based on their activities. **(p. 17)**

▼Capstone Exercise

This chapter's exercise is based on a model that allows you to assess the structure of any industry. The methodology was developed by Michael Porter, and is called Five Forces of Competitive Position. The Five Forces include the following:

- Bargaining power of suppliers
- Bargaining power of buyers
- Threat of new entrants
- Threat of substitutes
- Rivalry among competitors

The Five Forces provide a way to understand the business models of industries. How competitive is the industry? What does it take to succeed? How easy is it to get into the business? How do they make money? Taken together, these answers give you a way to understand the likelihood of success and the potential for profit in this industry. It is important to understand the key factors to be successful. Those key factors also help determine whether or not a certain industry could be successful.

To fully understand this process, choose an industry and then do the research to produce a one-page version of the Five Forces of Competitive Position.

▼Application Exercises

Complete the following exercises:

1. Define the marketing environment for Starbucks (www.starbucks.com). Keep in mind that a company's marketing environment consists of the actors and forces outside marketing that affect marketing management's ability to build and maintain successful relationships with target customers.

2. What are the fundamental differences between consumer markets and business markets?

3. By 2050, Hispanics will constitute an estimated 24% of the U.S. population. How will this impact the manner in which some products are marketed?

4. Describe the differences in products that appeal to the middle class, working class, and upper class.

chapter 3

Part 1 Explaining **(Chapters 1, 2, 3, 4)**
Part 2 Creating **(Chapters 5, 6, 7, 8)**
Part 3 Strategizing **(Chapters 9, 10)**

Part 4 Managing **(Chapters 11, 12, 13, 14, 15)**
Part 5 Integrating **(Chapters 16, 17)**

Planning and Marketing in an Organization

Chapter Overview In the initial chapters, you considered marketing, marketing functions, and the marketing environment. This chapter expands those concepts by considering the marketing function within an organization. The marketing activity plays a pivotal role in connecting consumers to businesses by developing an understanding of customer requirements. Marketing also performs a critical function within businesses to concentrate every business activity on generating desired financial results based on fulfilling consumer requirements. The concept of marketing in an organization is considered through exploring the planning process and how businesses manage marketing planning.

▼ Chapter **Outline**

Planning Process pp. 23–24 ⟵ **Objective 1.** How do businesses manage systems to achieve their goals?

Strategic **Planning** pp. 24–26 ⟵ **Objective 2.** How do organizations determine their overall goals?

Marketing **Planning** pp. 26–28 ⟵ **Objective 3.** How do businesses connect to the environment in which they function?

PLANNING PROCESS (pp. 23–24)

> ▼ **DEFINED** **Planning process** *is the series of steps businesses take to determine how they will achieve their goals.*

▼ **EXPLAINED**

Planning Process

Businesses consist of many functions, such as marketing, finance, and operations. These business functions can be considered **systems**, a group of interacting related parts that perform a specific function.

Business planning is a decision process for people and businesses to manage systems to achieve an objective. By understanding the systems that influence a business and making decisions based on that understanding, businesses increase the likelihood of a desired outcome, such as increased market share or higher profits. All businesses, from a one-person shop to a large multinational conglomerate, should engage in the planning process. The complexity of the process can depend on the size of the business and the number of different products and services offered. Large businesses may have multiple committees to initiate, review, and approve plans, yet a single individual may handle that function at a small business. The length of time addressed by business planning also differs, based on the nature of competition in the specific business market and the characteristics of the products or services the business offers. However, business planning is an ongoing effort and typically addresses some specific short-term objectives as well as some longer-term objectives. A short term may be weeks or months for some high-tech products, but a short term may also be a year or more for major capital goods such as large appliances or automobiles. The aim of business planning is the creation of a business plan.

A **business plan** is a written document that defines the operational and financial objectives of a business over a particular time. A marketer contributes a variety of inputs to the business plan, including the following:

- A comprehensive review and assessment of a business's marketing environment
- An explanation of what the marketing function is attempting to achieve in support of the business plan
- A discussion of how a business intends to achieve its marketing objectives
- A process to allocate resources and monitor results

Although marketers provide critical inputs to the business plan, the marketing function also must work with other business functions, such as finance, manufacturing, and human resources. These other areas may support or resist marketing initiatives due to different strategic visions for the business or the desire to control resources. As a marketer, remember the importance of your position and advocate that you perform an essential activity of injecting customer requirements into the many systems within an organization. That customer connection is fundamental in linking businesses to consumers.

▼ **APPLIED**

Planning Process

"Good fortune is what happens when opportunity meets with planning." Thomas Edison's quote identifies the potential that businesses can realize by choosing to plan. The opposite is also a possibility; by failing to plan, a business risks the potential for bad fortune in the future. That is not to say that planning guarantees success or that failing to plan guarantees failure. Businesses practice varying forms of planning and have varying levels of success. Some businesses have elaborate planning processes with entire staffs dedicated to developing business plans, while others have little or no resources dedicated to planning. Many resources can be devoted to the planning process. However, it is the level of involvement of the various activities within a business in developing and implementing the business plan that most influences the potential for success.

Whole Foods Market, the world's largest natural and organic foods retailer with 270 locations in North America and the United Kingdom, articulates its business mission through the following motto: Whole Foods, Whole People, Whole Planet. The company's stated core values elaborate on this motto:

- Selling the Highest Quality Natural and Organic Products Available
- Satisfying and Delighting Our Customers
- We Support Team Member Happiness and Excellence
- Creating Wealth Through Profits & Growth
- Caring About Our Communities & Our Environment
- Creating Ongoing Win-Win Partnerships with Our Suppliers

Whole Foods Market's business vision includes leadership in the quality food business. The vision also includes being a mission-driven company that aims to set standards of excellence for food retailers. Whole Foods sets objectives, develops its portfolio, and manages its business based on its mission and vision. The company has enjoyed success with annual sales exceeding $6.5 billion.[1]

PHOTO: Hannamariah

Strategic **Planning** (pp. 24–26)

>
> **DEFINED** **Strategic planning** *determines the overall goals of the business and the steps it will take to achieve them.*[2]

▼ **EXPLAINED**

Strategic Planning

Business planning can be categorized into two different levels:

- Strategic planning is typically completed by the top management of a business as opposed to tactical planning that is typically done within the various functions within a business. Nike is engaged in strategic planning when it evaluates growth potential in different athletic shoe segments, such as cross-training, running, and basketball, and decides that an opportunity exists for a new entry in the basketball segment.
- **Tactical planning** is the process of developing actions for various functions within a business to support implementing a business's strategic plan. Tactical planning occurs when the Nike marketing department decides to introduce Nike Hyperdunk Basketball Shoes and determines the characteristics of the product, the price of the product, the method of distribution, and the types of promotion to support the launch.

The strategic planning process includes the following four critical elements:

- Establish the business mission.
- Identify the business vision.
- Define the business objectives.
- Develop the business portfolio.

A **business mission** is a statement that identifies the purpose of a business and what makes that business different from others. The mission statement should be neither trite nor verbose. The scope of the mission should not be so broad that any strategy could be developed within that scope. It should also not be so specific that flexibility to take advantage of market opportunities is restricted. The mission should at least reflect the compelling benefit that a business offers to consumers. Starbuck's business mission is the following: "Establish Starbucks as the premier purveyor of the finest coffee in the world while maintaining our uncompromising principles while we grow."

A **business vision** is a statement in a strategic plan that identifies an idealized picture of a future state a business is aiming to achieve. A business vision complements a mission statement by providing a description of the end state if the strategic plan is implemented successfully. A business vision is generally targeted for use within a business, as opposed to the mission statement, which is directed at all stakeholders. Microsoft co-founders Bill Gates and Paul Allen had a vision of "A computer on every desk and in every home." General Electric's vision is "To become #1 or #2 in every market we serve and revolutionize this company to have the speed and agility of a small enterprise." Delphi, the world's largest automotive parts manufacturer, has the following vision: "Be recognized by our customers as their best supplier."

After establishing a business mission and business vision, to translate the mission and vision throughout a business, objectives must be developed. A **business objective** is something a business is attempting to achieve in support of an overarching strategy. Successful objectives include the following:

- **Specific**—Does the objective refer to a unique event?
- **Measurable**—Can the objective's achievement be determined using established metrics?
- **Achievable**—Is the objective possible, given business constraints?
- **Relevant**—Will the objective support a desired business strategy?
- **Time-bound**—Is there a duration for attaining the objective?

Objectives can be established to address many different requirements, including financial requirements such as sales revenue and profitability, operational requirements such as productivity and efficiency, and marketing requirements such as market share and brand awareness. Examples of some objectives include "to increase sales by 25%" and "to expand retail locations to every country in Europe."

The products or services that a business presents to consumers must reflect the business's mission, values, and objectives. A business portfolio, also known as a product portfolio, is a collection of products, services, and their corresponding brands that a business manages to achieve stated goals. A business portfolio that reflects the strengths of a business and limits its weaknesses provides the best opportunity for a business to realize success. The more products and services a business offers, the more opportunities there are to serve different consumers. However, there are also higher costs to manage all the products and services. **Portfolio analysis** is the process that a business uses to evaluate the different combinations of products and services that the business offers, based on business objectives.

▼ **APPLIED**

Strategic Planning

There are varieties of tools that can assist businesses to complete their strategic planning processes. These range from traditional to contemporary models. A classic model for conducting a portfolio analysis is the Boston Consulting Group (BCG) Growth-market matrix. The BCG matrix (see Figure 3.1) assists in identifying which products or services should receive more or less investment, and which market sectors could benefit from more or fewer product or service offerings. The BCG matrix includes two variables: market share on the x-axis and market growth rate on the y-axis. The ranges, typically referred to as high and low, should be set relative to economic realities, such as the rate of inflation, as well as the characteristics of the market sectors, such as the number of competitors and leading market share, being analyzed.

FIGURE 3.1	BCG Growth-market Matrix

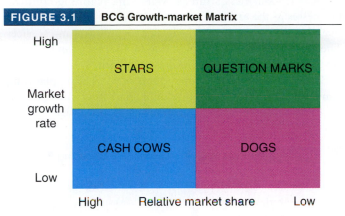

Stars represent products or services with high growth and high market share. Placement in this category indicates tremendous strategic value to a business. The number of consumers and the potential for significant profits in this sector require strong consideration for investment of resources. Money generated from this sector can support products or services in other sectors. An important strategy for Stars is to ensure that the products or services remain relevant to consumers.

Cash Cows are products or services with high market share and low growth opportunities. Stars often become Cash Cows when competitors enter their market and growth slows. Cash Cows do not require the level of investment that Stars require, because there is limited potential to grow. Instead, the current position is managed to generate money to support other aspects of a business.

Question Marks are products or services with low relative market share in a sector with high growth. While there is potential in this sector, a significant financial investment is required to take advantage of that potential. Question Marks could evolve into Stars, but they could also drain resources from other potential investments within the portfolio.

Dogs are products or services with low relative market share in a low growth sector. Although there is limited potential, there is an opportunity for a product or service to maintain its position. Little or no additional investment is warranted unless products or services in this sector are connected to products or services in a higher potential sector. Strategies for offerings in this sector are often selling this part of the portfolio or reducing financial support while removing cash and then divesting.

The BCG matrix has limitations, including the consideration of only two dimensions: market share and market growth rate. High market share does not guarantee financial profits, and limited market share does not guarantee poor financial results. Growth is not the only indicator of market attractiveness, and investment or divestment decisions made solely using the BCG matrix may be shortsighted.

EXAMPLE	STRATEGIC PLANNING, BCG MATRIX

Deckers Outdoor Company entered into an agreement in 1985 with Teva founder Mark Thatcher to produce and distribute Teva sandals. Teva's portfolio has grown from its iconic sport sandal to include a wide range of products, including trail-running shoes, adventure shoes, casual shoes, casual sandals, and water shoes.[3] As Teva considers a new product or a new market segment, the growth rate and market potential of that product are charted to determine how each will serve the overall goals and objectives of the company. A hypothetical classification of Teva's portfolio using the BCG matrix is presented graphically and discussed individually within each element of the BCG matrix.

Stars: Although the trail-running shoes entered the market segment facing strong competition, Teva's reputation for outdoor performance has extended to the trail-running shoe. The market share and the growth rate have exceeded goals and Teva's product is a Star.

Cash Cows: The Teva sport sandal continues to be the Cash Cow for the business.

Question Marks: The introduction of Teva's casual shoe has been less impressive. The competition in this category is significant and quality control has proved challenging. The casual shoe is a Question Mark. Casual sandals and adventure shoes are also in this category because of a low market share in growing markets.

Dogs: The Teva water shoe is struggling. Consumers do not seem to differentiate between the traditional sport sandal and the water shoe. The water shoe has relatively high production costs and a higher retail price than the sport sandal. Management is considering exiting this category.

Sample BCG Growth-market Matrix for Teva Products

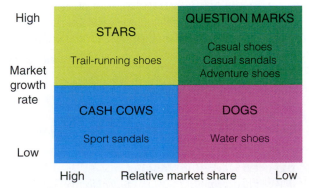

FIGURE 3.2

PHOTO: Dick Stada

>> END EXAMPLE

A contemporary model assisting strategic planning efforts is **the balanced scorecard**, developed in the early 1990s by Robert Kaplan and David Norton as a management system to relate business vision and mission to individual business activities.[4] The balanced scorecard considers a business from four different perspectives, including financial and nonfinancial measures:

- Customer perspective—How do customers view us?
- Internal business perspective—What must we do well?
- Innovation and learning perspective—Can we continue to grow and generate value?
- Financial perspective—How do shareholders view us?

The scorecard identifies the relationships between the different perspectives and business vision and strategy. Each is influenced by the business vision and strategy, and each perspective influences all the other perspectives.

EXAMPLE STRATEGIC PLANNING, TEVA BALANCED SCORECARD

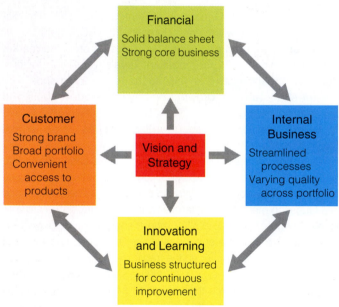

FIGURE 3.3

A hypothetical example for the Teva portfolio is illustrated in Figure 3.3. For each perspective, a list of objectives derived from the strategic plan is identified. Measures of success and a list of initiatives to achieve the objectives also are identified.[5]

>> END EXAMPLE

Marketing **Planning** (pp. 26–28)

 DEFINED **Marketing planning** *includes those activities devoted to accomplishing marketing objectives.*

▼ **EXPLAINED**
Marketing Planning

Strategic planning identifies the overall direction of a business. Individual functions within a business must develop plans to support the business strategy. Marketing planning connects businesses to the environments in which they function, in particular to the consumers of the business's products and services. The ability for marketing planning to address changes in the environment is an essential business function.

There are four major components of marketing planning: marketing objectives, marketing audit, marketing strategies, and allocating resources and monitoring (see Figure 3.4).

FIGURE 3.4   Four Major Components of Marketing Planning

A **marketing objective** is something that a marketing function is attempting to achieve in support of a strategic business plan. A marketing function can select a wide range of possible objectives, including building awareness of a product or service, increasing sales, increasing market share, and reducing resistance to a product or service. Examples of marketing objectives include the following:

- Increase sales of high-end navigation systems among owners of European luxury cars by 10% in one year. This can be measured through analyzing annual sales data
- Increase market share of a specific brand of office furniture within the business market by 5% in six months. This can be measured through industry data published by an office furniture trade association.
- Create awareness of a new wetsuit line among high school swimmers. This can be measured through a questionnaire given to high school swimmers.

EXAMPLE MARKETING PLANNING

Speedo launched the LZR Racer swimsuit, a full-body suit, in 2008, several months in advance of the Beijing Olympics. After 25 world records were broken at the 2008 Olympics, second

only to 30 world records in the 1976 Olympics when goggles were first allowed, initial demand for the new swimsuit by athletes of all levels skyrocketed. Speedo's marketing objective was to use the Olympics to launch the new product. Speedo collaborated with NASA to help design the suit that dramatically reduces drag in the water. Even though the suit noticeably improved swimming times, some swimming organizations have banned full-body suits for competitions because the suits are considered unfair performance-enhancing gear. In spite of the potential competitive restrictions and a price tag exceeding $500, demand for the product continues to grow.[6]

PHOTO: Schmid Christophe

>> END EXAMPLE

After marketing objectives are established, the next step is the marketing audit. A **marketing audit** is the comprehensive review and assessment of a business's marketing environment. An important part of the marketing process is that a business understand the external and internal forces that can influence its success.

Once the marketing audit has been completed, the marketing function is responsible for developing marketing strategies. A **marketing strategy** is a statement of how a business intends to achieve its marketing objectives.[7] A marketing strategy includes two critical functions:

- Select a target market.
- Create an appropriate marketing mix for the target market.

A **target market** is a group of consumers that a business determines is the most viable for its products or services. Consumer wants, needs, and business resources and strategies all contribute to the selection of a target market. In some cases, several targets are selected. (This topic will be explored in detail in Chapter 9.) A **marketing mix** is a group of marketing variables that a business controls with the intent of implementing a marketing strategy directed at a specific target market. As discussed in Chapter 1, the most common variables of the marketing mix include product, place, pricing, and promotion.

A **product strategy** identifies the product and service portfolio, including packaging, branding, and warranty for its target market. An automobile manufacturer creates a product strategy when it decides to offer consumers a choice of a diesel or hybrid engine in a new vehicle. This strategy helps meet growing consumer demands for a wider choice of engine types. A **place strategy** identifies where, how, and when products and services

are made available to target consumers. A newspaper publisher develops a place strategy when it decides to offer customers newspapers in newsprint and online. A **pricing strategy** identifies what a business will charge for its products or services. A company creates a pricing strategy with its clothing brand when that company decides to charge more for products sold in its retail stores than for the same products sold through the company Web site. A **promotion strategy** identifies how a business communicates product or service benefits and value to its target market. A perfume manufacturer develops a promotion strategy when that manufacturer decides to advertise a new brand of perfume both in-store and on television.

Following the development of marketing strategies, the next step is allocating resources and monitoring performance. People and money both must be assigned to support implementation of marketing strategies. The monitoring process is essential to determine if the target market is responding to marketing strategies. Proper monitoring requires identifying performance measures so that actual performance can be compared to expected performance. Performance measures can include different variables, for example, customer satisfaction, average value of customer orders, and level of advertising recall.

The result of marketing planning is the creation of a marketing plan. A **marketing plan** is a document that includes an assessment of the marketing situation, marketing objectives, marketing strategy, and marketing initiatives. The marketing plan is discussed in detail in Chapter 10.

▼ APPLIED

Marketing Planning

In practice, marketing planning is subject to the same challenges as business planning, including a potential lack of focus on business objectives, a lack of involvement of all aspects of the marketing activity in the planning process, and the failure to track performance against objectives. The structure and culture of a marketing activity has much to do with managing these potential challenges. Clear roles and responsibilities regarding planning responsibility and the level of understanding of a business's environment contribute significantly to successful marketing planning.

SWOT analysis is a tool that helps identify business strengths, weaknesses, opportunities, and threats. A SWOT analysis can assist in the marketing planning process, particularly with the marketing audit.

Strengths and weaknesses are based on internal characteristics, and opportunities and threats are external. Strengths and opportunities can be considered potential advantages, but weaknesses and threats are problems to be addressed. Strategically, weaknesses must be examined to search for opportunities. Strengths should be managed against potential threats. The Five Forces of Competitive Position Model, discussed in the previous chapter, can also assist in completing a marketing audit.

Marketing performance must be evaluated relative to objectives, as well as against the overall financial investment in the marketing activity. Increasingly, marketing is being asked to justify its contribution to business performance through identifying a return on marketing investment. Marketing planning should be designed to identify the relative contributions of each aspect of the marketing activity, including advertising and promotions, toward achieving overall objectives. **Return on marketing investment (ROMI)** is the impact on business performance resulting from executing specific marketing activities. Funding can then be allocated to the most efficient investment option.

EXAMPLE   **MARKETING PLANNING, SWOT**

Strengths	Weaknesses
• Well-recognized global brand • Cult-like following • Unique positioning for most products	• Challenging financial situation with parent company • Third-party evaluations have been mixed
Opportunities	**Threats**
• Potential to expand to international markets • Potential to move into higher demand product segments	• Uncertainty of fuel prices • Changing consumer preferences away from trucks and sport utility vehicles

FIGURE 3.5 | **Chrysler LLC's Jeep Brand SWOT Anaylsis**

Studying the Jeep SWOT analysis leads to questions about the appropriateness of the portfolio and the potential for new market segments that might be viable. Price sensitivity among consumers, as well as shopping patterns and promotional opportunities that leverage brand strength, should also be considered.

PHOTO: Andres

>> END EXAMPLE

▼**Visual** Summary

Chapter 3 Summary

Building on the concepts of marketing, marketing functions, and the marketing environment, this chapter expanded those concepts by considering the marketing function within an organization, and particularly its role in planning. The planning process includes specific actions undertaken and methods used to determine the best way to accomplish an objective. The strategic planning process includes four critical elements:

- Establish the business mission
- Identify the business vision
- Define the business objectives
- Develop the business portfolio

Marketing planning includes activities devoted to accomplishing marketing objectives. There are four major components of marketing planning:

- Marketing objectives
- Marketing audit
- Marketing strategies
- Allocating resources and monitoring.

Planning Process pp. 23–24

steps

The planning process refers to a set of steps, or actions, businesses take to figure out how to meet, or exceed, their organizational, unit, divisional, or corporate goals.

Strategic Planning pp. 24–26

how & when

Strategic planning involves the development of big picture concepts that determine how and when a company will achieve its objectives and goals.

Marketing Planning pp. 26–28

development

Marketing planning involves the development of steps or actions necessary to achieve overall marketing objectives.

Capstone **Exercise** p. 31

▼Chapter Key Terms

Planning Process (pp. 23–24)

The **planning process** *is the series of steps businesses take to determine how they will achieve their goals.* *(p. 23)* **Opening Example (p. 23)**

Key Terms (p. 23)

Business plan is a written document that defines the operational and financial objectives of a business over a particular time and how the business plans to accomplish those objectives. **(p. 23)**

Business planning is a decision process for people and businesses to manage systems to achieve an objective. **(p. 23)**

Systems are groups of interacting related parts that perform a specific function. **(p. 23)**

Strategic Planning (pp. 24–26)

Strategic planning *determines the overall goals of the business and the steps the business will take to achieve those goals.* *(p. 24)* **Example: Strategic Planning, BCG Matrix (p. 25) Example: Strategic Planning, Teva Balanced Scorecard (p. 26)**

Key Terms (pp. 24–26)

Business mission is a statement that identifies the purpose of a business and what makes that business different from others. **(p. 24)**

Business objective is something that a business attempts to achieve in support of an overarching strategy. **(p. 24)**

Business vision is a statement in a strategic plan that identifies an idealized picture of a future state a business is aiming to achieve. **(p. 24)**

Cash Cows are products or services with high market share and low growth opportunities. **(p. 25) Example: Strategic Planning, BCG Matrix (p. 25)**

Dogs are products or services with low relative market share in a low growth sector. **(p. 25) Example: Strategic Planning, BCG Matrix (p. 25)**

Portfolio analysis is the process a business uses to evaluate the different combinations of products and services that the business offers based its objectives. **(p. 24)**

Question Marks are products or services with low relative market share in a sector with high growth. **(p. 25) Example: Strategic Planning, BCG Matrix (p. 25)**

Stars represent products or services with high growth and high market share. **(p. 25) Example: Strategic Planning, BCG Matrix (p. 25)**

Tactical planning is the process of developing actions for various functions within a business to support implementing a business's strategic plan. **(p. 24)**

The balanced scorecard is a management system that relates a business's vision and mission to individual business activities. **(p. 26) Example: Strategic Planning, Teva Balanced Scorecard (p. 26)**

Marketing Planning (pp. 26–28)

Marketing planning *is the part of business planning devoted to connecting a business to the environments in which that business functions in order to accomplish the business's goals.* *(p. 26)* **Example: Marketing Planning: SWOT (p. 28) Example: Marketing Planning (p. 26)**

Key Terms (pp. 26–28)

Marketing audit is the comprehensive review and assessment of a business's marketing environment. **(p. 27)**

Marketing mix is a group of marketing variables that a business controls with the intent of implementing a marketing strategy directed at a specific target market. **(p. 27)**

Marketing objective is something that a marketing function is attempting to achieve in support of a strategic business plan. **(p. 26)**

Marketing plan is a document that includes an assessment of the marketing situation, marketing objectives, marketing strategy, and marketing initiatives. **(p. 27)**

Marketing strategy is a statement of how a business intends to achieve its marketing objectives. **(p. 27)**

Place strategy identifies where, how, and when products and services are made available to target consumers. **(p. 27)**

Pricing strategy identifies what a business will charge for its products or services. **(p. 27)**

Product strategy identifies the product and service portfolio, including packaging, branding, and warranty for its target market. **(p. 27) Example: Marketing Planning (p. 26)**

Promotion strategy identifies how a business communicates product or service benefits and value to its target market. **(p. 27)**

Return on marketing investment (ROMI) is the impact on business performance resulting from executing specific marketing activities. **(p. 28)**

SWOT analysis is a tool that helps identify business strengths, weaknesses, opportunities, and threats. **(p. 27) Example: Marketing Planning: SWOT (p. 28)**

Target market is a group of consumers that a business determines to be the most viable for its products or services. **(p. 27)**

▼Capstone Exercise

The planning process is a complicated process, but it can be simplified as follows: How does your company plan to get from where you are as a company today to where you want to be in the future? The tools described in this chapter help you understand the business environment in which your company operates and understand where your organization fits regarding the market and your competitors. A critical part of marketing planning is the marketing audit, a process that helps a business understand external and internal forces that can influence its success.

Perform a brief marketing audit on your educational institution. Some sample questions you should ask include the following:

1. Is your institution growing, and at what rate? How many students were in the incoming freshman class this year versus past years?

2. Who are your school's biggest competitors? What are the overlap schools?

3. Is the current economic climate good or bad for your institution?

4. How much of a role do tuition costs play in your admissions?

5. Does the institution have a clear marketing message? State that marketing message in your own words.

6. What is the institution's competitive advantage? How is it different from your competitors'? What are you known for?

7. Look at the school Web site and then go to the admissions office to study the material used to recruit students. Does the school have a consistent message? What can be done to improve that message?

8. How effective are news media relations? How frequently do you see your school in the local/regional/national media? What are your suggestions for improvement?

9. Go to the Alumni Office and get copies of the publications the school sends to alumni. How effective are alumni communications?

▼Application Exercises

Complete the following exercises:

1. Create a SWOT analysis for a business of your choice and discuss the implications on elements of the marketing mix.

2. A business portfolio is the collection of businesses or products that make up the company. Take a look at Ford's portfolio (www.ford.com). Describe Ford's business portfolio in terms of businesses and products.

3. Using the Boston Consulting Group's Growth-market matrix, place Ford's vehicles on the grid. Which vehicles are the Stars, the Cash Cows, the Question Marks, and the Dogs?

4. What are some of the problems with using a matrix approach (such as the BCG matrix)?

A Broader Perspective on
Marketing

Chapter Overview The previous chapters examined the purpose of marketing in commerce, including marketing's business functions, its application to consumer and business markets, and its role within an organization. This chapter discusses marketing from a broader perspective by examining its social, legal, ethical, and global aspects. Additionally, this chapter considers marketing's relationship to society as well as how laws are used to regulate marketing. Finally, this chapter also discusses the ethical implications of marketing, corporate social responsibility, and globalization.

▼ Chapter **Outline**

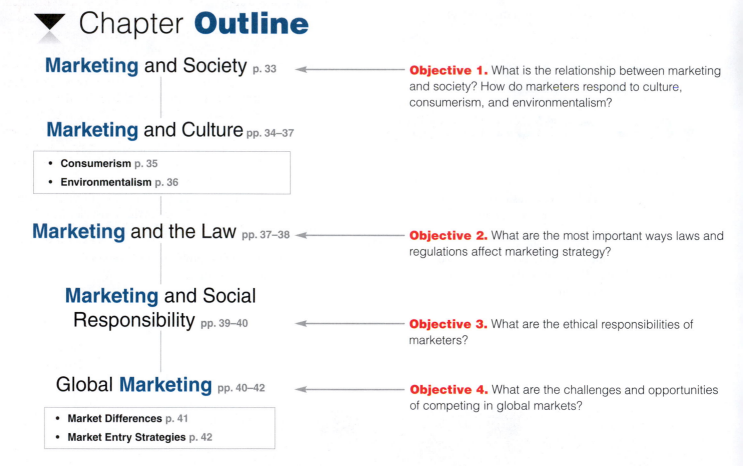

Marketing and Society p. 33 ← **Objective 1.** What is the relationship between marketing and society? How do marketers respond to culture, consumerism, and environmentalism?

Marketing and Culture pp. 34–37

- **Consumerism** p. 35
- **Environmentalism** p. 36

Marketing and the Law pp. 37–38 ← **Objective 2.** What are the most important ways laws and regulations affect marketing strategy?

Marketing and Social Responsibility pp. 39–40 ← **Objective 3.** What are the ethical responsibilities of marketers?

Global **Marketing** pp. 40–42 ← **Objective 4.** What are the challenges and opportunities of competing in global markets?

- **Market Differences** p. 41
- **Market Entry Strategies** p. 42

> ▼ **DEFINED** *A* **society** *is a community, nation, or group that shares common traditions, institutions, activities, and interests.*

▼ EXPLAINED

Marketing and Society

Maybe you enjoy a cup of coffee in the morning, brewed at home or in your local coffee shop. If you stop to think about it, you might realize that the coffee you are savoring is the result of an interconnected series of marketing actions. A coffee grower (probably in a far-away country) cultivated, harvested, and shipped the beans to a manufacturer. The manufacturer then roasted, packaged, and passed along the coffee to its retailers and distributors. Grocers stocked the shelves of their stores with attractive packages of the beans, and then consumers transformed the beans into cups of piping hot coffee.

Except for products and services provided by governments or institutions, everything in our modern consumer society is the result of marketing. Products must be developed, manufactured, distributed, advertised, and priced. Based on statistics from the Organization for Economic Cooperation and Development (OECD) for 2006, the United States is the largest single economy, with a **Gross Domestic Product (GDP)** of over $13 trillion. The combined GDP for all OECD nations (including various European and Asian nations) was over $35 trillion, reflecting part of the worldwide nature of commerce.[1]

Given marketing's economic importance, the interests of society are complex. On the one hand, a competitive marketplace and creative marketing can improve customer satisfaction. On the other, governments and institutions take a keen interest in consumer safety, public safety, and anticompetitive or unethical business practices.

▼ APPLIED

Marketing and Society

The United States is described as a "consumer society" because much of it is organized around commerce and consumer satisfaction. Modern society binds together a variety of groups and individuals in a web of interrelated activity:

- Consumers enjoy benefits from the variety of product choices brought to them through marketing. They also determine the success or failure of businesses by deciding which products to buy.
- Businesses market products and services for consumption by consumers and other businesses. Their livelihood depends on these purchases, and boundaries are set on their actions by governments and other organizations.
- Governments collect taxes from consumers and businesses and attempt to promote the welfare of the economic system by regulating any anticompetitive behavior by marketers.
- **Nongovernmental organizations (NGOs)**, like Consumers Union (CU) or People for the Ethical Treatment of Animals (PETA), are groups of private individuals that monitor the behavior of marketers or governments. They use their influence to achieve social goals such as product safety or animal rights.

With marketing so intertwined with society, it makes sense to pause and view the subject from a broader perspective. Three aspects of marketing and society worth exploring in more detail are culture, consumerism, and environmentalism.

The Consumer Product Safety Commission (CPSC) is responsible for protecting American consumers from unsafe products. During the Christmas holiday season of 2007, the number of product safety recalls by the CPSC increased dramatically. Toys produced by Chinese manufacturers were found to contain tiny magnets that could endanger children who swallowed them. Some toys had been coated in lead paint, which the CPSC banned for use on toys or furniture in 1978. Other products from China that were recalled include pet foods, drugs, and recreational products. In at least half of these cases, the problem did not originate with the Chinese firms, who were simply acting as contract manufacturers. Instead, the defects were traced to their American partners' inadequate engineering and design. In an effort to improve its political and business relationship with the United States, the Chinese authorities have begun to aggressively enforce product safety regulations. In the wake of the recalls, export licenses were revoked from 103 electronics manufacturers, 57 toy plants, and 98 food-processing firms. China's product safety agency also increased its testing and product inspection budget.[2]

PHOTO: Shutterstock

Marketing and Culture (pp. 34–37)

▼ **DEFINED** **Culture** *is the shared values, beliefs, and preferences of a particular society.*

▼ **EXPLAINED**

Marketing and Culture

Although each of us is an individual, with our own clear likes and dislikes, we are also members of larger groups (or societies). Being together and interacting with other people is a normal part of life. Psychological research into social conformity tells us that individual views and behavior can be strongly influenced by other people. As market researcher Mark Earls said, "We are a 'we' species, laboring under the illusion of 'I.'"[3]

▼ **APPLIED**

Marketing and Culture

Culture can be discussed at the national level (for example, the United States), regional level (for example, the Midwest), local level (for example, Chicago), or in terms of subcultures (for example, skateboarders). Some defining aspects of American culture include the following:[4]

- The right to choose your own destiny
- Taking control of yourself and your environment
- Egalitarianism ("All people are created equal.")
- Change equals progress
- "Time is money"
- Charity and "giving back"
- Strength in diversity

Companies craft products and services to fit nicely into this cultural landscape. State and private universities in the United States market their services as a way for students to take control of their personal destinies. Whenever a product is advertised as "new and improved," it addresses cultural beliefs that change and progress are good things. Overnight delivery services and online banking are built upon a "need for speed" among Americans, who believe that wasted time means lost opportunities.

Marketing is both a reflection of a culture and a powerful influence upon it. Clever marketers tune into what is happening within a culture (sometimes called the *zeitgeist*), and transform their insights into profitable marketing opportunities.

Certainly the most visible form of marketing is advertising. On any given day, you are exposed to hundreds of ad messages through mediums such as TV, the Internet, cell phones, billboards, transit (for example, buses, airport boards), magazines, and newspapers. Not all of these messages are noticed or remembered, but every so often an ad is successful at more than just selling a product. Its content taps into a shared feeling among members of a society, and its catchphrases are repeated in situations having almost nothing to do with the original ad.

In December 1999, Budweiser launched an advertising campaign that quickly became part of American culture and language. A group of four real-life Bud-drinking guys carry on a phone conversation, greeting each other with the now famous line "Wazzup?" The hilarious ad was so popular that it inspired dance singles and a worldwide Internet frenzy. At the height of its popularity, Budweiser's Web site logged 300,000 hits a day by consumers eager to watch the spot (and share it with others). By becoming part of the broader culture, the Wazzup? campaign created goodwill and millions of dollars worth of word-of-mouth publicity for Budweiser. As Keith Reinhard, then CEO of DDB Worldwide said, "Of the millions of words spoken in advertising, none has come close to matching the power of the simple but hip one-word question.... Nor is it likely that any word or phrase in any language will every again incite such a global phenomenon."[5]

PHOTO: Shutterstock

>> END EXAMPLE

Fashion is another way that marketing influences culture. Designers like Zara or Juicy Couture introduce new fashion styles on a regular basis, and their ideas affect what consumers feel is new, fresh, and exciting. Fashion brands are built upon image, and this foundation must be continually reinforced or it becomes stale.

eMarketer estimates that by 2010 there will be more than 210 million Americans on the Web.[6] The Internet and World Wide Web have taken the globe by storm, with marketing playing a major role in their lightning-fast adoption by consumers. E-mail has replaced traditional letter writing and phone calls. Customers sit on their couches and shop e-retailers such as Amazon.com or BestBuy.com instead of driving to their local mall. Each of these demonstrates marketing introducing products based on new technology that eventually becomes a daily part of our shared culture.

Not everyone thinks that the interaction between marketing and culture is beneficial. Marketing is seen by many people as encouraging consumption, which can become excessive or even addictive. Product packaging is sometimes wasteful and harmful to the environment. Advertising to children may exploit those members of society who are unable to make fully informed decisions. If marketers do not consider the impact of their actions on society, then, in some cases, society may decide to regulate marketing behavior. Two parts of our culture are interconnected: consumerism and environmentalism.

Consumerism

Consumerism describes the organized efforts on the part of consumer groups or governments to improve the rights and power of buyers in relation to sellers.[7] Consumerism does not need to be coordinated in any formal manner. One example of consumerism is when consumers decide, each on his or her own, to stop buying a company's products due to its business practices. In some instances, organized collective actions (called **boycotts**) can be very effective in correcting what consumers believe to be unethical or harmful marketing behavior. Boycotts work because they result in lowered sales and profitability, directly attacking something very precious to businesses: their pocketbooks. Another way boycotts influence corporate behavior is through any negative publicity they may generate. Firms that ignore or resisted boycotts have been depicted as insensitive bullies in the news media. Due to their harmful impact on financial situations and brand image, companies tend to avoid boycotts if possible.

Although consumerism in the United States has roots as far back as the early 1900s, the latest period of consumer activism began in the mid-1960s. Rising inflation led many consumers to question the real value of their purchases. More and more, they sought protection from false advertising, poor-quality products, and deceptive pricing practices.[8] At the forefront of this movement were authors like Ralph Nader, whose 1965 book *Unsafe at Any Speed* argued that owners should be protected from potentially dangerous automobiles like General Motors' Chevrolet Corvair. Upset by the negative publicity, the automaker hired private detectives to follow the author. GM's president later publicly apologized to Nader for its actions, but many observers attribute the passage of tougher automotive safety legislation to this incident.[9]

Recognizing this rising wave of consumerism, governments tried to codify the rights of individual consumers. The Consumer Bill of Rights (identified in Table 4.1) was outlined in President John F. Kennedy's 1961 inaugural speech. The bill was intended to explicitly define the four basic rights to which each and every consumer is entitled, including the right to be *safe*, to be *informed*, to be *heard*, and to *choose freely*. Many federal organizations and laws, such as the Consumer Product Safety Commission and the Truth in Lending Act, came into existence as a result of these four tenets. In 1985, the concept of consumer rights was endorsed by the United Nations and expanded to eight basic rights.[10]

Advocacy groups such as Consumers International, Consumers Union, and the Better Business Bureau act on behalf of consumers to promote their rights in the marketplace. Although they lack the legal authority of government bodies, these groups can bring substantial pressure on marketers through the media, by political lobbying, or by organizing consumer boycotts. At its core, consumerism is a signal that customers are not all happy, docile, and satisfied. Militant customers are quite willing to take aggressive action, and wise marketers attempt to be prepared for the results.[11]

EXAMPLE   CONSUMERISM

Between 1988 and 1995, over 200 companies and 1,000 products were boycotted in the United States. Boycott targets cover a wide range of industries and issues, such as the following:

- **Environmental safety**
  Since 1999, boycotts by groups such as the Rainforest Action Network have influenced over 400 large retailers and users of timber to phase out all products using wood from old-growth forests.

- **Genetically modified foods**
  Greenpeace and other organizations threatened boycotts of food marketers, including Heinz, Gerber, Frito-Lay,

Table 4.1 Eight Basic Rights

The right to safety	To be protected against products, production processes, and services that are hazardous to health or life
The right to be informed	To be given facts needed to make an informed choice, and to be protected against dishonest or misleading advertising and labeling
The right to choose	To be able to select from a range of products and services, offered at competitive prices with an assurance of satisfactory quality
The right to be heard	To have consumer interests represented in the making and execution of government policy, and in the development of products and services
The right to satisfaction of basic needs	To have access to basic essential goods and services, adequate food, clothing, shelter, health care, education, and sanitation
The right to redress	To receive a fair settlement of just claims, including compensation for misrepresentation, shoddy goods, or unsatisfactory services
The right to consumer education	To acquire knowledge and skills needed to make informed, confident choices about goods and services while being aware of basic consumer rights and responsibilities and how to act on them
The right to a healthy environment	To live and work in an environment that is nonthreatening to the well-being of present and future generations

McDonald's, and Burger King to ensure that their products are free of genetically modified ingredients.

- **Animal rights**
  Boycotts by PETA persuaded McDonald's, Burger King, and Wendy's to require humane production practices from their suppliers of chickens, eggs, and other meats.

Research by Davidson, Worrell, and El-Jelly found evidence that boycotts can be effective in changing corporate behavior. Boycotts send a strong signal to marketers' wallets, resulting in a type of "stakeholder capitalism" where consumers discover empowerment in their wallets.[12,13]

PHOTO: G. Lancia

>> END EXAMPLE

Environmentalism

Each year, about 90 million people are born, placing even greater demands on our planet's resources. Societal concerns over climate change, diminishing natural resources, and pollution are causing a growing number of consumers to question their consumption habits.

Environmentalism is an organized movement of citizens, businesses, and government agencies to protect and improve our living environment. As a social movement, environmentalism is expressed in a variety of ways, from consumer boycotts of environmentally unfriendly products to formal government legislation.

Green marketing is a catchall phrase describing how marketing has responded to the environmental movement by offering more ecologically responsible products and services. Being "green" can mean many things, from ensuring that your product is free of harmful chemicals, to arranging a means to recycle or reclaim some of your product's ingredients at the end of its useful life. Environmentally responsible questions for marketers include the following:

- What chemicals or processes will be used to create this product?
- How much energy will be consumed in its creation?
- Can the product be used safely and with minimal impact on the environment?
- Can the product be disposed of or recycled in a manner that poses minimal or no risk to the environment?
- Is there a more environmentally sound alternative to this product?

EXAMPLE   **ENVIRONMENTALISM**

A growing number of consumers will only use cleaning products made from environmentally friendly ingredients. This "green cleaning" movement accounted for about $300 million in sales, or 2% of the total market for household cleaning products in 2006.

Method is a company that sells biodegradable cleaning products, including laundry detergent, dish soap, spray cleaners, and scented plug-ins. Combining thoughtful design with "green" ingredients at an affordable price, Method's slogan is "people against dirty." The company's watchwords are *environment*, *safety*, *efficacy*, *design*, and *fragrance*.

Products come in appealing packages with fresh scents like lavender or ylang-ylang. One of Method's most innovative products is the omop, which is a nontoxic, microfiber floor cleaner. In keeping with the growing importance of "green" products, Method can be found at large retailers such as Target, Office Depot, and Costco in the United States, Canada, and the United Kingdom.

According to market research firm Kline & Company, Method was one of the fastest-growing companies of its type in 2006, with sales of $85 million (up 140%).[14,15,16]

PHOTO: Michal Bednarek

>> END EXAMPLE

The market for environmentally and socially responsible products can be divided into distinct customer segments. A segmentation study conducted by the Natural Marketing Institute in 2007 identified the following five core groups in the United States based on lifestyles of health and sustainability (LOHAS):[17]

FIGURE 4.1	**Five Core Groups**

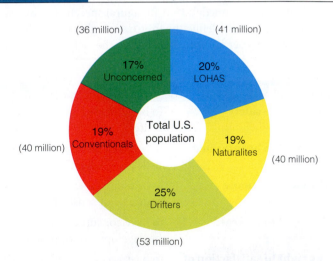

- **LOHAS** are dedicated to the health of themselves and the planet. They purchase environmentally friendly products and are active in related causes.
- **Naturalites** focus on natural and organic products, especially food and beverages.
- **Drifters** mean well, but they are price sensitive and trendy regarding their purchases. They have several rationalizations for not buying environmentally friendly products.

- **Conventionals** are practical and do not have overtly "green" attitudes, but they will recycle, conserve energy, and engage in other mainstream eco-behaviors.
- **Unconcerned** do not make protecting the environment or improving society a priority. They demonstrate no environmentally responsible behavior.

In 2008, about 20% of Americans could be classified as members of a LOHAS segment. They spent 10% more in warehouse clubs and bought more cereal, jelly, pasta, produce, and soup than "nongreen" consumers. The economic impact of consumers who have adopted an environmental mindset can be tremendous. According to research by Mambo Sprouts Marketing, 7 in 10 consumers are willing to spend up to 20% more for "green" sustainable products.[18]

Organic foods are those grown without the use of pesticides or synthetic fertilizers. These products are considered better for the environment because they reduce pollution and conserve water and soil. The market for organic foods was $4.4 billion annually in 2008, and is expected to increase to $6.8 billion by 2012.[19] Smart marketers are paying attention to the social risks, and the economic rewards, presented by the environmental movement.

Marketing and the Law (pp. 37–38)

 DEFINED Laws *are rules of conduct or action prescribed by an authority, or the binding customs or practices of a community.*

 **EXPLAINED**
Marketing and the Law

Although the vast majority of businesspeople conduct themselves in a responsible and ethical manner, the risks are too great to assume that everyone will do so. To protect consumers and maintain economic stability, the U.S. government periodically institutes laws and regulations to deter harmful marketing behavior. Areas of marketing that are of particular interest to legislators include the following:

- False advertising
- Deceptive pricing practices
- Tobacco advertising
- Children's advertising
- Product safety
- Nutritional labeling
- Consumer privacy
- Fairness in lending practices

A broader definition of "law" also includes social practices or customs. Whether as individuals or in organized groups, from time to time, consumers themselves attempt to limit some business activities and encourage others. As of 2006, there were approximately 20,000 NGOs outside the United States and about 2 million in the United States.[20] Although these actions lack the official rule of law, they can be equally (or more) effective in governing marketing behavior if a business is truly consumer-oriented.

 APPLIED
Marketing and the Law

The federal government has created several official agencies to protect the interests of consumers and the general public. These agencies are taken very seriously, because businesspeople who violate the agencies' standards can be affected professionally and personally, and face fines or imprisonment. Each of the following regulatory bodies has influence over areas of policy related to marketing:[21]

- **Consumer Product Safety Commission (CPSC)**—This agency monitors product safety and issues recalls for unsafe products. It also establishes standards for product safety.
- **Environmental Protection Agency (EPA)**—The EPA develops and enforces regulations to protect the environment, some of which affect the materials and processes marketers may use to manufacture products.
- **Federal Communications Commission (FCC)**—Any firm that uses broadcast media (telephone, radio, or television) for marketing is affected by FCC rules.
- **Federal Trade Commission (FTC)**—The FTC enforces laws against deceptive advertising and product labeling regulations.
- **Food and Drug Administration (FDA)**—This agency enforces laws and regulations on foods, drugs, cosmetics, and veterinary products. Before introducing new drugs and other products into the marketplace manufacturers must first obtain FDA approval.
- **Interstate Commerce Commission (ICC)**—The ICC regulates all interstate bus, truck, rail, and water operations. ICC regulations and policies can impact the efficiency of marketing distribution channels.

A **regulation** is a rule or order issued by an official government agency that has proper authority that carries the force of law. Marketers must learn to successfully operate within constraints imposed by these requirements. Table 4.2 contains some major federal laws that have fostered regulations on marketing activity.[22]

From a consumer perspective, the most visible areas of government regulation on marketing are advertising, pricing, and product safety. The FTC is responsible for ensuring compliance with a wide range of regulations on pricing and promotion. Examples of federal regulation in these areas include the following:[23]

- Advertisers must have documented proof of any claims made in an advertisement before the ad runs—letters from satisfied customers are usually not sufficient.
- It is illegal to say that a product has a "retail value of $15.00, your price: $7.50," if $15.00 is not the prevailing price for the product in the retailer's geographic area.

Table 4.2 Major Federal Laws and Regulations

Law	Area of Marketing Regulated by Law
Sherman Antitrust Act (1890)	Distribution (for example, exclusive territories)
	Pricing (for example, price fixing, predatory pricing)
Food and Drug Act (1906)	Product safety (for example, food and drugs)
Clayton Act (1914)	Distribution (for example, tying contracts and exclusive dealing)
Federal Trade Commission (FTC) Act (1914)	All areas of marketing that result in unfair business practices
Robinson-Patman Act (1936)	Pricing (for example, price discrimination)
Wheeler-Lea Amendment to FTC Act (1938)	Promotion (for example, deceptive or misleading advertising)
Lanham Trademark Act (1946)	Branding (for example, brand names and trademarks)
Fair Packaging and Labeling Act (1966)	Packaging (for example, truth in labeling)
National Traffic and Motor Vehicle Safety Act (1966)	Product safety (for example, automobile and tire safety)
Cigarette Labeling Act (1966)	Product (for example, cigarette package warnings)
Child Protection Act (1966)	Product safety (for example, children's product safety)
Child Protection and Toy Safety Act (1969)	Packaging (for example, child-resistant packages)
Consumer Credit Protection Act (1968)	Promotion (for example, credit terms, loan terms)
Fair Credit Reporting Act (1970)	Information sharing (for example, credit reporting)
Consumer Products Safety Commission Act (1972)	Product safety (for example, safety monitoring, recalls, safety standards)
Magunuson-Moss Consumer Product Warranty Act (1975)	Product (for example, warranties)
Children's Television Act (1990)	Promotion (for example, children's advertising)
Nutrition Labeling and Education Act (1990)	Packaging (for example, food and drug labeling)
National Do Not Call Registry (2003)	Promotion (for example, telemarketing)

- It is illegal to advertise any product when a company has no plans to sell it, but instead plans to switch customers to another item at a higher price (called a bait-and-switch).

The FTC looks at advertising from the point of view of a reasonable consumer and asks, "Would a typical person looking at this ad be fooled or harmed by this?" If the answer is yes, the FTC may issue a cease and desist order, forcing the marketers to stop running the deceptive ad. It may also invoke civil penalties (which can range from thousands to millions of dollars) and might even force the company to create new ads to correct any misinformation.

Marketers do have a bit of leeway in making statements and claims regarding their products and services. Claims of product superiority that cannot be proven as true or false are called **puffery**, and are a generally accepted marketing practice. For example, saying "ABC cola tastes great!" is puffery, but saying "ABC water filters remove harmful chemicals from tap water" is not. On the other hand, **exaggerated claims** are restricted by the FTC. Every marketer that makes an explicit or implicit claim about its products or services should have substantiation or a reasonable basis for that statement. For example, ads for health products may boast that a product is a "medical breakthrough" or that it was "tested across the world." By law, anyone making these claims should have solid evidence in place before running these ads.

EXAMPLE   REGULATIONS

Makers of the dietary supplement Airborne advertised and labeled their product as an effective treatment to prevent illnesses contracted when traveling on airplanes or in other public environments. The FTC investigated and found that Airborne "did not have adequate evidence to support its advertising claims in which its effervescent tablet was marketed as a cold prevention and treatment remedy." As a result, the makers of Airborne reached a $30 million settlement with the FTC, and consumers who purchased the product were able to file claims for refunds.[24,25]

PHOTO: Mark Stout Photography

>> END EXAMPLE

Another organization that issues regulations that affect marketing is the Consumer Product Safety Commission (CPSC). The CPSC is a watchdog organization whose charter is the protection and safety of consumers. It issues regulations on the ingredients and processes marketers can use when manufacturing their products. It also carries the authority to ban or seize potentially harmful products. Marketers who violate its regulations face severe penalties.

Marketing and Social Responsibility *(pp. 39–40)*

▼ **DEFINED** Social responsibility *is concern for how a person's (or company's) actions might affect the interests of others.*

▼ **EXPLAINED**
Marketing and Social Responsibility

A business cannot be separated from the society in which it operates. A business's influence is felt through its products and services, its production methods, its pricing, its advertising, its distribution methods, and how it distributes its profits. Recognizing the interrelationships between companies and society, many firms have adopted a policy of **corporate social responsibility (CSR)** that encourages decision makers to take into account the social consequences of their business actions.

Profitability has been the traditional yardstick used to measure the success, or failure, of a business. As a result of using such a yardstick, the interests of society become secondary to monetary goals. Proponents of corporate social responsibility argue that companies should earn profits in an ethical manner that respects people and communities. They also suggest that companies ought to promote **sustainability** through careful stewardship of our natural resources and the environment.

Some people believe that marketing should not only avoid creating harm to society, but should also be used to benefit society. The **social marketing concept** asserts that marketing techniques may be employed for more than selling things and making a profit. Marketing tools can be applied to causes that improve the lives of individuals and society. One of the best examples of social marketing in action is the TRUTH antismoking advertising campaign. Using a variety of nontraditional and traditional media such as TV, promotional items (T-shirts), posters, and graffiti, TRUTH ads were credited with significant reductions in the number of middle- and high-school students who began smoking.

▼ **APPLIED**
Marketing and Social Responsibility

"To my mind, industry must aim for, exist for, and everlastingly operate for the good of the community. The community cannot ride one track and business another. The two are inseparable, interactive, and interdependent."
Cleo F. Craig, President, AT&T (1951–1956)

Corporate social responsibility is not a notion confined to textbooks and academia. Many major corporations now accept the tenets of CSR, and weigh their marketing decisions accordingly. Coca-Cola, Ford Motor Company, Marathon Oil, Bayer, Colgate-Palmolive, Nestlé, Motorola, and Starbucks are just a few companies that have issued formal corporate social responsibility reports.

CSR is closely related to principles of ethical business behavior. **Ethics** are a system of moral principles and values, as well as moral duties or obligations. A simple way to think about ethics is that they determine which actions are "good," or correct from a philosophical or social point of view. A similar set of principles, called **marketing ethics**, are rules for evaluating marketing decisions and actions based on marketers' duties or obligations to society (see marketing ethics below).

CSR assumes that marketers have a responsibility to behave in an ethical manner, and that decisions that negatively impact society are often unethical. There is even talk about a "triple bottom line," asserting that firms should be evaluated not only on their economic performance but also on their environmental and social impacts. Ethics codes, like the one published by the American Marketing Association, are an attempt to lay down general norms and guidelines for ethical marketing behavior.[26]

Sometimes what is permitted legally is not necessarily ethical. For instance, a company might stop selling a product in developed nations where consumer safety regulations are strict and the product is found to be harmful. Although the firm could begin selling its product in less developed countries where legal restrictions are more lax, some people might find this action unethical. If a product is unsafe for human consumption in one country, it is equally unfit for another. An ethical lapse such as this sometimes happens because it is difficult to choose between what is legally permitted and what is ethical when profits or personal advancement are at stake.

General Norms

1. Marketers must do no harm. This means doing work for which they are appropriately trained or in which they are experienced so that they can actively add value to their organizations and customers. It also means adhering to all applicable laws and regulations and embodying high ethical standards in the choices they make.

2. Marketers must foster trust in the marketing system. This means that products are appropriate for their intended and promoted uses. It requires that marketing communications about goods and services are not intentionally deceptive or misleading. It suggests building relationships that provide for the equitable alignment and/or redress of consumer grievances. It implies striving for good faith and fair dealing so as to contribute to the efficacy of the exchange process.

3. Marketers must embrace ethical values. These basic values are intended to be values to which marketers aspire and include *honesty*, *responsibility*, *fairness*, *respect*, *openness*, and *citizenship*.

EXAMPLE   SOCIAL RESPONSIBILITY

Food marketing is big business, and young people are a particularly attractive target. Soda, snacks, candy, fast food, and other high-energy but nutrient-poor foods have been marketed to youth in North America, Europe, and Australasia (New Zealand, Australia, Papua New Guinea, and neighboring islands in the Pacific Ocean) for years. In the United States, over $10 billion is spent annually marketing food to young consumers; a new emphasis has been placed on promotion in schools and on the Internet. In 2006, the Institute of Medicine concluded that food and beverage marketing is a "likely contributor to less healthful diets" and that it "may contribute to negative diet-related health outcomes and risks among children and youth." Childhood obesity has become a worldwide problem, with 10% of children worldwide estimated to be overweight or obese. Given the link between marketing, food choices, and health problems among youth, what should companies such as Coca-Cola, Frito-Lay, and Burger King do? Should they take a short-term view, focus on profits, and continue with "business as usual" while contributing to a growing health problem? Or, should they focus on long-term social benefits by offering healthier food options, but possibly alienating customers who have been conditioned to prefer less healthy foods?[27]

PHOTO: Amy Walters

>> END EXAMPLE

Defenders of CSR suggest that a company's reputation depends on the totality of its actions, and that "doing the right thing" at all times will have long-term economic benefits. Surveys have indicated that consumers are willing to pay a higher price for products from firms that give priority to ethical behavior.[28] However, businesses in poorer countries or those in financial distress may be faced with the choice of either complying with CSR principles or going out of business. Like most conceptual frameworks, the application of ethics and social responsibility in the real world is sometimes a delicate balance.

EXAMPLE   CORPORATE SOCIAL RESPONSIBILITY

When you think of corporate social responsibility, a bank may not be the first business that comes to mind. For years, Wells Fargo has provided financial services such as banking, insurance, investments, and mortgages while still guiding its marketing

decisions by CSR principles. Here are some examples of socially responsible marketing actions taken by Wells Fargo in 2007:[29]

- **Serving customers responsibly**—The company adopted responsible lending principles and marketing practices for education financing.
- **Supporting homeownership**—The company launched Hope Now, an alliance of mortgage servicers, not-for-profit counselors, and investors in the capital markets to help homeowners at risk of foreclosure.
- **Building communities**—The company invested $337 million in community-development projects for affordable housing, schools, economic development, community revitalization, and job creation.
- **Volunteering**—During 2007, 20,000 Wells Fargo team members volunteered 796,000 hours worth $14.7 million in person hours.
- **Financial education**—In addition to its Hands on Banking financial education curriculum, Wells Fargo launched the Teen Checking project to improve young people's financial knowledge.
- **Protecting the environment**—Committed to purchasing 550 million kilowatt-hours of renewable energy certificates each year for three years, making Wells Fargo the second largest purchaser of renewable energy.
- **Putting our people first**—Wells Fargo offers flexible work arrangements and work/life programs to support team members. *BusinessWeek* ranked Wells Fargo among the top 50 best places to launch a career in 2007.

PHOTO: Kristian Sekulic

>> END EXAMPLE

Global **Marketing** (pp. 40–42)

 DEFINED Global marketing *includes all marketing activities conducted at an international level by individuals or businesses.*

 EXPLAINED

Global Marketing

Our world today is made up of about 6.5 billion people who are connected by global communications networks and relatively inexpensive transportation. **Globalization** is the outcome of cultures intermingling, sharing experiences, news, and commerce. Richard N. Haass, president of the Council on Foreign Relations, described globalization as "the increasing volume, speed, and importance of flows across borders: people, ideas, greenhouse gases, manufactured goods, dollars, euros, television and radio signals, drugs, germs, emails, weapons, and a good deal else."[30]

International trade (and marketing) is one of the driving forces behind globalization. China and India are quickly strengthening their ability to compete in the global marketplace, and their influence on mainstream American culture is already beginning to be felt. The growing popularity of Indian Bollywood films and Japanese *manga* comics are just two examples. Some of the benefits of global trade to businesses and nations include the following:

- Access to new and possibly growing consumer markets
- Obtaining scale economies (that is, reducing costs by increasing production volume)
- Access to lower cost labor or materials
- Ability to offset domestic economic cycles
- Enhanced brand image and perceptions
- Ability to overcome trade barriers (for example, tariffs or quotas on imports)
- Access to foreign investment incentives

Even on a global scale, the basic functions of marketing do not change. A product must still be offered at a fair price whether it is sold in Paris, France or in Paris, Texas. But a "fair price" could be defined quite differently in those two locations. National, regional, and local differences make global marketing more complex and difficult.

When consumer tastes differ at a local level, marketers are tempted to modify products, services, prices, distribution methods, and communications to cater to those tastes. However, extensive customization also defeats one of the primary benefits of global trade, which is to lower production costs through standardization. Successful global marketers do not think solely in terms of "local" versus "global." Instead, they are "**glocal**"— acting either globally, locally, or both, as needed. About 60% of McDonald's products sold in India are international, while 40% of its items, like the Paneer Salsa Wrap or McAloo Tikki, are specially designed to satisfy local tastes.[31]

 APPLIED

Global Marketing

When conducting global marketing, the first step is to decide whether a company actually needs a global marketing strategy. The primary motivations for embarking on global marketing are to offset sluggish economic growth in a home market, capitalize on market opportunities abroad, or directly compete with other global competitors. Some firms are completely local in nature, and conducting business on an international scale would add unnecessary cost and complexity.

The next step involves looking at potential markets, assessing their differences, and selecting some (or all) for eventual market entry. This is a critical step, as an incorrect market assessment could lead a firm to invest heavily in a market with little potential. The third step is to decide the method of entry into each selected market. Some markets are attractive only if they are handled at arm's length through exporting, while others are ripe for full-scale investment. Once the entry method has been selected, the firm can then develop and execute marketing strategies for each market. At this point, global marketing for the company has begun.

Market Differences

A **market** is a place, either physical or virtual, where buyers and sellers come together to exchange goods and services. Nations, regions, localities, or portions of the Web are all markets. It is not uncommon for large companies to operate in dozens of markets. The Coca-Cola Company sells products in more than 200 markets, including Fiji, Morocco, Nigeria, and Bulgaria. More than 70% of Coca-Cola's net operating revenues come from its operations outside the United States.[32]

Not every market is equally attractive. The economic, political, and cultural situation in a market may help or hinder business activities. Some important differences and questions to consider when evaluating a market are as follows:[33]

- Market potential
- Customer characteristics
- Competition
- Local culture
- Economic outlook
- Political outlook
- Government policies
- Financial requirements
- Labor market
- Taxation
- Legal environment
- Crime and corruption
- Infrastructure
- Foreign trade environment
- Current and future costs of building a business and brand

In developed markets like the United States or Europe, it has become harder to sustain high rates of GDP growth. For example, revenue growth among developed countries averages around 1–4%. Marketers are subsequently exploring opportunities in emerging markets like Russia, China, and the Middle East. In 2004, firms in Iran or Dubai were averaging 10–25% growth and Chinese or Russian companies were averaging 20–35% growth.[34]

EXAMPLE   MARKET DIFFERENCES

Samsung is a global manufacturer of consumer electronics, producing TVs, PDAs, mobile phones, DVD players, and other consumer electronics and appliances. By the late 1990s, Samsung decided to take aggressive action to close the gap between itself and market leader Sony in the international marketplace.

Formulating a global marketing strategy was daunting. Samsung marketed products in 14 different categories in more than 200 countries. To allocate resources and maximize return on investment, Samsung needed to prioritize each and every

market and category. Data collected for each region included the following:

- Overall population and target buyer population
- Spending power per capita
- Category penetration rates
- Overall growth of categories
- Share of each of Samsung's brands
- Media costs
- Previous marketing expenditures
- Category profitability
- Competitor metrics

Samsung then created an information repository, called M-Net, that could be accessed by each region's marketing group, as well as Samsung headquarters. Using analytic engines, marketing executives built predictive models to tell them both the current and the estimated future position of each market.

As a result, Samsung found that it was overinvesting in North America and Russia, and spending too little in Europe and China. Three product categories—mobile phones, vacuums, and air-conditioners—were also consuming too many marketing resources relative to their growth potential. Other categories, such as DVDs, TVs, and PC monitors, held greater growth and profit potential.

Based on its analysis of market differences, Samsung reallocated marketing resources and launched a new global branding campaign. Afterward, Samsung saw increases in its global brand equity and sales and net income both rose sharply. Interbrand reported that Samsung had become the fastest-growing global brand name.[35]

PHOTO: Shutterstock

>> **END EXAMPLE**

Market Entry Strategies

When selecting a market entry strategy, marketers balance how much risk, cost, and profitability they are willing to accept. Lower-risk strategies are usually cheaper, but profit opportunities are limited. Higher-risk strategies can be more expensive, but have the potential for higher rewards. Figure 4.2 illustrates three categories of market entry strategies:[36]

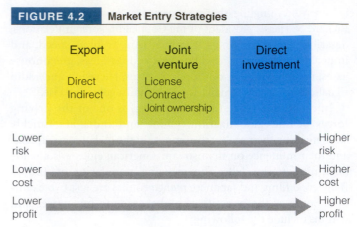

FIGURE 4.2   **Market Entry Strategies**

- **Exporting**—A common form of market entry, **exporting** occurs when a company produces in its home market and then transports its products to other nations for sale. Exporting may be either **indirect** (when a firm sells through intermediaries) or **direct** (when it establishes its own overseas sales branches). This entry strategy insulates marketers from risk because they remain distant from the market and allows them to avoid costs associated with other forms of entry. However, it also limits profit potential, because exporting partners must be paid for their services.
- **Joint Ventures**—Marketers engaged in a **joint venture** must be willing to accept more risk, because this entry strategy means they are teaming with a host company in the particular market they are entering. Under a **licensing** approach, marketers are paid fees or royalties by partner firms in the host country for the right to use a brand, manufacturing process, or patent. Marketers may also directly hire **contract manufacturers** in the host nation to manufacture products on their behalf. The most expensive and risky form of joint venture is **joint ownership**, which occurs when a firm joins with a foreign investor to build its own local business. In some cases, joint ownership may even be required by a host country.
- **Direct Investment**—The riskiest and most expensive market entry strategy is **direct investment**. Firms pursuing a direct investment strategy establish foreign-based manufacturing facilities. Some benefits of direct investment include taking advantage of local cost differences and gaining better knowledge about the wants and needs of consumers in the local market. Because marketers do not need to share revenues with local partners, profit opportunities are greatest under a direct investment scenario.

Multinational companies use a variety of market entry strategies. McDonald's uses a form of licensing called **franchising**, in which local firms purchase the right to use its processes and brand in their restaurants. Automotive manufacturers like GM directly invest in markets, in part to gain a better understanding of local customers and to satisfy government requirements for local content in its products.

▼ **Visual** Summary

Chapter 4 Summary

From a broader perspective, marketing involves society, the legal environment, ethics, and international trade. Consumers, companies, and culture interact in ways that can be either mutually beneficial or destructive. The force of law, both official and unofficial, is intended to curb marketing excesses and to encourage proper conduct. Consumer-driven agendas, such as consumerism, environmentalism, and corporate social responsibility, are topics companies must learn to integrate into their marketing strategies. Global markets present complicated challenges for marketers, along with great opportunities and risks.

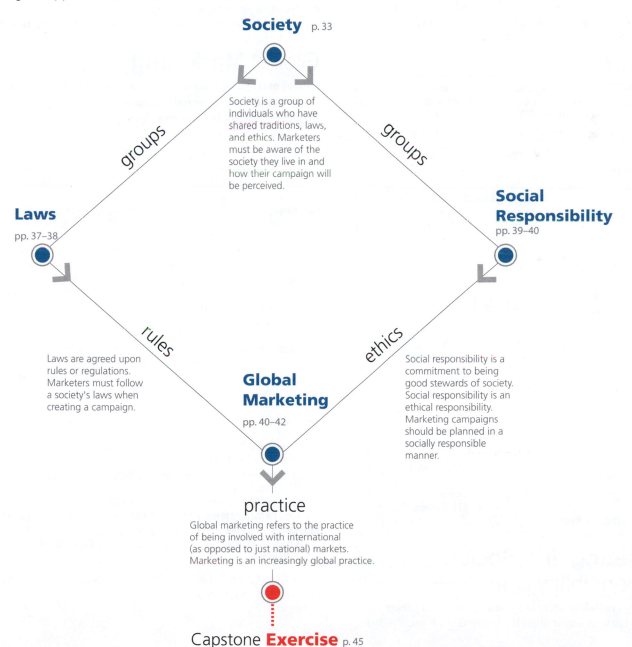

Society p. 33

Society is a group of individuals who have shared traditions, laws, and ethics. Marketers must be aware of the society they live in and how their campaign will be perceived.

groups   groups

Laws
pp. 37–38

Social Responsibility
pp. 39–40

rules   ethics

Laws are agreed upon rules or regulations. Marketers must follow a society's laws when creating a campaign.

Global Marketing
pp. 40–42

Social responsibility is a commitment to being good stewards of society. Social responsibility is an ethical responsibility. Marketing campaigns should be planned in a socially responsible manner.

practice

Global marketing refers to the practice of being involved with international (as opposed to just national) markets. Marketing is an increasingly global practice.

Capstone **Exercise** p. 45

▼**Chapter** Key Terms

Marketing and Society (p. 33)

Society refers to a community, nation, or group that shares common traditions, institutions, activities, and interests. (p. 33)
Opening Example (p. 33)

Key Terms (pp. 33)

Gross Domestic Product (GDP) measures the total dollar value of goods and services a country produces within a given year. **(p. 33)**

Nongovernmental organizations (NGOs) are groups of private individuals that monitor the behavior of marketers or governments. **(p. 33)**

Marketing and Culture (pp. 34–37)

Culture refers to the shared values, beliefs, and preferences of a particular society. (p. 34) **Example: Culture (p. 34)**

Key Terms (pp. 34–37)

Boycotts happen when consumers refuse to do business with a company or nation in order to signal their disapproval of its actions and encourage change. **(p. 35) Example: Consumerism (p. 35)**

Consumerism is the organized efforts on the part of consumer groups or governments to improve the rights and power of buyers in relation to sellers. **(p. 35) Opening Example (p. 33) Example: Consumerism (p. 35)**

Environmentalism is an organized movement of citizens, businesses, and government agencies to protect and improve our living environment. **(p. 36) Example: Environmentalism (p. 36) Example: Consumerism (p. 35)**

Green marketing refers to marketing efforts to product more environmentally responsible products and services. **(p. 36) Example: Environmentalism (p. 36)**

Organic foods are foods grown naturally without the use of pesticides or synthetic fertilizers. **(p. 37)**

Marketing and the Law (pp. 37–38)

Laws are rules of conduct or action prescribed by an authority, or the binding customs or practices of a community. (p. 37)
Example: Regulations (p. 38)

Key Terms (pp. 37–38)

Exaggerated claims are extravagant statements made in advertising, either explicitly or implicitly, that have no substantiation or reasonable basis in truth. **(p. 38) Example: Regulations (p. 38)**

Puffery refers to claims of product superiority that cannot be proven as true or false. **(p. 38)**

Regulations are rules or orders issued by an official government agency with proper authority that carries the force of law. **(p. 37) Opening Example (p. 33) Example: Regulations (p. 38)**

Marketing and Social Responsibility (pp. 39–40)

Social responsibility refers to a concern for how a person's (or company's) actions might affect the interests of others. (p. 39)

Example: Corporate Social Responsibility (p. 40) Example: Social Responsibility (p. 40)

Key Terms (pp. 39–40)

Corporate social responsibility (CSR) is a philosophy that encourages decision makers to take into account the social consequences of their business actions. **(p. 39) Example: Corporate Social Responsibility (p. 40)**

Ethics are a system of moral principles and values, as well as moral duties or obligations. **(p. 39) Example: Corporate Social Responsibility (p. 40)**

Marketing ethics are rules for evaluating marketing decisions and actions based on marketers' duties or obligations to society. **(p. 39) Example: Social Marketing Responsibility (p. 40)**

Social marketing concept asserts that marketing techniques may be employed for more than selling things and making a profit. **(p. 39) Example: Corporate Social Responsibility (p. 40)**

Sustainability is a term used to describe practices that combine economic growth with careful stewardship of our natural resources and the environment. **(p. 39)**

Global **Marketing** (pp. 40–42)

Global marketing includes all marketing activities conducted at an international level by individuals or businesses. (p. 40)
Example: Market Differences (p. 41)

Key Terms (pp. 40–42)

Contract manufacturers are manufacturing firms that a company hires to manufacture products on its behalf. **(p. 42)**

Direct exporting occurs when a firm establishes its own overseas sales branches to export to a foreign country. **(p. 42) Example: Market Differences (p. 41)**

Direct investment occurs when a firm establishes its own foreign-based manufacturing operations and businesses. **(p. 42)**

Exporting occurs when a company produces in its home market and then transports its products to other nations for sale. **(p. 42) Opening Example (p. 33) Example: Market Differences (p. 41)**

Franchising occurs when a company sells the rights to use its brand or processes in a service business. **(p. 42)**

Indirect exporting occurs when a firm exports its products through intermediaries in a host country. **(p. 42)**

Globalization is the effect of an intermingling of international cultures sharing experiences, news, and commerce. **(p. 40) Opening Example (p. 33) Example: Market Differences (p. 41)**

Glocal is a slang term used to describe the tension between uniform global and customized local business strategies. **(p. 41)**

Joint ownership occurs when a company joins with an investor to build its own local business. **(p. 42)**

Joint venture refers to the situation in which one company teams with another for the purposes of conducting business and marketing. **(p. 42)**

Licensing is the practice of a company receiving fees or royalties from partner firms for the right to use a brand, manufacturing process, or patent. **(p. 42)**

Market refers to a place, either physical or virtual, where buyers and sellers come together to exchange goods and services. **(p. 41) Example: Market Differences (p. 41)**

▼Capstone Exercise

How do marketers deal with marketing socially controversial products such as cigarettes, liquor, firearms, gambling, and pornography? Depending on your personal views, selling these products can be perfectly fine, or not. Without debating the issues relating to these products, your exercise is to understand how regulation and ethics affect the marketing of such products. Do companies have a social responsibility to not sell such products?

We focus on the marketing of cigarettes in this example. Starting in 1964, the surgeon general of the United States issued a report raising the issue of cigarettes and their harmful effect on the nation's health. Since then, a variety of organizations have pushed to limit the sales of cigarettes to the public in general and to certain age groups. These restrictions have included health warnings on packages, limits on the age to purchase cigarettes, limits on the types of promotion and advertising, and imposing taxes that raise the price of the product. Yet the tobacco industry still exists, with an increasing number of young people still starting smoking.

This chapter's exercise is to decide the following:

- If you were the marketing manager for a tobacco company, how would you feel about your job and its duties and why?

- How would you deal with government-imposed restrictions limiting your choices of media? Should the government impose limits on the sale of such products? Who are your target markets, and why? What media would you use to reach them, and why?

- What are the issues in increasing your global marketing efforts in countries where there are few or no government regulations that affect the sale of these products?

▼Application Exercises

Complete the following exercises:

1. Spirited debates about the relationship of marketing to society can be very interesting. Organize a series of debates in your class between individuals or small teams of two or three students. Have each person or team prepare to argue an opposing point of view on an issue concerning society and marketing. Some ideas for topics are as follows:
   - Is society helped or harmed by marketing?
   - Does marketing exploit certain members of society (for example, children, lower-income consumers)?
   - To what degree should marketers act according to a strict code of ethics in all places and situations?

   You could also invent your own topic based on the material in this chapter. You may want to conduct a bit of research and prepare notes before holding an open debate in class.

2. Write a paper answering the question "Is environmentalism more of an opportunity or threat for marketers?" Use your library or the Internet to find instances where environmentalism either helped or hurt marketing efforts. Be sure to take a stand one way or the other on this question, and support your conclusion with clear arguments.

3. Corporate reputation or image can be seen as society's assessment of the sum of all actions taken by a company. Research firms like Harris Interactive regularly conduct surveys to assess corporate reputation and report the results. A quick search of the Web using keywords such as "corporate reputation survey" and the current year should bring up one or more examples. Who has the best reputation? Who has the worst? What actions by each company led to its relative ranking? How much do you think marketing has to do with a company's ranking? Regarding the lower-ranked company, is there any way marketing could be used to improve its position?

4. Global marketing is a complex task, because companies must juggle differences in language, consumer tastes, income levels, infrastructure, customs, and laws. Choose a country or region other than your own that you find interesting. Do some research to understand how that market is similar to or different from where you live. Does your research suggest any major implications for marketing? Be prepared to talk about your findings in class.

chapter **5**

Part 1	Explaining (Chapters 1, 2, 3, 4)		Part 4	Managing (Chapters 11, 12, 13, 14, 15)
Part 2	Creating (Chapters 5, 6, 7, 8)		Part 5	Integrating (Chapters 16, 17)
Part 3	Strategizing (Chapters 9, 10)			

Value for **Customers**

Chapter Overview This chapter examines the principles that drive today's customer-focused companies, specifically those principles regarding creating value for the customers. When customers receive value in excess of their expectations, their level of customer satisfaction with the brand is high, they are more likely to continue buying the brand, and they form a customer loyalty to the brand. Successful companies seek to develop customer loyalty in an effort to build long-term relationships, which leads to higher revenue and greater profitability. To strengthen customer loyalty, companies focus their efforts on relationship marketing so as to fully understand customers and to stay abreast of their changing needs. The implementation of relationship marketing requires using customer relationship management techniques that allow companies to stay connected with their customers.

Chapter **Outline**

CUSTOMER VALUE (pp. 47–48)

> ▼ **DEFINED Customer value** *is the difference between the benefits a customer receives and the total cost incurred from acquiring, using, and disposing of a product.*

Customer Value

The number of products that are available to potential buyers has increased dramatically in recent decades. Products are offered with a variety of features, at different levels of quality, and at various prices. With so many different options, how do buyers select which products to purchase? At the most basic level, buyers make a purchase decision based on the value they perceive a product will deliver. Buyers accomplish this by weighing the differences between the perceived costs of the product and the perceived benefits gained from owning the product. This can be shown with the following formula:

Customer Perceived Value = Perceived Benefits – Perceived Costs

Because each buyer will have different perceptions as to the benefits a product will deliver, as well as different interpretations of the perceived costs, the perceived value that a product will deliver varies between groups of customers. In most cases, buyers select the brand that they perceive will provide them with the greatest value. Some buyers will therefore select the high-quality, high-priced product that is loaded with features, while other buyers will opt for a product that has fewer features and a lower price. This is one of the principal reasons there are so many different brands available in the market.

Customer Value

Benefits are delivered in ways other than just a product's functional use. **Functional use** can be described as the purpose for seeking a product. For example, the functional use of a drill bit is to drill a hole. Other benefits a product provides can come from elements such as the brand name, product features, and product warranty. The elements of a product will be explained in much greater depth when product strategies are discussed in Chapter 11.

A product's cost has multiple elements that include more than the purchase price. There are often additional costs associated with owning a product, such as the expenses involved with using, maintaining, and disposing of a product. For example, in addition to its higher purchase price, the total cost of owning an SUV is much higher than that of owning a smaller, more fuel-efficient automobile. These additional costs, such as operating costs (due to lower fuel efficiency) and higher disposal costs (due to lower resale values), have resulted in many buyers having a reduced perceived value for SUVs. That reduced value has resulted in a dramatic drop in the sales of SUVs and an increase in the sales of smaller vehicles that are less expensive to operate. The tradeoff between benefits and price is shown in Figure 5.1.

Since its founding in 1997, Netflix has shipped over 1 billion movies to its 8.4 million customers. The company's success is due primarily to delivering superior customer value by reducing the total cost associated with renting a DVD. Instead of two trips that used to be required to rent and return a movie, customers now have movies delivered directly to their homes via the postal service. This saves customers not only time, but also gasoline. According to company estimates, Netflix customers save over 800,000 gallons of gasoline per year.
PHOTO: Paul Sakuma

FIGURE 5.1 Customer Perceived Value

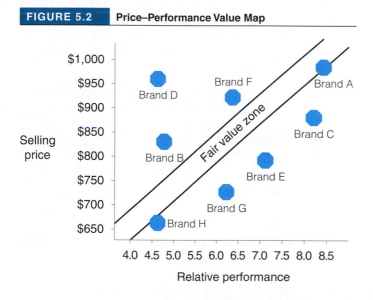

To better understand the concept of customer value, the **value map** shown in Figure 5.2 examines the tradeoffs customers make between costs and benefits (performance in this example) when making a purchase decision. Products that fall within the **fair value zone** are perceived to deliver benefits equal to the products' total cost. Products below, or to the right of the zone, are perceived to have greater benefits than their associated costs. Products above the line are perceived by buyers to deliver fewer benefits than what the products cost.

FIGURE 5.2 Price–Performance Value Map

Managers use a value map to track and manage the perceived value customers assign to their brands, as well as to competitors' brands. The value map shown in Figure 5.2 highlights a market with eight competitors, each of which has various levels of performance and price. Brands B, D, and F all fall to the left of the fair value zone, which indicates low customer perceived value. The low perceptions by customers will translate into low market share for these brands. Brands C, E, and G are rated by customers as having high customer perceived value. Brands A and H are rated as having performance benefits equal to their selling price. In this example, brand C is priced around $200 higher than brand H. Is brand C worth the added cost? One could make the case that because brand C has a much higher performance rating, the additional $200 is acceptable.

Companies can alter the customer perceived value in one of three ways: increase the perceived benefits, decrease the perceived cost, or a combination of the two. For example, perceived benefits can be increased by adding new features to a product while either maintaining the current price or increasing the price only slightly. Perceived costs can be altered through a price reduction or by improving a product's efficiency. An example of the latter would be an automobile manufacturer improving the gas mileage of one of its models. Improved fuel efficiency lowers the overall operating expenses, thereby reducing the perceived cost of the vehicle. Even if the perceived benefits remain the same, the reduction in overall costs results in an increase in the perceived value.

Customer
Satisfaction (pp. 48–51)

▼ **DEFINED** Customer satisfaction *is the degree to which a product meets or exceeds customer expectations.*

▼ **EXPLAINED**

Customer Satisfaction

The emotional experience that a customer has with a purchase will fall within one of three categories; the experience will either be positive, neutral, or negative. A negative feeling, or dissatisfaction, is the result when the product's performance does not live up to expectations. A neutral outcome occurs when a product's performance matches expectations. In this situation, a buyer has reached the baseline level of satisfaction. If expectations are exceeded, then a positive experience has occurred, leaving the buyer highly satisfied. This high level of satisfaction is referred to as delighted. The varying levels of satisfaction, and likely outcomes associated with each, are shown in Figure 5.3.

FIGURE 5.3 Outcomes of Varying Degrees of Satisfaction

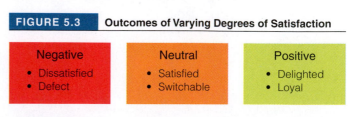

The initial level of satisfaction is normally determined at the time a product is purchased. However, for some products, the level of satisfaction may change over time. For example, the purchase and consumption of a new flavor of soft drink will result in an initial level of satisfaction. In most cases, customers will make up their minds as to whether they would purchase that brand again in the first few sips. It is unlikely that a week after trying the new flavor, that a person would alter his or her level of satisfaction without having a new experience with the product. This is not be the case for other types of products. For instance, take the purchase of an ink-jet printer. At first, the buyer may experience a high level of satisfaction due to finding the product at a low price. Once the product has been brought home and installed, the level of satisfaction could increase, based on the quality of the printed pages. However, over time, the level of satisfaction may diminish as the customer seeks to replace the ink cartridge and finds the price to be much higher than expected. Where once there was initial delight, dissatisfaction takes over. For products where long-term ownership is expected, the company's product and customer service quality play an important role in customer satisfaction.

▼ **APPLIED**

Customer Satisfaction

Creating satisfied customers requires that the company manage customer expectations, as well as the quality of their products or services. Companies strive to manage expectations in an effort to not "overpromise and underdeliver." Increasing the expected perceived benefits may create more initial sales, but if the expected benefits are not delivered, customers will experience dissatisfaction with the brand and probably will not buy that brand in the future. Customers who are merely satisfied can be persuaded to switch to a competitor's product. It is only customers who are delighted by their experience who can be counted on to remain loyal to the brand.

Companies with highly satisfied or delighted customers generate significant benefits for themselves in the form of the following benefits:[2]

- **Loyalty**—Customers who are satisfied are likely to continue to purchase the same brands, or do business with the same service provider.
- **Product champions**—Satisfied customers cannot wait to share their experiences with anyone who listens.
- **Reduced costs**—The costs benefits of having satisfied customers is found in multiple areas, from lower warranty expenses (satisfied customers have fewer problems, hence lower warranty expenses) to fewer phone calls to customer service representatives.
- **Larger share of wallet**—Satisfied customers are more likely to purchase other products from a company to which they are loyal.

These benefits in turn lead to greater profitability for the company, as well as an increase in revenue due to satisfied customers purchasing other products from the company. Satisfied customers may also become product advocates by referring the brand to their friends and colleagues. This word-of-mouth, or viral, advertising carries much greater weight with potential buyers than any advertising campaign a company could develop.

Measuring Customer Satisfaction

Because of its importance for long-term growth, companies make an effort to measure the satisfaction levels of their customers. The measurement of satisfaction can take the form of surveys where customers are asked to rate their level of satisfaction on a scale of 1–10. These types of surveys traditionally ask respondents questions such as the following: How satisfied are you with the product or service? Do you intend to purchase the product in the future? Would you recommend the product to a friend? Capturing ratings for customer satisfaction provides managers with insights into how well the company is performing in the marketplace. However, the data alone are of little use unless they are compared against the company's previous ratings or against the satisfaction ratings competitors have earned.

Independent rating organizations such as J.D. Power and Associates and the American Customer Satisfaction Index (ACSI) are also involved in the assessment of customer satisfaction. The ACSI conducts more than 65,000 customer interviews annually and links customer expectations, perceived quality, and perceived value to develop an overall ACSI score. Measures are taken across a wide variety of consumer product categories, allowing managers to see their customers' level of satisfaction in relation to industry averages and specific competitors.

EXAMPLE | CUSTOMER SATISFACTION

According to the American Customer Satisfaction Index, Southwest Airlines customers are the most satisfied of the major air carrier customers in the United States. Southwest accomplishes this by delivering at or above the expectations customers have, which in turn leads to high levels of customer satisfaction. In 2007, Southwest Airlines was named a "customer service champ" by *BusinessWeek*, and has earned similar honors from the *Wall Street Journal* (2007). Customers know exactly what to expect from Southwest: low fares, open seating, and limited amenities (you get a bag of peanuts and a soft drink). Southwest Airlines has shown a profit for 36 consecutive years, a record that has been unmatched in the airline industry.[3]

PHOTO: Mikeal Damkier

>> END EXAMPLE

Customer Loyalty

Customer loyalty is the degree to which a customer will select a particular brand when a purchase from that product category is being considered. Customer loyalty can be described as a buyer's feeling of attachment to a particular product, brand, or company. Buyers exhibit varying degrees of loyalty toward the brands they purchase. Some buyers have high levels of loyalty to a particular brand and will purchase only that brand, no matter what. Other buyers may split their loyalty among two or three brands in a category. Still others may hold loyalty to no brand, and select perhaps the lowest priced product when a purchase decision must be made. It is the first group of customers, those who are loyal to a specific brand, that organizations strive to create and expand by delivering high levels of customer satisfaction. Companies also seek to ensure that highly loyal customers remain loyal. At the same time, companies try to move those customers who are only somewhat loyal into a state of high loyalty. To accomplish this, companies seek to ensure continued relationships with select groups of customers.

It can be assumed that loyal customers will generate a profit for the company, but that does not mean they are the most profitable customers. Nor is it the case that the largest customers are the most profitable. In fact, customers who purchase the most may be doing so only because of special deals or price promotions. Large customers may also require additional company resources, such as higher levels of customer service or special product specifications. These additional resources result in higher costs and, thus, lower profitability. To determine which customers are profitable and which are not, an in-depth customer profitability analysis should be conducted. A profitability analysis of customers involves assigning actual marketing costs to customers, based on the actual costs that are required to perform various marketing activities, such as sales calls and product shipping. Looking at customers in this light allows the company to determine the overall value, in terms of profitability, that a customer generates for a company.

The Value of a Customer

It is important to note that not all customers are created equal. According to the Pareto Principle, or what is commonly referred to as the 80/20 rule, 80% of a company's profits are generated by 20% of their customers. Another 60% of customers generate the remaining profits for a company. This leaves an additional 20% of customers who generate a loss for the company. This observation has led many companies to offer tiered levels of service, with the most profitable customers receiving high levels of customer service and unprofitable customers receiving minimal levels of service. For example, credit card companies ensure that a "live" customer service representative answers a highly valued card holder's phone call in a matter of seconds; a phone call from a card holder that generates less value is routinely answered by an automated phone system.

Customer Lifetime Value

Customer lifetime value (CLV) is the present value of all profits expected to be earned in the future from a customer. To determine the value of a customer, companies utilize metrics such as customer lifetime value. The benefit for using CLV can be seen in a simple example of a loyal Blockbuster customer who rents two movies a week. At an average price of $2.99 per rental, this customer will generate over $1,200 in revenue for Blockbuster over a four-year period. If Blockbuster earns an average of 10% profit on customer revenue, then the customer generates a profit of $120. At the most basic level, the $120 profit can be taken as the customer lifetime value. If the cost to recruit and retain the customer is less than $120, then this would be a profitable customer for Blockbuster.

Customer lifetime value goes much deeper than the preceding example demonstrates. Companies must also take into account the fact that revenue collected in the future is worth less than if that revenue were collected up front. To account for this, companies use what is known as a discount rate, which averages between 10% and 15%. The concept behind the discount rate is also referred to as the time value of money.

To calculate customer lifetime value, a company must know five pieces of information:

1. Customer average purchases per year
2. Profit margin earned on those purchases
3. Costs to service the customer
4. Customer retention rate (percentage of customers who remain customers)
5. The firm's discount rate

Customers represent different levels of value in terms of the amount of profits they generate for an organization. Because of the high expense and effort required, companies use metrics such as customer lifetime value (CLV) to determine which customers should receive the focus of the company's relationship marketing efforts. Perhaps equally important, knowing a customer's lifetime value also allows a company to know with which customers to not seek to build relationships. For example, some companies have opted to "fire" unprofitable customers. Take the 2007 case of Sprint, which identified and terminated the contracts of over 1,000 customers who repeatedly contacted the company's customer service department an average of 40 times per month, some even after the original complaint was resolved. This move generated a great deal of negative publicity for Sprint, but other cell phone providers acknowledged that they had also cancelled customer contracts for similar reasons.[4]

Customers can add value to a company in addition to their lifetime value, because many highly satisfied customers may become champions for the products they buy. These loyal customers will go out of their way to refer a brand to anyone who will listen.[5] Research conducted by Purdue's Center for Customer Driven Quality shows that 87% of consumers follow the opinion of their friends and family.[6]

Customer Retention

Companies are continuously seeking to attract new customers to increase sales and profits. For many companies, attracting new customers is necessary to replace customers who defect to competing products, or who leave the market entirely. This is especially the case for those organizations that achieve low customer satisfaction scores, or even an entire industry, such as cellular phone service providers. Replacing lost customers is critical to growing a company's sales and profits, or to maintain current sales levels in those firms with high defection rates.

However, companies that work to retain current customers are reaching higher levels of profitability. A majority of a company's marketing efforts are often geared toward recruiting new customers, but, in addition, today's savvy businesses are turning their attention to retaining current customers.

EXAMPLE   **CUSTOMER RETENTION**

Searching for ways to connect with its "healthy, active, outdoor, aspirational," target customers, Nature Valley, a large health-oriented General Mill's cereal bar brand, called on consumers to post stories about their favorite nature activities, such as hiking and kayaking. The brand's Web site was redesigned in hopes of making the site a clearinghouse for information appealing to outdoor enthusiasts. Nature Valley also promoted a contest on YouTube where consumers posted videos highlighting their favorite place. The overall winner of the contest won two trips, one to Antarctica and the other to the North Pole. A total of 127 videos were submitted; they were viewed a total of 250,000 times.

The Web site and contest gave Nature Valley the means to build a relationship with a core customer group and to retain this group of customers.[7]

PHOTO: Andresr

>> END EXAMPLE

Relationship Marketing (p. 51)

 DEFINED **Relationship marketing** *is the organizational commitment to developing and enhancing long-term, mutually beneficial relationships with profitable or potentially profitable customers.*

EXPLAINED
Relationship Marketing

In the past, companies would determine the value of customers based on their most recent purchase. Previous purchases or future purchases were of lesser concern. This transaction-based view gave way to the relationship-based view of an exchange with the emergence of the marketing concept. Today's successful companies have sought to focus their marketing efforts on building long-term, mutually beneficial relationships with profitable or potentially profitable customers. The primary goal for developing customer relationships is to increase customer loyalty and retention. In thinking about long-term customer relationships, companies understand that customer profitability may be limited or even at a loss at the beginning of a relationship, but over time,

profits increase. Relationship marketing is especially important, given the following data:[8]

- A company can lose up to 50% of its customers over a five-year period.
- It costs 6–7 times more to recruit new customers than it does to retain existing customers.
- Even small increases in customer retention rates can have a profound impact on a company's profits.

According to Michael Porter, a world-renowned strategy guru, a business can differentiate itself from competitors based on the following: (1) the core product or service, (2) price, and (3) the total relationship and customer experience. Companies are finding that the first two are difficult in today's competitive environment, and are focusing on the importance of developing strong customer relationships. Relationship marketing, or one-to-one marketing, requires that an organization be committed to the development of a customer relationship.

APPLIED
Relationship Marketing

Developing relationships with customers requires a complete, committed effort on the part of the organization. This is because a relationship requires the delivery of superior customer value that results from high product quality and exemplary customer service. Building relationships with customers is not a short-term undertaking; it requires a long-term plan and strong commitment from the organization, as well as the proper investment. It is important to understand that customers will have different reasons for seeking to develop a relationship with a company. Some customers will enter a relationship for the added value they receive, reduced anxiety throughout the purchase/repurchase process, and to achieve a sense of belonging.

EXAMPLE   **RELATIONSHIP MARKETING**

Seeking to establish a community with loyal customers, Patrón Spirits launched an online social networking Web site. The Patrón Social Club provides tequila aficionados with a central gathering place for Patrón (Spanish for "the good boss") enthusiasts. The site is interactive and open to members only. With the help of a worldwide, integrated marketing campaign, the brand is meeting the desires of its top customers. The information the company has gained from hosting the site has led to members receiving invitations for exclusive events and parties, including Super Bowl XLII. The addition of the Web site and the marketing campaign have raised awareness of the brand 61% from the previous year, and increased case sales by 45%.[9]

PHOTO: Roman Sigaev

>> END EXAMPLE

Customer Relationship Management (pp. 52–53)

DEFINED Customer relationship management *is comprised of the activities that are used to establish, develop, and maintain customer sales.*

EXPLAINED

Customer Relationship Management

Customer relationship management (CRM) seeks to ensure that every effort an organization undertakes has as its purpose the development and maintenance of a profitable customer relationship. The practice of CRM requires internal and external processes. External processes are those that connect the company with its customers, while internal processes involve the management of information acquired from customers. A breakdown in either process will result in the CRM experience not meeting the expectations of either the company or the customer.

APPLIED

Customer Relationship Management

Perhaps the most critical element of practicing CRM is in the information such a system can provide the organization. Companies should not only collect information regarding their customers, such as demographics and usage patterns, but also seek to gain information to help assess the customers' needs. The information that a company collects is stored in a customer database, which is an organized collection of information about a customer. The information in this database must be constantly updated and should be designed for ease of use.

There are four steps in the development of one-to-one relationships with customers:[10]

1. Identify and gather as much detail as possible about your customers.
2. Differentiate customers based on their needs and the levels of value they bring to the company.
3. Talk to your customers to find ways of improving cost efficiencies as well as the customer-interaction experience.
4. Customize your products or services for each customer segment.

Customer Identification

For many companies, such as those in the business-to-business market (B2B market), taking the first step of identifying and collecting information about customers is relatively simple.

However, the effort in the consumer market is much more challenging. In the B2B market, firms know who their customers are because of previous purchases. For example, ArcelorMittal, the world's largest steel manufacturer, can easily pull up a customer list from a previous order and begin building the necessary information needed for their CRM systems. However, in the consumer market, companies must take great effort to even identify their customers. Imagine the difficulty that Procter and Gamble (P&G) has determining which consumers purchase Tide detergent or Crest toothpaste. Although some of this information may be available from supermarkets that have implemented a loyalty program, issues abound when sharing information among firms.

In the process of identifying customers and collecting pertinent information, companies should seek to err on the side of having too much information, rather than too little. Information that should be collected includes the standard names and contact information, as well as other data that may be specific to your brand, company, or industry. For example, a consumer products company may benefit from knowing whether a customer is married, has children (along with their ages), or the type of job he or she holds. This information may allow the company to promote other products the company produces. Companies should also focus on ways to determine a customer's needs, for example, how the product is perceived, what features the customer finds valuable, and how the product is used. Perhaps the most critical piece of information that should be collected, either directly from the customer or from other sources, involves a customer's purchase history. This information will allow the company to perform a customer profitability analysis that, along with the other information mentioned, will be valuable in the next step of the process.

Customer Differentiation

The ability to differentiate customers based on the value they bring to the company in the form of profits and based on the customers' needs gives the company the means to find groups of customers who share similar characteristics. The information collected in Step one (customer identification) allows the company to identify its top customers in terms of sales and profitability. The differentiation step allows a company to detect customers whose purchases have been significantly fewer this quarter than they were last quarter. This might indicate that the customer has become less satisfied with the products. The company then might contact the customer to prevent the loss of this customer to a competitor. Companies that do not utilize a CRM system may not find out about a dissatisfied customer until it is too late.

Customer Interaction

Every contact a company has with a customer provides an opportunity to either strengthen or damage a relationship. Companies that make the effort to improve customer relationships look at their customer interactions as ongoing conversations. They seek to understand ways to improve customers' experiences with the company, for example, seeing a trend in the types of questions customers ask and including this information on a company Web site or automated information systems. Through customer interactions, companies can identify methods to deliver the resources that customers require in the most cost-effective ways, thus reducing overall costs and increasing customer profitability.

Customization

The first three steps, when implemented properly, can provide the company with increased revenue, decreased costs, and ultimately higher profitability. However, the fourth step may be the source of the greatest benefits to the organization. Taking the information learned and using this information to deliver what customers actually need generates enormous goodwill and loyalty. Customers see the value in continuing the relationship, and their degree of loyalty increases. Companies are better able to craft marketing messages through personalized direct-mail pieces, which leads to higher success rates for such advertising programs.

Loyalty Programs

Some brands lend themselves well to developing loyal customers based on the quality, customer service, or even price of the product. However, some product categories find that building repeat business requires the development of reward or loyalty programs. These types of efforts are found in many product categories and among retailers. They represent an attempt to entice customers to repurchase from the company in exchange for various rewards. Companies also benefit from loyalty programs by collecting information about customers, including contact information and a customer's spending habits. This type of information may even be the most beneficial part of a loyalty program. The various types of programs that are used include frequent flyer miles (airlines), cash back (credit cards), discounts on select products (supermarkets), and discounts on purchases (department stores), just to name a few. According to Jupiter Research, more than 75% of consumers are enrolled in at least one loyalty program. Consumer product manufacturers are also using various programs to build some degree of loyalty among their customers. Coca-Cola offers its customers free merchandise for the continued purchase of their beverages (see Mycokerewards.com). Retailers such as Nordstrom and Best Buy have implemented programs to encourage customer loyalty.

EXAMPLE LOYALTY PROGRAMS

To combat declining sales, Starbucks has joined a growing list of companies that have rolled out a customer rewards program. The Starbucks Card Rewards programs offers free refills on brewed coffee, free beverages with purchase of a whole bean coffee, and two-hours of daily Wi-Fi access.[11]

PHOTO: Denis Miraniuk

>> END EXAMPLE

Technology

Implementing and utilizing a customer relationship management system requires a major investment in computer systems, including specialized software that allows for in-depth analysis of the information that is collected. Dedicated employees are also needed to manage the flow of information from customers to managers. Although a CRM system can provide managers with an instantaneous view of customers, these systems can be expensive. It has been estimated that over $13 billion was spent on CRM programs in 2006.

Formal CRM systems can be too expensive for small firms, but those companies can still realize the same benefits by using other, less expensive, methods such as basic databases created in Excel. Much greater effort is needed to generate the same level of information as systems costing millions, but companies may see greater returns because they might place a higher value on the information they receive. It is important to remember that no matter how much a company invests in its CRM program, if customer information is not maintained, the benefits will be minimal. A well-maintained database offers companies the potential to uncover market opportunities through the use of **data mining**. This statistical technique has been used successfully in direct marketing to uncover individuals or groups of individuals who are most likely to respond to an offer and the types of offers that will elicit a response. Data mining has helped reduce costs by eliminating duplicate customer entries. Retailers have also benefited from data mining techniques that identify local buying patterns, thus allowing them to tailor the types of merchandise carried by individual stores.

Special precautions must be taken with the sensitive information contained in databases because customers have great concern regarding privacy and security issues. There have been numerous incidents of customer information being compromised through security breaches or lost laptops. The expenses incurred because of lost or stolen customer information can reach into the millions, not counting the losses associated with the negative publicity. It is estimated that a company can incur a cost between $30 and $300 for every customer record that is compromised. A security breach at retailer TJMaxx in 2007, where over 45 million customer credit card and debit card numbers were stolen by computer hackers, cost the company more than $250 million.

▼**Visual** Summary

Chapter 5 Summary

A company's marketing efforts should be focused on developing profitable and loyal customers. Building customer loyalty is the result of delivering value to the customer in excess of their expectations. Exceeding expectations creates feelings of satisfaction with the brand or company. Higher levels of satisfaction, or delight, cause customers to continue to purchase the brand. Customer loyalty can be enhanced through the use of relationship marketing, where the focus is on the individual customer, not only at a single point in time, but over the lifetime of the relationship. However, not all customers are worthy of the effort and expense required to build a long-term relationship. It is only through in-depth analysis of customer lifetime value that a company can decide with which customers to build a relationship and which customers to fire.

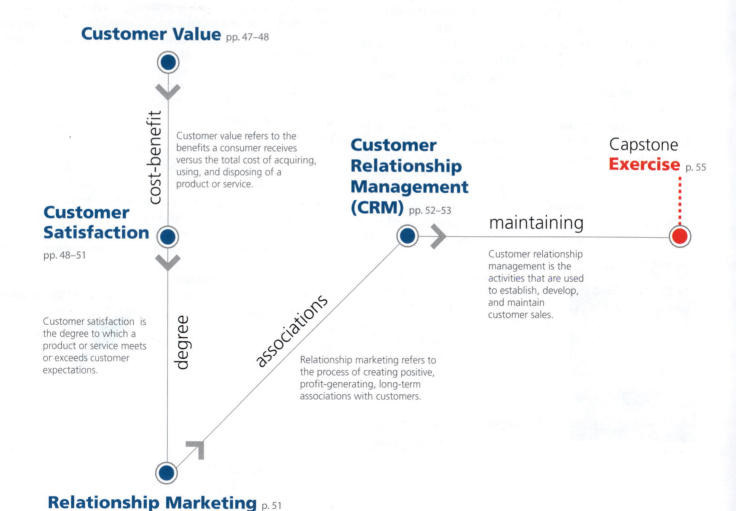

Customer Value pp. 47–48

cost-benefit

Customer value refers to the benefits a consumer receives versus the total cost of acquiring, using, and disposing of a product or service.

Customer Satisfaction

pp. 48–51

degree

Customer satisfaction is the degree to which a product or service meets or exceeds customer expectations.

Customer Relationship Management (CRM) pp. 52–53

associations

Relationship marketing refers to the process of creating positive, profit-generating, long-term associations with customers.

maintaining

Customer relationship management is the activities that are used to establish, develop, and maintain customer sales.

Capstone **Exercise** p. 55

Relationship Marketing p. 51

▼ **Chapter** Key Terms

Customer Value (pp. 47–48)

Customer value (customer perceived value) *is the difference between the benefits a customer receives and the total cost incurred from acquiring, using, and disposing of a product. (p. 47)*
Opening Example (p. 47)

Key Terms (pp. 47–48)

Fair value zone is the area on a value map where customers' perceived benefits equal the customers' perceived cost. **(p. 48)**
Functional use is the purpose for seeking a product. **(p. 47)**
Value map is a graphical representation of the ratio between customers' perceived benefits and the perceived total cost of a product. **(p. 48)**

Customer Satisfaction (pp. 48–51)

Customer satisfaction *is the degree to which a product meets or exceeds customer expectations. (p. 48)* **Example: Customer Satisfaction (p. 49) Example: Customer Retention (p. 51)**

Key Terms (pp. 50–51)

Customer lifetime value is the present value of all profits expected to be earned from a customer over the lifetime of his or her relationship with a company. **(p. 50)**

Customer loyalty is the degree to which a customer will select a particular brand when a purchase from that product category is being considered. **(p. 50)**

Relationship Marketing (p. 51)

Relationship marketing *is the process of developing and enhancing long-term relationships with profitable customers. (p. 51)*
Example: Relationship Marketing (p. 51)

Customer Relationship Management (pp. 52–53)

Customer relationship management (CRM) *is the activities that are used to establish, develop, and maintain customer relationships. (p. 52)*

Key Term (p. 53)

Data mining is the statistical analysis of large databases seeking to discover hidden pieces of information. **(p. 53)**

▼ **Capstone** Exercise

Customer loyalty is critical to a business's continued success. Loyalty programs have been popular in recent years, but the original customer loyalty program was S&H Green Stamps. The S&H Green Stamps reward program was started in the 1930s and was popular during the 1950s and 1960s. The next major advance in loyalty programs was the American Airlines AAdvantage frequent flyer program, which was started in 1981. To fully understand the scope and size of this program, go to www.aadvantage.com.

A key concept in designing loyalty programs is to reward consistent buying habits. As with much of the marketing field, knowledge about your customers is the key to being successful. However, for this exercise, you'll have to make assumptions.

We have the following three scenarios with which to work:

1. A credit card company is aware that if a husband and wife are both active card users, they are much less likely to change cards.

2. A local independent hardware store wants to compete with The Home Depot and Lowe's.

3. A dentist wants to increase the number of patients coming to his or her practice.

What customer loyalty programs, if any, would you put into place, and why? Try to provide details of how they would work and what tactics you would use.

▼ **Application** Exercises

Complete the following exercises:

1. Visit the American Customer Satisfaction Index (ACSI) Web site (http://www.theacsi.org/) and examine the ASCI scores for industries with which you are familiar. Look at the scores of the various brands. How well do they fit with your experiences?

2. Think about your first visit to a new restaurant. What were your expectations before entering the door? What was the source of

your expectations? What was your level of satisfaction after completing your meal? Would your satisfaction level be different if your expectations were based on an advertisement for the restaurant, versus if they were based on a word-of-mouth recommendation from a trusted source, such as a roommate?

3. What are the distinguishing features of relationship marketing?

A Perspective on **Consumer** Behavior

Chapter Overview In the previous chapter, you considered how companies create value for consumers and how businesses cultivate and maintain consumer relationships. To realize the potential of the value that can be created between consumers and companies, it is essential to understand how consumers behave, specifically how they make decisions and how they solve problems. In this chapter, we explore the consumer decision-making and problem-solving processes to help us better understand consumer behavior.

 ## Chapter **Outline**

Consumer Behavior p. 57   ⟵   **Objective 1.** What is consumer behavior?

Consumer Decision-Making Process pp. 58–63   ⟵   **Objective 2.** How do consumers identify and evaluate choices?

- **Personal Influence on Decision Making** pp. 59–60
- **Psychological Influence on Decision Making** pp. 60–61
- **Situational Influence on Decision Making** p. 61
- **Social Influence on Decision Making** pp. 61–63

Consumer Problem Solving p. 64   ⟵   **Objective 3.** What are the different categories of consumer problem solving?

CONSUMER BEHAVIOR (p. 57)

 **DEFINED Consumer behavior** *is the dynamic interaction of affect and cognition, behavior, and the environment in which human beings conduct the exchange aspects (product and service purchases) of their lives.*[1]

 EXPLAINED

Consumer Behavior

Consumer behavior represents the psychology of marketing. **Psychology** involves the study of the mind. The way a person's mind is wired plays an essential role in making purchase decisions. The process of how purchase decisions are made can be challenging to understand because the decisions consumers make are related to underlying human behavior. Consumer behavior has been explored through the lenses of marketing actions (for example, advertising and sales) and social psychology. **Social psychology** is a process used to understand social phenomena and their influences on social behavior. The Theory of Planned Behavior, a social psychology theory, attempts to explain how attitudes, behaviors, and norms influence consumer behavior.[2] Attitudes toward behavior, social norms, and perceived control (as opposed to the amount of control one actually has) are determining factors of a consumer's intention. A consumer's intention is considered an indicator of how he or she will behave.[3]

APPLIED

Consumer Behavior

Consumer behavior is a familiar personal experience because consumers make product and service decisions on a regular basis. Consumers have considerable choices across a wide range of product and service categories. Consumers make purchase decisions based on several factors, for example, convenience, price, product or service characteristics, blogs about the product or service, and word-of-mouth recommendations. The decision-making process is often a combination of rational and emotional factors. Companies attempt to understand the consumer's process when that consumer makes a decision. Companies then develop marketing strategies to increase the likelihood that their products or services will be selected.

Consumer behavior involves not only a decision about purchasing a product or service, but it also involves the shopping process itself: how the relationships with the product and company evolve (including service and maintenance), how individual and societal perceptions of the product change, and how the relationship with the product develops over time.

Starbucks, the leading retailer, roaster, and brand of specialty coffee in the world, claims it is not selling coffee, but an experience. That pursuit of delivering the desired experience often encounters challenges in areas as subtle as identifying special drinks for different markets, to dramatic ones, such as challenging the pace of an entire society. In Japan, Starbucks launched a Green Tea Cream Frappuccino after the product enjoyed success in other Asian markets. Starbucks also began offering soymilk in Japan because of consumer demand and competitive actions. Beyond identifying niche products, Starbucks also launched an attack on European café society. One of the first targets was Vienna, considered by many to be the home of Europe's coffeehouse traditions. Located across from the famous Vienna State Opera House, the Starbucks coffee-to-go model has run head on into a society that is known for coffeehouse visits that last hours. Growth has been slow, but Starbucks continues to evaluate its business model in Austria, and to adjust this model relative to various cultures and business practices around the world.
PHOTO: Sandra Cunningham

Consumer Decision-Making Process (pp. 58–63)

▼ **DEFINED** *The* **consumer decision-making process** *is the steps that consumers take to identify and evaluate choice options.*

▼ **EXPLAINED**

Consumer Decision-Making Process

The consumer decision-making process can range from a simple, low-involvement decision made without much investigation, to a programmed response to a complex high-involvement cognitive task. Involvement is primarily classified into two segments: high and low. High involvement is typically considered a cognitive and verbal process that is referred to as left-brain processing.[5] Consumers under high-involvement conditions often reach deeper levels of information processing due to the significance of the decision being made.[6] However, some high-involvement situations may be considered nonverbal, emotional, and even metaphorical; these are referred to as right-brain processing.[7] Low-involvement situations are much like hypnotic suggestion and involve links to brain pathways that have been formed from prior experiences.[8] This is common with routine purchases that offer little risk.

EXAMPLE   **CONSUMER DECISION MAKING**

The purchase of a vehicle is a high-involvement choice. Saturn, a division of General Motors, has implemented several practices to make consumers more comfortable with the vehicle-purchasing process. Saturn offers no-haggle pricing, where the price listed is the price that is charged. Taking the negotiation out of the purchase process is a big relief to many consumers. Saturn also offers test drive programs that involve bringing a vehicle to a consumer's home for evaluation and live online chats with customer service representatives. Each of these actions is intended to make the decision process easier for consumers. A positive ownership experience tends to build loyalty and satisfaction, which is relatively strong at Saturn.

PHOTO: Kristian Sekulic

>> END EXAMPLE

Decision making, influenced by involvement, is a problem-solving process that requires a selection of a particular type of behavior.

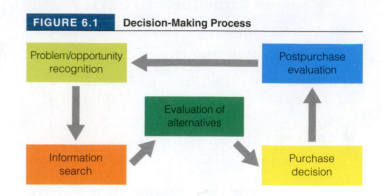

FIGURE 6.1   **Decision-Making Process**

The problem/opportunity recognition phase begins when a need or want is determined, such as the desire for a vacation. Information search involves exploring different sources of information to fulfill the need or want. In the case of a vacation, examples of information sources include travel agencies and travel Web sites. Different options are identified, based on certain criteria in the next step in the decision-making process. Travel choices could include places such as Florida, Mexico, or Puerto Rico. Those options could be evaluated based on criteria such as cost, ease of getting to and from the destination, and available activities at the destination. The purchase decision is made after evaluating alternatives. Postpurchase evaluation occurs when determining if the correct choice was made. Decisions on subsequent similar needs and wants, such as a vacation, are influenced by current experience.

▼ **APPLIED**

Consumer Decision-Making Process

Developing marketing strategies that reflect an understanding of consumer decision making is important from a business perspective because strategies based on an understanding of consumer behavior enable marketing professionals to optimize the effectiveness of their investments. Effectiveness, even if strategically constructed and behaviorally aligned with consumer needs, can be either enhanced or limited by the type of product or service category, as well as by the interest level of certain consumers.

Products (and services) can be divided into three distinct categories based on how consumers interact with the respective categories. "Approach" products consist of products that consumers gain enjoyment from using and include categories such as automobiles, fashionable clothing, fine jewelry, and entertainment.[9] "Avoidance" products are those products that consumers would not regularly consider unless the use of such a product would reduce the likelihood of something unpleasant occurring.[10] Examples of avoidance products include insurance, automotive service, medical services, and deodorants. A third category includes "utilitarian" products that are products neither enjoyed nor used as a precaution.[11] Examples of utilitarian products include paper, pencils, and paper clips. It is much easier to create emotional connections with consumers when marketing approach products.

Consumer purchase decisions are influenced by personal, psychological, situational, and social factors. The extent to which businesses can understand these influences is significant when determining success. Each of these areas of influence is discussed in the following sections.

Personal Influence on Decision Making

Consumer behavior is influenced by a variety of personal characteristics. These personal characteristics include self-identity, personality, lifestyle, age and life stage (shared life events), vocation, and level of affluence (material comfort or wealth).

Self-Identity

Self-identity is an individual's understanding that he or she is unique. The implication is that through that uniqueness, different behavior can be expressed relative to other individuals. That behavior reflects personal values and is demonstrated through consumption choices. Self-identity has been shown to predict intentions, which we have previously shown extend to purchase behavior.[12] Individuals tend to select products and services that are consistent with their perception of self-identify.

Personality

Personality involves a "sense of consistency, internal causality, and personal distinctiveness."[13] Through interaction with one's environment, personality is expressed through particular patterns of behavior. Personalities can range from "rugged individualists" to "practical conformists." Products and services are often expressed, through characteristics of the product or service or through advertising, as having personalities that are relevant to the consumers identified as offering the most value to the company.

Lifestyle

Lifestyle is a way of life that individuals express by choosing how to spend their time and personal resources. Lifestyle is expressed through one's choices, for example, a home, car, travel, and music. Companies seeking to form deep emotional connections with consumers have worked to position their products and services in the environment in which those consumers live. Whether marketers are trying to reach scuba divers or dirt bike riders, they can connect with consumers through a variety of forms, including sponsoring events or advertising in lifestyle magazines.

Age and Life Stage

A person's age and age group influence consumer behavior. Different ages bring different societal requirements and product and service opportunities. Generation X consists of people born between 1965 and 1981, while Generation Y consists of people born between 1982 and 1994. Both groups have grown up experiencing successful and challenging economic times, but the groups have differences. Members of Generation X are moving into different life stages with more established careers, while many Generation Y members are still entering or becoming

established with their careers. Experience with media is also different because Generation Y members are more immersed in social media than are Generation X members. This media experience changes the methods businesses use to communicate with these groups. Depending on your age and other factors, such as income, particular retirement investment choices are available. Age can also enable membership in certain organizations or the ability to live in certain communities where services are aimed at the typical member of that age group.

AARP is a membership organization that operates in every state, the District of Columbia, Puerto Rico, and the U.S. Virgin Islands for people aged 50 and over. People aged 50 and older are the fastest-growing population in the United States and control the majority of America's financial assets. Therefore, it is it critical that marketers are aware of how to reach this segment of the population. AARP provides a wide range of lifestyle-related information and services, ranging from travel to health. They operate a Web site, a magazine, and a monthly bulletin, as well as a Spanish-language newspaper. AARP also is involved in advocacy for its members on issues such as health care and Social Security.

PHOTO: Monkey Business Images

>> END EXAMPLE

In additional to chronological age, cognitive age contributes greatly to understanding an individual's perspectives, attitudes, and behaviors.[14] **Cognitive age**, also referred to as subjective age, is the age that one *feels*. Cognitive age influences one's self-image.[15] Cognitive age can link a 35-year-old with a 55-year-old and create marketing opportunities for particular products and services. For example, adventure sports such as triathlons, cycling, and skiing attract participants of varying ages. Interest in participating in such events has much to do with how one feels and how one is willing to work toward a particular goal.

Life stage, similar life events experienced by a group of individuals of varying chronological and cognitive ages, is yet another factor that influences consumer behavior. People can be in different life stages relative to their work or family life. With respect to family life, the traditional life-stage model has evolved to reflect alternative lifestyles. Childless couples, same-sex couples, and families with multiple generations living together all create opportunities for a wide range of consumer expectations.

Vocation

A person's occupation also influences consumer behavior. A corporate executive typically purchases different work-related products than a member of the clergy, an emergency room surgeon, or a factory worker, for example. Some occupations also provide more room for individual expression. An occupation might have great influence on work-related products, but it may have less influence on a person's personal choices outside the work environment.

Affluence

An individual's financial means determines the opportunity to purchase certain products or services, or the limitations on such purchases. Although some products, such as a Ferrari, are impossible for most individuals to afford, other products, such as a Burberry purse, are relatively expensive, yet possible for a broader range of people to purchase. The challenge for marketers of luxury products is to develop and manage an image of quality and prestige, while appealing to as broad a group of consumers as possible.

The process in which consumers purchase and consume luxury products is different from other products.[16] The consumer decision-making process for luxury items focuses on an item's meaning to the consumer and not necessarily on the physical presence of the item.[17] Meaning and corresponding motivation have changed over time. Instead of status and style as motivations for luxury purchases, other emotional factors now influence luxury purchases, ranging from jewelry to clothes and even homes, cars, and vacation clubs. The Boston Consulting Group has identified three emotional factors that influence the affluent purchase decision process:

- **Adventure or journey of reinvention**—This is the idea that individuals seek products and services, such as exotic vacations, that create excitement or enable introspection.
- **Desire to foster heath and wellness**—This idea is that individuals seek products and services such as spas and yoga retreats that are designed to assist in understanding and improving one's health.
- **Connecting and building personal relationships**—This is the idea that individuals seek products and services, such as team-building retreats and event planning, that engender shared experiences.

EXAMPLE AFFLUENCE

 Golden Door, an upscale network of spas, has designed multiday health and wellness programs for affluent consumers. Capitalizing on the increased focus on improving health, Golden Door has expanded, with six locations across North America. The services range from personal fitness consulting to yoga, hiking, massage, and beauty services. Focusing on the desire for building relationships, Golden Door offers special events during their men's, women's and co-ed weeks.

PHOTO: Hywit Dimyadi

>> END EXAMPLE

Psychological Influence on Decision Making

Consumer behavior is influenced by a variety of psychological characteristics. These personal characteristics include perception, motivation, attitudes and beliefs, and learning.

Perception

Perception is a cognitive impression of incoming stimuli that influences the individual's actions and behavior.[18] The stimuli are generated through the senses: hearing, smelling, tasting, seeing, and touching. How the information is processed through the senses is unique to each person. Stimuli, such as an advertisement with a picture of a new boat, or a magazine with the scent of a new perfume, must pass through a filtering process. With all the stimuli from the external environment as well as advertising, businesses try to understand those stimuli that generate desired responses from consumers.

Although stimuli are processed overtly, they can also be processed subconsciously. **Subliminal perception** is the processing of stimuli by a recipient who is not aware of the stimuli being received. The original intent of subliminal perception, which originated in the 1950s, was to influence behavior with embedded images in various forms of advertising. After significant research, this concept was proven to be ineffective other than to help remind people to do something they already were interested in doing. Subliminal advertising is considered unethical and is illegal in many countries.

Motivation

Although perception essentially involves working from the outside in to interpret external stimuli, motivation involves working from the inside out to match current conditions to a desired condition. Any gap between the current and desired state is a motive for action. **Motivation** is the set of conditions that creates a drive toward particular action to fulfill a need or want. Maslow's hierarchy of needs provides a context to understand motivation. The hierarchy is based on a theory that individuals need to secure their most basic needs, such as food and security, before trying to realize any higher-order needs, such as belongingness, self-esteem, or self-actualization.

Attitudes and Beliefs

Attitude is a state of readiness, based on experience, that influences a response to something. Attitudes involve a like, dislike, or ambivalence toward an idea, product, service, or just about anything. There are three components of attitudes, including what one feels, what one does, and what one knows. While attitudes are generally consistent over time, there are opportunities to influence attitudes through experience or education. A **belief** is a sense of truth about something. Beliefs are what an individual knows and can influence attitudes.

Learning

Learning is knowledge that is acquired through experiences. The learning process includes drive, cue, response, and reinforcement.

- **Drive** is an internal stimulus that encourages action.
- **Cue** is an environmental stimulus that influences a particular action.

- **Response** is a consumer's reaction to drive and cues.
- **Reinforcement** is a reduction in drive resulting from a positive-response experience.

Businesses can use the learning process to create positive customer experiences and cultivate loyalty. For example, the need for a course textbook creates the drive to obtain one. Seeing the required textbook in the bookstore is a cue that can influence the purchase action. The actual purchase of the textbook is the response. Reinforcement occurs through using the textbook and eliminating the underlying drive to obtain the required course textbook.

Situational Influence on Decision Making

Consumer behavior is influenced by a variety of situation-specific characteristics. These characteristics include the purchase environment, digital environment, time, and context.

Purchase Environment

The shopping environment has considerable influence on consumer behavior. Energetic music can stimulate shoppers to make bold choices, whereas slow-paced music might encourage leisurely shopping that might translate into more purchases than might have otherwise been made. A shelf's organization can discourage shopping or encourage the education process for new products. Many businesses design aisles and overall store traffic flow to maximize the total purchase size.

EXAMPLE   PURCHASE ENVIRONMENT

AutoZone, founded in 1979 with a single retail auto parts store, now has over 3,000 stores across the United States. Several years ago, AutoZone standardized how its stores used Plan-O-Grams (a map of how products should be displayed in a store environment). The idea was to place certain products that appeal to a particular customer next to each other instead of the more traditional way of displaying similar products next to each other. Instead of managing product lines independently, the entire portfolio is managed based on customer shopping behavior. For example, all chrome products used to be grouped together. Chrome tips were moved next to muffler clamps and hangers, allowing an easy purchase of the products necessary to update an automotive exhaust system, resulting in an overall increase in margin, based on the new merchandising strategy.[19]

PHOTO: Andrjuss

>> END EXAMPLE

Time

After the product decision is made, the length and amount of effort in the shopping process influence consumer behavior. If a consumer knows that a preferred product is in a store that typically has long lines and the secondary or tertiary product in a particular category is at a location that has short or efficient lines, the consumer may elect to purchase one of the less-desired products to avoid the long lines. Whether it is same-day dry-cleaning, fast food, or one-hour photo processing, circumstances have the potential to override possible negative factors, such as lower quality, associated with the services.

Digital Environment

The digital environment influences consumer behavior through online social networking, blogs, product-ratings sites, and other activities that assist in online research, evaluation, and purchase. There is a tremendous wealth of information, of varying reliability, available instantly in the digital realm for consumers to consider when making decisions.

EXAMPLE   DIGITAL ENVIRONMENT

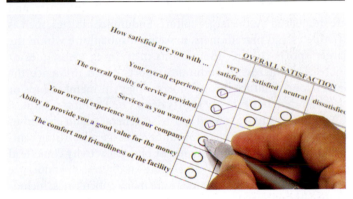

Epinions, a popular Web-based consumer reviews platform, is an example of how digital media is influencing consumer behavior. A service of Shopping.com, an eBay company, Epinions provides detailed product evaluations and personalized recommendations. Whether or not consumers purchase products online, consumers are increasingly conducting online product research prior to making purchases.

PHOTO: Ragsac

>> END EXAMPLE

There is also a wide range of choices that are presented to consumers through digital technology, including emerging mobile applications.

Context

An individual may have very strong opinions about desired quality or ingredients. Depending on circumstances, the individual may create a different set of requirements for his or her purchases. If a consumer purchases only organic products, but is asked to purchase products for an office party, he or she may not elect to pay the price premium of the organic products because others may not expect or even appreciate the additional investment.

Social Influence on Decision Making

Consumer behavior is influenced by a variety of social characteristics. These characteristics include culture, subculture, global, groups, social class, gender roles, and family.

Culture

Culture refers to the shared values, beliefs, and preferences of a particular society. Culture can be reflected through and influenced by religious beliefs, morality, artistic expression, and even habits. Culture can be formally established through laws and informally encouraged by societal actions and reactions. Cultures can also exist within a larger whole. Consider the wide variety of cultures in the United States.

Culture is fundamental in the initial wiring of an individual's behavior. The influence of culture exists in all countries, but it varies in terms of the level of influence. Businesses must understand the extent to which culture influences consumer expectations and behavior.

Subculture

Subcultures are groups of people within a broader society who share similar behaviors and values. Subcultures influence, and are influenced by, the larger culture. Endurance athletes, such as triathletes and marathoners, make up a subculture within the larger sports culture. Innovations in training techniques or increasing interest in endurance sports could influence the larger sports culture through increasing gym memberships or through demand for new sports drinks or training products. Changes in attitudes toward sports, in general, could also influence the endurance athlete subculture. A large advertising campaign supporting the importance of physical activity could lead to more people eventually developing an interest in endurance sports. In the United States, there are many subcultures, including a wide range of ethnic and age groups, as well as religious, gender, professional status, and geographic subcultures.

By 2050, it is estimated that over 47% of the U.S. population will be comprised of ethnic minorities.[20] Today, ethnic minorities account for more than 50% of the population in 48 of the 100 largest U.S. cities.[21] Hispanics and Asians will account for more than 45% of population growth in the United States through 2020.[22] The Asian population, the most affluent U.S. subculture, is growing at a rate of 9% annually, faster than Hispanics, but Hispanics are the largest minority in the total population.[23] African Americans have been supplanted as the largest minority group, and the African American population segment is growing at a much slower rate than Hispanics. Still, African Americans continue to increase their level of affluence, which should approach $1 trillion by 2010.

The subculture implications for marketers are that the various ethnic minorities do not necessarily follow general market-consumption patterns. AT&T has developed marketing programs to meet the needs of over 30 different cultures in 20 languages.[24] A unique marketing mix is necessary for each group, and there are opportunities to make a brand stand for different things to different groups, although at a significant cost.[25]

There is yet another factor when considering the ethnic minority subcultures. In 2000, seven million Americans considered themselves mixed-race, as recorded by the U.S census.[26] More mixed-race babies are born in Washington, California, and other Western states than any other group except Caucasians.[27] Prominent individuals, such as Tiger Woods, Keanu Reeves, Christina Aguilera, Alicia Keys, and Anne Curry, all identify themselves as mixed-race people.[28]

EXAMPLE   SUBCULTURE

Matt Kelley, a 19-year-old freshman at Connecticut's Wesleyan University, launched MAVIN magazine in 1999. At the time of its inception, it was the only magazine dedicated to mixed-race people and families. Today, the MAVIN Foundation is involved in communities across the country through awareness-building and educational activities.[29]

PHOTO: Monkey Business Images

>> END EXAMPLE

The youth market can also be considered a subculture. Fifty million 13- to 23-year-old consumers spend over $150 billion annually.[30] However, the youth market influences a far greater number of expenditures by other people. Teenagers and young adults ages 13-21 exert varying degrees of influence on family decision making regarding different product or service categories.[31] In the clothing sector 89% decide or influence the purchase decision, 77% of 13- to 21-year-olds influence software decisions, and 61% influence vehicle purchase decisions.[32]

America's youth have generally been exposed to more of a variety of cultures than previous generations.[33] These diverse cultures are often integrated into the lives of the youth market and diverse messages are welcome and actually expected. Is it these youth who are defining diversity, as opposed to marketers?[34]

Global

There is considerable variety in an individual country's marketplace, and there is even more variety in a global market. Although the variations are vast, common behavioral characteristics assist in understanding global consumer behavior. These behaviors are often an expression of personal values. *Culture's Consequences*, written by the Dutch author Geert Hofstede, who explored the relationship between national and organizational culture, discusses "mental programs" that develop early in life and are reinforced through national culture.[35] Five dimensions are identified to assist in differentiating cultural values:

- **Power distance**—Involves whether individuals are comfortable participating in decision making regardless of position
- **Uncertainty avoidance**—Involves the desire to minimize uncertainty
- **Individualism versus collectivism**—Involves the prevalence of people feeling comfortable making decisions with or without the input of group members

- **Masculinity versus femininity**—Involves traits that are considered either masculine or feminine
- **Long-term versus short-term orientation**—Is the importance of the past versus the future

Behavior can be demonstrated either by a group or by an individual. Thus, by applying Hofstede's cultural perspective, the differences between societies can be explored. Consider the differences between collectivist societies such as the People's Republic of China and individualist societies such as the United States:

- Chinese consumers spend more time searching for products than U.S. consumers.
- Chinese consumers consider more brands per product than U.S. consumers.[36]
- Chinese consumers are more risk-adverse than U.S. consumers.[37]
- Chinese consumers rely on personal sources of information, as opposed to U.S. consumers who tend to rely on market-provided information.[38]
- Symbolism is important for Chinese consumers and can greatly influence purchase decisions.[39]

Understanding these differences is essential when developing marketing propositions for collectivist countries such as China.

Group

Throughout their lives, individuals will be influenced by a variety of groups. The extent of the influence will vary by group. Initially, group influence will come from one's parents, which will then expand to small groups of friends, and then to activities and organizations. In a particular group, there are standards of behaviors called **norms** that are imparted to members; norms in a group define membership into the group. One can also perform a particular role or roles within a group. In a group context, **roles** are specific actions expected from someone in a group as a member or from a particular position held. Through either belonging to or holding a position within a group, one can achieve status. **Status** is the position of one individual relative to others.

A **reference group** consists of people who directly or indirectly influence how an individual feels about a particular topic. Reference groups can provide a new perspective on how to live one's life. Businesses that understand the reference group dynamic can work through reference groups to link their products and services with changes in lifestyle. Within a given reference group, there are opinion leaders who can serve as the connection between consumers and businesses. **Opinion leaders** are individuals who have the greatest influence on the attitudes and behaviors of a particular group. The fact that consumers often look to opinion leaders for insight and direction provides marketers with opportunities to work through opinion leaders either directly, through paid activities, or simply by tracking consumer reactions to evolving trends. Opinion leaders can include celebrities, experts, or others who possess characteristics that individuals admire or respect. Social media, such as blogs, wikis, or networking sites, provide a forum for opinion leaders to establish their positions. For those opinions already established, social media provide a mechanism to quickly communicate perspectives on various topics.

EXAMPLE GROUP

Oprah Winfrey, media celebrity and philanthropist, launched Oprah's Book Club in 1996. Each month, Oprah recommends books to millions of members. Over 50 of Oprah's recommended books have achieved best-seller status. Oprah functions as an opinion leader to book club members.

PHOTO: Ragne Kabanova

>> END EXAMPLE

Social Class

Social classes are characteristics that distinguish certain members of a society from others, based on a variety of factors, including wealth, vocation, education, power, place of residence, and ancestry. It is possible to change membership in a social class, such as an income class, but in some cases changing social class is not possible. For example, you cannot change family history. Membership in a particular social class generally influences how one presents oneself to society and influences consumer behavior in many lifestyle-related categories.

Gender Roles

Society defines expectations of appropriate attitudes and behaviors to men and women. Different societies have different gender roles that can affect the workplace and home. Gender roles can change or evolve over time. Only half of all women between the ages of 25–54 worked outside the home just 40 years ago; now that number is over 80%. Gender roles also differ depending on sexual orientation and gender identity.

Family

Family members are the first influencers of group behavior on an individual. The family group is considered one of the most important influencers of consumer behavior. Just as with other groups, there is normative behavior and distinct roles of family members. Norms and behavior can vary from one family to another and can evolve from one's birth family to one's family constructed through choice later in life. In a traditional family structure, one spouse can handle decision making for virtually all decisions, the decision making can be product and service specific, or both spouses may jointly make decisions. The construction of families has changed greatly from the traditional married household with children, and now includes same-sex households with or without children and an increasing number of single households.

Consumer Problem Solving (p. 64)

DEFINED **Consumer problem solving** *is how someone comes to a conclusion about a situation. This is determined by what kind of decision a consumer is facing.*

EXPLAINED
Consumer Problem Solving

Problem solving can be classified into three categories: limited problem solving, significant problem solving, and routine response problem solving. **Limited problem solving** occurs when a consumer is prepared to exert a certain amount of effort to make a purchase decision. This situation can occur when a consumer has considerable experience with a category and then encounters a new product option. **Significant problem solving** occurs when a consumer is prepared to commit considerable effort to make a purchase decision. This type of problem solving occurs when a new product is encountered that possesses characteristics that cause a consumer to reflect on his or her current perceptions of a category. Another scenario that warrants significant problem solving occurs when the product is expensive and there are great implications if a poor choice is made. **Routine response problem solving** occurs when a consumer has a well-developed process associated with fulfilling a need or want. An example of this problem-solving process is when a consumer purchases a new DVD from a series with which the consumer is familiar and enjoys. Each type of problem solving involves some level of risk. The more problem solving is involved in decision making, the more risk that must be managed.

APPLIED
Consumer Problem Solving

In practice, businesses constantly try to position products in such as a way that the problem-solving process works to their advantage. If a business has a strong position in a particular market, that business is trying to make as many purchases as routine as possible. Alternatively, if a business is trying to grow significantly in a market, management may concentrate efforts on making consumers reconsider the characteristics that define the product category with respect to the attributes of its products or services.

EXAMPLE   **CONSUMER PROBLEM SOLVING**

Eco-labels such as Energy Star, Fair Trade Certified, and the recycled logo are being used by a wide range of companies, including Marriott Hotels, Kohl's Department Stores, and Hewlett-Packard (HP), to differentiate their products from competitors. Responding to consumer demand for more socially and environmentally friendly products, HP has created its Eco Highlights label for select HP products. Through disclosing energy-saving features and certifications, HP intends to help businesses and consumers "reduce the environmental impact of their imaging and printing." By focusing on the eco-friendly characteristics of its products, HP is hoping that consumers will prefer its "green" products to those of competitors.[40]

PHOTO: Binkski

>> END EXAMPLE

▼Visual Summary

Chapter 6 Summary

The concepts underlying consumer behavior are built on value creation and customer relationship management. Companies that understand the factors that influence consumer behavior as it is expressed through decision making can implement strategies based on consumer behavior. Decision making is influenced by personal, psychological, situational, and social factors. A consumer's decision-making process includes five main steps: problem/opportunity recognition, information search, evaluation of alternatives, purchase decision, and postpurchase evaluation. Depending on the type of decisions being made, certain levels of problem solving can occur, including limited problem solving, significant problem solving, and routine response problem solving. A commitment to understanding consumer behavior and implementing consumer behavior-based strategies can provide a business with the information necessary to create financially rewarding relationships with consumers.

Consumer Behavior p. 57

Consumer behavior is simply the study of how business and final consumers shop for products, services, and ideas. Marketers are especially interested in the psychology of the consumer, as well as the geographic and demographic characteristics of their target markets.

how

Consumer Decision-Making Process pp. 58–63

way

The consumer-decision making process refers to the way consumers make purchase choices. There are many different models that explain consumers' behaviors in different shopping situations.

Consumer Problem Solving p. 64

conclusions

Consumer problem solving is related to the consumer decision-making process, but specifically relates to how consumers come to buying conclusions.

Capstone **Exercise** p. 67

▼**Chapter** Key Terms

Consumer Behavior (p. 57)

Consumer behavior *is the dynamic interaction of affect and cognition, behavior, and the environment in which human beings conduct the exchange aspects of their lives.* (p. 57) **Opening Example** (p. 57)

Key Terms (p. 57)

Psychology involves the study of the mind. **(p. 57)**
Social psychology is the process to understand social phenomena and their influence on social behavior. **(p. 57)**

Consumer Decision-Making Process (pp. 58–63)

Consumer decision-making process *is the steps that consumers take to identify and evaluate choice options.* (p. 58) **Example: Consumer Decision Making (p. 58) Example: Age and Life Stage (p. 59) Example: Affluence (p. 60) Example: Purchase Environment (p. 61) Example: Digital Environment (p. 61) Example: Subculture (p. 62) Example: Group (p. 63)**

Key Terms (pp. 59–63)

Attitude is a state of readiness, based on experience that influences a response to something. **(p. 60)**
Belief is a sense of truth about something. **(p. 60)**
Cognitive age, also referred to as subjective age, is the age that a person feels. **(p. 59)**
Cue is an environmental stimulus that influences a particular action. **(p. 60)**
Culture refers to the shared values, beliefs, and preferences of a particular society. **(p. 62)**
Drive is an internal stimulus that encourages action. **(p. 60)**
Learning is knowledge that is acquired through experiences. **(p. 60)**
Life stages are similar life events experienced by groups of individuals of varying chronological and cognitive ages. **(p. 59) Example: Age and Life Stage (p. 59)**
Lifestyle is a way of life that individuals express through choosing how to spend their time and personal resources. **(p. 59)**
Motivation is the set of conditions that creates a drive toward a particular action to fulfill a need or want. **(p. 60)**

Norms are standards of behaviors imparted to members of a particular group that define membership. **(p. 63)**
Opinion leaders are those individuals who have the greatest influence on the attitudes and behaviors of a particular group. **(p. 63) Example: Group (p. 63)**
Perception is a cognitive impression of incoming stimuli that influences the individual's actions and behavior. **(p. 60)**
Personality involves a sense of consistency, internal causality, and personal distinctiveness. **(p. 59)**
Reference group consists of people who directly or indirectly influence how an individual feels about a particular topic. **(p. 63) Example: Group (p. 63)**
Reinforcement is a reduction in drive resulting from a positive response experience. **(p. 61)**
Response is a consumer's reaction to his or her drive and cues. **(p. 61)**
Roles are specific actions expected from someone in a group as a member or from a particular position held. **(p. 63)**
Self-identity is the understanding by an individual that he or she is unique. **(p. 59) Example: Age and Life Stage (p. 59)**
Social classes are characteristics that distinguish certain members of a society from others, based on a variety of factors, including wealth, vocation, education, power, place of residence, and ancestry. **(p. 63) Example: Affluence (p. 60)**
Status is the relative position of one individual relative to others. **(p. 63)**
Subcultures are groups of people, within a broader society, who share similar behaviors and values. **(p. 62) Example: Subculture (p. 62)**
Subliminal perception is the processing of stimuli by a recipient who is not aware of the stimuli being received. **(p. 60)**

Consumer Problem Solving (p. 64)

Consumer problem solving *is how someone comes to a conclusion about a situation. This is determined by what kind of a decision a consumer is facing.* **Example: Consumer Problem Solving (p. 64)**

Key Terms (p. 64)

Limited problem solving occurs when a consumer is prepared to exert a certain amount of effort to make a purchase decision. **(p. 64)**
Routine response problem solving occurs when a consumer has a well-developed process associated with fulfilling a need or want. **(p. 64)**
Significant problem solving occurs when a consumer is prepared to commit considerable effort to make a purchase decision. **(p. 64) Example: Consumer Problem Solving (p. 64)**

▼Capstone Exercise

This chapter deals with consumer behavior. The issue in this chapter is to understand the factors that influence a person's buying decisions. Why do people buy what they buy? For example, why would one woman spend $200 on a sweater when another comparable sweater could be bought for $50? To explore the buying process and how it works, it is helpful to talk to an individual who has bought a product or service and then dissect the buying decision.

This chapter's exercise is to interview two people who are not members of your marketing class. Preferably, the people should be from different demographic groups—age, income, education, and occupation. Don't just pick your fellow students, or that will skew your findings. Of the two people, one needs to have made a purchase decision of $25.00 or less, and the other a purchase decision of $100.00 or more. Evaluate and prioritize the information that influenced their purchase decisions.

Your task is to "get in the person's head." Try to understand why they bought what they did. Question the reasons they used to make their decisions.

Write a 1–2 page paper on each interview. Describe the person, what he or she bought, and what factors contributed to the person's purchase decision. Be creative in the questions that you ask. To get you started, here are some questions to ask:

- Was it an individual or family decision?
- Was it a want or a need?
- What motivated the purchase?
- What features or benefits seemed important to the buyer?
- Was it a first-time decision? Has the person bought this product before?
- How much thought went into the buying decision?
- Did the person search the Internet or speak to friends? Did he or she read reviews on a site such as Amazon or www.epinions.com?
- How did the person gather the information he or she used to make the decision?
- Was the choice a low- or high-involvement purchase?
- How many alternatives were evaluated?
- Was the person happy with his or her choice? Why, or why not?
- Did service play a factor with the choice?
- Did the product/service meet the person's expectations? If so, why? If not, why not?
- What role did the brand name play?

▼Application Exercises

Complete the following exercises:

1. Select a product and service and apply the decision-making process to that product or service. Discuss each step.

2. Explain the consumer decision-making process for luxury products and provide an example.

3. Every culture contains smaller subcultures. In the United States, the rapidly increasing Hispanic market holds opportunities for many businesses. Look around your community and make a list of the businesses that may well prosper from this increasing subculture. Why do you think this is so?

4. Within the U.S. Hispanic market, there exist many distinct subsegments. Research these subsegments and detail the characteristics unique to each.

Consumer Insight

Chapter Overview In the previous chapter, you considered how consumers made decisions and behaved in the marketplace, and you explored how that behavior extended globally. The reasons consumers behave the way they do, and the underlying motivations for that behavior, need to be understood for a company to make effective marketing decisions. This chapter considers the concepts, tools, and processes that companies can use to learn more about their customers (and potential customers). By exploring marketing research and marketing information systems, the concept of consumer insight will be developed.

 Chapter **Outline**

Consumer Insight pp. 69–70 ⟵ **Objective 1.** How do companies use the information they get from consumer interactions?

Marketing Research pp. 70–77 ⟵ **Objective 2.** What is marketing research? How does it help decision makers make better decisions?

- **Define the Problem** p. 71
- **Design the Research** p. 71
- **Conduct the Research** p. 76
- **Analyze the Research** p. 76
- **Address the Problem in a Research Report** p. 77

Marketing Information System pp. 77–78 ⟵ **Objective 3.** What is a marketing information system? How does it help to establish, develop, and maintain customer relationships?

CONSUMER INSIGHT (p. 69–70)

>  **DEFINED** **Consumer insight** *is perceived meanings of data collected from the study of consumer behavior.*

 EXPLAINED

Consumer Insight

With the increased competition for space on the shelves of retailers and the sheer number of new products entering the market each year, understanding what consumers want and why they want it is an essential marketing practice. Consumer insight is not insight that consumers have; it is insight about consumers. Consumer insight includes a broad range of information that is obtained and interpreted to create detailed perspectives on customers and other market members. **Insight** is defined as the act or result of apprehending the inner nature of things, or of seeing intuitively.[1] From this definition, we can see that insights are far more valuable than mere information. Insights place information in context; that context can extend to both consumers and businesses. The study of business behavior, for those involved in business-to-business activities, is just as important as the study of consumer behavior is to those involved in business-to-consumer activities.

The American Marketing Association (AMA) defines **consumer market insight** as "an in-depth understanding of customer behavior that is more qualitative than quantitative. Specifically, it describes the role played by the product/brand in question in the life of its consumers—and their general stance toward it, including the way they acquire information about the category or brand, the importance attached to generic and specific values, attitudes, expectations, as well as the choice-making process. It refers to a holistic appreciation, which used to be traditionally split by market researchers and brand managers as qualitative and quantitative research."[2] This definition illustrates the relationship of consumer insight to the study of consumer behavior. Exploring consumer behavior involves conducting marketing research and managing a marketing information system. Each of these topics will be addressed in subsequent sections.

APPLIED

Consumer Insight

Consumers interact with companies in many different ways, including responding to direct marketing, using call centers, shopping at retail outlets, using service locations, and responding to advertising. Each of these activities provides data (insights) that help companies determine who the most desirable consumers are, where they are, how best to talk to them, how to keep them happy, and how to sell them more things at higher margins.

Although consumer information is generated from many different areas within an organization, the responsibility for consumer insight is typically assigned to a person or group within the marketing or strategy departments. The specific department titles vary widely from Knowledge Management, Consumer Innovation, Marketing Intelligence, and Marketing Research to Consumer Insights. The specific functions of these groups may be similar, but this textbook treats the concepts of marketing intelligence, marketing research, and consumers insight differently.

In practice, consumer insight can address a wide range of questions, including the following:

- What do people think about my brand?
- What do people think about the competing brands?

OnStar is the nation's leading provider of in-vehicle safety, security, and communication services using wireless technology and the Global Positioning System (GPS) satellite network. OnStar regularly uses consumer insight to support its product development, marketing, and strategic planning processes. Founded in 1995 as a collaboration between General Motors, EDS, and Hughes Electronics Corporation, OnStar utilizes methods such as data mining, online communities, qualitative research, survey research, and analytics to assess consumer loyalty, brand health and advertising effectiveness.
PHOTO: Courtesy of U.S. Department of Defense Visual Information Center

- What do people expect from my brand?
- What opportunities and threats exist for my brand?
- What factors influence purchase considerations for my brand?
- What types of advertising work best for communicating the essence of my brand?
- How consistently does price change with demand for my brand?
- With what other brands could my brand collaborate for mutual benefit?
- What is the personality of my brand, and how does that influence purchase consideration?
- Who are my brand's most loyal customers?
- What market conditions exist such that I have either greater or lesser opportunities than I did recently?

Understanding these consumer insights can lead to responsive product development processes, targeted marketing strategies, and efficiencies throughout the supply and distribution channels, as well as in marketing expenditures.

Marketing Research (pp. 70–77)

> **DEFINED Marketing research** *is the acquisition and analysis of information used to identify and define marketing opportunities that connect consumers to marketers.*[3]

 EXPLAINED
Marketing Research

One of the first marketing research projects occurred in 1879 when advertising company N.W. Ayer & Son applied marketing research when creating ads for the Nichols-Shepard Company, makers of agricultural machinery. N.W. Ayer & Son wired state officials and publishers around the country asking for information on grain production.[4] The first continuous marketing research study is credited to Charles Parlin for his work with Curtis Publishing Company, beginning in 1911 and continuing for 27 years, to collect information about customers to help Curtis sell more magazine advertising for the *Saturday Evening Post*.[5]

Research is defined as "the studious inquiry or examination; *especially*: investigation or experimentation aimed at the discovery and interpretation of facts, revision of accepted theories or laws in the light of new facts, or practical application of such new or revised theories or laws."[6] Research can be classified as either applied or pure. **Applied research** attempts to answer questions related to practical problems. If a small business owner wants to know where to locate his or her new restaurant, the owner would conduct applied research on a variety of topics including competition, traffic patterns, and level of consumer affluence near the proposed locations. **Pure research** attempts to expand understanding

of the unknown. Scientists searching for a cure for AIDS or cancer are conducting pure research. Applied research is much more common in business. Many different disciplines, from law to political history, utilize research, but marketing research is classified as either consumer marketing research or business-to-business marketing research. Consumer marketing research considers the behavior of individual consumers or groups of consumers. Business-to-business marketing research considers the behavior of businesses transacting with other businesses.

APPLIED
Marketing Research

The purpose of marketing research is to help decision makers make better decisions. Marketing research can produce valuable information, but that information is most valuable when it is effectively translated into consumer insight. Marketing research information is a tool that can be used to launch successful new products and assist in the creation of effective advertising. The uses of marketing research include the following:[7]

- Identify and define marketing opportunities and problems.
- Generate, refine, and evaluate marketing actions.
- Monitor marketing performance.
- Improve understanding of marketing as a process.

While potentially valuable, marketing research can also be misrepresented when not placed into proper context. The *Chicago Tribune* used a still-growing technology, the telephone, to project the winner of the 1948 presidential election. Collecting responses from a high-income, mainly Republican, group of telephone owners produced a skewed representation of the population. The result was the infamous front-page headline "Dewey Defeats Truman" running the day after the election, when, in fact, Harry Truman won the presidential election against New York Governor Thomas Dewey.[8]

EXAMPLE   MARKETING RESEARCH

An example of misinterpretation of research is the 2000 Presidential election between George W. Bush and Al Gore. The results were announced, changed, changed again, and then thrust into confusion for many weeks. The election of George W. Bush was only made final after the Supreme Court case *Bush v. Gore* was decided in Bush's favor. Television network projections were incorrect for a variety of reasons, including incorrect information obtained from exit polling, sample results, and unofficial election returns from election sites throughout Florida. The rush to be the first network to announce election results and a lack of understanding of the methodology of how certain data was obtained caused much of the confusion.

PHOTO: Sergieiev

>> END EXAMPLE

The Internet has provided additional means to collect marketing research. The traditional methods of telephone, door-to-door, and mail have, although still used, essentially given way to Internet-based marketing research. Given the speed to administer, ability to tailor questioning based on prior responses, opportunity to show pictures, cost-effectiveness for midsized to large surveys, and speed of responses, the Internet is transforming marketing research. One of the major concerns regarding Internet marketing research is the ability to translate results obtained from the Internet to the general population. Some argue that people on the Internet are different from the rest of the population because lower-income individuals have limited access to the Internet. A historical perspective on the current Internet research applications debate extends from the in-person versus telephone debate of the 1960s and 1970s. When phone penetration exceeded 90%, the argument became moot. Clearly, the Internet is moving in that direction. Internet penetration in the United States is about 74%, compared to a global average of 22%, European average of 48%, African average of 5%, and Asian average of 15%. Companies that operate worldwide should understand that the Internet does not offer similar research opportunities in all countries.

When an organization has questions, marketing research may be appropriate. A formal process should be followed to determine if marketing research is warranted and, if warranted, then how best to structure and conduct the marketing research. There are five major steps in the marketing research process:

- Define the problem.
- Design the research.
- Conduct the research.
- Analyze the research.
- Address the problem in a research report.

These steps are each necessary and generally linear in nature, but there should be considerable feedback to ensure that no assumptions have changed during the research process.

Define the Problem

The first step in the marketing research process is the most important. It is the step when the specific problem is determined. At that time, the decision is made whether marketing research is necessary and viable as well as how to set limits on what will be studied. The **research question**, the question the research is designed to answer, is also defined in this step. Properly addressing this step provides necessary clarity for subsequent steps in the marketing research process.

Developing the problem statement involves considering the known facts as they relate to what is occurring and why. For example, a common trigger for a marketing research request is a significant decrease in sales of a product. Although the symptom of reduced sales is observed, there also may be other symptoms. The challenge lies in isolating symptoms from causes. The causes could vary, including a competitor's actions, a decrease in the size or number of distributors, a reduction in productivity of the sales force, or a production or operations issue. If I believe the perception of my product has changed, then the research question should evolve from "I need to know why my sales are

down" to questions like the following: "How do customers evaluate my product relative to my competitors?" "What are the perceived strengths or weaknesses of my product?"

In some cases, research is not appropriate. Examples of marketing research being neither necessary nor viable include the following:

- The net benefit from conducting the research is significantly less than the cost of conducting the research, for example, when a business considers spending $50,000 to study the impact of purchasing $5,000 in computer software.
- The business is either unwilling or unable to take advantage of any potential results from the research, for example, when a business decides to test consumer interest in two advertising campaigns, even though the business has already committed to one of the campaigns.
- The business does not have time to wait for research before a business decision must be made or the time to implement changes suggested by the research. An example is when a business has 24 hours to react to a competitor's dramatic price change and the business begins a viability study that will take several weeks to complete.

Once the appropriateness of conducting marketing research is determined, the next task involves designing the research.

Design the Research

With a clear research question determined, it is important to identify any available information that may assist in answering all or part of the question. Such information might be previous research or research conducted by others, for example, the government and trade associations. There may be also information available to help further clarify the research question. This information may come from within or outside the company. There are two classifications of information sources to consider:

- Primary data
- Secondary data

Primary data is information that is collected to address a current research question. Primary data can be obtained through a variety of marketing research activities, including surveys and observational techniques. The techniques to obtain primary data will be discussed later in the chapter. **Secondary data** is information that has been previously collected for another purpose. Secondary data comes from a wide range of sources, including company reports, previous marketing research studies, sales performance reports, the Internet, government publications, and libraries. Private research companies can provide primary, secondary, or both types of information. The data that private research companies provide is often called syndicated research. **Syndicated research** is information collected on a regular basis using standardized procedures and sold to multiple customers from a related industry. In many cases, secondary data can provide "close enough" answers to business questions. Quite often, businesses have considered the same research questions repeatedly. Determining the level of precision required to address a specific research question will indicate if secondary research might be acceptable, if the secondary research exists.

J.D. Power and Associates offers a variety of syndicated studies, including the Initial Quality Study for its automotive clients. the Initial Quality Study (IQS) provides in-depth diagnostic information on new-vehicle quality after 90 days of ownership. Owners and lessees are surveyed regarding problems with their new vehicles. Automotive brands use this secondary data to make business decisions instead of creating their own independent studies. Automotive brands consider the cost savings of secondary research over primary research and the ability to compare research results across automotive brands.[9]

PHOTO: Nigel Carse

>> **END EXAMPLE**

Research Design Categories

Based on the research question, a research design can be developed. A **research design** is a framework or plan for a study that guides the collection and analysis of the data.[10] There are three general categories of research designs:

- Exploratory
- Descriptive
- Explanatory

Exploratory research is a marketing research design used to generate ideas in a new area of inquiry. This design is most useful in dividing a broad research problem into smaller problems for subsequent research. An example of exploratory research could involve a series of personal interviews with select consumers to determine why they purchase a particular product or service.

Descriptive research is a marketing research design that is used to describe marketing variables by answering who, what, when, where, and how questions. Descriptive research is more structured than exploratory research. An example of descriptive research could involve a survey among specific consumers that explores where they purchase groceries and how often they go shopping.

Explanatory research is a marketing research design used to understand the relationship between independent and dependent variables. This type of research, also known as causal research, is typically used to further study relationships identified from descriptive or exploratory research. An example of explanatory research could involve an experiment where

a direct marketing campaign is tested against sales performance to determine effectiveness.

Research Types

Depending on the research design selected, a research classification will be selected. There are two types of research:

- Qualitative
- Quantitative

Qualitative research is a collection of techniques designed to identify and interpret information obtained through the observation of people. Qualitative research is generally considered subjective. It can be used in concert with **quantitative research**, a process to collect a large number of responses using a standardized questionnaire where the results can be summarized into numbers for statistical analysis. The analysis results can be used either to provide perspective prior to quantitative research or to further explore results from quantitative research. There are a variety of qualitative research techniques, including the following:

- Focus groups
- Structured interviews
- Ethnographic research

Focus groups are collections of a small number of individuals who were recruited using specific criteria with the purpose to discuss predetermined topics with qualified moderators.

Structured interviews are a series of discussions held between a trained interviewer and individuals, on a one-on-one basis. The individuals are recruited using specific criteria with the purpose to discuss predetermined topics. **Ethnographic research** is a type of observational research where trained researchers immerse themselves in a specific consumer environment. Researchers using ethnographic research techniques may visit someone in their home and watch how breakfast decisions are made, or they may ride along in someone's vehicle to observe how shopping locations are selected when running errands.

On-Site Research Associates has been involved with digital ethnography for over 20 years. The company pioneered the use of nonobtrusive ethnographic techniques that do not require a videographer to record consumer reality in a person's home or in a retail environment. The company uses a small "hand cam" so it can record what consumers actually do with a given product. In 2004, On-Site conducted a cross-country ethnographic learning journey (The Pulse Of America) to collect information on American attitudes and cultural insights. On-Site offers a variety of products, including a YouTube channel called Ethnovision.[11]

PHOTO: DeshaCAM

>> **END EXAMPLE**

The appropriate research technique depends on the scope of the project, the capabilities of the moderator/interviewer, the project timeline, and funding. The output from qualitative research can provide deep insight into the motivations of individuals. However, that output cannot be projectable to a larger group of similar people or to the general population.

Quantitative research is essentially survey research. The results are intended to be statistically valid and projectable to a larger group of the general population. While qualitative research tends to be more exploratory, quantitative research is more descriptive and explanatory.

Once a research classification is selected, a data-collection method must be identified. Several examples of qualitative techniques were identified earlier. Focus groups are typically conducted in person, but they are increasingly being conducted online. Much has changed since American Dialogue conducted the first documented online focus group in 1993. Many of those changes are due to the advent of broadband and other high-speed Internet options, as well as greater acceptance from businesses.[12] Still, individual interviews and ethnographic research are primarily conducted in person.

There are a variety of data-collection options when conducting quantitative research. These options include the following:

- Telephone
- In person
- Mail
- Online

Telephone interviewing can provide quick feedback, and the ability exists to react to specific responses. However, response rates are decreasing and there can be variability in how different interviewers ask questions and interpret responses. In-person interviewing can also provide quick feedback and flexibility to follow up to responses, but it can suffer from variability in interviewer questioning, and it is very expensive. Mail questionnaires can be relatively cost effective and are not subjected to interviewer variability, but questionnaires have no flexibility for follow-up questions and can take a considerable amount of time to complete. Online questionnaires offer the lowest relative cost of all options and provide rapid responses. At the same time, online questionnaires control interviewer variation and allow some flexibility to follow up, based on some predetermined responses. Online questionnaires do not have the flexibility of in-person and telephone methods to deal with any respondent comprehension issues. Online questionnaires require valid e-mail addresses or access to a well-managed Internet panel. Response rates are considered lower for Internet research, unless an Internet panel is utilized, than other data collection options.[13]

Online research is one of the most popular forms of marketing research because an increasing number of consumers are online and an increasing amount of marketing and advertising investment is being made in the online environment. The four primary motivations for Web use by consumers are as follows:[14]

- Researching
- Shopping
- Socializing
- Surfing

Each of these motivations provides businesses with opportunities to connect with their customers. Marketing research can access consumers in any of these environments.

While a wide range of research can be conducted on the Internet, for example, online focus groups or tracking Web site visits, the decision on whether to conduct survey research on the Internet requires that several critical questions be answered. These questions include the following:[15]

- Can the survey be self-administered?
- Can the information about the product or service be effectively communicated on a computer monitor?
- Can the target respondent be reached through e-mail?
- Can members of the online population reflect the desired target market?

An Internet research panel can directly address the final two questions. An **Internet research panel** is a collection of individuals who agree, for some predetermined incentive, to participate in questionnaires on a variety of topics as determined by the owner and manager of the panel. These panels are typically owned and managed by marketing research companies and are used to provide services to their clients. A number of Internet research panels have been established for a single client of a marketing research company. These panels are known as online communities.

EXAMPLE MARKETING RESEARCH, INTERNET RESEARCH PANEL

e-Rewards, Inc. operates an invitation-only online marketing research panel with over 700 clients and 2.6 million panelists. e-Rewards offers panelists the opportunity to complete surveys, after matching individual profiles with specific business sponsor requirements, for e-Rewards currency that can be redeemed for gift cards. Joining e-Rewards is free, but consumers join through one of e-Rewards sponsors such as Continental Airlines OnePass frequent flyer program.[16]

PHOTO: Karen Roach

>> END EXAMPLE

It is important to understand that research collected from an Internet research panel is not typically representative of any given population because probability sampling is not used to recruit members. Internet research panels are often used to recruit specific types of people, such as adventurous individuals or owners of boats. Members often are invited from a variety of sources, including media placements or other Web sites. It is possible that special sampling, weighting, and other statistical techniques can be used to create representative data for certain populations. Panel maintenance is a critical issue to retain viability of the panel. Aspects of panel management include the following:

- Panelist relationship management (keeping panelists engaged in the panel)
- Incentive program development and administration
- Maintaining historical record of panelist activity
- Monitoring completion rates and response times of surveys
- Cleaning and refreshing the panel
- Periodic reprofiling
- Regular reporting on composition and response rates
- Compliance with laws and regulations

Many large businesses have transitioned much of their marketing research to the Internet. Brand-tracking studies, advertising copy tests, and customer satisfaction studies are all being conducted in an online environment. Some marketing research studies have transitioned easily, but others have had to be adjusted for the online environment. Some new marketing research techniques have evolved solely in an online environment. Virtual shopping environments can be created and used to simulate the actual choices that a consumer has in a store. The results can influence product development and positioning issues.

Much of the current work in moving marketing research from one data-collection method to another is from telephone to Internet. There are many differences between these two methods. It is often considered that online research limits the ability of a respondent to express emotion. However, the anonymity provided by an online environment does provide the opportunity for realistic opinions.[17] The Internet also uses a wider range of response types and can be considered less invasive and more satisfying for the respondent than other methods.[18]

Question structure can contribute significantly to accessing the benefits of Internet research. Core elements of a brand and advertising tracking study include questions relating to the consumer purchase funnel, brand imagery, and advertising recall and classification demographics and psychographics. Table 7.1 provides examples of the different wordings of questions for each topic.

Measurement

Measurement is the process of quantifying how much one variable's set of features or characteristics are possessed in another variable. A measurement plan involves two primary elements, including determining those features or characteristics, referred to as properties, that best represent the concept being studied from the research question. The second element of the plan is determining the appropriate scale to use to measure questions about the concept. The two aspects are closely linked by statistical requirements.

The first requirement is to determine what is to be measured. Will it be tangible (direct) or intangible (subjective)? The former allows for a direct rating, such as a demographic question of household income or age of respondent. The latter involves a respondent using a rating scale to choose which point on the scale best reflects the way they feel. This could involve a question such as the following: Which of the following statements best reflects the way that you feel about your vehicle's quality with respect to all vehicles? The possible responses would be as follows: Better than average. Average. Below Average.

The second requirement involves selecting the type of scale to use. There are four types of scales:

- Nominal
- Ordinal
- Interval
- Ratio

A **nominal scale** is a measurement in which numbers are assigned to characteristics of objects or groups of objects solely for identifying the objects.[19] The nominal scale is often used for classification and, therefore, is limited for analysis that can be conducted with the data. An **ordinal scale** is a measurement in which numbers are assigned to characteristics of objects or groups of objects to reflect the order of the objects,[20] such as the results of a 100-yard running race (John Smith came in first, Jack Johnson came in second, Jerry Jackson came in third). An ordinal scale allows rankings (first, second, third), but it does not allow us to know the specific differences between rankings; for example, John Smith finished in 10.5 seconds, Jack Johnson finished in 10.8 seconds, and Jerry Jackson finished in 11.1 seconds.

An **interval scale** is a measurement in which the numbers assigned to the characteristics of the objects or groups of objects legitimately allow comparison of the size of the differences among and between objects.[21] An interval scale allows us to compare John Smith's time against Jack Johnson's time and Jerry Jackson's time. Interval scales are often used to rate satisfaction levels with some aspect of a product or service. A **ratio scale** is a measurement in which the numbers assigned to the characteristics of the objects have an identifiable absolute zero.[22] An example would be the number of days spent traveling in one calendar year. There is an absolute zero, so a person could travel one-third as much or twice as much as someone else could.

Questionnaire Development

A **questionnaire** is an organized set of questions that a researcher desires respondents to answer. Questionnaires perform a range of functions, including the following:

- Keeping respondents motivated to complete the survey
- Translating research objectives into research questions
- Providing a consistent question format for each respondent
- Facilitating ease of data analysis

Table 7.1 Survey Question Format: Phone versus Internet

Question Topic	Phone Question	Internet Question
Unaided brand awareness	Now, thinking of different makes and models of motorcycles, which make and model comes to mind first? Which comes to mind next? Which others?	Thinking of different makes and models of motorcycles, which makes and models come to mind? Please type in both the make AND the model for each motorcycle you can think of.
Familiarity	Now, I'd like to know how familiar you are with these various motorcycles. For each make and model I mention, can you tell me if you...?	Which of these statements most applies to how familiar you are with the following?
Overall rating	Overall, how would you rate the...?	Overall, how would you rate the...?
Purchase consideration	Now, I'd like to know how likely you are to buy or lease these various motorcycles. For each make and model I mention, can you tell me if...?	Thinking about the next time you purchase or lease a new motorcycle, how likely are you to purchase or lease the following?
Brand image	Based on anything that you've seen or heard or any impressions you may have... Which of these makes and models, if any...?	We'd like you to indicate which motorcycle (companies/makes/models) is best described by the following statements. You can choose as many or as few as you wish, or none at all. Which is best described by these statements?
Advertising recall	Have you seen a commercial that (detailed description of commercial)?	We are now going to show you some pictures from a TV commercial. Have you seen this TV commercial before? Please wait for the images to completely load before answering the question.
Income	Is your total annual income before taxes over or under $50,000?	Please choose the category that roughly includes your total annual household income before taxes.
Age	For statistical purposes only, may I have your age please? ...That is, are you...?	Which of the following group includes your age?
Ethnicity	Are you (read list of ethnicities)?	To ensure that we have a fair representation of diverse ethnic backgrounds, are you...? Please select all that apply. If other, please specify your ethnic heritage.
Gender	Record respondent's gender.	Are you? (male/female)
Psychographics	I am going to read you a list of statements that people have made about motorcycles and about what they are looking for when they are buying or leasing their vehicle. Please tell me if you agree strongly, agree somewhat, neither agree nor disagree, disagree somewhat, or disagree strongly that the statement describes you. The first statement is...	The following statements describe the way different people approach selecting the motorcycles they are going to buy. Please choose the one statement that best describes you.

The development of a questionnaire requires a decision on the answer choices presented to consumers. A **closed-ended question** has specific survey answer choices available to respondents. The numbering of the answer choices for each question is known as **coding**. For example, "How many four-credit university courses do you anticipate registering for next term?" The choices are the following: A-0, B-1 to 2, C-3 to 4, and D-5 or more. An **open-ended question** allows for unrestricted survey responses. For example, "If you were the governor of your state, what would be your top policy priority?" Regardless of the choice of closed-ended, open-ended, or a combination of question types, the questions must be carefully worded, concise, and clear, so that respondents understand the precise meaning of each question being asked and that responses are not biased by leading questions.

After determining the individual question structure, the overall design of the questionnaire must be considered. The primary elements of a questionnaire include the following:

- **Introduction**—An overview that introduces the general context of the survey
- **Screening**—If any restrictions exist on the desired respondents for the survey, the restrictions are applied through screening questions

- **Warm-up**—Opening questions that determine general knowledge of the topic of the questionnaire
- **Body**—Main collection of survey questions
- **Classification questions**—Questions that group respondents into various categories, such as age, income, gender, or level of education

Sample Plan

The next design decision involves creating a sample plan. It is seldom either financially viable or physically possible (nor is it statistically necessary) to survey everyone within a specific consumer segment. A sample, if correctly identified, can represent the opinion of a broader population. A **sample** is defined as a specific part of the population that is selected to the represent the population. A **population** is defined as the total group of individuals that meet the criteria being studied. A **census** is a survey that collects responses for each member of the population.

The **sample plan** identifies who will be sampled, how many people will be sampled, and the procedure that will be used for sampling. For example, if a company is interested in determining purchase consideration for its products relative to competitors, the company could ask a specific demographic target toward which its product is positioned, or the company could ask only those within that target who are aware of the brand and competitive brands in the category. The company then can select between a census and a sample. The actual number of the people in the target depends not only on the overall group being studied, but also any subgroups within the overall group, such as gender or particular age cohorts. The calculation for the sample size is beyond the scope of this book. Ultimately, the sample plan should manage the risks of bias entering the marketing research project. **Sample error** refers to any differences between the sample results and the actual results that would emerge from a census of the population.

The **sampling procedure** involves selecting either a probability sample or a nonprobability sample as part of your sample plan. A **probability sample** is a procedure whereby each member of a population has a known and nonzero chance of possibly being selected to a sample. There are several probability sampling procedures, including simple random sampling where each person has an equal chance of being selected, systematic sampling where a skip interval is used from a list of the population to select the sample, and stratified sampling where the population is subdivided into specific groups and random samples are selected from those groups.

A **nonprobability sample** is a procedure whereby each member of a population does not have an equal chance, or, in some cases, any chance, of being selected to a sample. Results from nonprobability samples can describe only the characteristics of the sample and not the population. There are several nonprobability procedures, including a convenience sample, where samples are created out of convenience; a purposive sample, where judgment is used to create the sample based on a perception that the respondents meet the necessary requirements; a snowball sample, where respondents help identify subsequent respondents for the sample; and a quota sample, where predetermined categories are used to identify respondents based on that predetermined criteria.

Conduct the Research

Implementing the research design begins with data collection. Assuming that the survey instrument has been appropriately designed, the next concern is how to obtain viable data for analysis. If the collection is through the mail, then the area to watch is when data is transferred from the mail to a computer file. If collection is directly online, then the area to watch is the program that aggregates and analyzes the data, as well as the process to move the data from one program to another, if relevant.

When interviewers are involved, through either a telephone interview or an in-person interview, there are other concerns. The interviewer may not consistently execute the survey, either intentionally or unintentionally, the interviewer may record the responses incorrectly, the researcher may not understand the responses, or the researcher may improperly clarify or incorrectly clarify a question. **Nonsampling error** is any bias that emerges in the study for any reason other than sampling error. Nonsampling error includes not only interviewer error, but also respondent errors such as confusion, fatigue, or deceit.

The overarching concerns with the quality of the marketing research involve the levels of validity and reliability of the results. **Validity** is the strength of the conclusion. Were the results correct? **Reliability** is the level of consistency of the measurement. Is the marketing research repeatable with the same conditions? A variety of techniques is available to measure these factors, depending on how the scales were developed.

Analyze the Research

Analyzing the data involves creating a data file with the results and eliminating data-entry errors through cleaning and executing the warranted appropriate statistical analysis, given the scale of the data and the nature of the research question. With ratio data, there is the greatest flexibility to use a wide range of statistical techniques. The broad range of statistical techniques includes descriptive statistics used to describe findings and relationships, inferential statistics used to generalize sample results to a larger population, and other techniques that consider relationships between variables, differences between groups, and advanced modeling.

Address the Problem in a Research Report

Once the entire research process has been completed, it is essential to do more than simply document the results. Findings must be evaluated and conclusions developed. Most important, it is essential to attempt to answer the original research question. Think about who is receiving this information and understand that they may not have a marketing research background. Be sure to consider the findings of the research from various perspectives and ultimately try to synthesize the most viable recommendations from the findings and conclusions.

Marketing Information System (p. 77–78)

 DEFINED *A* **marketing information system** *is a series of steps that include collection, analysis, and presentation of information for use in making marketing decisions.*[23]

 **EXPLAINED**

Marketing Information System

A marketing information system functions much like a management information system except in support of the marketing activity. A management information system is a set of procedures and methods for the regular, planned collection, analysis, and presentation of information for use in making management decisions.[24] A marketing information system is intended to bring together various streams of marketing data within an organization. But a marketing information system is more than a repository of data. It is an ongoing collaboration of "people, equipment, and procedures."[25] The level of complexity can vary greatly from a manual system to a series of mainframe computers.

There are four primary elements of the marketing information system:

- Internal company data
- Market intelligence zystems
- Marketing decision support systems
- Marketing research systems

Internal company data includes everything from order status, stock levels, and production schedules to financial performance, human resource status, direct-mail redemption details, and Web site click-through details. These seemingly separate pieces of data can be combined to influence a wide range of marketing decisions, including product pricing, advertising copywriting, distribution partner selection, and packaging changes.

A **market intelligence system** is a system that gathers, processes, assesses, and makes available marketing information in a format that allows the marketing activity to function more effectively.[26] The information from a market intelligence system can also assist strategic planning and policy development. The procedures of a marketing intelligence system identify critical areas to be monitored, including market activity and trends, consumers, customers, and competitors. **Competitive intelligence** involves the systematic tracking of competitive actions and plans and is a significant activity within a business. Good competitive intelligence can help fend off a competitive attack or blunt a competitor's launch of a new product.

A **marketing decision support system** (**MDSS**) is the software and associated infrastructure that connect the marketing activity to company databases. This system is an important component of a marketing information system because it contains the analytical tools to provide critical data to marketing decision makers. An MDSS often contains modeling capability to create different marketing and financial models.

A **marketing research system** is a collection of the results of marketing research studies conducted by a company. The contents of this system are much more specific than those of the market intelligence system. The breadth of possible marketing research is discussed earlier in this chapter.

 APPLIED

Marketing Information System

In practice, a marketing information system is often referred to as a customer relationship management (CRM) system. CRM is comprised of the activities that are used to establish, develop, and maintain customer relationships. There are many similarities because CRM is designed to create more valuable customer contact using databases. The two work together, but a marketing information system is more holistic; it includes more marketing inputs than with CRM. Also, the sheer number of inputs into a marketing information system is growing. In addition to the many traditional sources of information feeding a marketing information system, the rapid proliferation of discussion forums, blogs, and other types of social media is forcing marketing information systems to evolve to keep up.

The sophistication of the marketing information system provides a marketing activity with everything needed to manage the portfolio, from scanner data from an individual store, to brand-switching data at a regional level, to cookies from online stores. Scanner data collected at the many retail checkout counters across the country can provide instant feedback on sales promotions and purchasing trends. Each person who uses a pharmacy or supermarket loyalty card provides inputs into a marketing information system when that card is swiped through a retail scanner. Scanner purchase data can be analyzed at the store level and at the state, regional, and national levels. **Cookies** are small files containing certain personal information and are sent from Web servers to a consumer's computer to be accessed the next time a consumer visits a particular Web site. Cookies are used to facilitate the completion of forms on Web sites, and they are also used to store online shopping cart information. Increases in online marketing and e-commerce practices have expanded the use of cookies and their importance as inputs to marketing information systems.

EXAMPLE | **MARKETING INFORMATION SYSTEM**

Costco Wholesale, the largest wholesale club operator in the United States, uses a scanner-based point-of-sale tracking system developed by Information Resources, Inc. The Costco Collaborative Retail Exchange program provides information on sales performance, inventory control, and promotion performance.

PHOTO: Marcin Balcerzak

>> **END EXAMPLE**

▼Visual Summary

Chapter 7 Summary

The process of generating and utilizing consumer insight builds on the previous chapter's discussion of how consumers make decisions and behave in the global marketplace. Without a strong commitment to practicing a consumer-insight philosophy, businesses cannot effectively understand how they are perceived in the marketplace. Useful consumer insight builds on an active marketing research practice that identifies and defines marketing opportunities and problems, generates, refines, and evaluates marketing actions, monitors marketing performance, and improves understanding of the process of marketing. The marketing research is then included with market intelligence, internal reporting data, and the marketing decision support system to support a marketing information system. Ultimately, timely and detailed consumer insight is useful not only to the marketing function, but also to the business itself.

Consumer Insight pp. 69–70

Consumer insight is part of a process where marketers try and make meaningful interpretations of consumer data in order to fully understand their markets. Consumer insight generally is based upon softer (qualitative) data.

Marketing Information System pp. 77–78

Capstone **Exercise** p. 81

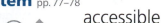

actionable   accessible

Marketing Research pp. 70–77

Marketing research involves the collection and analysis of data related to issues important to marketing managers. The purpose is to provide "actionable" information (or data) to marketing decision makers.

A Marketing Information System is a series of steps designed to acquire information about current and potential customers. The information is acquired, then stored. Marketing managers (and others with information needs) can then access the systems in order to help them solve relevant questions and problems related to their daily marketing activities.

▼Chapter Key Terms

Consumer Insight (pp. 69–70)

Consumer insight *is perceived meanings of data collected from the study of consumer behavior.* *(p. 69)* **Opening Example** **(p. 69)**

Key Terms (p. 69)

Consumer market insight is an in-depth understanding of customer behavior that is more qualitative than quantitative. **(p. 69)**

Insight is the act or result of apprehending the inner nature of things, or of seeing intuitively. **(p. 69)**

Marketing Research (pp. 70–77)

Marketing research *is the acquisition and analysis of information used to identify and define marketing opportunities that connect consumers to marketers.* *(p. 70)* **Example: Marketing Research (p. 70)**

Key Terms (pp. 70–76)

Applied research attempts to answer questions related to practical problems. **(p. 70)**

Census is a survey that collects responses for each member of the population. **(p. 76)**

Closed-ended question is a question that has specific survey answer choices available to respondents. **(p. 75)**

Coding is the numbering of the answer choices for each survey question. **(p. 75)**

Descriptive research is a marketing research design that is used to describe marketing variables by answering who, what, when, where, and how questions. **(p. 72)**

Ethnographic research is a type of observational research where trained researchers immerse themselves in a specific consumer environment. **(p. 72)** **Example, Marketing Research, Ethnographic Research (p. 72)**

Explanatory research is a marketing research design used to understand the relationship between independent and dependent variables. **(p. 72)**

Exploratory research is a marketing research design used to generate ideas in a new area of inquiry. **(p. 72)**

Focus groups are collections of a small number of individuals recruited by specific criteria with the purpose to discuss predetermined topics with qualified moderators. **(p. 72)**

Internet research panel is a collection of individuals who agree, for some predetermined incentive, to participate in questionnaires on a variety of topics as determined by the owner and manager of the panel. **(p. 73)** **Example, Marketing Research, Internet Research Panel (p. 73)**

Interval scale is a measurement in which the numbers assigned to the characteristics of the objects or groups of objects legitimately allow a comparison of the size of the differences among and between objects. **(p. 74)**

Measurement is the process of quantifying how much of a variable's set of features or characteristics are possessed in another variable. **(p. 74)**

Nominal scale is a measurement in which numbers are assigned to characteristics of objects or groups of objects solely for identifying the objects. **(p. 74)**

Nonprobability sample is a procedure where each member of a population does not have an equal chance, or, in some cases, any chance, of being selected to a sample. **(p. 76)**

Nonsampling error is any bias that emerges in the study for any reason other than sampling error. **(p. 76)**

Open-ended question is a question that allows for unrestricted survey responses. **(p. 75)**

Ordinal scale is a measurement in which numbers are assigned to characteristics of objects or groups of objects to reflect the order of the objects. **(p. 74)**

Population is defined as the total group of individuals who meet the criteria that is being studied. **(p. 76)**

Primary data is information that is collected to address a current research question. **(p. 71)**

Probability sample is a procedure where each member of a population has a known and nonzero chance of possibly being selected to a sample. **(p. 76)**

Pure research attempts to expand understanding of the unknown. **(p. 70)**

Qualitative research is a collection of techniques designed to identify and interpret information obtained through the observation of people. **(p. 72)**

Quantitative research is a process to collect a large number of responses using a standardized questionnaire where the results can be summarized into numbers for statistical analysis. **(p. 72)**

Questionnaire is an organized set of questions that a researcher desires that respondents answer. **(p. 74)**

Ratio scale is a measurement in which the numbers assigned to the characteristics of the objects have an identifiable absolute zero. **(p. 74)**

Reliability is the level of consistency of a measurement. **(p. 76)**

Research is the studious inquiry or examination; *especially*: investigation or experimentation aimed at the discovery and interpretation of facts, revision of accepted theories or laws in the light of new facts, or practical application of such new or revised theories or laws. **(p. 70)**

Research design is a framework or plan for a study that guides the collection and analysis of the data. **(p. 72)**

Research question is the question the research is designed to answer. **(p. 71)**

Sample is defined as a specific part of the population that is selected to the represent the population. **(p. 76)**

Sample error refers to any differences between the sample results and the actual results that would emerge from a census of the population. **(p. 76)**

Sample plan identifies who will be sampled, how many people will be sampled, and the procedure that will be used for sampling. **(p. 76)**

Sampling procedure involves selecting either a probability sample or a nonprobability sample as part of your sample plan. **(p. 76)**

Secondary data is information that has been previously collected for another purpose. **(p. 71)**

Structured interviews are a series of discussions held between a trained interviewer and individuals, on a one-on-one basis, recruited by specific criteria, with the purpose to discuss predetermined topics. **(p. 72)**

Syndicated research is information collected on a regular basis using standardized procedures and sold to multiple customers from a related industry. **(p. 71)** **Example: Marketing Research, Syndicated Research (p. 72)**

Validity is the strength of a conclusion. **(p. 76)**

Marketing Information System (pp. 77–78)

Marketing information system (MIS) *is a series of steps that include collection, analysis, and presentation of information for use in making marketing decisions.* *(p. 77)* **Example: Marketing Information System (p. 78)**

Key Terms (pp. 77–78)

Cookies are small files containing certain personal information that are sent from Web servers to a consumer's computer to be accessed the next time a consumer visits a particular Web site. **(p. 78)**

Competitive intelligence involves the systematic tracking of competitive actions and plans and is a significant activity within a business. **(p. 77)**

Marketing decision support system is the software and associated infrastructure that connects the marketing activity to company databases. **(p. 77)**

Marketing intelligence system is a system that gathers, processes, assesses, and makes available marketing information in a format that allows the marketing activity to function more effectively. **(p. 77)**

Marketing research system is a collection of the results of marketing research studies conducted by a company. **(p. 77)**

▼Capstone Exercise

To be able to make good marketing decisions, you need to understand your target customers. How do you understand your target customers? One of the classic ways to understand target customers is to conduct marketing research. The fundamental process of marketing research is usually completed by observing customer behavior or by asking customers questions. Then, the data is tabulated and interpreted, to arrive to some conclusions you would use in making your marketing strategies.

The most commonly used methods of primary research are surveys, interviews, and focus-group sessions.

The exercise is to design and run a small online survey. Your task is to design a 10-question online survey on a topic of your choice. However, before you design the survey, remember to decide what information you are trying to gather.

You need to get at least 10 responses and be able to write a short summary of your conclusions.

To make this task easier, here a few Web sites that allow you to do online surveys. Each one has a free option that allows you to do limited surveys.

- http://www.zoomerang.com
- http://www.surveymonkey.com/
- http://www.questionpro.com/

These are just suggestions; there are other sites that offer similar services.

To help you understand how to design your survey, see the following Web sites:

- http://www.questionpro.com/survey-design.html
- www.zoomerang.com/datasheet/Survey_Design_Checklist.pdf

▼Application Exercises

Complete the following exercises:

1. Qantas, an Australian-based airline, is considering offering flights between destinations within the United States. Assuming the airline has the legal ability to offer these flights, what types of consumer research should be conducted?

2. Procter & Gamble wants to offer en entirely new type of detergent. Although this new detergent has powerful ingredients and cleans better than competitors in lab tests, what information should P&G obtain from consumers before offering the product for sale?

3. Select a company and describe how that company might conduct explanatory, exploratory, and descriptive research.

The **Brand**

Chapter Overview In the previous section, you explored how companies create value, how consumers make decisions, and how consumer insights are generated. This chapter introduces the primary link between consumers and companies: the brand. The central concepts of branding will be discussed, including brand equity, building strong brands, and managing brands.

▼ Chapter **Outline**

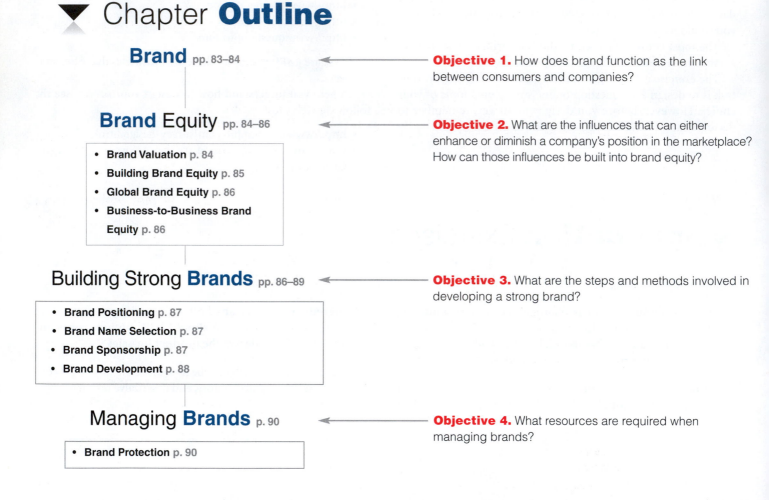

Brand pp. 83–84

Objective 1. How does brand function as the link between consumers and companies?

Brand Equity pp. 84–86

- **Brand Valuation** p. 84
- **Building Brand Equity** p. 85
- **Global Brand Equity** p. 86
- **Business-to-Business Brand Equity** p. 86

Objective 2. What are the influences that can either enhance or diminish a company's position in the marketplace? How can those influences be built into brand equity?

Building Strong **Brands** pp. 86–89

- **Brand Positioning** p. 87
- **Brand Name Selection** p. 87
- **Brand Sponsorship** p. 87
- **Brand Development** p. 88

Objective 3. What are the steps and methods involved in developing a strong brand?

Managing **Brands** p. 90

- **Brand Protection** p. 90

Objective 4. What resources are required when managing brands?

BRAND (pp. 83–84)

▼ **DEFINED** *A* **Brand** *is a promise to deliver specific benefits associated with products or services to consumers.*

▼ **EXPLAINED**

Brand

Based on the Nordic word *brandr*, meaning to burn, brands began as a mark of possession that was applied to cattle.[1] Over time, brands have evolved not only to represent ownership, but also to stand for specific attributes that mean something to consumers. When the attributes that a brand possesses form a connection with consumers' desires, a perception of value is created.

A brand is more than simply a name; it is a promise. This promise manifests itself in everything that consumers can sense about a brand. If the promise is continually kept, the brand's image is solidified by its reputation. A brand can be represented by a name or symbol and can be perceived positively, negatively, or ambiguously by consumers. This perception is influenced by both marketing communications and experiences with the brand.

Coca-Cola is sold in more than 200 countries. Produced by the Coca-Cola Company, its traditional soft drink product is often referred to simply as Coke. Originally intended as a patent medicine when Dr. John Pemberton created the product in the nineteenth century, Coca-Cola was eventually purchased by businessman Asa Candler, whose marketing efforts led Coke to its leadership in the world soft drink market throughout the twentieth and now twenty-first century. You probably recognized this brand without seeing the whole title because of its typeface and color. The Coke name may also convey certain meaning to you that increases value of, and interest in, the Coke product.

▼ **APPLIED**

Brand

A brand differs considerably from a product or service as it exists in a consumer's mind. Consider the following:

- A product is something produced in a factory, while a brand is created through marketing communications and experience.
- A product can be duplicated by a competitor, while a brand is unique.
- A product can become outdated, while a successful brand is often timeless.
- A product is a generic term, while a brand has personality, characteristics, and associations.

The personality, characteristics, and associations of a brand can be thought of as layers. These layers provide richness to a brand that creates an emotional connection that is not typically generated from a product. The initial layer represents tangible features, while inner layers represent benefits, attitudes, and values. This richness can translate into many opportunities for brands, including the following:[2]

- Ability to command price premium.
- Long-term financial strength.
- Greater market share.
- Higher perceived quality.
- Greater supply and distribution chain advantage.
- More **brand extension**, taking an existing brand into a new category, opportunities.
- Greater purchase frequency.

As consumers spend an increasing time online, the various mediums used to access online content are being targeted by brands. A **digital brand strategy** is a set of marketing activities that uses digital mediums to connect consumers to brands. A digital brand strategy is more than a Web site. Brand messages can be placed on many different digital devices including personal digital assistants (PDAs), mobile phones, and video games.

Brands are also being developed in a multicultural environment. Multicultural brands are brands that are created and managed to be relevant to more than one cultural group. For example, Yankelovich's 2007/2008 MONITOR Multicultural Marketing Study identified that Hispanic and African American consumers were likely to "enjoy looking at or listening" to advertising at a rate almost double of their peers of other races.[3] The study also revealed that marketing was generally perceived as neither culturally nor personally relevant.[4] The challenge for brands is to establish relevancy without over-commercializing culture.

Singapore, located in Asia near the equator, is the most densely populated country in the world and one of the 20 smallest countries. It has also been rated by the A.T. Kearney/FOREIGN POLICY Globalization Index as the most globalized country in the world. Known for its vibrant culture, nightlife, shopping, resorts, and its former ban on the sale and use of chewing gum, Singapore is a very popular destination for tourists from around the world. The Singapore Tourist Board (STB) is developing a digital brand strategy. The STB intends to connect with consumers in digital space to differentiate Singapore from other cities. Possible digital applications include interactive outdoor billboards and other mobile and sensory media.[5]

PHOTO: Colin and Linda McKie

>> END EXAMPLE

Brand Equity (pp. 84–86)

> **DEFINED   Brand equity** *is the power of a brand, through creation of a distinct image, to influence customer behavior.*[6]

Brand Equity

While brands are different from products and services, they definitely influence the perceived value of a company's products or services. This influence, or equity, can either enhance or diminish a company's position in the marketplace. Brand equity reflects the value consumers attach to the promise of the brand and evolves from the layers of the brand. Brand equity extends beyond products and services to include social movements, political parties, not-for-profit organizations, and individuals such as political candidates and other celebrities.

Keller defines brand equity as "the differential effect of brand knowledge on consumer response to the brand's marketing activities. **Brand knowledge** is the set of associations that consumers hold in memory regarding the brand's features, benefits, users, perceived quality, and overall attitude as a result of prior brand

marketing activities."[7] Effective marketing programs should apply Keller's brand equity definition to link desired images, perceptions, opinions, and feelings to their respective brands.[8]

▼ APPLIED

Brand Equity

Brand equity can provide a sustainable competitive advantage that can be capitalized on in both good and bad times.[9] Given a competitive industry, a strong brand has the potential to sustain a **price war**, which is when businesses cut prices to take sales from competitors. Price wars often occur in the airline industry and better-known brands often use aggressive pricing against start-up airlines. Essentially, the brand premium that exists for a strong brand provides a differential position among consumers that lesser-established brands cannot match. The lesser brands generally become identified by the lower price. The stronger brand can trade off its premium tactically by reducing its price, but not to the level of competitors, or it can reinforce the quality of its product and attempt to stabilize the price war. Alternatively, growth opportunities can be capitalized on by a strong brand identity that attracts a large number of brand loyal consumers. The situation facilitates less elastic demand which resists price changes and can translate into increased profits. Well-established supermarket brands are regularly faced with promotions by lesser-known brands and often use their equity to resist competitive discounting.

Although many companies acknowledge the financial potential of their brands, there is often a lack of understanding of many potential applications of brand equity. These applications include the following:[10]

- Brand alliances with other companies to expand marketing opportunities
- **Channel switching**, creating new product distribution or moving the distribution flow of products from one distribution channel to another, to project equity from one channel to another. (A **channel** is a system with few or many steps in which products and services flow from businesses to consumers while payment flows from consumers to businesses.)
- Relationship building to connect faster and closer to customers and distribution partners
- **Brand stretching**, extending a brand to new products, services, or markets, to spread brand building costs across a larger base of activities provided there is a fundamental fit with consumers' perceptions of the brand
- **Outsourcing**, procuring certain services from a third-party supplier, to lower costs and focus resources on core competencies

Brand Valuation

Discussion of the practical importance of branding and brand equity leads us to consider the methods that consumers and businesses use to ascribe value to brands. **Brand valuation** is the process of quantifying the financial benefit that results from owning a brand. This process is important as companies try to understand what drives value in their business.

Table 8.1 BusinessWeek/Interbrand's Annual Ranking of The Best Global Brands For 2007 [12]

Rank	Company	2007 Brand Value $MILLIONS	Percent Change (over 2006)	Country of Ownership
1	Coca-Cola	65,324	–3 %	United States
2	Microsoft	58,709	3 %	United States
3	IBM	57,091	2 %	United States
4	GE	51,569	5 %	United States
5	Nokia	33,696	12 %	Finland
6	Toyota	32,070	15 %	Japan
7	Intel	30,954	–4 %	United States
8	McDonald's	29,398	7 %	United States
9	Disney	29,210	5 %	United States
10	Mercedes-Benz	23,568	8 %	Germany

The history of modern brand valuation began in the mid-1980s when Interbrand began conducting a brand valuation for a United Kingdom business.[11] Interbrand continues to be involved with the brand valuation industry, including joining with BusinessWeek to publish a yearly ranking of the best global brands (see Table 8.1). Seven of the top-ranked global brands are owned in the United States.

Brand valuation has become increasingly important as certain countries require intangible items such as brand value to be included on a business balance sheet. There are two primary methods of brand valuation: additive and inclusive. The former, and more common application, refers to the idea that product and brand are separate, while the latter considers them to be one.[13] The problem with separation can be demonstrated by asking the questions "Can Coke be valued as a soda without the brand?" and "How many Jaguars would be sold without the brand versus with the brand?" An inclusive approach to brand valuation combines the brand with associated product attributes to determine true value. Product attributes can be translated into potential sales revenue in the inclusive approach.

Building Brand Equity

The process of creating or enhancing brand equity involves understanding the value of the brand as well those factors that can create a positive brand image. These factors include loyalty, commitment, and customer equity.

Loyalty

The equity ascribed to a brand is reflected behaviorally through loyalty. There are two components of **brand loyalty**: purchase loyalty and attitudinal loyalty. Attitudinal loyalty leads to a higher relative price while purchase loyalty leads to greater market share. These factors combine to influence brand profitability.[14]

Commitment

The psychological attachment that a consumer has to a brand will be a function of how relevant it is to that consumer, i.e., does it touch on things that are truly important to him or her. Brand relationships can be placed in a continuum of very committed users to uninterested non-users.

Customer Equity

Brand equity is also created from consumer knowledge that is translated into consumer behavior.[15] **Customer-based brand equity** is defined as the differential effect that brand knowledge has on the customer response to marketing efforts.[16] This concept is based on the idea that brand equity extends from what consumers have learned, heard, felt, and seen about a brand through their cumulative experiences. If this brand equity resides in the consumer's mind, managing and influencing experiences is critical.

EXAMPLE   BRAND EQUITY

Moët & Chandon, one of the largest producers of champagne and sparkling wine in the world, has built considerable positive brand equity since its beginnings in 1743. With an estimated brand value of almost $3.7 billion, this LVMH-owned company's products regularly appear at exclusive events and parties around the world. Moët & Chandon's brand image is built on its long history, its prestigious location in the Champagne region of France and its affiliation with high fashion. The fashion affilliation reaches back 200 years to Versailles. Today, there are exclusive activities during London Fashion Week and Milan Fashion Week, such as Moët & Chandon's own fashion awards and regular events with its LVMH sister-brand Christian Dior. These activities reinforce its current positioning "Be Fabulous," which ties the product into a lifestyle experience.[17]

PHOTO: Getty Images, Inc./Stockbyte Royalty Free

>> END EXAMPLE

Global Brand Equity

The concepts of loyalty, commitment, and customer equity and their contribution to building brand equity gain increased complexity when considered in a global context. Global brand equity is influenced by elements of the traditional marketing mix as well as additional issues such as geography, culture, legal and business environments, and political and economic realities. Four central ideas influence strategies to create global brand equity:[18]

- Identifying emerging global customers
- Building stronger links between country-specific marketing activities that support a global infrastructure
- Realizing opportunities to transfer products, brands, and ideas throughout various countries
- Gaining economies of scale by sharing human and financial resources in creating and managing brands

EXAMPLE GLOBAL BRAND EQUITY

IKEA, a Swedish furniture company, has cultivated unique global brand equity through its contemporary designs, creative promotions, and affordable pricing strategies. IKEA has grown steadily to over 220 stores in Europe, Asia, Australia, and North America by focusing on its consumers' lifestyles. The formula of quality, affordable contemporary furniture seems to reach across borders. IKEA endeavors to design and sell products that are aestetically pleasing yet inexpensive and functional. Founded in 1943, the brand has not always fared well entering new markets. An entry into the United States in the early 1990s was met with challenges including beds that were measured only in centimeters, sofas that were not deep enough, kitchens that did not accommodate U.S.-sized appliances, and curtains that were too short.[19]

PHOTO: Ryan McVay

>> END EXAMPLE

Business-to-Business Brand Equity

Brands are as important in the business-to-business (B2B) environment as they are in the business to consumer (B2C) environment. As has been discussed in previous chapters, the purchase process is more formal in the B2B markets versus the B2C markets. However, the question remains how certain brands are selected for inclusion in the sourcing process. That decision is often based on the unique requirements of the contract, past experiences with brands in the appropriate category, and the established brand equity of potential brands. Successful brands like Cisco, Intel, and Akamai have all established clear B2B positions and have translated those positions into financial success. Businesses selling to other businesses tend to present their products and services while discussing more rational elements, such as product characteristics, than B2C brands, but they also focus on both economic value and emotional benefits.

Building Strong Brands (pp. 86–89)

 DEFINED *A* **strong brand** *occupies a distinct position in consumers' minds based on relevant benefits and creates an emotional connection between businesses and consumers.*

 EXPLAINED

Building Strong Brands

Is there an innate purpose for brands? If there were such a reason, then companies could create demand for their brands by appropriately managing their image. It is possible that consumers are in need of brands as much as companies are in need of them. The clutter of products in the marketplace and the extensive choices available could drive consumers to look for reassurance in brands with which they have positive associations.[20]

Strong brands provide three things to consumers: they save time during the shopping process, they project the right message, and they provide an identity.[21] Consumers have established perspectives on known brands and, unless a unique new product or service has entered the market or there has been a large price adjustment or drastic change in the market, it is easy to re-purchase a brand that has previously been selected and performed as expected. A brand can be used to project security, convenience, quality, or something else to consumers that can reinforce the ability of a product or service to meet consumer needs. The brand provides consumers with the ability to project style and preferences to others through the choices made.

The large numbers of brands that have stood the test of time demonstrate the value of brands. Over 60% of the best-known brands in the United States are 50 years old or older.[22] The power of a long-lasting brand can often resist but not necessarily prevent decline if not properly supported. Research that tracks consumer memorability of brands often identifies a latent memory of a brand's advertising even if it has not advertised for months or even years. Still, it is possible for a brand to be damaged beyond repair, such as the failed former energy giant Enron. Enron grew through the 1990s to a $70 billion company by operating gas lines and power plants as well as engaging in trading businesses for a variety of commodities. In 2001, it was revealed that Enron had misstated its income and that its value was billions less than its balance sheet claimed. Enron claimed bankruptcy and ultimately went out of business.[23]

Apparently, brands are just as important to CEOs as to consumers. A Marsh Inc. and Oxford University study conducted in 2000 and based on input from senior business executives revealed that 85% considered brands to be their company's most important asset. de Chernatony has identified three essential elements of a powerful brand:

- The values that will characterize the brand
- The purpose for the brand other than making money, the brand's reason for being
- The future environment that the brand aims to facilitate

A business with a powerful brand understands what its brand should stand for, what it does stand for, and what it can stand for in the future.

 APPLIED

Building Strong Brands

How can a company capitalize on its brand and achieve a leading market position? This can be achieved, arguably, through a strong business model with desirable products and services of appropriate quality and a strong financial position, as well as strong brands. Strong brands can be built by considering competitive category, level, and type of competitors; ability to differentiate; relevance to consumers; management acumen; corporate strategy; and corporate assets.[24] The nature of the category dictates the success criteria for competing businesses including consumer desires. The existing competitive environment, whether filled with many or few competitors, also influences the creation of strong brands. The basis for a brand to differentiate from competitors through elements such as patents, expensive or unique production equipment, or weaker elements can assist in creating strong brands. The relevancy of the brand to consumers, often presented using advertising and the characteristics of the product or service, also influences the strength of the brand. Business capabilities such as having capable management, having a clear vision, and possessing financial and human assets are additional factors that influence the creation of a strong brand.

Brand Positioning

The creation of a strong brand involves several different steps that collectively answer the question "What should my brand stand for?" The first step involves placing the brand in a distinct position in consumers' minds. **Brand positioning**, the location that a brand occupies in the marketplace relative to competitors, can be achieved on a hierarchy of three levels (see Figure 8.2).[25]

FIGURE 8.2	Positioning Levels

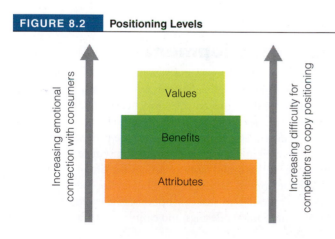

Attributes (either product or service) are the most basic levels of positioning and include smells, tastes, textures, and ingredients. Competitors can usually copy attribute positioning unless there is some type of intellectual property involved. The motivation for purchasing such products is typically what the attribute offers to the consumer instead of the brand itself.

The second level of positioning is benefit positioning, which involves focusing on the benefits that the attributes provide. Security, quality, performance, convenience, and value are all examples of benefits that products and service can provide. The benefits can also be communicated as a problem/solution position.

The third level is value positioning, which involves creating an emotional connection between the brand and consumer. Unlike beliefs and attitudes, values are the least likely to change. This type of positioning can appeal to aspirations as well. Each level creates value but the value positioning can create a relationship that engenders brand loyalty, commitment, and strong consumer equity.

Brand positioning is also strengthened if the positioning reflects the personality of the brand. **Brand personality** consists of characteristics that make a brand unique, much like human personality. Brand personalities vary widely, including rugged, sexy, and sophisticated.

Brand Name Selection

The right brand name can provide a tremendous advantage for the product or service. The brand name should fit with the attributes and benefits of the product or service and be relevant to the target consumers. Some important guidelines for brand name selection include the following:

- Use the name to distinguish as well as describe the product or service.
- Select a name that is memorable and distinctive yet appropriate for the category.
- Avoid limiting business opportunities to a particular market segment with a name that cannot be extended into new segments.
- Choose a name that is exportable to international markets.
- Ensure the name can be protected as intellectual property.

In many cases, a company is faced with a decision to create a new brand name for a new product or service or to add the product to an existing portfolio. This is a question regarding the company's brand architecture. **Brand architecture** involves the naming and organizing of brands within a broader portfolio. Sometimes these decisions are so critical that companies need to be hired to assist with naming research.

Brand Sponsorship

A product or service can be launched in two basic forms: manufacturer (national) brand and private label (retailer, reseller) brand. While the manufacturer, retailer, or reseller typically develops its own brand, some brands are licensed from other companies and others are co-branded with other brands. There are strategic advantages and disadvantages to each form and the most appropriate form must be carefully selected.

Comparing Manufacturers Brands to Private Label Brands

Manufacturer brands, owned by a manufacturer as opposed to a retailer or reseller, have traditionally dominated the brand choices available to consumers at retail stores. However, **private label**

brands created by either a retailer or reseller have increasingly appeared in the retail environment. Private label brands have almost completely absorbed the "generic" or non-branded products of the 1980s and 1990s by realizing that branding can provide incremental profitability that non-branded products cannot. It is difficult to attach a brand promise to an unbranded product. This growth of private brands has expanded to small and mid-size retailers primarily due to the profitability of these private label brands. Since retailers control more customer contact than manufacturers, they have the opportunity to realize the increased profit potential of private label products. Considerable effort goes into creating private brand products, from identifying and selecting a product to negotiating with the supplier and assessing and approving the product's level of safety and performance characteristics.

EXAMPLE   BRAND SPONSORSHIP

Trader Joe's, established in 1958, has grown to 280 stores in 23 states. The company's strategy has included offering innovative, hard-to-find food with employees wearing Hawaiian shirts and selling in an environment that feels like a local market. The company also brands over 80% of its offerings as private-label products, which allows development of the Trader Joe's brand as opposed to supplier brands and allows better control of advertising and promotion costs associated with the Trader Joe's brand. Trader Joe's private label strategy is part of the company's brand character. The net result is a loyal brand following translating into significant financial success. Interestingly enough, Trader Joe's has achieved its success without having to invest in traditional advertising. The company's only promotional effort is its newsprint circular.[26]

PHOTO: Comstock

>> END EXAMPLE

Licensing

An alternative to the significant expense of creating and developing a brand is **licensing**. Licensing involves assigning rights, generally for a fee, for one company to use another company's brand for specific products and for a specific period. An existing brand can be used to provide brand equity and enhance the chances for the new product to be more rapidly accepted by consumers. The primary motivator for choosing which particular brand to license, beyond affordability, is the stature of the brand (including awareness, familiarity, and opinion) and the consistency and relevancy of the image to the company's target consumers and category. Typical types of properties that are licensed include characters, corporate trademarks and brands, fashion, sports, and art.

EXAMPLE   LICENSING

Southern Comfort, a whiskey manufacturer, licensed its brand to Kemps Ice Cream, which created two products: Southern Comfort egg nog flavored ice cream and Southern Comfort vanilla spice flavored ice cream. Southern Comfort egg nog and Southern Comfort gourmet coffees are also in the marketplace. The benefit to the licensees is the unique brand flavor and brand equity. The Southern Comfort brand, founded in 1874, has also expanded to non-food product categories including apparel.[27]

PHOTO: Corbis RF

>> END EXAMPLE

Co-branding

Co-branding involves the collaboration of multiple brands in the marketing of one specific product. The idea is that the attributes of each brand can be blended and loyalty from the separate brands may extend to the co-branded product. Any shortcomings of one brand may also be mitigated by positive equity from the other brand. These types of arrangements are seen in market sectors including automotive, fashion, hotels, financial service, and food products. A co-branding strategy can work for different reasons including generating marketplace exposure, positioning against private label brands, and sharing promotion costs with a partner. Many co-branding efforts are based on brand alliances. **Brand alliance** is a relationship, short of a merger, that is formed by two or more businesses to create market opportunities that would not have existed without the alliance. A brand alliance is one form of a brand extension.

EXAMPLE   CO-BRANDING

Lay's KC Masterpiece barbecue potato chips is an example of co-branding. Lay's, a division of Frito-Lay and well known as a potato chip brand, and KC Masterpiece, a registered trademark of HV Food Products Company and leading brand of BBQ sauce, partnered to create a unique flavor of potato chip.[28]

PHOTO: Shutterstock

>> END EXAMPLE

Brand Development

Brand equity can be developed and maximized not only for a single brand but also for a portfolio of brands. When a company has multiple brands, the decisions on the correct combination of brand names and attributes across the entire portfolio is part of a comprehensive brand strategy. **Brand strategy** is the process where "the offer is positioned in the consumer's mind to produce a perception of advantage."[29] The brand strategy defines the brand architecture that is used for brand development. The development of brands involves several different strategic options: line extensions, brand extensions, multibrand offerings, and entirely new brands.

Line Extensions

A **line extension** is an addition to an existing product line that retains the currently utilized brand name. Companies often use line extensions because they believe such use will keep customers from switching brands and allow firms to retain or increase their margins.

There are two primary methods to extend product lines: horizontal and vertical. The product attributes selected to distinguish the products will determine which method is being used. A vertical line extension involves varying the product line by price and quality. A horizontal line extension maintains products within a similar price and quality level but varies other attributes such as flavor or smell. Line extensions can provide new opportunities to reach different consumers but it can also expose a brand to new levels of competition. Growth needs must be matched with any increased risks.

EXAMPLE   LINE EXTENSIONS

Crayola, known for its crayons that made their initial debut in 1903, has a variety of products including clay, paints, markers, and coloring books for children. Silly Putty is also a Crayola brand offering. Crayola practices vertical line extension with its portfolio products marketed to adults and artists with an upscale version of its drawing pencils, oil pastels, colored pencils, acrylic paints, and watercolors. The use of a vertical line extenion allows Crayola to present products to different market segments and to market different product characteristics and benefits while still building the overall Crayola brand.[30]

PHOTO: Andrew Bret Wallis

>> END EXAMPLE

Bundling is a way to present the portfolio to customers without necessarily adding to the product lines. **Bundling** refers to the "practice of marketing two or more products and/or services in a single 'package.'"[31] The principle behind bundling is that a bundled offering is perceived by customers to offer more value than the individual components of the bundle sold separately.

Brand Extensions

EXAMPLE   BRAND EXTENSIONS

 Entertainment and media giant Disney has extended its venerable brand with significant financial success. Disney uses its brand to enhance its relationships with its loyal customers by offering brand extensions such as Disney Vacation Club, Disney Cruise Line, and Radio Disney Network.[32]

PHOTO: Lourens Smak

>> END EXAMPLE

A **brand extension** involves taking an existing brand into a new category. This practice can save marketing investment in a new brand and could build additional brand stature. The risks include losing focus of the core attributes and positioning of the brand and failing in the new category, which could damage perceptions of the brand. The greatest chance for success is if the brand is well-positioned with consumers based on an emotional connection. Without an emotional connection, the brand can risk being overextended. Known for disposable razors, pens, and lighters, BIC attempted to extend its brand into women's underwear rather unsuccessfully.[33]

Multibrands

Some companies elect to launch several brands in the same category to appeal to the varying wants of the consumers and to take advantage of business conditions. In a fragmented market, a company may elect to compete with itself with the reasoning that owning 5 out of 14 brands will result in greater aggregate market share than owning 1 out of 10. Having individual brand names, while potentially expensive to develop, offers considerable flexibility in positioning different product attributes. Cannibalization is one particular problem associated with a multibrand approach. **Cannibalization** is the loss of sales of an existing product within a portfolio to a new product in the same portfolio. However, the risks of competing with oneself can be acceptable if there is a net overall gain. Many consumer product companies launch new products knowing that some sales will be cannibalized.

New Brands

A company can elect to create an entirely new brand because of an existing brand suffering from poor equity or because an existing brand does not extend well into a new category. New brands can offer a clean slate for positioning but require considerable financial investment to develop. Sometimes a new brand can be created based on the experience and positioning of another brand in the company's portfolio and positioned into a unique market niche.

EXAMPLE   NEW BRANDS

Starwood Hotels announced the aloft brand in 2005. The mid-scale lifestyle hotel that opened its first property in 2008 is based on the W Hotel concept and includes a technology focus with large, HDTV-ready flat-panel televisions, plug and play capabilities, and wireless internet throughout the hotel. Starwood launched its new aloft brand with a special event in 2006 hosted in Second Life, the 3D virtual world. The aloft brand plans to have 500 properties worldwide by 2012.[34]

PHOTO: Getty Images, Inc./Photodisc

>> END EXAMPLE

Managing **Brands** (p. 90)

 DEFINED **Brand management** *is the overall coordination of a brand's equities to create long-term brand growth through overseeing marketing mix strategies.*

 EXPLAINED

Managing Brands

Just as the creation and development of brand equity involves significant resources, the ongoing management of brands requires significant resources as well. The intangible and tangible brand value that extends from strong brand equity requires ongoing management.

Brand management utilizes brand equity to create a shortcut to address market needs as business conditions change. **Category management** involves the management of multiple brands in a product line and **category managers** have responsibilities that tend to include what was traditionally handled by product managers and **brand managers**, including portfolio decisions and marketing activities across different products.

 APPLIED

Managing Brands

The practice of brand management requires constant and consistent communication of a brand's desired positioning. That positioning is influenced not only by a brand's communication efforts but also by customer experience and more recently by social media. Blogs, discussion forums, and online evaluation services have considerable impact on the reputation of a brand. As a result, the media channels utilized by many companies have expanded and decentralized.

Even though social media has affected the relationship between consumers and brands, there are still opportunities for brands to use this media to their advantage. Just as small brands can look large to consumers by being active on the Internet, large brands can similarly look smaller to consumers when the Internet allows consumers to connect on an emotional level. Social relationships based on an emotional connection are some of the central principles of contemporary brand management.

Social media or not, it is still important to understand what a brand means to consumers. Just because a company brands its products does not guarantee that people will find the products either relevant or useful. With the average chief marketing officer's tenure at just over two years, the idea of either positioning or re-positioning a brand seems daunting, but the core principles of brand management remain.[35]

Brand Protection

One of the critical elements of brand management is the protection of the brand. Beyond making strategic decisions about the creation and nurturing of the brand, there must also be decisions about **brand protection** and securing the brand's inherent value, including intellectual property. **Intellectual property** is a collection of non-physical assets owned by an individual or company that are the result of innovation and are legally protected from being copied or used by unauthorized parties. Examples include patents and trademarks. Failure to protect a brand's intellectual property can result in significant long-term problems:

- Devaluing corporate brands—recalls and bad publicity can hurt the perception of a brand
- Reducing legitimate profits—long- and short-term profits are reduced by the high cost of fighting counterfeits
- Damaging consumer confidence—consumers may feel unsafe or reticent to purchase products
- Creating liability-related exposure—lawsuits may result from the use of counterfeit products

The **United States Patent and Trademark Office (USPTO)** is a federal agency responsible for assigning rights for limited times to individuals or companies to use innovations. Protection is granted for inventions and new applications for existing products. The primary tasks of the USPTO are processing trademark and patent applications and providing trademark and patent information. Counterfeiting is one of the most common forms of brand protection violations. **Counterfeiting** is the unauthorized copying of products, packaging, or other intellectual property of a registered brand. There are three main effects:

- Indirect harm to the economy through lost tax revenues or foreign investment
- Direct harm caused to the manufacturer and distribution channel members
- Indirect social cost due to the re-direction of public and private money to fight counterfeiting

Communication strategies can provide a front line of defense to fight counterfeiting. Examples of this include branded messages touting the risks of fake car parts and prescription drugs. By advertising the importance of purchasing the real product, quality, safety, durability, and other brand attributes can be leveraged on the demand side and subsequent pressure can be place on the supply side of counterfeiting.

EXAMPLE   **BRAND PROTECTION**

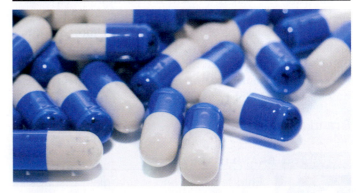

Pharmaceutical drugs are regular targets for counterfeiters. In 2005, the U.S. Attorney's Office for the Western District of Missouri announced 11 people were indicted for conspiracy to sell counterfeit and misbranded Lipitor, a cholesterol-reducing drug, among other drugs. Over 18 million Lipitor tablets were recalled as a result. Other targets for counterfeiters include Viagra and Cialis.[36]

PHOTO: Mashe

>> **END EXAMPLE**

▼Visual Summary

Chapter 8 Summary

The process of creating, cultivating, and strategically managing brands builds on concepts of value creation, consumer decision making, and consumer insights discussed in preceding chapters. Strong brands provide a consumer with relevant and desired benefits and possess a distinct position in the consumer mind. Ultimately, brands form a connection between companies and consumers that, if properly nurtured, can provide the means to realize the financial potential of the company.

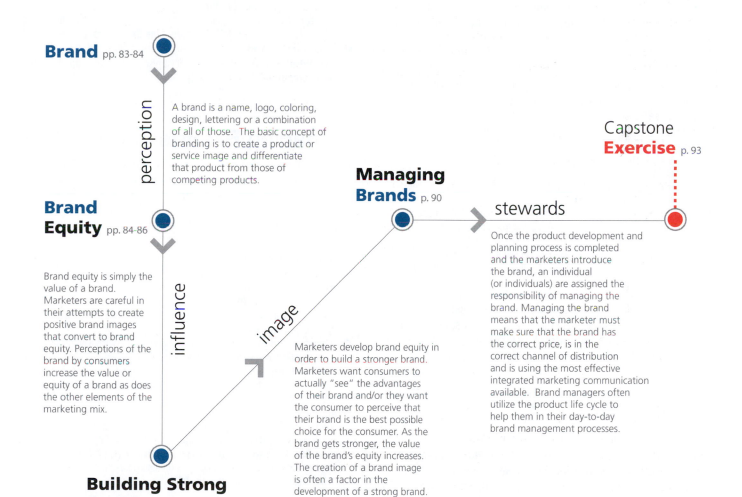

Brand pp. 83-84

perception

A brand is a name, logo, coloring, design, lettering or a combination of all of those. The basic concept of branding is to create a product or service image and differentiate that product from those of competing products.

Brand Equity pp. 84-86

Brand equity is simply the value of a brand. Marketers are careful in their attempts to create positive brand images that convert to brand equity. Perceptions of the brand by consumers increase the value or equity of a brand as does the other elements of the marketing mix.

influence

image

Building Strong Brands pp. 86-89

Marketers develop brand equity in order to build a stronger brand. Marketers want consumers to actually "see" the advantages of their brand and/or they want the consumer to perceive that their brand is the best possible choice for the consumer. As the brand gets stronger, the value of the brand's equity increases. The creation of a brand image is often a factor in the development of a strong brand.

Managing Brands p. 90

stewards

Once the product development and planning process is completed and the marketers introduce the brand, an individual (or individuals) are assigned the responsibility of managing the brand. Managing the brand means that the marketer must make sure that the brand has the correct price, is in the correct channel of distribution and is using the most effective integrated marketing communication available. Brand managers often utilize the product life cycle to help them in their day-to-day brand management processes.

Capstone **Exercise** p. 93

▼**Chapter** Key Terms

Brand (pp. 83–84)

Brand *is a promise to deliver specific benefits associated with products or services to consumers.* *(p. 83)* **Example: Brand (p. 86)**

Key Terms (p. 83)

Digital brand strategy is a set of marketing activities that uses digital mediums to connect consumers to brands. **(p. 83)**

Brand Equity (pp. 84–86)

Brand equity *is the power of a brand, through creation of a distinct image, to influence customer behavior.* *(p. 84)* **Example: Brand Equity (p. 86) Example: Global Brand Equity (p. 86)**

Key Terms (pp. 84–86)

Brand knowledge is the set of associations that consumers hold in memory regarding the brand's features, benefits, users, perceived quality, and overall attitude as a result of prior brand marketing activities. **(p. 84)**

Brand loyalty is the extent to which a consumer repeatedly purchases a given brand. **(p. 85)**

Brand stretching is extending a brand to new products, services, or markets. **(p. 84)**

Brand valuation is the process of quantifying the financial benefit that results from owning a brand. **(p. 84)**

Channel is a system with few or many steps in which products flow from businesses to consumers while payments flow from consumers to businesses. **(p. 84)**

Channel switching is creating new product distribution or moving the distribution flow of products from one distribution channel to another. **(p. 84)**

Customer-based brand equity is the differential effect that brand knowledge has on the customer response to marketing efforts. **(p. 85) Example: Brand Equity (p. 86) Example: Global Brand Equity (p. 86)**

Outsourcing is procuring certain services from a third-party supplier. **(p. 84)**

Price war occurs when businesses cut prices to take sales from competitors. **(p. 84)**

Building Strong **Brands** (pp. 86–89)

Strong brand *occupies a distinct position in consumers' minds based on relevant benefits and creates an emotional connection between businesses and consumers.* *(p. 86)*

Key Terms (pp. 87–89)

Brand alliance is a relationship, short of a merger, that is formed by two or more businesses to create market opportunities that would not have existed without the alliance **(p. 88) Example: Co-Branding (p. 88)**

Brand architecture is the naming and organizing of brands within a broader portfolio. **(p. 87)**

Brand personality consists of characteristics that make a brand unique, much like human personality. **(p. 87)**

Brand positioning is the location that a brand occupies in the marketplace relative to competitors. **(p. 87)**

Brand strategy is the process where the offer is positioned in the consumer's mind to produce a perception of advantage. **(p. 88)**

Bundling refers to the practice of marketing two or more products and/or services in a single package. **(p. 89)**

Brand extension takes an existing brand into a new category. **(p. 89) Example: Brand Extensions (p. 89)**

Cannibalization is the loss of sales of an existing product within a portfolio to a new product in the same portfolio. **Example: New Brands (p. 89)**

Co-branding is the collaboration of multiple brands in the marketing of one specific product. **(p. 88)**

Licensing is the practice of a company receiving fees or royalties from partner firms for the right to use a brand, manufacturing process, or patent. **(p. 88) Example: Licensing (p. 88)**

Line extension is an addition to an existing product line that retains the currently utilized brand name. **(p. 88) Example: Line Extensions (p. 89)**

Manufacturer brand is a brand owned by a manufacturer. **(p. 87)**

Private label brand is a brand owned by a reseller or retailer. **(pp. 87–88) Example: Brand Sponsorship (p. 88)**

Managing **Brands** (p. 90)

Brand management *is the overall coordination of a brand's equities to create long-term brand growth through overseeing marketing mix strategies.* *(p. 90)*

Key Terms (p. 90)

Brand manager is the person responsible for managing the marketing activities associated with a brand. **(p. 90)**

Brand protection involves securing the brand's inherent value, including its intellectual property. **(p. 90)**

Category management involves the management of multiple brands in a product line. **(p. 90)**

Category manager is the person responsible for managing a product line that may contain one or more brands. **(p. 90)**

Counterfeiting is the unauthorized copying of products, packaging, or other intellectual property of a registered brand. **(p. 90) Example: Brand Protection (p. 90)**

Intellectual property is a collection of non-physical assets owned by an individual or company that are the result of innovation and are legally protected from being copied or used by unauthorized parties. **(p. 90)**

United States Patent and Trademark Office (USPTO) is a federal agency responsible for assigning rights for limited times to individuals or companies to use innovations. **(p. 90)**

▼Capstone Exercise

In this chapter, you learned about the various issues relating to brands and how marketers develop brands. To better understand these concepts, let us examine the company that invented brand and category management. Founded in 1837 in Cincinnati, Ohio, as a soap- and candle-making venture, Proctor & Gamble is now a huge company. Proctor & Gamble, or P&G, has 23 brands with a combined revenue of over a billion dollars. In fact, P&G originated the term "soap opera" when it sponsored daytime TV shows and used them to sell soap.

Leading brands are based on consumer trust and loyalty and they are successful because they offer superior value. Sometimes, better value is measured by a more competitive price. Or, better value could be found in superior customer service or even because the product is unique.

Go to www.pg.com and look at the wide range of products and notice the brand names that are in the P&G product portfolio. Did you realize that all of these are P&G products?

The Chapter 8 learning objectives are

Objective 1. How does brand function as the link between consumers and companies?

Objective 2. What are the influences that can either enhance or diminish a company's position in the marketplace? How can those influences be built into brand equity?

Objective 3. What are the steps and methods involved in developing a strong brand?

Objective 4. What resources are required when managing brands?

All of these are related to how P&G operates as a premier consumer products company.

Questions

1. Why do you think P&G emphasizes the brand name and not the company name?

2. Pick a P&G brand and explain what the image of the brand is and how P&G creates and conveys that image to the consumer.

3. As a P&G brand manager how do you improve your odds that when the customer makes the buying decision he or she will pick your brand and not your competitors'?

▼Application Exercises

Complete the following exercises:

1. Many manufacturers are producing "green" products. As the many green products enter the market, how will the various brands differentiate from each other and how will they maintain success? Cite some examples.

2. Discuss the risks in failing to protect one's brand as well as the specific risks that counterfeiting poses.

3. Select two companies and discuss their potential to co-brand a new product. Be sure to consider the situations where co-branding can be most effective.

4. What is your all-time favorite brand? What do you most like about the product and/or brand name? What (if anything) do you dislike? What image does the brand have in your mind? How loyal are you toward the brand? Why?

5. Go to the supermarket and take a look at the brand extensions that exist for Coke. Do you think this makes sense or not? When is brand extension a good strategy? When is it a poor one?

Segmenting, Targeting, and Positioning

Chapter Overview In the previous chapter, you explored the brand-building process. The successful management of brands depends on an understanding of market potential. How efficiently a firm capitalizes on market potential can dictate success. This chapter introduces concepts related to the way brands can efficiently interact with consumers. The central elements of an efficient marketing strategy include the division of consumer markets into meaningful and distinct customer groups: segmenting, the selection of particular customer groups to serve; targeting; and positioning, the placement of the product or service offerings in the minds of consumer targets.

 Chapter **Outline**

Segmentation pp. 95–96

Objective 1. What are the best ways to divide a consumer market into meaningful and distinct groups?

Segmentation Base pp. 96–98

- **Segmenting Business Markets** pp. 97–98
- **Segmenting International Markets** p. 98

Targeting pp. 98–101

Objective 2. How do marketers evaluate market segments and choose the best ones to serve?

- **Undifferentiated Marketing** p. 99
- **Differentiated Marketing** pp. 99–100
- **Niche Marketing** p. 100
- **Global Targeting** p. 100
- **Selecting a Target** pp. 100–101

Positioning pp. 101–102

Objective 3. How do marketers create value propositions to meet the requirements of target customers?

- **Using a Perceptional Map** p. 102
- **Selecting a Position** p. 102
- **Developing a Brand Position Statement** p. 102

SEGMENTATION (pp. 95–96)

> ▼ DEFINED **Segmentation** (*also referred to as* **market segmentation**) *is the division of consumer markets into meaningful and distinct customer groups.*

▼ EXPLAINED

Segmentation

There was a time when large companies such as McDonald's, Procter & Gamble, and Coca-Cola could market and sell their products by considering only the broad wants and needs of large groups of the U.S. population, if not the entire market. These companies could advertise their messages through a small number of radio and television stations that reached much of the population. This strategy is known as mass marketing.

Mass marketing is communicating a product or service message to as broad a group of people as possible with the purpose of positively influencing sales. The idea of mass marketing is that the broader the audience, the more potential for sales. In the past, this strategy proved successful for some businesses. Today, there are several problems with mass marketing. For one, there is no longer the ability to easily reach a large audience. Secondly, there is an increasingly vast number of product and brand choices for the consumer.

Communicating with the entire U.S. market or a large segment within the market was much easier decades ago. For example, in the 1960s, businesses could run advertising on three major television networks, ABC, CBS, and NBC, and reach 80% of U.S. women.[1] Reaching a similar level today would require advertising on over 100 television channels.[2] Even if a business purchased enough advertising and was able to reach such a large audience, it is not enough to tell consumers that the business exists and invite them to buy its products or services. Many product categories contain hundreds of different brand choices and consumers are often overwhelmed with options. Consider a typical supermarket shelf. Many brands in product categories offer specific attributes that appeal to certain consumers, but do not appeal to others.

Consumers differ in their wants, needs, perceptions, values, and expectations. It is these differences that form the foundation for segmentation. Segmentation identifies groups of consumers who have similar market responses, such as reacting to advertising or personal selling, within their group, but whose responses differ from other groups.[3] A response could be to product characteristics, or to a projected image, or the way a group learns about, purchases, and consumes a product or service.

To qualify as a true segment, a group should fulfill several criteria:[4]

- Be a homogeneous set
- Be different from other segments
- Be a critical mass
- Have core similarities of attitude, behavior, and economics
- Be robust and replicable over time

▼ APPLIED

Segmentation

Market segmentation allows businesses to look at consumers as several different groups, instead of one mass market. Correctly segmenting consumers allows companies to target their marketing dollars effectively. The value of market segmentation can be measured through increased market share for a given segment, for example, an increase in sales for women ages 24–35.

Red Bull has revolutionized the energy drink beverage segment. Launched in Europe in 1987 and in the United States in 1997, Red Bull claims about 40% market share in the North American supermarket energy drink segment. The energy drink segment, totaling over $1 billion in annual sales, accounts for almost 5% of the North American nonalcoholic beverage market and includes over 200 brands. Red Bull initially targeted Generation Y in the United States, focusing in particular on the "Millennials," who reached the age of 18 at the turn of the century. Due to a generally recognized resistance by Millennials to traditional marketing, Red Bull sponsored events that are important to youth culture, including many extreme sports activities, and worked to create a "buzz," or growing interest, among its target segment by placing the product in trendy bars and at college hangouts. The current segment of target consumers consists of young adults and teenagers, with a particular emphasis on males, who make up the largest group of energy drink purchasers.[5]

PHOTO: David Young/Wolff

The most basic form of market segmentation involves demographic or psychographic criteria, such as age or gender. However, consumers seldom make purchase decisions based solely on demographics or psychographics. Instead, they rely on a wide range of other criteria, such as attitudes or values. There are similar levels of complexity in segmenting business markets (for B2B transactions) and segmenting international markets.

Businesses generally conduct market segmentation through marketing research studies among consumers or businesses. Large numbers of consumers or businesses are surveyed on a wide range of issues and the results are used to create segments based on a variety of factors. Additional information on various research techniques is included in Chapter 7.

Segmentation
Base (pp. 96–98)

 DEFINED *The **segmentation base** is a group of characteristics that is used to assign segment members.*

 EXPLAINED

Segmentation Base

The choice of a segmentation base can be one of the most critical decisions that influences the success of market segmentation. Consumers are divided into groups for marketing purposes. For example, if you market Red Bull, as we saw in the opening example, then you would market to members of Generation Y, or young adults. You would focus your marketing in an effort to sell more units of Red Bull. Consumers are typically divided into groups by demographic, psychographic, values, behavioral, and needs variables.

Demographic segmentation divides the market into groups, based on criteria such as age, gender, family size, family life cycle, income, occupation, education, religion, ethnicity, generation, nationality, and sexual orientation. For example, some companies offer distinct products or marketing approaches for different age cohorts or life-stage groups, such as selling child insurance policies to new parents. Some may market to affluent consumers with premium goods or services. Others may market to men or women with gender-specific products or services.

Demographic criteria provide the most common bases for segmenting customer groups and, while use of such criteria is typically the initial method of segmenting, other criteria can be used within demographic segments. Demographics can be the easiest information to obtain, but may not provide the greatest amount of insights into why consumers behave differently. A hypothetical example of demographic segmentation output that reflects the percentage of age groups that watch 20 hours or more of television each week is shown in Figure 9.1.

FIGURE 9.1

Percent of Age Groups that Watch 20 or More Hours of Television Each Week

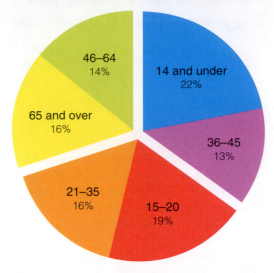

46–64 14%
14 and under 22%
65 and over 16%
36–45 13%
21–35 16%
15–20 19%

EXAMPLE DEMOGRAPHIC SEGMENTATION

Curves, the largest fitness franchise in the world, is designed to provide one-stop fitness facilities and exercise and nutritional information for women. With over 10,000 locations in 60 countries serving 4 million women, Curves offers a variety of products, including its 30-minute workout. By segmenting the market by gender, Curves has carefully defined itself to consumers and has made many women, both experienced athletes and novices alike, feel more comfortable about working out.[6]

PHOTO: Andy Crawford © Dorling Kindersley

>> END EXAMPLE

Psychographic segmentation assigns buyers into different groups, based on lifestyle, class, or personality characteristics. People belonging to a particular demographic group can have dramatically different psychographic characteristics. For example, 18- to 24-year-old males represent a wide range of lifestyles that can dramatically influence the likelihood of whether they will select one type of product or service over another. Some may be adventurous and go camping when traveling, while others may enjoy staying in luxury hotels. In fact, these distinct groups of people may have more in common with people from a wide range of age groups rather than their fellow 18- to 24-year-olds.

PSYCHOGRAPHIC SEGMENTATION

Moosejaw began as a small outfitter in Keego Harbor, Michigan. Over time, it became an iconic cult brand with sales across the country. Moosejaw flags are a common promotional tool and the company combines a savvy knowledge of consumer behavior with a broad range of products. Moosejaw uses lifestyle, a psychographic segmentation variable, to create an emotional connection with its customers; that connection is called Moosejaw madness. Moosejaw madness involves a variety of activities, such as reviewing proposed advertising copy and having people send in pictures of themselves with a Moosejaw flag in places around the world.[7]

PHOTO: Dana E. Fry

>> END EXAMPLE

Values segmentation considers what customers prefer and what motivates customer response to marketing activities. Values segmentation criteria can be used to segment consumers effectively by reflecting consumer perception. Examples of values variables include an interest in life-long learning, integrity, respect, and honesty.

Behavioral segmentation allocates consumers into groups, based on their knowledge, attitudes, uses, or responses to a product or service. For example, buyers can be grouped according to occasions or life events, such as graduations, when they get the idea to buy a product or service, actually make their purchase, or use the purchased item. Markets can be segmented into nonusers, ex-users, potential users, first-time users, and regular users of a product. Consumers could be grouped into high levels of usage or lower levels of usage. A market can be segmented by loyalty because consumers can be loyal to distribution outlets or product or service brands.

Needs segmentation assigns consumers into groups, based on their current and desired level of interaction with a particular market category. Consumers classified by needs segmentation are asked to rate their level of agreement with statements about how they feel about aspects of the category being studied. Automotive consumers can be classified based on their needs for storage space, horsepower, towing capacity, and many other characteristics of products in the automotive category.

▼ **APPLIED**

Segmentation Base

The selection of a segmentation base is sometimes done by default if a business is unaware of the different ways to classify customers. Businesses may use readily available information, usually demographics, to conduct segmentation without considering if that available information best represents how consumers think about and interact with their business and the larger category. In many cases, more complex segmentation

bases should be considered, such as psychographic, values, behavioral, and needs. Quite often, a combination of different bases provides the most useful segmentation.

Needs segmentation could be utilized to identify specific groups, but those groups could then be classified by demographic, psychographic, and behavioral characteristics. It is important to use a variety of criteria in creating segments because they may overlap in classification criteria. For example, two segments could both be females between the ages of 25 and 35, but the product needs could be completely different. One group may want to drive convertibles and the other group may consist of moms who want minivans. This would certainly require different marketing activities for each group.

Companies, however, can be wrong when trying to determine what different segments want. For example, a company could believe that it has a product that 18- to 25-year-olds will want, but in which 30- to 45-year-olds will not be interested. Believing this, the company targets its ads to the younger age group. However, sales information may indicate that both groups bought the product. For example, Toyota launched the Scion brand assuming young adults would be the primary purchasers. Ultimately, Toyota found that people of all ages were purchasing the product.

Marketers seldom restrict their segmentation analysis to variables from only one type of segmentation base, such as demographic. Instead, they are increasingly using multiple segmentation bases to locate better-defined target groups. For example, a jewelry designer could identify a group of individuals earning over $1 million each year who are interested in his or her products and, within that group, the designer could identify a large subgroup that enjoys tennis. By combining demographic and psychographic bases, the jewelry designer could produce products for high-income individuals that are either created in tennis themes or are marketed and sold at tennis events. Instead of simply targeting high-income individuals, there is another connection—tennis—that creates a stronger level of interest among certain consumers.

Segmenting Business Markets

Business markets can often be segmented using variables similar to consumer markets. The primary business segmentation variables include the following:

- **Demographics**—Business size, industry group
- **Geographics**—Regional, national, international locations
- **Benefits sought**—Desire for extensive service support, cutting-edge technology, financing terms
- **Loyalty**—Share of total purchases
- **Usage rates**—Amount, frequency of purchases

There are some unique business market variables that include the following:

- **Customer operating characteristics**—Customer capabilities and processes, and technology requirements
- **Purchasing approaches**—Where power resides in an organization and general purchasing policies

- **Situational factors**—Size of order, sense of urgency of order
- **Personal characteristics**—Loyalty, risk aversion of customer

Depending on the product, some businesses may place a high value on the service support offered by the supplier. That level of service may make the price less important. Like consumer markets, a combination of variables may provide the most effective segmentation.

EXAMPLE   **SEGMENTING BUSINESS MARKETS**

JPMorgan Chase is a leading global financial services firm with assets of $1.8 trillion. Operating in over 60 countries, Chase offers consumer and business banking offerings. Business services include credit, payroll services, retirement services, and payment processing services. In addition, Chase offers special programs for certain business segments, including not-for-profits (through tax-exempt business retirement program management and access to potential grants through the JPMorgan Chase Foundation) and CPAs (through a dedicated CPA hotline and online access to client banking information). The programs are designed to meet the unique needs of these segments.[8]

PHOTO: David Gilder

>> **END EXAMPLE**

Segmenting International Markets

Consumers in one country's market can have more in common with certain segments in another country's market than with consumers in their own country. This could be due to immigration and shared heritage. Some Hispanic consumers in parts of the United States and some consumers in Mexico have the same brand preferences and consume similar media. Global marketing strategies can be successful by identifying consumer needs and wants that span national boundaries by increasing the overall market potential. Segments that span national boundaries can sometimes be more valuable to companies than segments that exist in a single country.

Countries, even those in close proximity, may differ significantly in their cultural, economic, and political composition. The basis for grouping consumers, whether across country borders or across county borders, involves identifying distinct buying needs and behaviors.

EXAMPLE   **SEGMENTING INTERNATIONAL MARKETS**

Nokia, the world's leading mobile phone manufacturer, has sold over 1 billion phones in over 140 countries. Nokia has a global portfolio that is adapted to meet local customer needs as well as infrastructure and legal requirements. In the Middle East, Nokia launched a selection of mobile applications for the holy month of Ramadan. The Ramadan offering enables users to search, read, bookmark, and listen to Qur'an recitation. Locations of major mosques in Saudi Arabia, Egypt, Morocco, Pakistan, Jordan, and the United Arab Emirates are included through Nokia Maps. Additional mobile content includes wallpaper, ringtones, and Islamic songs. About 14% of Nokia global sales come from the Middle East and Africa.[9]

PHOTO: Josh Gow

>> **END EXAMPLE**

Targeting (pp. 98–101)

 DEFINED **Targeting** (also referred to as **market targeting**) is the process of evaluating and selecting the most viable market segment to enter.

 EXPLAINED

Targeting

Once the segmentation possibilities have been identified, the next step is to determine which customer groups to serve. Businesses often select more than one customer group based on criteria such as the following:

- Ability to meet requirements of the customers
- Overall cost to meet customer requirements
- Potential profitability of serving different customer groups

As many brands face an increasingly competitive and crowded market, the challenges are both strategic and tactical. Strategic questions generally involve "where" and "who" types of questions, such as "Who are those consumers who are most interested in what my brand stands for?" Tactical questions typically involve "what" and "how" types of questions, such as "What type of marketing offer would be most desired by those consumers who are most interested in my brand?"

Although market targeting often begins with an established product or service, target marketing occurs when a business identifies a market segment it wants to serve and then develops a product or service that is appropriate for that segment. For example, Baby Einstein, owned by Disney, has a wide product offering of DVDs and toys, and markets its portfolio to moms, with a particular focus on first-time moms. The targeting process involves an understanding of the characteristics of the various segments and draws considerably from the choices made during segmentation. Ultimately, the concept of targeting involves the prioritization of segments and the allocation of resources.[10]

▼ APPLIED
Targeting

Targeting allows businesses to build efficiencies through the use of appropriate advertising media and relevant messages for a given target. Targeting can be accomplished in a variety of methods, but ultimately should be based on the understanding of consumer preferences and needs. The result can be a competitive advantage that is essential to the overall marketing strategy.

With the growing number of ways to segment customers, targeting choices are also increasing. Generational marketing involves grouping consumers by age and socioeconomic factors. Cohort marketing looks at individuals with similar life experiences at different times in their history. Life-stage marketing considers those common events that individuals and families face regardless of age. Behaviors are another aspect, beyond age, that can provide valuable targeting options.

Behavioral targeting is a recent development that optimizes the online advertising potential for products and services. The ultimate idea is to increase interest in a particular product at a point when the consumer is actively shopping within the product category. Behavioral targeting works by placing a cookie, information that a Web site places on your computer to identify you at a later time, on a user's computer. The cookie then makes a note of the user's online behavior. An example would be a consumer searching a variety of automotive sites and then receiving an offer for vehicle insurance.

In some cases, products or services are developed before a market opportunity is sought. There is considerable risk with this scenario, particularly with technology companies.

EXAMPLE   TARGETING

Iridium LLC, supported by Motorola, spent $5 billion to launch a system of satellites and to establish other infrastructure to support the development of a satellite telephone network in 1998. The global satellite telephone market proved unsustainable for Iridium and others in the late 1990s. Iridium filed for bankruptcy in 1999. While there was some demand for satellite telephones, the pricing structure, performance, and substitute products made companies such as Iridium not viable.[11]

PHOTO: Alistair Cotton

>> END EXAMPLE

There are several specific targeting choices available, but there are essentially three market coverage choices when targeting: **undifferentiated**, **differentiated**, and **niche marketing**.

Undifferentiated Marketing

Building on the concept of mass marketing introduced at the beginning of this chapter, undifferentiated marketing is when a company treats the market as a whole, focusing on what is similar among the needs of customers, rather than on what is different. By using this strategy, companies create products or services to appeal to the greatest number of potential buyers. The benefit of an undifferentiated strategy is that it can be cost-effective because a limited portfolio results in reduced production, advertising, research, inventory, and shipping costs. This strategy is typically most successful when used in a market with limited or no competition or when the product or service has wide appeal and the market is rapidly growing. A wide range of organizations could be classified as having practiced undifferentiated marketing at some point in their history; examples include local libraries, public utilities, Coca-Cola, and Disney.

EXAMPLE   UNDIFFERENTIATED MARKETING

Henry Ford's early financial backers encouraged him to build cars for the rich to maximize his profits, just as the hundreds of other automotive start-ups were doing. Instead of taking this advice, Ford bought out his backers and embarked on a path that led to the launch of what Ford referred to as "the universal car." The Ford Model T was introduced in 1908 with the intention of being affordable for the general population. Over 15 million Model Ts were produced between 1908 and 1927. Ford practiced undifferentiated marketing that is best represented by his quote: "The customer can have any color he wants, so long as it's black." An excerpt from another quote acknowledges that he understood the market as well: "All Fords are exactly alike, but no two men are just alike...." Ford was able to practice undifferentiated marketing because the automotive market was expanding rapidly and he had a unique selling proposition based on affordability, quality, and safety in the context of the time.[12]

PHOTO: Dave King © Dorling Kindersley, Courtesy of the National Motor Museum, Beaulieu

>> END EXAMPLE

Differentiated Marketing

A firm practicing a differentiated strategy separates and targets different market segments, with a unique product or service tailored to each segment. The result is a distinctive marketing plan for each segment. With a differentiated marketing strategy, companies can generally increase total sales because of broader appeal through greater relevance across market segments and a stronger position within each segment. Sometimes referred to as multisegment marketing, the strategy not only increases sales potential, but it also increases costs associated with targeting different market segments with relevant messages. Still, if done effectively, there is the potential for greater loyalty, resulting in repeat purchases.

EXAMPLE   DIFFERENTIATED MARKETING

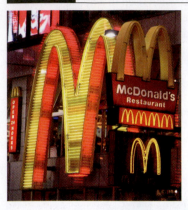

Just a decade ago, many people could have argued that McDonald's practiced undifferentiated marketing. McDonald's had a standard product portfolio that consisted of foods such as hamburgers, french fries, chicken nuggets, and fish sandwiches, and essentially targeted the mass market with a standard marketing mix strategy. In recent years, McDonald's has taken steps to make its brand relevant to increasingly fragmented consumer segments by expanding its offerings. Those now include items such as salads and yogurt parfaits. Simply thinking beyond the core product of a hamburger led McDonald's to realize that convenience and enjoyment were reasons that its customers frequented its stores. These points became the foundation for McDonald's marketing. Today, McDonald's targets a wide range of consumer segments, from diversity groups to young people, to healthy people of all ages. A recent entry into the coffee market has targeted yet another segment of the population.[13]

PHOTO: Jim Lopes

>> END EXAMPLE

Niche Marketing

The third market coverage strategy is known as the niche strategy. Also referred to as concentrated marketing, or focused marketing, **niche marketing** is serving a small but well-defined consumer segment. It is best suited for companies with limited resources, or companies with exclusive products. This approach allows companies to gain a strong position within their segments because they have a better understanding of consumer needs in those specific segments. The marketing plans for niche markets can be quite specialized.

EXAMPLE   NICHE MARKETING

Movado Group, Inc., was founded in 1967 and designs, markets, and distributes jewelry and watches. The organization's portfolio includes popular watch brands such as Ebel,

Condord, Movado, ESQ, Coach, HUGO BOSS, Juicy Couture, Tommy Hilfiger, and Lacoste. In 2007, Movado moved to retarget its premium offering, the almost 100-year-old Concord brand, to an even more upscale target. The Concord offering was reduced to a single line, the recently launched C1. The number of retail outlets were reduced significantly and average retail prices almost tripled to over $9,000. Concord's target was stated to be "hardcore watch aficionados and enthusiasts."[14]

PHOTO: Igor Grochev

>> END EXAMPLE

Global Targeting

There are many different ways that brands can adopt a global strategy. These methods include the following:

- Standardizing core products or services with limited localization for all markets
- Creating value-added elements for selective markets
- Practicing specific competitive-based strategies for each market
- Implementing a universal targeting strategy and marketing mix

Many luxury brands are practicing the strategy of targeting a group that exhibits similar characteristics across national boundaries. While this may be efficient, most brands are adopting some level of standardization with localization as necessary to reflect local conditions.

Selecting a Target

When choosing an appropriate market for a given product or service, three general factors should be considered:

- Attractiveness
- Size and growth potential
- Brand objectives and resources to form the basis for competition

The attractiveness of the segment is determined by the level of competition within the segment and the various strategies used by the brands competing in the segment. If many large competitors that practice differentiated marketing exist, it may be difficult for a smaller brand to stake out a particular market space. Alternatively, a small brand may have tremendous successes by entering an undifferentiated market with a specific point of differentiation.

The size and growth potential for the segment includes the variability and viability of the segment. A segment may be subjected to significant technology or legislative changes that might redefine opportunity in the near future. Brand objectives and resources represent the basis on which the company has to compete. There may be limited flexibility in the product portfolio, or there may be limited funding for advertising. Either reality might limit the potential for the brand to succeed, depending on the market being entered.

Positioning (pp. 101–102)

 DEFINED **Positioning** *is the placement of a product or service offering in the minds of consumer targets.*

 EXPLAINED

Positioning

Positioning involves the development of marketing programs to meet the requirements of target customers.[15] Ultimately, positioning is how your target customers define you in relation to your competitors. Therefore, customer perceptions have much to do with a brand's positioning. The process to establish positioning, provided you are not already positioned precisely where you want, involves competing with all your competitors' marketing communications. Communication of a **unique selling proposition (USP)** can provide a good basis for successful positioning. A USP is an expression of the uniqueness of a brand in a succinct manner. It can be a commitment that others cannot match, or it can be some distinct aspect of your product or service. There are three types of positioning:

- **Functional positioning** is based on the attributes of products or services and their corresponding benefits and is intended to communicate how customers can solve problems or fulfill needs. An example would be high quality.
- **Symbolic positioning** is based on characteristics of the brands that enhance the self-esteem of customers. An example would be the concept of physical appearance.
- **Experiential positioning** is based on characteristics of the brands that stimulate sensory or emotional connections with customers. An example would be the feeling of joy.

 APPLIED

Positioning

The positioning of a brand results in a value proposition being presented to the target market. The value proposition is the entire set of benefits upon which the brand is differentiated. Similar to the USP, the value proposition is also unique. However, unlike the USP, it is intended to be specifically relevant to the target. Although a product can be unique, such as being organic or made in the United States, the brand target for that product may not value those characteristics. That same product may be of exceptionally high quality, which may be a desired benefit that could be

conveyed in a value proposition. Value can be created from many different positioning strategies. Positioning strategies can be based on specific product attributes, different ways the product or service can be used, different types of users, differences between the product and a competitor's product, and a comparison to other product classes.

Sometimes a position needs to evolve, based on customer response. Federal Express invented the concept of delivering packages overnight. A significant point of differentiation was identified to be that the company owned its own fleet of planes. However, customers and potential customers did not care if Federal Express owned its own planes. Once the company determined that the primary benefit was the overnight delivery, the positioning was cemented and the success of Federal Express has been well documented.

EXAMPLE **POSITIONING**

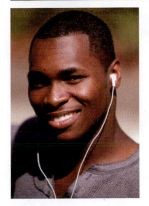

The Apple iPod, with over 100 million units sold, controls the leading position in the global digital music player industry. Launched by Apple Computers in 2001, the iPod has enjoyed success from building on the Apple brand and using the Apple computer as a digital hub for consumers. The idea of a digital hub is that consumers will purchase additional Apple products to connect to their Apple computer. Beyond iPod, iTunes, and iPhone, there is iLife, iWork, iWeb, and iPhoto, not to mention Apple TV (renamed from iTV). While the iPod basically performs the same functions as the many different brands of MP3 players, it separates itself from other brands by being used by many different influential celebrities, from presidents to rock stars and by generally being considered "cool." Being positioned as cool and being associated with celebrities has made the product iconic in countries across the world. Just as being popular has helped the iPod increase sales, it is that ubiquity that could, potentially, cause at least some of its consumers to look for less common brands of MP3s to express their individuality. That is where the digital hub strategy is designed to keep adding new and relevant products to the overall Apple offering.[16]

PHOTO: Michael Ledray

>> END EXAMPLE

Positioning is also important in an online environment. Since Internet search engines such as Google, Cuil, and AltaVista have become ubiquitous, it makes sense to optimize one's position in this important medium. **Search engine optimization**, the process of enhancing Web site traffic through either organic or compensated means, can be an effective marketing tool and can assist in the positioning of your product or service during the consumer shopping process. The critical element of effective search engine optimization is the selection of the keywords, which should be based on the positioning of the product or service.

Using a Perceptual Map

A **perceptual map** defines the market, based on consumer perceptions of attributes, or characteristics, of competing products. Also referred to as a positioning chart, a perceptual map visually represents consumer perceptions of a group of brands by evaluating category attributes such as price, quality, speed, fuel economy, and appearance. Brands can be positioned in the context of competing brands on a perceptual map. The perceptual map can identify important competitors and indicate if the current positioning needs to be changed.

EXAMPLE **PERCEPTUAL MAP**

A perceptual map for the relationship between *Consumer Reports'* overall road-test scores and fuel economy ratings for a select list of compact sedans is as follows:

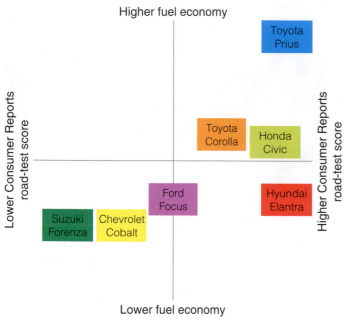

FIGURE 9.2

This particular perceptual map combines subjective consumer road-test ratings with established fuel-economy numbers. The map could also have been constructed with two subjective criteria, such as consumer road-test ratings and consumer appearance ratings. In this example, although the Hyundai Elantra has the highest road-test score, the Toyota Prius has a similar road-test score, but with much higher fuel economy. The Toyota Corolla and Honda Civic are clear competitors for those consumers who consider road-test scores and fuel economy as the primary factors in their purchase decisions. This perceptual map assumes that road-test scores and fuel-economy ratings are the only relevant attributes in selecting a vehicle. This is seldom the case. Status, appearance, and ride could all factor into an evaluation. Still, Prius is the leading hybrid vehicle sold in the United States, and Civic and Corolla are two of the leading models in overall sales.[17]

>> END EXAMPLE

Selecting a Position

The selection of a position should reflect an understanding of the external marketing environment and the competitive advantage that can be created as a result of differentiation. It is necessary to understand how the brands, products, and services satisfy the needs of the target segment, as well as to switch costs for those target consumers who are using competitive products or services. Ultimately, the position selected should do the following:

- Deliver a valued benefit to the target.
- Be distinctive with respect to competitors.
- Offer a superior benefit that can easily be communicated.
- Be difficult for others to copy.
- Be affordable to the target.
- Provide required revenues and profits to the brand.

One way to communicate your position is through a brand position statement.

Developing a Brand Position Statement

The **brand position statement** is a summary of what your brand offers to the market. This statement is not seen by the public and is not the advertising tagline, although the tagline should support the brand position statement. The statement is a guide for marketing communication development and should be developed using the following form: To (consumer segment) our (brand) is (business concept) that (basis for differentiation).[18]

EXAMPLE **BRAND POSITION STATEMENT**

Focus: HOPE has been active as a Detroit-based community organization since 1967. Its brand position statement directed to potential donors is the following:

To socially aware people and organizations who desire to financially support an organization dedicated to overcoming racism, poverty, and injustice. Focus: HOPE is the preeminent community-based organization that has a long history of addressing those issues through a holistic process by providing education and training for the disadvantaged, distributing packaged food to low-income seniors and young families, and revitalizing neighborhoods.[19]

PHOTO: Kuzma

>> END EXAMPLE

▼**Visual** Summary

Chapter 9 Summary

The process of segmenting, targeting, and positioning builds on concepts of building a brand and a marketing philosophy. Without a strong brand to which consumers ascribe equity and a company philosophy that places a brand at the forefront of its business, no segmentation effort can be successful. Well-crafted segmentation can provide a company with the means to efficiently identify and target consumers with a value proposition that is differentiated from its competitors. The process of identifying and selecting segments can be expensive and time-consuming, but the rewards can be significant. Ultimately, segmentation advances the marketing goals and creates an organization that grows with its customers.

Segmentation
pp. 95–96

classifying

Segmentation is the process of subdividing a company or organization's target market into smaller, homogenous sub-groups.

Capstone
Exercise p. 105

Positioning
pp. 101–102

Targeting pp. 98–101

selecting

Marketers identify each of their potential market opportunities and then target, or select, the best possible opportunities for marketing exploitation.

Influencing

With positioning, marketers attempt, usually through research, to identify how consumers view their products. Consumers often rank companies and their product offerings. With positioning, some consumers would see certain products as the best, some products as second best, third best, etc. Companies need to know how consumer's perceive their products in order to position the product.

▼Chapter Key Terms

Segmentation (pp. 95–96)

Segmentation (also referred to as **market segmentation***) is the division of consumer markets into meaningful and distinct customer groups. (p. 95)* **Opening example** **(p. 95)**

Key Terms (p. 95)

Mass marketing is communicating a product or service message to as broad a group of people as possible with the purpose of positively influencing sales. **(p. 95)**

Segmentation Base (pp. 96–98)

Segmentation base is a group of characteristics that is used to assign segment members. (p. 96)

Key Terms (pp. 96–97)

Behavioral segmentation allocates consumers into groups, based on their knowledge, attitudes, uses, or responses to a product or service. **(p. 97)**

Demographic segmentation divides the market into groups, based on variables such as age, gender, family size, family life cycle, income, occupation, education, religion, ethnicity, generation, nationality, and sexual orientation. **(p. 96)** **Example: Demographic Segmentation (p. 96)**

Needs segmentation allocates consumers into groups, based on their product or service needs. **(p. 97)** **Example: Segmenting Business Markets (p. 98)** **Example: Segmenting International Markets (p. 98)**

Psychographic segmentation assigns buyers into different groups, based on lifestyle, class, or personality characteristics. **(p. 96)** **Example: Psychographic Segmentation (p. 97)**

Values segmentation considers what customers prefer and what motivates customer response to marketing activities. **(p. 97)**

Targeting (pp. 98–101)

Targeting (also referred to as **market targeting***) is the process of evaluating and selecting the most viable market segment to enter. (p. 98)* **Example: Targeting (p. 99)**

Key Terms (pp. 98–100)

Behavioral targeting optimizes the online advertising potential for brands. **(p. 99)**

Differentiated marketing separates and targets several different market segments with a different product or service geared to each segment. **(p. 99)** **Example: Differentiated Marketing (p. 100)**

Niche marketing is serving a small but well-defined consumer segment. **(p. 100)** **Example: Niche Marketing (p. 100)**

Undifferentiated marketing is when a company treats the market as a whole, focusing on what is common to the needs of customers rather than on what is different. **(p. 99)** **Example: Undifferentiated Marketing (p. 99)**

Positioning (pp. 101–102)

Positioning is the placement of a product or service offering in the minds of consumer targets. (p. 101) **Example: Positioning (p. 101)**

Key Terms (pp. 101–102)

Brand position statement is a summary of what a brand offers to the market. **(p. 102)** **Example: Brand Position Statement (p. 102)**

Experiential positioning is based on characteristics of the brands that stimulate sensory or emotional connections with customers. **(p. 101)**

Functional positioning is based on the attributes of products or services and their corresponding benefits and is intended to communicate how customers can solve problems or fulfill needs. **(p. 101)**

Perceptual map defines the market, based on consumer perceptions of attributes of competing products. **(p. 102)** **Example: Perceptual Map (p. 102)**

Search engine optimization is the process of enhancing Web site traffic through either organic or compensated means. **(p. 101)**

Symbolic positioning is based on characteristics of the brand that enhance the self-esteem of customers. **(p. 101)**

Unique selling proposition (USP) is an expression of the uniqueness of a brand. **(p. 101)**

▼Capstone Exercise

In this chapter, you learned about segmenting markets and positioning your products to appeal to your best target customers. We will look in greater depth at how to apply these concepts by doing three exercises

We will focus on another dominant consumer products company—Coca-Cola. Go to www.coca-cola.com to see the depth of products and the international areas served. Coca-Cola has 450 brands and does business in over 200 countries. Pick one of the international areas and see the brands offered there.

Go to www.virtualvender.coca-cola.com/vm/Vending.jsp to see the range of products to do the following exercises. From the virtual vendor page, pick soft drinks with all countries. Notice that the company sells 76 different brands of soft drinks worldwide. Look at each brand and notice the product description and how the company differentiates each brand in ways other than geography. This is clearly an example of differentiated marketing.

1. Think about the characteristics of the segment that Coke is trying to reach with each product. Pick four soft drinks and, based on the part of the chapter on **Segmentation Applied**, decide which of the major segmentation strategies apply and be prepared to identify which segment belongs to each product.

2. Make a perceptual map (see page 000) and plot 12 brands on this map. Remember that the trick is to think of what the axes represent.

3. Review the **Positioning Applied** section of the chapter. Decide how you want to position your four chosen brands in consumers' minds. Also decide what associations/images you want consumers to have when shown each bottle, for example, healthy, tasty, refreshing.

▼Application Exercises

Complete the following exercises:

1. Virgin Galactic touts itself as the world's first spaceline. Its plan is to develop the market for affordable suborbital space tourism. When its creation was announced in 2004, company founder Sir Richard Branson estimated an initial market of around 3,000 individuals for its $200,000 product. Identify and discuss the segmentation, targeting, and positioning strategy that Virgin Galactic used for its marketing plan. What if, in the near future, the price could be reduced to $10,000 per trip? What might be the impact on positioning?

2. Ferrari manufactures and sells a variety of vehicles priced well over $200,000. Founded in 1947, the brand is known for its racing heritage, technological innovations, and distinctive design. Despite its great success over the years, Ferrari's corporate identity and logo were redesigned in 2002. Discuss the possible motivations to change the corporate identity and logo. What might the impact of this change be on the company's market positioning?

3. Go to iTunes (http://www.apple.com/itunes/) or Rhapsody (www.rhapsody.com). What unique market segments appear to be the target of specific genres of music? How did you determine the segments?

4. Collect advertisements that demonstrate the positioning of different watch brands. Sort the various brands into categories of brands with similar positions.

5. You have agreed to help a friend with a home furnishings business to segment his or her market. Suggest a way to segment the market for your friend. Select a target market to go after, keeping in mind segment size and growth, structural attractiveness, and probable company resources. What target marketing strategy would you use? Explain your answers.

chapter 10

Part 1   Explaining (Chapters 1, 2, 3, 4)   Part 4   Managing (Chapters 11, 12, 13, 14, 15)
Part 2   Creating (Chapters 5, 6, 7, 8)   Part 5   Integrating (Chapters 16, 17)
Part 3   Strategizing (Chapters 9, 10)

The **Marketing Plan**

Chapter Overview At this point in the book, you have built a solid marketing foundation through explaining, creating, and strategizing fundamental aspects of marketing. This chapter provides a structure to document the marketing situation, marketing objectives, marketing strategy, and marketing initiatives through the creation of a marketing plan. Integrated throughout this chapter is a marketing plan for a fictitious company, Interior Views LLC. Interior Views, a home accessories shop specializing in fabrics and complementary services, is a relatively new company that has aggressive growth targets. Interior Views has a diverse group of competitors and distributes products both online and through a storefront location. Interior Views, unknown by many potential customers and dealing with emerging and evolving trends, is promoting itself through a variety of media channels. This focus on Interior Views provides a vibrant example to support exploring the elements of a marketing plan.

In addition, components of the marketing plan and business plan are introduced and contrasted. In subsequent chapters, you will be introduced to management and integration issues based on specific marketing mix elements. As you are exposed to those concepts, it would be helpful to apply the framework of the marketing plan covered in this chapter to assist in building a holistic perspective on marketing.

▼ Chapter **Outline**

BUSINESS PLAN (pp. 107–108)

▼ **DEFINED** *A* **business plan** *is a written document that defines the operational and financial objectives of a business over a particular time, and defines how the business plans to accomplish those objectives.*

▼ **EXPLAINED**
Business Plan

The business plan is a comprehensive document that identifies the nature of the business. Varieties of plans exist within the business plan, including the marketing plan. The business plan also contains objectives, decision-making processes, and policies. A well-crafted business plan guides optimal utilization of resources within a business. The elements of a business plan generally include the following:

- Title Page
- Executive Summary
- Business Overview
- Product or Service Overview
- Market Overview
- Competitive Overview
- Operations Overview
- Management Overview
- Financial Overview

Depending on the type of business, the business plan may include different sections. The identified sections are common for an established business. A start-up business would also need to include start-up expenses and information on capitalization. Not-for-profit businesses also benefit from developing a business plan. A not-for-profit business plan should identify the capacity of the business to benefit its customer target.

▼ **APPLIED**
Business Plan

A business plan is a road map, based on current business and market understanding, to navigate the near future. It is used to guide decisions and to communicate the performance and direction of the business to potential investors and to stakeholders, people who are, or may be, affected by actions a business takes. A business plan is different from individual department plans, such as marketing or finance. A business plan identifies responsibilities of management and how those responsibilities pertain to each area. The plan also identifies the capital requirements to manage each area. Marketers contribute a variety of inputs into the business plan, including the following:

- A comprehensive review and assessment of a business's marketing environment
- An explanation of what the marketing function is attempting to achieve in support of the business plan
- A discussion on how a business intends to achieve its marketing objectives
- A process to allocate resources and monitor results

In July 2005, shortly after being awarded the 2012 Olympic Games, London began translating its bid proposal into specific plans. The London Olympics will sponsor 26 Olympic sports in 34 venues and 20 Paralympic sports in 21 venues, while hosting 10,500 Olympic athletes and 4,200 Paralympic athletes, along with 20,000 members of the press. It is anticipated that over 9 million tickets will be sold.

One specific area of planning relates the marketing activities associated with the games. Both the London 2012 Organizing Committee and the International Olympic Committee will share in the revenues and costs, to varying extents, associated with the 2012 Olympic and Paralympic Games. The London 2012 Organizing Committee receives a share of the broadcasting revenue from the global sales of TV rights to the games and a share from The Olympic Partners program. The Olympic Partners is an International Olympic Committee program featuring companies that have purchased international marketing rights of association with the Olympic movement. Those companies include Coca-Cola, Acer, Atos Origin, GE, McDonald's, Omega, Panasonic, Samsung, and Visa. The London 2012 Organizing Committee will also receive income from domestic sponsorship, ticketing, and merchandising programs, including coins, stamps, official mascots, clothing, and pins.[1]

PHOTO: Johnny Lye

Most business plans include three types of financial statements: the income statement, cash-flow statement, and balance sheet. The income statement identifies business revenues, expenses, and profits. The cash-flow statement identifies how much cash is needed to meet financial obligations and the source of that cash. The balance sheet is used to determine the net worth, which is the assets less liabilities, of a business.

As few as one individual to an entire staff create business plans. It is not the number of people involved in creating the business plan that matters, but how the various activities within a business are represented throughout the planning process. The support of the various levels of management is also essential for successful development and implementation of the business plan. Businesses should have a business plan in place at inception, and may have one well in advance of start-up if external financing is required. That plan must be reviewed on a regular basis if either external market or internal company conditions change.

EXAMPLE   BUSINESS PLAN

Petfinder.com built its business plan on its reputation as being "The temporary home of nearly 250,000 adoptable pets." Established in 1995, Petfinder.com is a searchable database of a variety of pets from thousands of shelters and foster groups. Petfinder.com was sold to Discovery Communications in 2006 as part of an acquisition strategy included in Discovery's business plan. The Web site is now part of Discovery's Animal Planet Media Enterprises and is featured on Discovery's and Animal Planet's Web sites.[2]

PHOTO: Suponev Vladimir Mihajlovich

>> END EXAMPLE

Marketing Plan (pp. 108–117)

 DEFINED *A* **marketing plan** *is a document that includes an assessment of the marketing situation, marketing objectives, marketing strategy, and marketing initiatives.*

EXPLAINED

Marketing Plan

A marketing plan can be an independent document, or it can be contained within a business plan. The marketing plan outlines those actions that are intended to communicate value, generate interest, and persuade target customers to purchase specific products or services. Many of the inputs to the plan come from consumer insight, market intelligence, marketing research, and strategic thinking. There can be one or more marketing plans, depending on the product or service portfolio. A **marketing program** is a consolidated plan of all individual marketing plans. A marketing program is intended to ration and optimize resources across brands, products, or services in a portfolio.

The marketing plan consists of six basic sections:

- Executive Summary
- Company Description, Purpose, and Goals
- Marketing Situation
- Forecasting
- Marketing Strategy
- Measurement and Controls

Creating and updating the marketing plan is the responsibility of the marketing department. Just as with business plans, the breadth of activities and levels of management represented in the marketing plan process are essential. Implementation of the marketing plan requires support of the entire business.

APPLIED

Marketing Plan

Marketing plans are used, just as are business plans, to guide decisions and provide valuable information to stakeholders. In practice, some businesses confuse the roles of the business and marketing plans, while others pay little attention to developing either plan. Still others commit resources and time to developing, implementing, and monitoring successful plans. The most successful marketing plans meet the following criteria:

- The plan is realistic and achievable.
- The plan can be measured.
- The plan has committed organizational resources for implementation.
- The plan requirements are clear.

We will now look at a marketing plan section-by-section. As each of the sections of the marketing plan is introduced, the corresponding section from Interior Views LLC's marketing plan is presented.

Executive Summary

The executive summary provides a brief overview of the primary goals, recommendations, and planned actions included in the marketing plan. The executive summary is intended to communicate essential information to senior leadership and business stakeholders.

INTERIOR VIEWS LLC EXECUTIVE SUMMARY

Interior Views is a home accessories shop specializing in fabrics and complementary services that is now in its third year. This destination store offers the advantages of providing fabrics specifically designed for home decorator use in fabric widths of 54 inches and greater. Over 900 fabrics are available on the floor at any time with more than 3,000 sample fabrics for custom "cut" orders. Customers see, touch, feel, and take the fabric to their home as they work through their purchase decision. Market research indicates a specific and growing need in the area for the products and services Interior Views offers in the market it serves. The market strategy will be based on a cost-effective approach to reach this clearly defined target market. The three-phase approach will utilize resources to create awareness of the store and encourage customers to benefit from the convenience and services it offers. Interior Views will focus on its selection, accessibility of product, design services, and competitive pricing. The marketing objective is to actively support continued growth and profitability through effective implementation of the strategy.

>> END EXAMPLE

Company Description, Purpose, and Goals

The company description identifies the history of the business, its portfolio, and value proposition. The core competencies of the business, those characteristics that create a competitive advantage, are identified in this section, as is the purpose for the business to exist and its goals, both financial and nonfinancial.

INTERIOR VIEWS LLC COMPANY DESCRIPTION, PURPOSE, AND GOALS

The Company—Interior Views is a home accessories shop specializing in fabrics and complementary services that is now in its third year. This destination store offers the advantages of providing fabrics specifically designed for home decorator use in fabric widths of 54 inches and greater. Over 900 fabrics are available on the floor at any time with more than 3,000 sample fabrics for custom "cut" orders. Customers see, touch, feel, and take the fabric to their home as they work through their purchase decision.

Judy Wilson, the owner, is the one primarily responsible for marketing activities. This is in addition to her other responsibilities, and she does depend on some outside resources for mailing (Donna at Postal Connection) and some graphic design work. Judy does delegate responsibilities to Julie Hanson to assist with television advertising. Julie and the other staff members are also responsible for at least one special event throughout the year.

The Mission—Interior Views LLC is a store for discerning, quality-conscious buyers of decorator fabrics and complementary home accessories and furniture. The store celebrates the home through the color and texture of fabric. The experience informs, inspires, and shows people how to transform their home into a unique and personalized expression of themselves. Interior Views seeks to encourage people to imagine what can be, and help make their vision a reality.

The Offer—Our primary points of differentiation offer these qualities:

- The most extensive access to in-stock, first-quality decorator fabrics within 100 miles of our primary geographic market and offered at affordable prices
- The largest selection of special-order fabrics, with arrangements to have most of those products shipped to the store within 10 days of placing the order
- Personal assistance from a design-oriented staff that is qualified and capable of meeting the needs of discerning customers with high expectations
- Complementary product offering, including hard-covering window treatment, hardware, home accessories, made-to-order upholstered furniture, and antiques that are designed, selected, and displayed in a way to emphasize the use of fabric in home design

Interior Views will qualify for the most attractive retail discount through select suppliers, offering greater profit margins and more competitive pricing for bolt purchases in quantities of 50 to 60 yards, or in half of that yardage with a "cutting fee" that increases cost per yard by an average of 50 cents. The primary product lines will include fabrics from the following textile sources:

- Robert Allen Fabrics
- Fabricut
- Waverly Fabrics
- Spectrum
- Art Mark
- Covington
- P/Kaufmann

Complementary accessories, including fabric trims, drapery hardware, and hard-covering window treatments, are supplied from the following sources:

- Hunter Douglas—Hard-window coverings
- Kirsch—Rods and selected window hardware and accessories
- Conso—Trims and Fabric Accessories
- Petersen-Arne—Trims and Accessories
- Graber—Selected window hardware
- Grumman—Threads

Positioning—For the person creating a personalized and unique impression of his or her home, Interior Views is the best local source for selection and price points of the fabric, customer-oriented design services, and a variety of other home accessory and furniture products. Customers will be impressed with, and return for, the great in-stock selection, value-oriented pricing, and excellent customer service. Unlike JoAnn's, Warehouse Fabric, or catalogs, Interior Views is a pleasant and tasteful resource that encourages everyone in the process of decorating their home. Unlike employing an interior decorator, Interior Views allows the individual to participate in design choices to the extent he or she chooses, and realize greater value for the dollars the individual invests.

Value Proposition—Interior Views sells more than fabric, it sells a personalized and unique vision for your home. Interior Views helps you revive your home and your living experience.

Goals -

- Achieve growth rate in sales of 12% for the year 2005, to total in excess of $341,200 in total revenues
- Generate average sales per business day (305 days per year) in excess of $1,000
- Reduce the existing credit line by a minimum of $26,400
- Maintain a gross margin of 45% each month
- Generate an average of $1,000 of sales each business day each month
- Experience a $5,000 increase in quarterly sales with each newsletter
- Realize an annual growth rate of approximately 25% in the year 2000

>> END EXAMPLE

Marketing Situation

The marketing situation section includes an assessment of customers, competitors, product portfolio, distribution channel, business, and the marketing environment, including economic, political, legal, cultural, social, and technological factors. Tools such as the SWOT analysis, BCG growth-market matrix, and the Five Forces of Competitive Position model, discussed in earlier chapters, can also assist in completing the marketing situation section.

EXAMPLE INTERIOR VIEWS LLC COMPANY
MARKETING SITUATION

Situation Analysis—Interior Views is a retail store heading into its third year of operation. The store has been well received, and marketing is now critical to its continued success and future profitability. The store offers the most extensive selection of in-stock decorator fabrics as well as a resource for special-ordered fabrics. The basic market need is to offer a good selection of decorator fabrics at reasonable prices, for the "do-it-yourself" and the "buy-it-yourself" customers, through a personalized retail store that offers excellent service, design assistance, and inspiration for people to redecorate their homes.

Market Needs—Interior Views is providing its customers the opportunity to create a home environment to express who they are. They have the choice to select their fabric and go whatever direction they choose—to fabric it themselves or have it done for them. They have the opportunity to actively participate in the design, look, and feel of their home. They desire their home to be personal, unique, and tasteful as well as communicate a message about what is important to them. We seek to fulfill the following benefits that we know are important to our customers:

- **Selection**—The company carries a wide choice of current and tasteful decorator fabrics.
- **Accessibility**—The buyer can walk out of the store with the fabric he or she needs to begin a project.
- **Customer Design Services**—Employees have a design background to make them a resource for the customer. This enables customers to benefit from suggestions regarding the selection of their fabric and related products in a manner to complement their design choice.
- **Competitive Pricing**—All products will be competitively priced in comparison to stores in the Portland, Oregon market (best price comparison) and other channels of distribution, such as catalog sales.

The Market—We possess good information about our market, identified in Table 10.1, and know a great deal about the common attributes of our most prized and loyal customers. We will leverage this information to better understand who we serve, their specific needs, and how we can better communicate with them.

Market Demographics—The profile of the Interior Views customer consists of the following geographic, demographic, psychographic, and behavior factors:

- **Geographics**—Our immediate geographic market is the Boise area, with a population of 168,300. A 50-mile geographic area is in need of our products and services. The total targeted area population is estimated at 568,800.
- **Demographics**—The typical Interior Views customer is female, married, has children but not necessarily at home, has attended college, has a combined income in excess of $50,000, age range of 35–55 years with a median age of 42 and owns a home, townhouse, and/or condominium valued at over $125,000. If the customer works from home, it's by choice in a professional/business setting. The individual belongs to one or more business, social, and/or athletic organizations, which may include:

- Downtown Athletic Club
- Boise Country Club

Table 10.1 Market Analysis

Potential Customers	Growth	Year 1	Year 2	Year 3	Year 4	Year 5
Country Club Women	25%	73,500	91,875	114,844	143,555	179,444
Boomers in Transition	20%	28,500	34,200	41,040	49,248	59,098
Professional Youngsters	18%	23,000	27,140	32,025	37,790	44,592
Home Builders	12%	18,000	20,160	22,579	25,288	28,323
Total	21%	143,000	173,375	210,488	255,881	311,457

- Junior League of Boise
- American Business Women's Association

We know the following regarding the profile of the typical residents of Boise:

- 67% have lived in Boise for 7 years or more
- 23% are between the ages of 35 and 44
- 40% have completed some college
- 24% are managers, professionals, and/or owners of a business
- 53% are married
- 65% have no children living at home
- 56% own their residence

- **Psychographics**—The typical Interior Views customer believes the appearance of his or her home is a priority, enjoys entertaining and showing his or her home, perceives him- or herself as creative, tasteful and able, but seeks validation and support regarding decorating ideas and choices. The customer reads one or more of the following magazines:

  - *Country Living*
  - *Martha Stewart Living*
  - *Home*
  - *House Beautiful*
  - *Country Home*
  - *Metropolitan Home*
  - *Traditional Homes*
  - *Victoria*
  - *Architectural Digest*
  - *Elle Decor*

- **Behaviors**—The customer takes pride in having an active role in decorating his or her home. The customer's home is a form of communicating "who he or she is" to others. Comparisons within social groups are made on an ongoing basis, but rarely discussed.

Market Trends—The home textile market, considered to include sheets, towels, draperies, carpets, blankets, and upholstery, accounts for 37% of all textile output. The trade publication "*Home Textiles Today*" estimates the size of the U.S. home textiles market at the wholesale level, excluding carpets, to be between $6.5 billion to $7 billion annually. The industry is expected to realize a steady increase over the next few years.

The industry is driven by the number of "household formations," which is expected to continue for several years. This is primarily due to the solid growth in the number of single-parent and non-family households. This growth also comes from baby boomers needing bigger houses to accommodate growing and extended families and, as people get older, they are buying homes rather than renting to realize tax and equity-building benefits. Favorable mortgage rates will also enable others to invest in their existing home.

The "do-it-yourself" (DIY) market continues to grow and closely parallels the professional home-improvement market. DIY market growth is attributed to an increased presence of products, the personal satisfaction experienced, and the cost savings customers realize. A portion of the do-it-yourself market is the "buy-it-yourself" (BIY) market. Consumers are buying the product and arranging for someone else to do the fabrication and/or installation. This is more expensive then the do-it-yourself approach, but less costly than buying finished products from other sources.

Market Growth—The publication, *American Demographics*, projected the number of U.S. households will grow by 16% between 1995 and the year 2010, an increase from 98.5 million to 115 million. Of the households composed of people from 35 to 44 years old, almost half are married couples with children under the age of 18. Based on research by *American Demographics*, households in the 45 to 65 age range were estimated to grow to 34 million by the year 2000. These households will increase another 32 percent to 45 million in 2010 as baby boomers add to this peak-earning and spending age group. With approximately 46.2% of the nation's 93.3 million dwellings built before 1960, many of these homeowners are also expected to update. These factors contribute to an increased need for home decorator fabrics for window treatment, upholstering, pillows, bedding, and other fabric accessory needs.

One important factor is that married couples in the 35 to 65 age range represent a growth segment and enjoy larger incomes than other family structures. They enjoy the choice to spend their disposable income on life's amenities. They may demonstrate "cocooning" by making their home a more comfortable and attractive haven. They choose to spend resources here rather than on vacations and other discretionary options. This group represents a larger subsegment of the target market.

Macroenvironment—The following trends and issues influence the success of Interior Views:

- **National economic health**—The store does better when the country experiences "good times" regardless of its direct impact on the local economy. Sales decrease when the stock market falls. An upbeat State of the Union address correlates with an increase in sales.
- **New home construction activity**—More closely related to what is taking place in our local economy, new home construction has a significant impact on sales across all product lines.
- **Shifts in design trends**—Major changes in design trends increase sales. The Boise market lags behind metropolitan design trends by 6 to 12 months. This offers a buying advantage for the store, offering a preview of what is coming and how we should adjust our in-stock inventory.

SWOT Analysis—The following SWOT analysis captures the key strengths and weaknesses within the company, and describes the opportunities and threats facing Interior Views.

- **Strengths**
  - Strong relationships with suppliers that offer credit arrangements, flexibility, and response to special product requirements
  - Excellent and stable staff, offering personalized customer service
  - Great retail space that offers flexibility with a positive and attractive atmosphere
  - Strong merchandising and product presentation

- Good referral relationships with complementary vendors, local realtors, and some designers
- In-store complementary products through "The Window Seat" and "Antique Bureau" add interest, stability, and revenue
- High customer loyalty among repeat and high-dollar purchase customers

- **Weaknesses**
  - Access to capital
  - Cash flow continues to be unpredictable
  - Owners are still climbing the "retail experience curve"
  - Location is not in a heavily traveled, traditional retail area
  - Challenges of the seasonality of the business

- **Opportunities**
  - Growing market with a significant percentage of our target market still not knowing we exist
  - Continuing opportunity through strategic alliances for referrals and marketing activities
  - Benefiting from high levels of new home construction
  - Changes in design trends can initiate updating and therefore sales
  - Increasing sales opportunities beyond our "100-mile" target area
  - Internet potential for selling products to other markets

- **Threats**
  - Competition from a national store, or a store with greater financing or product resources could enter the market
  - Catalog resources, including Calico Corners and Pottery Barn, are aggressively priced with comparable products
  - Continued price pressure, reducing contribution margins
  - Dramatic changes in design, including fabric colors and styles, creates obsolete or less profitable inventory

Competition—Competition in the area of decorator fabric comes from three general categories: traditional fabric retail stores, catalog sales, and discounters. The other local fabric retailers are direct competition, but we have seen strong indirect competition from catalog sales and discounters.

- **Retail Stores**
  - **House of Fabrics**—Nationwide recognition and buying power of numerous types of dated fabric with strong product availability. This store has experienced financial difficulty in recent years and has closed several locations throughout the country.
  - **Warehouse Fabrics**—Locally owned, offering low-cost products with a wide selection of discontinued fabrics and only a limited number of "current" fabrics. This warehouse concept offers marginal customer service with what many "upper-end" customers consider to be an "undesirable" shopping environment.
  - **JoAnn's**—Nationwide chain with strong buying power. The company has a broad fabric selection for clothing with a limited number of in-store decorator fabrics available. Its primary target markets are the clothing seamstress, with an increasing emphasis on craft items.

- **Interior Designers**—Interior Designers make profit off mark up of fabric in addition to its hourly services charges. Its costs per yard are typically higher since they do not benefit from retail or volume discounts. Therefore, the costs to the customer are often two to four times higher than the price per yard from Interior Views.
- **Web site providers**—Fabric sales over the Web are limited at this time, and this will be a source of competition for the future to watch. Currently, there is no measurable impact on our market through competitive Web sites.

- **Catalog Competitors**—An increasing level of competition is anticipated from catalog sales. Recent trends, such as those demonstrated in the well-established but evolving catalog *Pottery Barn*, indicate increased interest in offering decorator fabric, window designs, and other home decorating products through this increasingly popular channel of distribution. Catalog sources do not offer customers the option to see, touch, and have the fabric in their homes. Price is the most significant competitive factor this product source presents. The most aggressive catalog competitor is *Calico Corners* followed by *Pottery Barn* and other home-accessory-based providers.
- **Discounters**—Channels of distribution continue to shift in favor of discounters, who account for a significant portion of the growth in the industry. As consumers experience lower levels of disposable income, discounters leverage frequent store promotions to entice frugal, value-oriented consumers. One of the biggest criticisms of discounters is their failure to offer a quality service experience and their failure to present inviting displays to promote sales. These discounters, along with specialty store chains, present one of the most severe competitive threats for individually owned specialty stores. This is partially due to extensive promotional efforts, price advantages, and established relationships with their vendors. One example of these discounters is the "home improvement" chains, such as Home Base. This aggressive retailer has adopted a strategy to include complete decorator departments in their metropolitan stores. Currently existing in the Los Angeles market, this strategy is anticipated to be introduced into the Seattle area and other select metropolitan markets within the year. Although the Boise Home Base store sells basic curtain rod hardware and other hard-cover window treatment, there are no known plans at this time for the Boise Home Base store to implement this in the foreseeable future. This will be an important issue to monitor for competitive purposes.

>> END EXAMPLE

Forecasting

The forecasting section includes the anticipated outcomes based on achieving predefined marketing goals. Revenues and expenses are both forecasted in this section. A mix of judgment and data analysis is used to consider past performance and the characteristics influencing that performance, as well as current and future opportunities and threats. The outcome of the forecasting process is essential when exploring alternative marketing strategies.

EXAMPLE INTERIOR VIEWS LLC FORECASTING

Financials—Our marketing strategy is based on becoming the resource of choice for people looking for decorator fabrics, do-it-yourself, and buy-it-yourself resources to create a look in their home. Our marketing strategy is based on superior performance in the following areas:

- Product selection
- Product quality
- Customer service

Our marketing strategy will create awareness, interest, and appeal from our target market for what Interior Views offers our customers.

This section will offer a financial overview of Interior Views as it relates to our marketing activities. We will address break-even information, sales forecasts, expense forecasts, and how those link to our marketing strategy.

- **Break-even analysis**—The break-even analysis (detailed in Tables 10.2, 10.3, and the Break-Even Analysis figure) illustrates the number of single sales, or units, that we must realize to break even. This is based on average sale and costs per transaction.

Table 10.2 Fixed Costs

Utilities	$ 400
Web Site Hosting	$ 200
Recurring Marketing Expenses	$1,200
Payroll	$6,000
Rent	$1,500
Total	$9,300

Table 10.3 Break-even Analysis

Monthly Revenue Break-even	$20,427
Assumptions:	
Average Percent Variable Cost	54%
Estimated Monthly Fixed Costs	$ 9,300

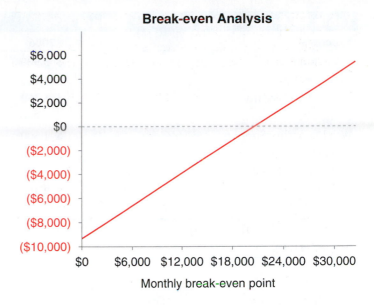

Break-even Analysis

Monthly break-even point

Break-even point = where the line intersects with 0

- **Sales Forecast**—The sales forecast (Table 10.4) is broken down into the four main revenue streams: direct sales, Web sales, consignment sales, and sub-lease revenues. The sales forecast for the upcoming year is based on a 25% growth rate. This is a slower growth rate than what was experienced in previous years at 33%, and also less than what is expected for future sales, estimated to be approximately 28%. These projections appear attainable and take the increasing base into consideration. Future growth rates are based on percentage increases as follows:

- Direct sales 20% growth rate per year
- Web sales 50% growth rate per year
- Consignment sales 20% growth rate per year
- Sub-lease revenues 10% growth rate per year

- **Expense Forecast**—Marketing expenses (Table 10.5) are to be budgeted at approximately 5% of total sales. Expenses are tracked in the major marketing categories of television advertisements, newspaper advertisements, the newsletter

Table 10.4 Sales Forecast

Sales	2006	2007	2008	2009	2010
Direct Sales	$322,000	$386,400	$463,700	$556,400	$667,700
Web Sales	$ 12,500	$ 18,750	$ 28,125	$ 42,190	$ 63,280
Consignment Sales	$ 1,360	$ 1,632	$ 1,960	$ 2,350	$ 2,820
Sublease Revenue	$ 5,340	$ 5,600	$ 6,165	$ 6,780	$ 7,460
Subtotal Direct Cost of Sales	$341,200	$412,382	$499,950	$607,720	$741,260
Direct Cost of Sales	**2006**	**2007**	**2008**	**2009**	**2010**
Direct Sales	$178,850	$214,000	$255,500	$307,000	$370,000
Web Sales	$ 6,875	$ 10,400	$ 12,000	$ 18,000	$ 20,000
Consignment Sales	$ 71	$ 85	$ 102	$ 123	$ 150
Sublease Revenue	$ 60	$ 66	$ 73	$ 80	$ 88
Subtotal Direct Cost of Sales	$185,856	$224,551	$267,675	$325,203	$390,238

Table 10.5 Marketing Expense Budget

Expenses	2006	2007	2008	2009	2010
Television Ads	$ 3,900	$ 4,600	$ 5,620	$ 6,740	$ 8,200
Newspaper Ads	$ 1,800	$ 2,160	$ 2,592	$ 3,110	$ 3,800
Newsletter/Postcard	$ 6,450	$ 7,700	$ 9,200	$11,150	$13,400
Printed Promotional Materials	$ 960	$ 1,150	$ 1,380	$ 1,660	$ 2,000
Web Marketing/Support	$ 1,500	$ 1,950	$ 2,535	$ 3,295	$ 4,300
Public Relations	$ 240	$ 345	$ 415	$ 500	$ 600
Promotional Events	$ 1,700	$ 1,950	$ 2,300	$ 2,800	$ 3,400
Web Site Expenses	$ 2,400	$ 2,600	$ 2,800	$ 3,000	$ 3,000
Other	$ 400	$ 480	$ 575	$ 700	$ 850
Total Sales and Marketing Exp.	$19,350	$22,935	$27,417	$32,955	$39,550
Percent of Sales	5.67%	5.56%	5.48%	5.42%	5.32%

and postcard mailings, Web marketing support, printed promotional materials, public relations, and other.

Marketing expenses are evenly allocated based on the type of inventory in the store. Marketing expenses are allocated 60% to invest in our current customer base, 30% in prospective customers that match our known profile, and 10% in creating greater awareness in the community. A key component of our marketing plan is to try to keep gross margins at or above 45%.

>> END EXAMPLE

Marketing Strategy

The marketing strategy section identifies the procedures that businesses intend to follow to meet their marketing objectives. The section also identifies the target market, positioning, marketing-mix strategies, and investment requirements. An example might be a company targeting 25- to 35-year-old females with a new personal care product that is positioned as a premium offer against the current market leader. If the brand is new, then the expenditure might be significant to support a wide range of marketing-mix strategies. Detailed marketing-mix strategies, including product, promotion, distribution, and pricing, will be discussed in subsequent chapters.

EXAMPLE **INTERIOR VIEWS LLC MARKETING STRATEGY**

Target Market Strategy—The target markets are separated into four segments: Country Club Women, Boomers in Transition, Professional Youngsters, and Home Builders. The primary marketing opportunity is selling to these well-defined and accessible target market segments that focus on investing discretionary income in these areas:

- **Country Club Women**—The most dominant segment of the four is composed of women in the age range of 35 to 50. They are married, have a combined income of greater than $80,000, own at least one home or condominium, and are socially active at and away from home. They are members of the Boise Country Club, the Downtown Athletic Club, the Junior League of Boise, AAUW, and/or the Doctor Wives

Auxiliary. They have discretionary income, and their home and how it looks is a priority. The appearance of where they live communicates who they are and what is important to them. This group represents the largest collection of "Martha Stewart Wannabees," with their profile echoing readers of *Martha Stewart Living* magazine, based on the current demographics described in the *Martha Stewart Living Media Kit*.

- **Boomers in Transition**—This group, typically ranging in age from 50 to 65, is going through a positive and planned life transition. The members of the group are changing homes (either building or moving) or remodeling due to empty nest syndrome, retirement plans, general downsizing desires, or to just get closer to the golf course. Their surprisingly high level of discretionary income is first spent on travel, with decorating their home a close second. The woman of the couple is the decision maker, and often does not always include the husband in the selection or purchase process.

- **Professional Youngsters**—Couples between the ages of 25 and 35 establishing their first "adult" household fall into this group. They both work, earn in excess of $50,000 annually, and now want to invest in their home. They seek to enjoy their home and communicate a "successful" image and message to their contemporaries. They buy big when they have received a promotion, a bonus, or an inheritance.

- **Home Builders**—People in the building process, typically ranging in age from 40 to 60, are prime candidates for Interior Views.

Messaging—Interior Views can help you create the personalized and unique vision you have for your home, with the best local source for fabric selection and price, customer-oriented design services, and a variety of other home accessory and furniture products. Revive your home today!

Table 10.6 Target Market Messaging

Country Club Women	Make your home new again
Boomers in Transition	It's time for a new look
Professional Youngsters	It's your first home—make it yours
Home Builders	Presentation is everything

Branding—Our name is our brand. "Interior Views" represents our mission of celebrating the home through the color and texture of fabric. The brand invokes the fact that the home should be a unique and personalized expression of the person living there. The home is a "view" of the home's owner. The word "view" also evokes the vision of what a homeowner wants their home to be. In addition to our name, our logo reflects the architectural quality of the work that we do. Our products are more than just decoration; they enhance and reflect the home itself.

Objectives and Strategies—The single objective is to position Interior Views as the premier source for home decorator fabrics in the Greater Boise area, commanding a majority of the market share within three years. The marketing strategy will seek to first create customer awareness regarding the products and services offered, develop that customer base, establish connections with targeted markets, and work toward building customer loyalty and referrals. Interior Views's four main marketing strategies are as follows:

- Increased awareness and image
- Leveraging existing customer base
- Cross selling
- New home construction promotion

Marketing Mix—Our marketing mix is composed of these approaches to pricing, distribution, advertising and promotion, and customer service.

- **Pricing**—A keystone pricing formula plus $3.00 will be applied for most fabrics. The goal is to have price points within 5% of the list price of Calico Corners's retail prices. This insures competitive pricing and strong margins.
- **Distribution**—All product is distributed through the retail store. The store does receive phone orders from established customers and we will be developing a Web site.
- **Advertising and Promotion**—The most successful advertising has been through the *Boise Herald* and through ads on *Martha Stewart* and *Interior Motives* television shows. The quarterly newsletter has also proven to be an excellent method to connect with the existing customer base, now with a mailing list of 4,300 people.
- **Customer Service**—Excellent, personalized, fun, one-of-a-kind customer service is essential. This is perhaps the only attribute that cannot be duplicated by any competitor.
- **Product Marketing**—Our products enable our customers to experience support, gather ideas and options, and accomplish their decorating goals. They will be able to create a look that is truly unique to their home. They will not be able to do this in the same way through any other resource.
- **Pricing**—Product pricing is based on offering high value to our customers compared to most price points in the market. Value is determined based on the best quality available, convenience, and timeliness in acquiring the product. We will consistently be below the price points offered through interior designers and consistently above prices offered through the warehouse/seconds retail stores, but we will offer better quality and selection.

- **Promotion**—Our most successful advertising and promotion in the past has been through the following:

  - **Newspaper Advertisements**—*Boise Herald*
  - **Television Advertisements**—*Martha Stewart* and *Interior Motives* television shows
  - **Quarterly Newsletter and Postcard**—A direct-mail, 4-page newsletter distributed to the customer mailing list generated from people completing the "register" sign up in the store. The mailing list now totals more than 4,300 people.
  - **In Store Classes**—"How-to" classes, most of which are free, have been successful because of the traffic and sales they generate after the class. Typically 90 minutes in length and most held on Saturday, these are the most popular classes.

- **Advertising**—Expand newspaper advertisements to surrounding towns, and buy two half-page ads every month. Continue television ads.
- **Public Relations**—Our public relations plan is to pitch a twice-monthly column in the "Home" section of the local paper, covering our in-store classes, with profiles of our customers and their redecorated rooms. Readers will see how our classes directly relate to individual decorating projects.
- **Direct Marketing**—Improve the quality of the newsletter, increase the number of one-time customers who sign up for it, and offer an email-newsletter option to catch the more tech-savvy customers.
- **Web Plan**—Over 1,000 fabrics are available on the floor at any time with more than 8,000 sample fabrics for custom orders. The goal of this Web plan is to extend the reach of the store to others outside the area and add to the revenue base. Interior Views currently has a Web site but has not given it the attention or focus needed to assess its marketing potential. The site offers basic functions and we consider it to be a crude version of what we can imagine it will become through a site redesign that will produce revenue and enhance the image of the business. Market research indicates a specific and growing need in the area for the products and services Interior Views offers in the market it serves and there are indications that Web sales will play an increasing role in connecting customers with sellers. The most significant challenge is that the core target customer, women between the ages of 35 and 50, are some of the least likely of groups to shop on the Web. Shopping for decorator fabric presents an additional challenge. The online marketing objective is to actively support continued growth and profitability of Interior Views through effective implementation of the strategy. The online marketing and sales strategy will be based on a cost effective approach to reach additional customers over the Web to generate attention and revenue for the business. The Web target groups will include the more Web-savvy younger customer base that the store currently serves (women between the ages of 25 and 35) and out-of-area potential customers that are already shopping on the Web for the products Interior Views offers. The Web site will

focus on its selection, competitive pricing, and customer service to differentiate itself among other Internet options.

- **Web site Goals**—Our Web site will generate revenue through initiating product sales to the targeted audience that we would not have realized through the retail store. It will be measured based on revenue generated each month compared to our stated objective. On a secondary basis, we will also measure and track traffic to the site and document what activities that traffic contributes to the other objectives of the site, including sales leads and information dissemination.
- **Objectives**—Increase revenues through Web-based sales by $2,400 per month with a 5% growth rate thereafter. Enhance "information channels" with the established customer base to provide additional options to receive information from the store. Meet the needs of customers outside the immediate serving area through Web accessibility.
- **Web Site Marketing Strategy**—Our Web site strategy will be to reach these key groups listed in order of importance based on their expected use and purchases from the site.

1. **Professional Youngsters**—Expected to be the most likely of the targeted segments to use this resource because of their relatively high Internet use compared to the other segments. This group should offer the greatest online revenue opportunity.
2. **Outsiders**—Composed of people outside the area with Internet access that have come in contact with the physical store or learned of it though a referral or promotion. This group, most commonly located in rural areas of the Western U.S. and Hawaii, are expected to be a small but faithful sector of buyers.
3. **Online Fabric Shoppers**—Most often find the site through search engines and these online decorator fabric shoppers are browsing multiple sites for a best buy or access to discontinued and hard-to-find fabric. They hold potential, but are typically the most work for the lowest return.
4. **Internet Learners**—Represents all of the targeted segments that are just beginning to become familiar with the site and will increase their use of the Internet over time. Revenue expectations from this group are low at this point and it is viewed as an investment in the future.

Three Web strategies have been developed:

Strategy #1—Increasing Awareness and Image
Informing those not yet aware of what Interior Views offers.

- Search engine presence
- Leveraging the newsletter and mailing programs

Strategy #2—Leveraging Existing Internet-Savvy Customers
Our best sales in the future will come from our current customer base.

- Newsletter information
- Web-only promotions

Strategy #3—Upselling and Cross-selling Activities
Increasing the average dollar amount per transaction.

- Additional and complementary fabric
- Other product sales:
  - Additional sales of trims, notions, and accessories
  - Promoting sales of furniture

Service—The first goal is to recognize everyone as they come into the store. If the person is a repeat customer, he or she is referred to by name. If he or she is a new customer, the person is asked, "How did you hear about us?" Help is always available and never invasive. The store is staffed to be able to dedicate time and energy to customers that want assistance when they need it. The store is designed so a customer can sit as long as he or she wants to look at books, fabric samples, and review the resources in the store. The customer's children are also welcome, with a television, VCR, and toys available in the children's area in clear view of the resource center. We provide service in a way that no other competitive retail store can touch. It is one of our greatest assets and points of differentiation. Insight, ideas, inspiration, and fun are the goals. Repeat, high-dollar purchases from loyal customers is the desired end product.

Implementation Schedule—Table 10.7 identifies the key activities that are critical to our marketing plan. It is important to accomplish each one on time and on budget.

>> END EXAMPLE

Measurement and Controls

The measuring and control section identifies the process to monitor achievement toward attaining the marketing objectives. The objectives are attained through successful implementation of the marketing strategies. Measuring and controlling considers both financial and nonfinancial factors. Underperforming products and services can be identified and necessary actions taken in context to overall marketing objectives. Information can be collected and processed through market intelligence systems to address a wide range of issues, from customer satisfaction to loyalty. Operational control, considering results with respect to the stated marketing plan or marketing program, and strategic control, considering the appropriateness of overall strategies based on internal and external conditions, should be addressed in this section.

EXAMPLE **INTERIOR VIEWS LLC MEASUREMENT AND CONTROLS**

Controls—The following will enable us to keep on track. If we fail in any of these areas, we will need to reevaluate our business model:

- Gross margins at or above 45%
- Month-to-month annual comparisons indicate an increase of 20% or greater
- Do not depend on the credit line to meet cash requirements
- Continue to pay down the credit line at a minimum of $24,000 per year
- Retain customers to generate repeat purchases and referrals
- Generate average sales in excess of $1,000 per business day

Table 10.7 Milestones

Marketing Activity	Start Date	End Date	Budget	Manager
Marketing Budget			$20,000	Tara
Television Ads	February 1	February 20	$ 3,000	Julie
Newspaper Ads	March 15	April 15	$ 1,000	Julie
Newsletter/Postcard	May 1	May 21	$ 3,000	Kandi
Special Event	June 10	June 10	$ 700	Julie
Printed Promotional Materials	July 13	July 26	$ 2,000	Kandi
Web Marketing/Support	August 1	August 30	$ 2,000	Pat
Public Relations	August 15	August 15	$ 300	Julie
Newsletter/Postcard	September 13	October 1	$ 3,000	Kandi
Promotional Events	Ongoing		$ 2,000	Kandi
Web Site Expenses	Ongoing		$ 3,000	Pat

Implementation—We will manage implementation by having a weekly milestones meeting with the entire staff to make sure that we are on track with our milestones and readjust our goals as we gather new data. Once a quarter, we will review this marketing plan to ensure that we stay focused on our marketing strategy and that we are not distracted by opportunities simply because they are different than what we are currently pursuing.

Market Research—The staff notes customer responses to the "How did you hear about us?" question. We attempt to correlate that with our advertising and promotional activities and referral-generation programs. The store suggestion box is another method to gain additional information from customers. Some of the most productive questions are as follows:

- What suggestion do you have to improve the store?
- Why did you visit the store today?
- What other products or services would you like to have available in the store?

We continually shop other stores. We visit each store in our market at least once each quarter for competitive information, we visit stores in the Seattle and Portland markets for merchandising and buying insight, and we subscribe to every catalog we know that has decorator fabrics as any part of their product line.

Contingency Planning
- **Difficulties and Risks**
  - Slow sales resulting in less-than-projected cash flow
  - Unexpected and excessive cost increases compared to the forecasted sales
  - Overly aggressive and debilitating actions by competitors
  - A parallel entry by a new competitor

- **Worst Case Risks Might Include**
  - Determining the business cannot support itself on an ongoing basis
  - Having to liquidate the inventory to pay back the bank loan
  - Locating a tenant to occupy the leased space for the duration of the five year lease
  - Losing the assets of the investors used for collateral
  - Dealing with the financial, business, and personal devastation of the store's failure

CRM Plans—Our best sales in the future will come from our current customer base. In order to build this customer base, we need to provide exceptional customer service when customers visit the store, have regular follow-up correspondence to thank them for their business (as well as to notify them of special promotions, etc.), and to provide personal shopper support so that each visit to the store meets their needs. In order to keep track of these activities, we will need to create a spreadsheet showing follow-up correspondence with customers and what, if any, feedback we have received from them. At least quarterly, we will plan to meet and discuss if we are, in fact, retaining our current customers and whether that base has grown, or what changes may need to be made.

SOURCE: Adapted from a sample plan provided by and copyrighted by Palo Alto Software, Inc. This plan was created using Marketing Plan Pro®.

>> END EXAMPLE

EXAMPLE   MARKETING PLAN

Bombardier Flexjet, Bombardier Aerospace fractional jet ownership activity, and Bombardier Skyjet, online booking service, created a strategic marketing agreement with Ultimate Resorts, a destination resort service. Each has named the other the "official" service for their businesses. The marketing plan application is for each business to increase access to the other's customers.[3]

PHOTO: Dragan Trifunovic

>> END EXAMPLE

▼**Visual** Summary

Chapter 10 Summary

By building on explaining, creating, and strategizing fundamental aspects of marketing, this chapter provided a structure to develop a marketing plan. The relationship between the business plan and marketing plan were discussed. A business plan is different from individual department plans, such as those for marketing or finance. A business plan identifies responsibilities of general management as they pertain to each functional area and identifies the capital requirements to manage each area. The marketing plan outlines actions that are intended to communicate value, generate interest, and persuade target customers to purchase specific products or services. The marketing plan consists of six basic sections:

- Executive Summary
- Company Description, Purpose, and Goals
- Marketing Situation
- Objectives and Forecasting
- Marketing Strategy
- Measurement and Controls

The most successful marketing plans meet several criteria:

- The plan is realistic and achievable.
- The plan can be measured.
- The plan has committed organizational resources for implementation.
- The plan requirements are clear.

Business Plan pp. 107–108

defining

A business plan is a document that defines the objectives of a business, especially in regard to finance, marketing, and operations.

Marketing Plan pp. 108–117

outlining

A marketing plan is a document that typically is part of the business plan. It outlines the marketing objectives, strategy, and tactical executions for the marketing portion of the business plan.

Marketing Strategy pp. 114–116

overall

The total number of marketing plans are placed together to create the overall marketing program of a business.

Capstone **Exercise** p. 119

▼ **Chapter** Key Terms

Business Plan (pp. 107–108)

Business plan *is a written document that defines the operational and financial objectives of a business over a particular time, and how the business plans to accomplish those objectives.* (p. 107)
Example: Business Plan (p. 108)

Marketing Plan (pp. 108–117)

Marketing plan *is a document that includes an assessment of the marketing situation, marketing objectives, marketing strategy, and marketing initiatives.* (p. 108) **Example: Interior Views LLC Executive Summary** (p. 109) **Example: Marketing Plan** (p. 117)

Key Term (p. 108)

Marketing program is a consolidated plan of all individual marketing plans. **(p. 108)**

▼ **Capstone** Exercise

This chapter brings you through the sections and content that are needed to put together a good marketing plan.

How does a business identify the information to include in the marketing plan? It is a complicated task to conduct the necessary research in order to create the plan. This exercise will provide you with some ideas on how to identify the data to complete the Marketing Strategy section.

The question "Who is my target customer?" drives this section. How do you identify information about your potential customers?

(If you are doing Application Exercise 2 in this chapter, you can use the following sources to complete that exercise.)

There are many places you can obtain demographic information. For this exercise, however, here are two particularly useful resources to better understand your potential market:

http://www.claritas.com/MyBestSegments/Default.jsp?ID=20
http://quickfacts.census.gov/qfd/index.html

Use either your school or home zip code and try to understand the different segments in that area.

Using this information, write a sample marketing strategy for either the case example, Interior Views LLC, or another business.

▼ **Application** Exercises

Complete the following exercises:

1. Discuss the three types of financial statements included in a business plan.

2. Identify the six parts of a marketing plan and create a sample plan for the Apple iPod.

3. Compare and contrast a marketing plan with a business plan.

Part 1 Explaining (Chapters 1, 2, 3, 4)
Part 2 Creating (Chapters 5, 6, 7, 8)
Part 3 Strategizing (Chapters 9, 10)

Part 4 Managing (Chapters 11, 12, 13, 14, 15)
Part 5 Integrating (Chapters 16, 17)

chapter 11

Product and Service Strategies

Chapter Overview The previous chapter explained how companies select target customers, position their brands, and construct a marketing plan. This chapter discusses how firms implement their marketing plan through product and service strategies. This effort involves effective management of new product development, a product portfolio, and the product life cycle.

 ## Chapter **Outline**

Objective 1. What are products and services? What are their categories?

Objective 2. How do firms manage all of their products and services? What are the steps in the best development process for new products?

Objective 3. What is the product life cycle, and how is it used?

PRODUCTS AND SERVICES (pp. 121–126)

▼ **DEFINED** **Products** *are items consumed for personal or business use.* **Services** *are activities that deliver benefits to consumers or businessess.*

Products and Services

In the United States, tens of thousands of new products are introduced every year: shampoos, video games, soups, T-shirts, credit cards, and home security systems, to name just a few. Every product is defined by a set of **attributes** that include its features, functions, benefits, and uses. For example, the Dyson DC07 vacuum cleaner has a brush control (a feature) that deactivates its brushes at the touch of a button (a function). This feature helps protect delicate rugs (a benefit) when vacuuming carpets and other floor surfaces (a product use). The following are other examples of product attributes: product design (including visual appearance and ease of use), brand name, level of quality and dependability, logos or identifiers, packaging, and warranty.

The basic purpose of a product is to deliver benefits to consumers. **Benefits** define a product's utility, or what that product *does* for a customer. When choosing between two or more products, consumers evaluate the attributes and benefits of each. They select the product that offers them the maximum set of benefits.

The term "product" is often used as an umbrella term to refer to both goods and services. According to the Department of State, services produced by private industry accounted for 67.8% of the U.S. gross domestic product in 2006.[1] Products can be thought of as falling on a continuum, from pure goods (for example, a hairbrush) to pure services (for example, a haircut). Most products are neither purely goods nor purely services, but a blend of both. Products that appear on the surface to be pure goods usually contain services, like the lifetime warranty on a Craftsman hammer. And services are often associated with goods, such as souvenir T-shirts at a Coldplay concert.

Four ways in which services differ from physical goods are as follows:

- **Intangibility**—A service cannot be perceived by the five senses before it is purchased and delivered.
- **Inseparability**—A service cannot be separated from whomever is providing the service. It must be bought, and then produced and used simultaneously.
- **Variability**—Service quality is sometimes inconsistent because it depends on factors that are difficult to control. For instance, the skill of the people providing the service can vary.
- **Perishability**—A service cannot be stored for later use. Once it is actually produced, it must be immediately consumed, or its value perishes forever.[2]

Products and Services

All parts of the marketing mix are important, but a sound product strategy is essential. It is through the sale and use of products or services that benefits are delivered to customers. Product strategy refers to all decisions that have an impact on a firm's product offerings, while service strategy refers to decisions about a company's services.

As an example of innovation Nintendo's Wii is the fastest-selling video game system in history. At a time when competitive consoles were focusing on faster gameplay and more detailed graphics, Nintendo designers added a revolutionary level of physical interaction between players and games. The secret is a handheld controller that resembles a TV remote but with fewer buttons. Built-in motion sensors translate players' physical movements into virtual ones. The controller can be swung like a tennis racket or turned like a steering wheel. The simplicity of the Wii and its playability make it popular with all age groups. Residents at senior centers around the United States compete in nationwide Wii bowling tournaments. According to Amazon.com, during the 2007 holiday season, the Wii sold at the rate of 1 every 17 seconds while the units were in stock.[3] **PHOTO:** © Aaron Harris / AP Wide World

Successful companies spend a large amount of time and effort on product management because it presents a great opportunity to grow sales, improve margins, and increase customer satisfaction. How should products be developed? What attributes and benefits should they have? Will they need to fit into a larger portfolio (or collection) of other products? What marketing strategies should be employed, based on product type? The answers to questions such as these compose a product strategy.

Levels of Product

Marketers recognize that consumers buy products for a variety of reasons and distinguish between various **levels of a product** (also called layers). At the most basic level, all sodas quench thirst. Beverage brands such as Pepsi or Mountain Dew add a level of differentiation to their products through unique combinations of color, flavor, sweetness, carbonation, packaging, and brand image. Products can be viewed on three levels[4]:

- **Core benefits**—The fundamental product benefits that the customer is buying. For instance, people buy cars to have a means of transportation.
- **Actual product**—The combination of tangible and intangible attributes that delivers the core benefits. Each automobile has a particular combination of attributes, such as horsepower and fuel economy, that determine its acceleration and cost of ownership. For some owners, the vehicle brand may also be a status symbol, for example, BMW or Lexus, and provide emotional rewards in addition to functional ones.
- **Augmented product**—Additional services or benefits that enhance the ownership of the actual product. For example, new vehicle purchases can also secure financing or extended warranties.

Looking beyond the core level of a product may create an opportunity to compensate for a product deficiency or to add a product benefit. Consider the case of Kia automobiles. To address concerns about its quality among U.S. consumers, Kia augmented its product by offering a 10-year/100,000-mile power train warranty. When all products in a category have similar core benefits, the appeal of one can also be enhanced by differentiating it at the actual or augmented level.

EXAMPLE   LEVELS OF A PRODUCT

Dell manufactures computers for the home and office. One of its most popular items is the laptop computer, used by many college students studying at home or away at school.

- At the core product level, a Dell laptop computer allows its user to manage information, enjoy personal entertainment, and connect to the Internet.

- Dimensions of the actual product include its color, screen size, weight, memory capacity, processor, software, and video card. The Dell brand image may also represent good value and quality to the laptop's owner.
- At the level of the augmented product, Dell offers financing, warranties, tech support, and customer service for every laptop that it sells.[5]

PHOTO: ArchMan

>> **END EXAMPLE**

Product Classifications

Marketers classify products based on customer behavior, as shown in Table 11.1. Depending on the classification, there are clear implications for shopping behavior, and thus marketing strategy. **Consumer products** are products that directly fulfill the desires of consumers and are not intended to assist in the manufacture of other products. **Convenience products**, such as potato chips or chewing gum, are bought frequently with little or no advanced planning. They usually have low prices and are widely distributed, so people can buy them easily when the mood strikes. For example, candy is usually prominently displayed near cash registers to motivate impulse purchases. Brand loyalty for convenience products is low, so manufacturers try to build awareness and preference through advertising and other forms of promotion, such as coupons.

Shopping products are more complex and are bought less frequently than convenience products. Consumers will spend more time cross-comparing product features and benefits, for example, product quality, brand name, and special features, before purchasing shopping products. Blue jeans or airline flights are examples of shopping products. Their prices are higher than convenience products and they are distributed through fewer locations, because customers are willing to make a greater effort to find them. Along with advertising, personal selling at point-of-sale plays a major role in promoting shopping products because salespeople are able to carefully explain product attributes and benefits.

Specialty products have unique characteristics, like highly prized brand names or one-of-a-kind features. Luxury cars, high-end designer clothes, and gourmet chocolates are some examples. Specialty products are purchased infrequently, and consumers are willing to expend more effort, search more locations, and spend more time to find exactly what they want. Because customers are willing to exert extra resources and effort, these items usually carry high prices and are distributed in far fewer locations. Promotional activities are highly targeted to particular audiences or lifestyles because mass communication would be far too inefficient.

Unsought products, such as life insurance or funeral planning, are items consumers often do not like to think about purchasing. People are generally unaware of brand names or specific product benefits. Purchases are made infrequently, often with a minimum amount of shopping effort. Price and distribution strategy will

Table 11.1 Consumer Product Classifications

Marketing Implications	Convenience Products	Shopping Products	Specialty Products	Unsought Products
Purchase frequency	Frequent	Less frequent	Infrequent	Infrequent
Amount of comparison and shopping effort	Minimal	Moderate	High	Minimal
Brand loyalty	Low	Higher	High	Low
Price	Low	Higher	High	Low to high
Distribution	Widespread	Fewer outlets	Few outlets	Low to high
Promotion	Mass promotion (for example, advertising, sampling) by manufacturer	Advertising and personal selling by manufacturer and retailer	Targeted promotion by manufacturer and retailer	Heavy advertising and personal selling by manufacturer and retailer
Examples	Chewing gum, potato chips, magazines	Blue jeans, TV sets, sofas	Luxury cars, deluxe vacations, fine crystal	Funerals, life insurance, retirement plans

vary, based on the type of product sold. Life insurance is relatively low priced and easily available, but funeral services are fairly expensive and available at only a few locations. Heavy promotion and personal selling are common marketing strategies, because consumers will not actively seek out these products and marketing messages must be aggressively taken to them.[6]

Industrial products sold to businesses and governments, like factory equipment or legal services, may also be classified. Types of products consumed by the business-to-business market are the following:

- **Equipment**—Factory buildings or copy machines are classified as equipment, and their marketing strategy frequently involves personal selling and product customization.
- **MRO products**—Items used for the maintenance, repair, and operation of a business are called MRO products. Because they are purchased frequently, prices for MRO products are kept as affordable as possible. Screws, nails, and washers are all MRO products.
- **Raw materials**—Raw materials include products such as lumber, wheat, or cotton. Offering lower prices and superior customer service are two common strategies for marketing raw materials.
- **Processed materials and services**—Firms also purchase processed materials and services, like fabric for clothing or copy-machine repair services.
- **Components**—These are finished products that organizations use to fabricate their own products. For example, liquid crystal displays are components in the manufacture of cell phones and computer monitors.[7]

EXAMPLE   PRODUCT CLASSIFICATIONS

Wrigley's chewing gum is perhaps the ultimate convenience product. The marketing strategy for Wrigley gum is an almost textbook example for how to market convenience products.

Chewing gum is purchased frequently, so every Wrigley product package is small and lightweight, making it easy to purchase and carry. On average, consumers spend 16 seconds shopping for confections such as candy or gum. Because consumers often buy on impulse with little or no product search, intensive distribution for these items is critical. Wrigley is committed to building strong relationships with its retailer partners, which helps to keep its products on shelves in locations as diverse as grocery stores, convenience stores, gas stations, drug stores, mass merchandisers, and wholesale clubs. Prices for Wrigley gum products are always affordable and competitive, so they are easily attainable for customers. Regarding promotion strategy, Wrigley follows the precept laid down by its founder William Wrigley Jr.: "Tell 'em quick, and tell 'em often." The company consistently invests in advertising and other promotional activities to support its brands. Traditional print and TV ads are combined with new media to reach on-the-go, tech-savvy consumers. By strengthening the equity of its brands, Wrigley is able to create primary demand for its gum and avoid excessive discounting.[8]

PHOTO: Pablo Eder

>> END EXAMPLE

New Product Development

For companies to remain vital, they must develop a steady stream of new products. Unfortunately, the failure rate for new products in the packaged goods sector is as high as 80%.[9] To improve these odds, a **new product development** process incorporates insight into a firm's customers and its environment. The steps involved in new product development follow and are illustrated in Figure 11.1:[10]

- **Idea generation**—Formulate an idea for a new product or service.
- **Idea screening**—Review the idea to ensure that it meets customer wants and company goals.
- **Concept development**—Concretely define the features and benefits of the new product.
- **Marketing strategy**—Create a marketing strategy for the product's introduction.
- **Business analysis**—Validate that the new product will meet all sales and profit objectives.
- **Concept testing**—Develop prototypes of the product for concept testing.
- **Commercialization**—Launch the new product in the marketplace.

Product concepts must pass through each stage of the process to move on to the next. At each step, ideas that fail to make the grade are weeded out. As a result, companies strive to generate a large number of ideas up front, knowing that only a few of those ideas will survive to commercialization. During the concept-development step, focus groups or other qualitative research techniques are often used to refine product ideas based on customer feedback. Before commercialization, a company may also invest in test marketing, during which actual products are introduced into select geographic areas. Test markets involve full-scale launch activities, including advertising, pricing, sampling, and distribution. Although costly, test markets help firms avoid more costly mistakes and can suggest ideas for product improvements.

EXAMPLE   NEW PRODUCT DEVELOPMENT

To broaden the appeal for their brand, marketers at Yoplait were looking to introduce a new product. At that time, yogurt was available in three styles: sundae-style (with fruit on the bottom), Swiss-style (with fruit mixed in), and plain. To uncover a new opportunity, Yoplait followed a classic product-development process:[11]

- **Idea generation**—According to market research, consumers liked Yoplait's flavor, but its smooth consistency led some to reject the brand. The Yoplait marketing team, along with its advertising agency, generated 26 new product ideas to address this problem.
- **Idea screening**—To pass through the screening stage, new product ideas had to meet specific sales volume objectives. Only 7 out of the original 26 ideas met those criteria.

FIGURE 11.1　Product Development Steps

	Idea generation	Idea screening	Concept development	Marketing strategy	Business analysis	Concept testing	Commercialization
Role of step in product development	Formulate ideas for new products	Review ideas with regard to customer wants and company goals	Define product features and benefits	Create a marketing strategy for product introduction	Validate that product will meet sales and profit objectives	Develop prototypes and test through market research	Product is advanced to formal launch stage
Requirements to advance to next step	Sufficiently large number of ideas that could survive idea screening	Idea appears to have market potential and is consistent with firm's capabilities and goals	Product has potential to be realized in concrete terms that deliver customer benefits	Marketing strategy can be crafted for intended customers including promotion, distribution, and pricing	Product cost, sales, and profitability meet the company's financial requirements	Confirmed product acceptance among intended customers	

- **Concept development**—The most promising idea was a new custard-style yogurt. The product needed to be firm and thick, yet smooth and creamy. Yoplait refined the product concept by experimenting with combinations of fat, fruit, color, and texture.
- **Marketing strategy**—Yoplait marketers were faced with several product strategy options:

  - Should the new product be positioned as a snack, meal substitute, or dessert?
  - Should it use the traditional conical Yoplait package?
  - Would a 4-oz or 6-oz serving be more appealing?
  - What should be the fat level (full or low)?

- **Product development**—Hundreds of prototypes were developed in search of the right combination of fruit, color, feel, and other attributes. Marketers sampled batches and used their judgment to narrow down the number of product concepts.
- **Test marketing**—Seven product concepts were tested in a minimarket test in Eau Claire/La Crosse, Wisconsin. Each concept used a different positioning and mix of package, size, and fat level. The "winning" alternative was positioned as a full-fat snack in a traditional 6-oz Yoplait package. Market test results suggested that the new product would add 36% incremental volume to the Yoplait line with a low risk of cannibalization.
- **Commercialization**—Based on favorable concept test results, Yoplait custard style yogurt was launched nationwide in six flavors.

As of 2007, sales for Yoplait products exceeded $1.1 billion. Yoplait custard style yogurt is now available in a dozen flavors, such as Key Lime Pie and Peaches 'N Cream.

PHOTO: David Davis

>> END EXAMPLE

Product-Development Steps— Roles and Requirements

There is no single, best way to encourage innovation and new ideas. Some firms establish new product teams that are multidisciplinary groups (including representatives from marketing, finance, manufacturing, and other departments) that meet on a regular basis to discuss new product ideas. Other companies maintain formal R&D (research and development) groups responsible for presenting new product concepts to brand managers.

Some new product ideas are **discontinuous innovations** that change our everyday lives in dramatic ways. Personal computers and portable phones are some examples. But innovations are not only revolutionary, breakthrough ideas. According to Peter Fisk, there are typically three kinds of new product ideas:[12]

- **Cosmetic change**—The most basic type of innovation, involving some evolutionary change to an existing product or service. New versions of existing automotive nameplates (such as Toyota Camry or Ford Escape) are introduced every few years, although they are rarely total product redesigns.
- **Context change**—When an existing product or service is taken into a new context or market. The context for the Bacardi Breezer was repositioned from a big bottle in the supermarket to a cool club drink.
- **Concept change**—This is an advanced innovation that changes everything. IKEA rethought home decoration and do-it-yourself shopping, and brought affordable Scandinavian design to the masses.

Ideas for new products come from almost anywhere. Mistakes can even be a source of innovation. In the 1970s, a researcher at 3M was trying to find a strong adhesive. His experiments led to an adhesive that was the opposite of strong; in fact, it was so weak that after sticking to a surface it could be easily removed. Years later, 3M came to understand the hidden potential in this discovery, and the product known as 3M Post-it Notes was born.

Another source of product innovation is packaging. One aspect is packaging design, which delights consumers by making products more attractive and easy to use. In 2006, CARGO Cosmetics won a DuPont Award for packaging for its ColorCards single-use portable eye shadows. Each ColorCard is the size of a credit card and employs a patented printing process that deposits a thin layer of eye shadow onto a 12-point decorated board. Marketers are also searching for ways to incorporate recyclable and environmentally safe ingredients into packages. The wedge-shaped Tetra Pak is designed to heat sauces in microwave ovens and is made with over 70% renewable materials.[13]

Product and Service Quality

Consumers will pay for a product (or service) only if it has an adequate level of quality at a fair price. But quality is in the eye of the beholder, and no two people define quality in exactly the same way. Quality is most frequently defined as the customer's overall reaction to the attributes of a product or service. For example, consider a trip to the dentist. For one patient, a quick visit with minimal discomfort is a "quality" experience, while another person will be satisfied only if their dentist also has an engaging, personable manner.

A product quality strategy, therefore, specifies a level of performance for each product attribute relative to the target market's perception of quality and value. Not every product needs to have superior performance on every attribute. In fact, few customers will pay for products that offer "the best of everything." Higher quality usually means higher costs, due to better engineering, superior materials, or a more highly trained workforce. A quality product for many people is one that excels on those few dimensions that are important to them, and is merely adequate on others. In this instance, they will give up some benefits for a lower price.

To implement a product and service quality strategy, marketers set performance level targets for attributes in alignment with customer wants and needs. Then, every activity of the firm, from research and development to customer service, is aligned to deliver those objectives. QFD (quality function deployment) is a method some companies use to translate customer needs into product and quality requirements. Process tools like Six Sigma use statistical analysis to continually reduce manufacturing defects. Firms compliant with ISO 9000 and ISO 9001 standards follow a strict set of rules governing internal processes from record keeping to annual reviews. A well-thought-out and well-executed product quality strategy will reduce costs, improve customer satisfaction, reduce customer defection, increase sales, and improve profitability.

Product Design

Although often overlooked, product design is a critical element of product strategy and has the potential to add differentiation and value. The term **product style** refers to the visual appearance of a product, but **product design** is a broader term that includes a product's style, its tactile appeal, and its usability. Consider two products with identical core benefits. The well-designed product is more pleasurable to look at, feels better in your hands, and is easier to use. The page you are currently reading was designed by graphic artists to make it legible and easy to understand.

Good design evokes positive feelings in the customer and is a source of strategic advantage. The OXO brand specializes in ergonomically designed tools for household tasks such as cooking, repairing, and gardening. Each OXO tool is designed to be visually appealing and comfortable to hold. Services as well as goods may be well-designed. Online marketers often apply experience design principles to improve their services. Amazon.com has redesigned the online buying experience by offering a "1-Click" feature that stores personal credit card information so returning customers can make quicker, easier purchases with a single mouse click.

EXAMPLE **PRODUCT DESIGN**

How can design be used to make an everyday product, such as a prescription bottle, more useful and attractive? After her grandmother accidentally took her grandfather's medication, designer Deborah Adler looked for a better way to design medicine bottles. Her ideas became the inspiration for the ClearRx prescription bottles offered exclusively through Target stores. Every ClearRx bottle has numerous features to improve the way medicine is used and stored:[14]

- An easy-to-read label with large type
- A color-coded ID ring with a color for each family member
- A top label with the name of the drug clearly printed for easy identification in case the bottle is stored in a drawer
- A slide-in information card with important patient and drug information
- An oral syringe to make measuring liquid doses easier
- Free flavoring for liquid medicine, with flavors such as watermelon or bubble gum
- A free magnifier to make label reading easier

PHOTO: Elena Ray

>> **END EXAMPLE**

Product Portfolio (pp. 126–127)

 DEFINED A **product portfolio** (also called a **product mix**) is the collection of all products and services offered by a company.

 EXPLAINED

Product Portfolio

Most companies sell more than one kind of product or service. If a product is successful, a firm usually introduces additional variations on the basic product, or additional new products, into its product portfolio. When a firm targets multiple customer segments, it may also need to offer a range of products tailored for each target group.

A company's product portfolio includes all of the brands, subbrands, and varieties of products or services that it offers. The number of products in a portfolio can add up quickly, so managing them might become overwhelming. A product that is popular today could go out of fashion tomorrow. The strategic challenge is to keep the firm's product portfolio fresh and relevant in the marketplace.

 APPLIED

Product Portfolio

Portfolio management comprises all of the decisions, or strategic wagers, a company makes regarding its portfolio of current and future products. Managing the product portfolio is an important component of the marketing strategy because company resources are finite. Even the most successful firms have limits on the amount of time and money they can devote to any one product. Resource-investment decisions are made based on which products the company believes have greater, or lesser, potential in the marketplace. The company must choose which products to keep within, remove from, or add to the portfolio. Because the success or failure of any particular product is uncertain, the resulting set of investment decisions adds up to a firm's collective wagers, or "bets," on the future performance of the portfolio.

When discussing product portfolios, several terms are used. A **product line** is a group of closely related products. Table 11.2 is an example of Sony's U.S. product lines in the fall of 2008.

Some organizations employ a **full-line product strategy** by offering a wide range of product lines within a product portfolio. Proctor & Gamble sells a variety of household products in categories such as oral care, cleaning products, and child care. Other companies pursue a **limited-line product strategy**, and focus on one or a few product lines. The product portfolio is managed along three dimensions:[15]

- **Product mix width** refers to the number of product lines a company offers.
- **Product mix length** is the total number of products offered.
- **Product mix depth** is the number of versions of products within a line.

Table 11.2 Sony U.S. Product Portfolio, Fall 2008

PRODUCT CATEGORY

	Computers	Cameras and Camcorders	TV and Home Entertainment	MP3 and Portable Electronics	Movies and Music	Games
PRODUCT LINES	VAIO notebooks VAIO desktops Digital Home Disc burners Location Free mylo Internet devices Software and media	Cyber-shot digital cameras Alpha Digital SLR cameras Handycam camcorders Digital picture frames Photo printers Photo services	Televisions Home theatre systems Blu-ray Disc DVD players Home Entertainment Servers (HES) Home audio components Mini stereo systems Location Free	Walkman Video MP3 players Rolly Reader Digital Book Sony Ericsson Mobile phones GPS navigation Portable DVD and CD players Bluetooth devices Radios and boom boxes Headphones Voice recorders iPod accessories Car audio mylo Internet devices	DVD movies Blu-ray Disc Movies UMD videos for PSP Music	PlayStation systems PlayStation 3 PlayStation 2 PlayStation Portable (PSP)

These terms are helpful when thinking about ways to expand or contract a portfolio. A firm may decide to change the width of its product mix by adding or eliminating a product line. **Line extensions** are additions to an existing product line and are one way to increase the depth of a product line. Developed as a stand-alone product, the popular Swiffer cleaning brush has inspired a series of line extensions, including Swiffer SweeperVac, Swiffer WetJet, Swiffer Dusters, and Swiffer CarpetFlick. Another way to increase the depth of a line is to stretch it upward (or downward) by introducing products of superior (or lesser) quality or price. **Line expansions** occur when entirely new lines are added to a product mix. For example, Pepsi added the Naked Juice health-drink line to its beverage portfolio by acquiring the brand's parent company in 2007.

EXAMPLE   PRODUCT PORTFOLIO

The Hershey Company is the largest maker of chocolate and sugar confectionery products in North America. Although it is most famous for its Hershey bars and Kisses, the Hershey Company maintains a product mix of great width, length, and depth. Reese's, Almond Joy, Cadbury, Mounds, Twizzlers, Heath, and Jolly Rancher are just a sampling of its chocolate and confectionery brands. The Hershey premium product lines include Cacao Reserve chocolate bars, Joseph Schmidt handcrafted chocolate gifts, and Dagoba organic chocolate products. Ice Breakers mints and Bubble Yum gum are some of Hershey's refreshment product lines.[16]

PHOTO: Joseph

>> END EXAMPLE

When adding products to a portfolio, marketers should pay attention to the possibility of cannibalization, which occurs when a new product takes market share from an established product. Cannibalization is not necessarily to be avoided, but it has the potential to ruin a business if a new, less profitable product is an attractive substitute for an older, more profitable entry. It could even become necessary when an aging product needs to be replaced by a newer, fresher alternative due to changes in consumer tastes or technological innovation. In the late 1990s, Charles Schwab recognized a potential opportunity in the emerging online stock-trading business. It deliberately cannibalized its own traditional brokerage business by instituting a common price for both online and offline stock trades. By cannibalizing itself, within 6 months $51 billion in assets poured into Charles Schwab and the firm captured 42% of the online stock-trading market.[17]

Product Life Cycle (pp. 128–130)

▼ **DEFINED** *The* **product life cycle (PLC)** *is a model that describes the evolution of a product's sales and profits throughout its lifetime. The stages of the product life cycle are as follows: Introduction, Growth, Maturity, and Decline.*

Product Life Cycle

The popularity of a product evolves over time, growing and fading as consumer tastes change or as a newer, more desirable product is introduced in that product's place. The PLC assumes that products follow a common pattern of evolution through a series of life stages. The PLC is based on an analogy taken from the realm of biology, where organisms evolve in a predicable pattern. Although only a model, or picture, of how the real world operates, the PLC can still be valuable because it contains implications for marketing strategy at each stage of evolution. The four stages of the PLC are as follows:

- **Introduction stage**—During this stage, a new product is introduced to the marketplace. Sales volume increases as potential customers gain awareness of the product.

  - Highly innovative cell phones (like Apple's iPhone) will continue to be in the introduction stage for the near future as new products come to market with even more exciting features.

- **Growth stage**—Many products fail during the introductory phase of the PLC. Those gaining acceptance in the marketplace progress to the growth stage, where sales increase rapidly. For marketers, this is an exciting time, because the new product also becomes very profitable.

  - Plasma or LCD widescreen TV sets are currently in the growth stage of the PLC, with a greater range of brands and models on sale as demand for these items continues to grow.

- **Maturity stage**—At some point, markets become saturated. Customers are sated with products and all of their variations. At this point, the product has graduated to the maturity stage, where sales growth peaks and eventually flattens. Although a few first-time buyers are coming to market, most product sales are replacements for previous purchases.

  - For many years, the DVD player has been in the maturity stage of the PLC. Prices are now so affordable that DVD players are within the budget of the majority of U.S. consumers. Many purchases are sales made to replace older or broken products.

- **Decline stage**—Every product eventually reaches a decline stage where sales and profits fall. A product may go into decline for many reasons, including technological obsolescence, an erosion of brand equity, increased competition,

and changes in customer preferences. One product may fade away slowly and gracefully, while another vanishes abruptly.

- In the mass consumer market, VHS players are in decline due to technological advances like DVD players, laptops with video capability, and TiVo. Previously easy to purchase and rent, VHS tapes and players are now difficult to find as manufacturers scale back models and production.

The PLC is not fixed, unchangeable, and true for each and every marketing situation. The PLC is a model for how products generally behave, based on past experience. Each product is unique; it has its own set of customers, benefits, competitors, brand names, and other attributes. Any of these could shorten, lengthen, or change the shape of an individual product's life cycle.

| FIGURE 11.2 | Product Life Cycle |

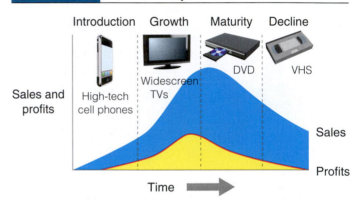

▼ **APPLIED**

Product Life Cycle

The PLC is a useful tool for marketers because it provides a clear, predictable framework for sales and profit levels over time. Marketers may take advantage of general rules or strategies that have been devised for each stage of the PLC. Although accurately estimating sales volume or profit at each stage can be difficult, and products may follow different life-cycle patterns, the PLC remains a useful source of ideas for marketing strategies throughout a product's lifetime.

Product Life Cycle and Marketing Strategies

The PLC model assumes that sales build through successive stages of the life cycle until a product reaches maturity, and that each stage has different implications for marketing mix strategy (product, pricing, placement, and promotion), as shown in Table 11.3. In contrast, profits are low (or negative) in the introduction stage, rise to a peak during growth, and then begin to decline over time, until they are essentially eliminated.

During introduction, the goal is to gain acceptance for the new product in the marketplace so companies will invest heavily in promotion and distribution. Prices may be high or low, depending on whether the firm has chosen to pursue a

Table 11.3 Stages of the Product Life Cycle

Marketing Implications	Introduction	Growth	Maturity	Decline
Sales	Low	Growing	Peak–Sales curve flattens out	Declining
Profit	Low or even negative	Rising	Falling	Low and eventually negative
Marketing goals	Build awareness for product category; encourage trial	Take advantage of growing demand; build brand preference	Maximize market share and profit	Eliminate product or reduce investment
Product	Basic	Add features and product line extensions	Diversify to attract new customers and extend life cycle	Reduce costs and slow-selling versions
Price	May be high or low	Lower	Low to meet competition	Low
Distribution	Selective, with few outlets	More outlets	Maximize number of outlets	Phase out unprofitable outlets
Promotion	Heavy expenditure to build targeted awareness	Mass communications to build general awareness	Mass communications to build brand preference	Reduce to minimum level

penetration strategy (holding price low to gain share) or a **skimming strategy** (keeping price high to maximize return).

Upon reaching the growth stage, the emphasis shifts to capitalizing on an expanding market opportunity. Competitors are attracted to the new profit opportunity and introduce their own variations of the successful product. Pioneer firms respond by attempting to build preference for their brands or by adding features to the basic product. Defending a high-market-share position during the growth stage can be expensive. Although investments in new product development or brand advertising may forfeit short-term profits, they can also leave a firm well-positioned to compete in the maturity stage.

As sales growth slows during the maturity stage, competitors struggle over a more finite pool of available customers. Downward pressure is exerted on profits as most firms are forced to invest in marketing incentives and/or to reduce prices. This is usually the longest stage because some products may remain in maturity for decades. Recognizing the challenges of the maturity stage, companies take steps to extend its duration as long as possible.

During the decline stage, some firms choose to simply pull out of the market, thus **divesting** themselves of a product. The declining product could be discontinued or sold outright to another firm. Others prefer licensing the brand name or product design to another company, allowing the original owners to maintain a degree of profitability without significant expense. LEGO licenses its brand name to the Clic Time Company, which manufactures clocks and watches using LEGO's distinctive colors and product design. **Harvesting** is a third option in which a firm continues to sell a product while gradually reducing, and eventually eliminating, all of its marketing investment.

Duration of the Product Life Cycle

Innovations take time to spread through the marketplace. Not every business or consumer is equally willing to try new things. **Diffusion of innovations** refers to the speed with which consumers and businesses adopt a particular product. Marketers segment populations into five groups with various degrees of openness toward innovations:

- **Innovators** (2.5% of population):
  The innovators are the most willing to adopt innovations. They are open-minded, adventurous, and tend to be younger, better educated, and more financially secure. They try new things just because they like having something new and unusual.
- **Early adopters** (13.5% of population):
  Early adopters are more socially aware than innovators and consider the prestige or social implications of being seen using a new product. They are media savvy, and more mainstream groups look to early adopters for cues as to what is the "next big thing."
- **Early majority** (34% of population):
  Members of the early majority do not want to be the first or the last to try a new product. Instead, they wait to see what excites the early adopters, and only then do they begin to buy a product. Once the early majority adopts a product, it is no longer a cutting-edge item, but has become part of the mainstream.
- **Late majority** (34% of population):
  Older and more conservative than other groups, the late majority will not adopt a product they consider to be too risky.

They will purchase something only if they consider it to be a necessity or when they are under some form of social pressure.

- **Laggards** (16% of population):
Laggards are heavily bound by tradition and are the last to adopt an innovation. By the time laggards take up a product, it may already have been rendered obsolete by another innovation.

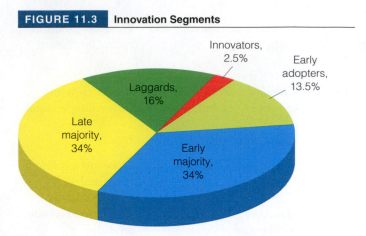

FIGURE 11.3 Innovation Segments

When launching a new product, marketers will focus their efforts on innovators and early adopters to get the diffusion process rolling. Depending on how readily these groups adopt the new product, the PLC may be quite short or very long.[18]

Although the average human lifetime is approximately 78 years, the estimated life cycle for a product or service is only 13 years.[19] Not every PLC is this short, however, because some products may be long lived. Colt pistols, Stetson hats, Vaseline emollient, and Pepsi-Cola have endured for more than 100 years. Marketers can extend a product's life span by doing the following:

- Promoting the product to new customers or markets
- Finding new uses or applications for the product
- Repositioning the product or brand
- Adding product features or benefits
- Offering new packages or sizes
- Introducing low-cost product variations and/or reducing price

Graphical representations of the PLC usually depict all four of its stages as roughly equal in duration. In reality, some stages might be longer or shorter than others. For example, when a product is a fad, it rapidly gains and then loses popularity in the marketplace, resulting in a PLC with a tall, narrow shape. The PLC graph for a style of product has a more wave-like appearance, as its popularity rises or falls over time. For instance, consider women's hemlines. Ankle-length skirts (or miniskirts) may be fashionable for a while, lose their appeal, and then become stylish again years later.

Limitations of the Product Life Cycle

One should keep in mind that the PLC is a model, or theory, about how products behave in the marketplace. Like most models or approximations of the real world, the PLC has limitations. In reality, the PLC is most applicable to classes of products (like the Blu-ray player category) and less predictive of behavior for individual products or brands (like Sony Blu-ray players). The PLC works best in modeling categories of product innovations, and not individual products. Determining the life stage for a class or category of products is fairly straightforward, because the sales and profits for all brands can be rolled up into a single metric. However, identifying the life stage for a particular brand can be more difficult. Although the overall product category may continue to hold appeal for consumers, not all brands may be equally preferred. Therefore, each one may perform differently.

It may also be difficult for marketers to identify the exact stage of their products in the life cycle because PLC curves come in many different shapes, for example, fads and styles. Your product's profit curve is rising, but does this mean it is progressing within the growth stage, or has it reached its peak of maturity? A "normal" life-cycle curve shows profits rising over a reasonable period of time, but in the case of a fad, sales and profits peak very quickly.

Perhaps the biggest controversy surrounding the PLC is that some say it stifles original marketing thought. If you believe a product is in decline, and you follow the suggestions of the PLC model completely, you will cut back R&D investment and promotion. Although the product may have had the potential to be resurrected, this disinvestment may simply force it into decline, as needed resources are pulled away. The PLC can serve as inspiration for marketing strategy, but it should never be the final word about what actions to take in each and every marketing situation.

▼ **Visual** Summary

Chapter 11 Summary

It is through the creation and management of products and services that a company delivers value to its customers. Portfolio management and new product development are two methods companies employ to keep their assortment of products and services relevant and vital. The product life cycle model suggests ways to improve performance at each stage in a product's life. Carefully formulated product and service strategies, when aligned with the marketing plan, will pave the way for the remaining elements of the marketing mix.

Products and Services pp. 121–126

classifications

Products are physical goods whereas services are non-physical. In other words when purchasing a car, you are purchasing a physical good and when purchasing a DVD on Netflix, you are purchasing the right to use the service and no title passes to the user. Examples of services would include a taxi cab ride or help with your income taxes. Examples of products would include the purchase of a Big Mac or textbooks for your classes. To facilitate the marketing process, marketers also classify products into different types to address different needs and wants. Thus, product classifications are developed that include convenience products, shopping goods, specialty goods, unsought goods. All of a companies products and services make up a company's portfolio.

Product Portfolio pp. 126–127

collection

Most companies have more than one product; the collection of all products and services offered by a company is the product portfolio. Companies may have dozens of products, so managing them can become overwhelming.

Product Life Cycle pp. 128–130

stages

After new products are commercialized (launched), they must be managed. One way to manage products is through the use of the product life cycle. The product life cycle assumes that products move through a series of stages from introduction to growth to maturity to decline. During each phase of the life cycle there are certain unique opportunities for marketers in terms of utilizing the marketing mix to provide the best product mix possible for the targeted market while at the same time looking at the potential income, margins, effects on other products, and potential success for a product or product line.

Capstone **Exercise** p. 133

▼Chapter Key Terms

Products and Services (pp. 121–126)

Products are items used or consumed for personal or business use. (p. 121)

Services are activities that deliver benefits to consumers or businesses. (p. 121)

Key Terms (pp. 121–126)

Actual product is the combination of tangible and intangible attributes that delivers the core benefits of the product. **(p. 122)**

Attributes are the unique characteristics of each product, including product features and options, product design, brand name, quality, logos, identifiers, packaging, and warranty. **(p. 121)**

Augmented product is additional services or benefits that enhance the ownership of the actual product. **(p. 122)**

Benefits, realized through product attributes, define the utility (or usefulness) of a product for the customer. **(p. 121)**

Business analysis is the process of validating that the new product will meet all sales and profit objectives. **(p. 124)**

Commercialization is the process of launching a new product in the marketplace. **(p. 124)**

Components are finished products companies employ to manufacture their own products, for example, microchips or engines. **(p. 123)**

Concept change is an advanced, breakthrough innovation that changes everything. **(p. 125)**

Concept development is the process of concretely defining the features and benefits of the new product. **(p. 124)**

Consumer products are products that directly fulfill the desires of consumers and are not intended to assist in the manufacture of other products. **(p. 122)**

Context change is when an existing product or service is taken into a new context or market. **(p. 125)**

Convenience products are products that are purchased frequently with little or no shopping effort, for example, grocery staples, paper products, and candy. **(p. 122)** **Example: Product Classifications (p. 123)**

Core benefits are the fundamental product benefits the customer receives from a product. **(p. 122)**

Cosmetic change is an evolutionary change to an existing product or service. **(p. 125)**

Discontinuous innovations are new product ideas that change our everyday lives in dramatic ways. **(p. 125)**

Equipment is a group of products used in the everyday operation of a business, for example, factories and copy machines. **(p. 123)**

Idea generation is the process of formulating an idea for a new product or service. **(p. 124)**

Idea screening is the process of reviewing a product idea to ensure that it meets customer wants and company goals. **(p. 124)**

Industrial products are products sold to business customers for their direct use or as inputs to the manufacture of other products. Classifications of industrial products include equipment, MRO products, raw materials, processed materials and services, and components. **(p. 123)**

Inseparability, in the context of a service, recognizes that a service cannot be separated from its means or manner of production. **(p. 121)**

Intangibility, in the context of a service, recognizes that a service cannot be perceived by the five senses (sight, hearing, touch, smell, or taste) before it is produced and consumed. **(p. 121)**

Marketing strategy is a statement of how a business intends to achieve its marketing objectives. **(p. 124)**

MRO products are products used in the maintenance, repair, and operation of a business, for example, nails, oil, or paint. **(p. 123)**

New product development is the process of creating, planning, testing, and commercializing products. **(p. 124)** **Example: New Product Development (p. 124)**

Levels of a product comprise all products. There are three levels—core benefits, actual product, and augmented product—and each additional level has the potential to add greater value for the customer. **(p. 122)** **Example: Levels of a Product (p. 122)**

Perishability, in the context of a service, recognizes that services cannot be stored for later use and must be consumed upon delivery. **(p. 121)**

Processed materials and services are products or services used in the production of finished products or services, for example, lumber, steel, or market research. **(p. 123)**

Product design is a product's style, tactile appeal, and usability. **(p. 126)** **Example: Product Design (p. 126)**

Product style is the visual and aesthetic appearance of a product. **(p. 126)**

Raw materials are unfinished products that are processed for use in the manufacture of a finished product, for example, wood, wheat, or iron ore. **(p. 123)**

Shopping products are products that are purchased with a moderate amount of shopping effort, for example, clothing, linens, housewares. **(p. 122)**

Specialty products are products with unique characteristics that are purchased with a high degree of shopping effort, for example, luxury items, vacations, and homes. **(p. 122)**

Test marketing is the process of developing prototypes of the product and using market research to evaluate customer acceptance. **(p. 125)**

Unsought products are products that consumers do not usually search for without an immediate problem or prompting, for example, life insurance, funerals, or legal services. **(p. 122)**

Variability, in the context of a service, recognizes that service quality may vary from experience to experience. **(p. 121)**

Product Portfolio (pp. 126–127)

*A **product portfolio** (also called a **product mix**) is the collection of all products and services offered by a company. (p. 126)*
Example: Product Portfolio (p. 127)

Key Terms (pp. 126–127)

Full-line product strategy is offering a wide range of product lines within a product portfolio. **(p. 126)**

Limited-line product strategy is focusing on one or a few product lines within a product portfolio. **(p. 126)**

Line expansions are the addition of entirely new product lines to a product mix. **(p. 127)**

Line extensions are additions to an existing product line that retains the currently utilized brand name. **(p. 127)**

Portfolio management comprises all of the decisions a company makes regarding its portfolio of current and future products. It involves deciding which products to add, keep, and remove from the overall product portfolio. **(p. 126)**

Product line is a group of closely related products. **(p. 126)** **Example: Product Portfolio (p. 127)**

Product mix depth is the number of versions of products within a product line. **(p. 126)**

Product mix length is the total number of products a company offers. **(p. 126)**

Product mix width is the number of product lines a company offers. **(p. 126)**

Product Life Cycle (pp. 128–130)

Product life cycle (PLC) *is the model that describes the evolution of a product's sales and profits throughout its lifetime. The stages of the product life cycle are as follows: Introduction, Growth, Maturity, and Decline. (p. 128)*

Key Terms (pp. 128–130)

Decline stage is the stage at which the demand for a product falls due to changes in customer preferences. Sales and profits eventually fall to zero. **(p. 128)**

Diffusion of innovations is a theory concerning how populations adopt innovations over time. **(p. 129)**

Divesting is the process of discontinuing the production and sale of a product. **(p. 129)**

Early adopters are consumers who are more socially aware than innovators and consider the prestige or social implications of being seen using a new product. **(p. 129)**

Early majority are middle-class consumers who do not want to be the first, or the last, to try a new product. They look to the early adopters for direction about product innovations. **(p. 129)**

Growth stage is the stage at which a product is rapidly adopted in the marketplace. Sales grow rapidly and profits peak. **(p. 128)**

Harvesting is the process of continuing to sell a product in spite of declining sales. **(p. 129)**

Innovators are consumers who are the most willing to adopt innovations. They tend to be younger, better educated, and more financially secure. **(p. 129)**

Introduction stage is the stage at which a new product is introduced to the marketplace. Sales begin to build, but profits remain low (or even negative). **(p. 128)**

Laggards are consumers who are heavily bound by tradition and are the last to adopt an innovation. **(p. 130)**

Late majority are older and conservative consumers who avoid products they consider to be too risky. They will purchase something only if they consider it to be a necessity or when they are under some form of social pressure. **(p. 129)**

Maturity stage is the stage at which the product has been purchased by most potential buyers and future sales are largely replacement purchases. Sales plateau and profits begin to fall. **(p. 128)**

Penetration strategy is the process of offering a product at a low price to maximize sales volume and market share. **(p. 129)**

Skimming strategy is the process of offering a product at a high price to maximize return. **(p. 129)**

▼Capstone Exercise

We will explore how different products are developed and product strategies are implemented. Go to http://www.caulksingles.com and study the site. As discussed, there are three kinds of new product ideas:

- Cosmetic change
- Context
- Concept change

Which one of the ideas best represents the idea of caulk singles? Could more than one idea fit? If yes, why?

Look at the Product Life Cycle Applied section on page 000. Because caulk singles are clearly a new kind of product, would you recommend using a **penetration strategy** or a **skimming pricing strategy**? Why? Please resist the temptation to peek ahead for the actual price for a caulk single; base your answer solely on your own analysis.

Clear design/packaging is a key factor in this product's future success. What are the benefits the marketing team will try to convey to the consumer? How would you advertise or promote this product when introducing it to the marketplace?

▼Application Exercises

Complete the following exercises:

1. Select a product or service that you enjoy using. What are its attributes and benefits? In what ways are these similar, or different, from the attributes and benefits of competitive products? Be prepared to discuss your product or service in class.

2. Visit the Web site of a company with many different products and product lines, for example, Proctor & Gamble, Johnson & Johnson, or Sony. How does this company organize its product portfolio? Find the firm's annual report and see if you can determine how each product line is performing in the marketplace. Which product lines should the company support with additional investment? Which, if any, should it drop?

3. In 2000, the U.S. census identified 4.2 million people as stay-at-home workers who conduct business out of their homes. This number was a 23% increase over 1990 and is apt to rise even more by the end of the decade. Try to put yourself "in the shoes" of a stay-at-home worker. What are his or her needs and wants? Can you think of at least three new product ideas that might be appropriate for this kind of customer? Be prepared to share your ideas in class.

4. Review the seven steps of new product development. You are the vice president of marketing at a brick manufacturing company. The CEO of the company has assigned you to come up with a type of brick other than the one traditionally used in building. Following the seven steps, come up with an idea for a new type of brick. Recognize that it will be difficult to complete Step 5, Business Analysis. You may assume that your new product idea is commercially feasible and will pass through the Business Analysis screen.

chapter 12

Part 1   Explaining (Chapters 1, 2, 3, 4)
Part 2   Creating (Chapters 5, 6, 7, 8)
Part 3   Strategizing (Chapters 9, 10)

Part 4   Managing (Chapters 11, 12, 13, 14, 15)
Part 5   Integrating (Chapters 16, 17)

Pricing Strategies

Chapter Overview The previous chapter addressed the product and service elements of the marketing mix. This chapter examines pricing and pricing strategies, which are critical to generating revenue and earning profits. It explains how to establish a price by understanding a product's value, its supply-and-demand curves, and its costs. General pricing practices are discussed, including the need to comply with legal requirements, price quotes, competitive bidding, and global pricing. The chapter concludes by exploring pricing strategies for specific marketing situations, such as the introduction of new products, online versus storefront pricing, auctions, portfolio pricing, and making price adjustments.

▼ Chapter **Outline**

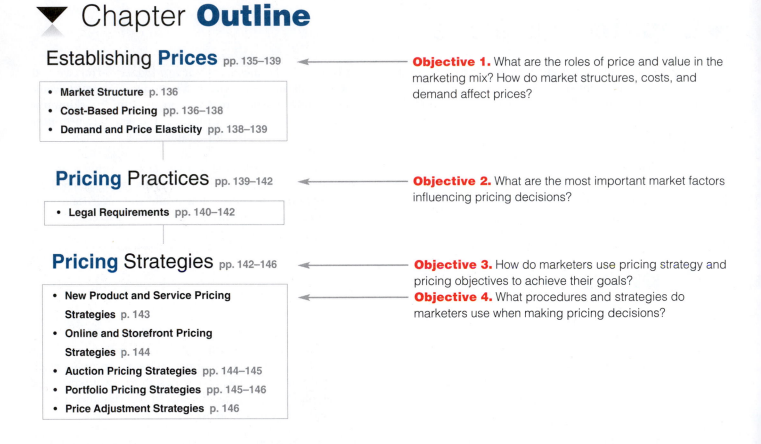

Objective 1. What are the roles of price and value in the marketing mix? How do market structures, costs, and demand affect prices?

Objective 2. What are the most important market factors influencing pricing decisions?

Objective 3. How do marketers use pricing strategy and pricing objectives to achieve their goals?

Objective 4. What procedures and strategies do marketers use when making pricing decisions?

ESTABLISHING PRICES (pp. 135–139)

> **DEFINED** *A **price** is the exchange value of a product or service in the marketplace.*

 EXPLAINED

Establishing Prices

Science fiction author Robert Heinlein is credited with popularizing the acronym TANSTAAFL, which stands for "There Ain't No Such Thing As A Free Lunch."[1] Whether you prefer to eat at Subway or Panera Bread, this saying holds true. Whenever you make a purchase, an exchange is taking place—you are giving up one thing in order to have another. A price is the formal expression of the value of this exchange.

Although consumers weigh a price carefully when making a purchase decision, the literal price is only part of a product's value. It is a product's perceived value that determines whether it will be purchased, not just its price. Value is a consumer's subjective evaluation of the ratio of the benefits of a product or service to its price. This concept is captured in a simple formula:

$$\text{Value} = \frac{\text{Benefits}}{\text{Price}}$$

A "good value" or a "good deal" is an instance where the ratio of product benefits to price is large. These benefits could be functional benefits, emotional benefits, or a combination of both. Your jacket may not only keep you dry in the rain (a functional benefit), but if it carries a prestigious brand name, it may also make you feel special when wearing it (an emotional benefit).

Price is the marketing mix variable that translates a product's or service's value into monetary terms. If a product is seen to have greater value, it should also have a higher price. The converse is also true, because marketers are forced to cut prices when items decline in perceived value.

Value is a relative concept, because customers will compare alternative products to find the one that offers the most benefits at the least cost. Because price is part of the value equation, whenever any competitor in a market raises (or lowers) its price, the value of every other product is affected. Beyond price, marketers add value for customers by improving the following:

- Product reliability
- Product performance
- Longevity
- Cost (both initial cost and lifetime cost)
- User and environmental safety
- Service (delivery reliability, speed, and flexibility)
- Superior aesthetics or design
- Prestige

Fair prices are those consumers perceive as offering good value and meeting personal and social norms. Unfair prices can evoke strong negative emotion. Companies must be careful to establish fair prices, which convey both value and fair dealing, or they risk alienating customers.

 **APPLIED**

Establishing Prices

Among the elements of the marketing mix, price is most closely linked with revenue. The activities of product development, promotion, and distribution are considered to be costs with, at best, only an indirect ability to encourage sales. For example, although a clever advertising campaign may encourage brand preference over the long term (and possibly an increase in sales), it is easier to understand how a price adjustment leads to a short-term change in revenue.

The Apple iPod has been an incredible success, with sales ranging from 50 to 60 million units per year. In addition to breakthrough design and innovative advertising, pricing has been a cornerstone of the iPod marketing strategy. Apple follows a price-lining strategy that positions newer versions of its players or those with the most advanced features at higher price points. For example, consider the following:

- The iPod Shuffle is the smallest and most portable version of the iPod, but has the least amount of storage. Its price begins at $49.
- The iPod Nano is larger than the Shuffle, but can hold more songs and play video. Its price starts at $149.
- The iPod Touch is Apple's newest music and video player with a price starting at $229. It responds to touch and movement, like Apple's iPhone.

By offering players at a range of prices, Apple has expanded the number of customers who can afford an iPod. An additional benefit is the opportunity to up-sell a consumer to a $149 Nano when that customer was originally interested in a $49 iPod Shuffle. Apple's profit stream does not end with the sale of its MP3 players. By selling individual songs on its iTunes Web site for only 99 cents, the company further extends its revenue stream over time and enhances the value of each iPod.[2]

PHOTO: Apple Computer, Inc.

Prices are dynamic and constantly changing, but they are a clear reflection of marketplace value in a free market system. They are affected by changes in economic conditions, such as recessions, in which the disposable incomes of consumers fall, or to the introduction of a new product by a competitor, which may offer customers a better value. Pricing must also be aligned with the firm's overall marketing strategy and the product's brand positioning. If the products of an upscale brand (like Gucci) are priced too low, are always on sale, or are a "deal," the company risks an erosion of its brand equity. Price can even be an indicator of quality or superiority. The **price–quality ratio** describes this relationship: Higher-priced products are assumed to have better quality. Lower-priced products are assumed to have lesser quality, regardless of actual product performance. Prices must be carefully calibrated with regard to pricing objectives, market structure, cost, and customer demand.

Market Structure

Market structure refers to the state of a market with respect to competition. Market structure defines the boundaries of a firm's pricing flexibility. In theory, an individual firm is either a price "maker" with the ability to set prices above competitors', or a price "taker" who must accept the marketplace price for its products or services. Economists recognize four types of market structures:

- **Monopoly**—A single firm is able to act as a price "maker," often due to product exclusivity (such as a patent) or high barriers to competitive entry. This gives a monopoly substantial **pricing power**, which is the ability to set a high price without a significant deterioration in market share. For example, patents on new drugs grant pharmaceutical companies monopoly power by restricting competition. Only the owner of a patent can sell the formulation of a drug, and any firms caught copying or simulating the patented product face legal sanctions. Although they are defended as essential for funding advanced drug research and development, monopolies resulting from patent protection can lead to prices almost 10 times above the competitive market price.
- **Oligopoly**—A small group of firms that shares pricing power through its collective ability to control prices, usually by restricting product supply. Cartels such as OPEC are the modern-day equivalent of oligopolies. For oligopolies to function, they depend on cooperation between member companies, who must agree to meet price and production targets. This can lead to a market price for the products of all member firms that is higher than any single company could achieve on its own.
- **Monopolistic competition**—A limited number of firms compete by offering products with varying degrees of differentiation. In this market structure, individual firms have a moderate ability to set higher prices, depending on customer demand for their specific brand. Nike, Reebok, and Adidas all make tennis shoes. But their products differ in terms of design, materials, and brand image. Each company may charge a price premium to the degree that its shoes are more appealing than its competitors'. At the same time, monopolistic competition cannot function like a monopoly because if prices are raised too high, customers will defect to competitors.
- **Pure competition**—A large number of producers sell mostly undifferentiated products, like wheat or soybeans. No particular brand of wheat or soybeans is preferred by consumers, so no producer has any appreciable pricing power. In purely competitive situations, companies usually deemphasize price as part of the marketing mix.

Due to globalization and the proliferation of product choices, today's marketplace is highly competitive. Evidence of this is the increasing failure of both start-up and long-standing businesses. Once-healthy and vibrant sectors like banks, automobiles, and airlines are under increasing pressure to reduce prices, cut costs, and consolidate operations. In response, some American firms have outsourced portions of their business, such as customer service or finance, to countries with lower labor costs. Economic cycles, globalization, the proliferation of product choices, and business failures lead to increased competition on the basis of price and downward pressure on profits. It is essential for marketing managers to aggressively manage costs in these situations.

Cost-Based Pricing

In addition to market structure, the cost to manufacture a product or deliver a service should be taken into account. Three common ways to group costs are as follows:

- **Fixed costs** (or **overhead**) are those costs associated with a product incurred regardless of any production or sales taking place.
- **Variable costs** are costs directly attributable to the production of a product or the delivery of a service.
- **Total cost** is the sum of fixed and variable costs.

For example, the Air Transport Association reports the Quarterly Cost Index on U.S. Passenger Airlines, which divides airline operating expenses into various categories. Variable costs such as fuel, food, labor, and marketing add up to about 85% of total operating cost. Insurance, landing fees, aircraft rents, and other miscellaneous items make up the remainder of the costs.[3]

To earn a profit, a firm must generate revenue that exceeds its total costs. The relationship between a company's profit, revenue, and costs is as follows:

$$\text{Profit} = \text{Revenue} - \text{Total Costs}$$

$$\underbrace{\text{Price} \times \text{Sales}}_{} \qquad \underbrace{\text{Fixed Cost} + \text{Variable Cost}}_{}$$

A product's **profit margin** is the difference between its price and total cost per unit. Because revenue is a function of sales volume times price per unit, improving the margin will also increase profitability. **Cost-based pricing** (or cost-oriented) approaches to pricing recognize the need to establish a price that offsets costs and results in a reasonable profit margin or rate of return.

A traditional cost-based method for setting margins is the **cost-plus pricing** approach, which adds a fixed amount to the cost of each item sufficient to earn a desired profit. The additional amount, or margin, added to each product is called a **markup** and is calculated as a percentage of unit variable cost. Although some people use the terms interchangeably, a markup is technically not the same thing as a margin. A markup determines a price based on product cost, while a margin is determined by the difference between the final price and unit cost. The following table compares margin and markup for a hypothetical product:[4]

Table 12.1 Relationship Between Margin and Markup

Price	Cost	Margin	Markup
$ 10.00	$ 9.00	10%	11%
$ 10.00	$ 7.50	25%	33%
$ 10.00	$ 6.67	33%	50%
$ 10.00	$ 5.00	50%	10%
$ 10.00	$ 4.00	60%	100%
$ 10.00	$ 3.33	67%	150%
$ 10.00	$ 2.50	75%	200%

Another cost-based technique for setting price is to calculate a product's **break-even point**, which is a projected price and sales volume where a company "breaks even," or earns revenue exactly equal to its total cost.

At the break-even point, profits are zero. If a firm can sell one additional unit beyond the break-even point, it will earn a profit equal to the margin on that product. Because each additional sale contributes to the bottom line, the gap between price and variable cost is also called a **contribution margin**. The formula used to calculate a break-even point (in units) is as follows:

$$\text{Break-Even Volume} = \frac{\text{Fixed Cost}}{\text{Price} - \text{Variable Cost}}$$

For instance, suppose a product sells for $50. If the product costs $10 per unit to manufacture, and the company's fixed costs are $60,000, then break-even volume is 1,500 units, or

$$1,500 \text{ units} = \frac{\$60,000}{\$50 - \$10}$$

Break-even analysis is helpful to marketers because it clarifies, for a given price, the minimum number of products a company must sell to stay in business. When performing a break-even analysis, marketers find it helpful to calculate the break-even formula at various price points. In the following graph, the firm's variable cost per unit is $5, fixed costs are $40,000, and price per unit is $10:

In this example, the break-even point is 8,000 units. It should be immediately apparent that any quantity to the left of the break-even point (below 8,000 units) will result in a net loss for the firm, because total cost will be greater than total revenue

FIGURE 12.1   The Break-even Formula at Various Price Points

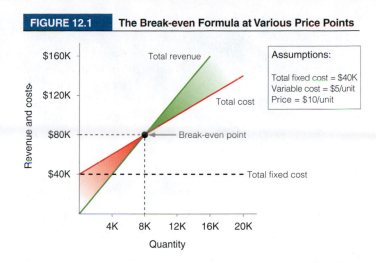

(represented by the red shaded area). Any sales volume above 8,000 units will be profitable (the green shaded area). Based on this information, the product price is adjusted upward or downward until a volume is reached that the marketing group believes is both achievable and profitable. A firm might use a rate of return on investment (such as 10% or 15% on total cost) or a target amount of profit as its criteria.

The main advantage to using cost-based pricing methods is that they are relatively easy to calculate. Once costs have been estimated, you simply determine the markup needed to earn a target amount of revenue (or offset fixed costs plus a satisfactory amount of profit). One drawback, however, is that this approach ignores customer demand for the product. It is based solely on cost and desired profit. If fixed or variable costs are too high relative to competition, then using a cost-based approach can lead to an uncompetitive price. If the products offered by competitors are comparable in terms of brand image and performance, a cost-based pricing method will dictate a price that is too high for the marketplace. Customers will not pay a higher price without added benefits. The marketing challenge then becomes how to find a way to make the product more attractive without adding cost, or to reduce fixed, variable, or total costs.

EXAMPLE   COST-BASED PRICING

Dr. Sarah Maxwell is an expert in the theory and practice of fair pricing. Two components of fairness are personal fairness and social fairness. Personal fairness is how people perceive that a price affects them personally. Social fairness is how people judge that a price is fair to society in general.

All price increases may be personally unfair to a degree, but the situation can be made worse, depending on how socially unfair they seem. Dr. Maxwell conducted an interesting study that asked two separate groups of people to consider two different imaginary pricing scenarios:

- The first group was told that a hardware store had been selling snow shovels for $15, but raised the price to $20 after a snowstorm. They were then asked to rate this action as completely fair, acceptable, unfair, and very unfair.

• For the second group, the scenario and questions were identical to the first, with the omission of any reference to a snowstorm.

When a storm was not mentioned, 69% of people in the second group found the price increase to be unfair, compared with 86% in the first group. Both groups perceived the price increase to be unfair, most likely due to the negative personal impact of paying a higher price (that is, personal fairness). But the second group also saw the price change as socially unfair, as evidenced by the 17% higher percentage who rated the store's action unfavorably. Raising prices to "take advantage" of a snowstorm was perceived as unfair both to individuals and to society.[5]

PHOTO: Fedor A. Sidorov

>> END EXAMPLE

Demand and Price Elasticity

Unless a company is a monopoly, it cannot set prices based solely on its own whims. Consumer preferences also must be factored into the pricing equation. A **demand curve** (or **demand schedule**) charts the projected sales for a product or service for any price customers are willing to pay. Each point along the curve represents the quantity demanded by consumers for a product at a given price. When plotted on a graph of quantity demanded versus price, a typical demand curve begins in the upper-left corner, and then slopes downward and to the right. This is because customers usually buy more of a product at lower prices than at higher ones.

FIGURE 12.2   The Demand Curve

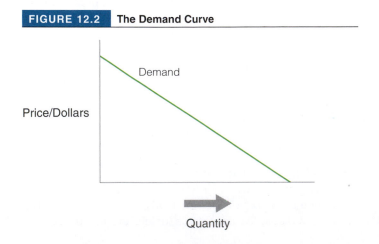

Using a break-even analysis, a marketer can estimate a target volume and price. The demand curve can then be employed as a quick validation of the feasibility of these assumptions. Are customers willing to purchase the target quantity at the desired price? If the price is too low, can it be changed without a substantial impact on sales? At first glance, the break-even price is sometimes below what a firm would like to charge to cover its fixed costs. Appropriate responses include reductions in fixed costs, variable costs, or tactics such as innovative advertising campaigns to enhance perceived product value.

Marketers may also attempt to stimulate customer demand for product categories or individual brands through nonprice methods. Developing improved versions of products or launching clever new advertising campaigns are just a couple of ways companies attempt to shift their demand curves upward, thereby maintaining higher prices.

EXAMPLE   DEMAND AND PRICE ELASTICITY

In 1993, the California Milk Processor Board (CPMB) decided that something needed to be done to turn around 15 consecutive years of falling milk sales. Although prices could be lowered to increase demand, this would be a short-term strategy at best and could threaten the survival of California's milk producers. Instead, the CPMB chose to use advertising to stabilize and reverse milk sales.

"Got Milk?" became the tagline for a memorable advertising campaign designed to stimulate demand for an entire category of products. Every ad was based on a single consumer insight: Milk is usually consumed along with food, and people care passionately about the product if it runs out while they are eating. Marquee TV ads included a game show contestant who eats a peanut butter sandwich but cannot give the winning answer because he has run out of milk.

The ad campaign achieved 90% awareness in California by 1995, aided by national news coverage. Tracking studies and sales figures from the California Department of Food and Agriculture showed that milk was being used more often. It may be quick and simple to lower prices to improve sales, but sometimes marketing techniques can shift the demand curve itself.[6]

PHOTO: Courtesy of Lowe Worldwide as agent for the National Fluid Milk Processor Promotion Board

>> END EXAMPLE

A product's **price elasticity** measures the percentage change in quantity demanded relative to a percentage change in price. Also called price elasticity of demand, this metric is helpful to marketers because it provides a guideline as to how much, or how little, a price should be increased or decreased. Elasticity can be measured at any point along the demand curve. The formula for estimating price elasticity is as follows:

$$\text{Price Elasticity} = \frac{\%\Delta \text{ Quantity}}{\%\Delta \text{ Price}}$$

Suppose demand falls by 6% when a price is increased by 2%. The price elasticity at this point along the demand curve is −3. This situation is said to be price **elastic** because the quantity is highly responsive to a change in price. Marketers consider lowering their prices when demand is elastic, because the relatively greater change in volume may lead to higher total profits. When elasticity is less than one, the situation is said to be price **inelastic**. Quantity demanded is largely unresponsive to a change in price. At inelastic points along the demand curve, marketers often increase prices and thus maximize profits. A monopoly has an inelastic demand curve, because it can raise prices with little fear that large numbers of customers will defect to other products.

By encouraging brand preference among their customers, some firms attempt to change the slope of their demand curves. Powerful brands are more price inelastic, allowing marketers to charge higher prices for moderately differentiated goods or services. For instance, a comparison of prices on Swivel.com from 2007 showed that a brand name 10 mg

tablet of a popular sleeping aid was $4.47, while generic versions of the identical drug averaged only $0.65.

Pricing Practices (pp. 139–142)

 DEFINED **Pricing practices** *are considerations (such as legal requirements or bidding practices) that must be taken into account when establishing a price for a product or service.*

▼ **EXPLAINED**
Pricing Practices

Establishing prices relies on an understanding of market structure, costs, and marketplace demand. Measuring price elasticity, in particular, requires data on customer demand at numerous price points. But it also requires marketers to consider other factors that may present constraints or opportunities for pricing strategy.

Marketers do not have total freedom when setting prices. But neither do they have to simply accept the market price for a product or service. Marketing can influence customer perceptions, and thereby affect prices. Products that are perceived as different and unique due to higher quality or a more exciting brand image often command higher prices.

A number of considerations to take into account when crafting a pricing strategy include legal requirements, the character of the competitive bidding process, and setting prices in a global marketing environment.

▼ **APPLIED**
Pricing Practices

Pricing practices are basically rules that marketers should follow when setting prices. Some of these, like legal requirements, restrict marketers' freedom of action. Others, like global pricing, allow marketers to maximize the effectiveness of their pricing strategies across national borders.

Implementing smart pricing practices and strategies represents a huge opportunity for marketers to improve the bottom line. In their book *Six Sigma Pricing* authors Manmohan Sodhi and Navdeep Sodhi estimate that well-managed pricing strategies add between 8% and 11% to operating profit, more than cost or sales volume (see Table 12.2).[7]

Table 12.2 Average Impact of 1% Improvement on Operating Profit		
Driver	**Compustat Companies**	**S&P 500 Companies**
Price management	11.1%	8.2%
Variable cost	7.8%	5.1%
Sales volume	3.3%	3.0%
Fixed costs	2.3%	2.0%

One of the more interesting aspects of pricing is its relationship to psychology. Beyond cost estimation, demand curves, and elasticity calculations, pricing strategy depends on how people make decisions. And this process is not always rational. For example, **odd-even pricing** is a practice that sets prices at fractional numbers instead of whole ones. An example would be when an item that is priced at $9.99 instead of $10.00. Logically, a price that is lower by one penny should make little difference, but research shows consumers will buy more of an item priced at $9.99 than $10.00.

Marketers also engage in **price bundling** to make two or more items appear more attractive at a single price than individually. A McDonald's value meal is a classic example of price bundling, where a sandwich, beverage, and fries are sold in a bundle. Computer manufacturers such as Dell and Gateway also sell computers with preinstalled devices, such as DVD drives along with preloaded software. In some instances, the price bundle offers a discount on the collected items. Another benefit for customers is the psychological effort they are saved in terms of product search and price evaluation.

Legal Requirements

The federal government, state governments, and private groups (like the Better Business Bureau) have taken an active interest in encouraging fair pricing practices. The goal of federal laws, state laws, and other guidelines is to promote fairness in pricing both for customers and for members of the distribution network. Marketers must keep one eye on their own strategic imperatives, for example, cost and marketplace demand, and the other eye on the legal requirements for fair pricing.

In terms of federal law, pricing is the most heavily regulated aspect of the marketing mix. **Antitrust law** is the catchall phrase for federal legislation meant to prohibit anticompetitive actions on the part of manufacturers, wholesalers, or resellers. The name for these laws dates back to the turn of the twentieth century, when industries like tobacco, oil, and steel were dominated by monopolies or oligopolies (also called "trusts"). A key assumption underlying this legislation is that actions on the part of private firms that lessen competition could force consumers, wholesalers, or resellers to pay unnecessarily inflated prices. The major U.S. antitrust laws are presented in Table 12.3.[8]

A violation of federal antitrust legislation can incur severe penalties. For example, individuals can be fined up to $350,000 and receive up to three years in prison for each offense under the Sherman Antitrust Act. Corporations can be fined up to $10 million for each offense, and fines can go even higher. Although the Clayton Act carries no criminal penalties, if found guilty of an infringement, a firm may be forced to pay triple damages as well as court and lawyer fees.

Types of unfair pricing activities prohibited by antitrust law are as follows:

- **Price fixing**—This occurs when two or more companies discuss prices in an effort to raise the market price for their products. Working together in this manner is also called collusion. Under the Sherman Antitrust Act, it is illegal to discuss prices with a competitor or even to mention prices in the competitor's presence, because this would reduce competition.
- **Price discrimination**—This occurs whenever a firm injures competition by charging different prices to different members of its distribution channel. Price discrimination that lessens competition in interstate commerce is illegal under both the Robinson-Patman Act and the Clayton Act. A marketer cannot offer a discount, rebate, coupon, or other benefit to one customer and not another, with a few exceptions. If a company has lower costs, a physically different product, or must adjust its price to meet competition, it is not considered to be guilty of price discrimination.
- **Predatory pricing**—When a firm sells its products at low prices to drive competitors out of the market, it is acting in a predatory manner. If the intention of an extremely low price is to bankrupt competitors and leave the low-priced firm as the sole survivor, this is considered to be a predatory strategy and is illegal under the Sherman Antitrust Act. An acceptable defense to these charges is that the firm has a more efficient cost structure that allows it to still earn a profit at much lower prices.

Antitrust cases may be brought against companies in one of three ways: by the Antitrust Division of the Department of Justice, by the Federal Trade Commission, or by private

Table 12.3 Summary of U.S. Antitrust Laws

Federal Legislation	Purpose of Legislation	Concerns
Sherman Antitrust Act of 1890	Make acts in restraint of trade illegal	• Price fixing • Bid fixing (rigging) • Monopolization (interstate)
Federal Trade Commission Act (FTC Act) of 1914	Establishes FTC in order to investigate unfair trade practices	• Price discrimination • Price fixing
Clayton Act of 1914	Outlaws unfair trade practices	• Price discrimination • Predatory pricing
Robinson-Patman Act of 1936	Outlaws price discrimination	• Price discrimination

parties against each other. Today, private firms initiate the majority of antitrust cases in an attempt to curtail what they perceive to be unfair pricing practices.

Price fixing is prohibited not only in the United States, but also in other countries. In 2002, the Hasbro toy company was found guilty of fixing prices on games such as Monopoly and on *Star Wars* merchandise. Hasbro was accused of forcing 10 of its distributors to enter price-fixing agreements. "These [price-fixing] agreements prevented the distributors from selling Hasbro toys and games below Hasbro's list price without permission," said a representative for Britain's Office of Fair Trading (OFT). As punishment, the OFT imposed its largest fine in history on the company—£4.95 million ($7.7 million).[9]

PHOTO: Gualbereto Becerra

>> END EXAMPLE

Other federal and state laws attempt to curtail **deceptive pricing**, which occurs when a price is meant to intentionally mislead or deceive customers. Deceptive pricing can take many forms. Perhaps the most well-known is **bait-and-switch pricing**. In this scenario, an unscrupulous marketer advertises a low price on a desirable product. When customers attempt to buy the advertised product, they discover it has "sold out," but that many higher-priced items just happen to be readily available. The law is that an advertised price must be a bona fide offer, or one made legitimately in good faith.

Some states have prohibited **loss-leader pricing** as an unfair sales act that harms consumers. Traditionally used as a form of **promotional pricing** by retailers such as grocery stores, loss-leading pricing involves selling items below cost to drive floor traffic. Laws restricting this kind of pricing are intended to protect smaller competitors whose cost structures do not allow them to conduct similar promotional activities.

Quotations, Competitive Bidding, and Negotiated Pricing

Every product and service has a price, whether it is sold to consumers or to businesses. A price offered by a business to a consumer is often called a **sticker price**, or an **MSRP** (**manufacturer's suggested retail price**). Prices for most consumer products are preestablished by the manufacturer or retailer. In some instances,

the seller may allow a customer to discuss a price, but in the vast majority of cases, this is not allowed. When purchasing paper towels, paint, or dog food, the average customer will accept the sticker price and not attempt to haggle.

In the business-to-business realm, the process for reaching a price acceptable to both buyer and seller is often complex. This is because businesses may need to acquire sophisticated and expensive products like buildings, machinery, or specialized components. Purchases are made by a group of employees instead of an individual and can take weeks, or even months. The purchasing process is usually initiated by a **request for quote** (**RFQ**), which specifies the characteristics of the product or service a company wants to purchase. A price **quotation** (or quote) is a supplier's response to an RFQ from a potential customer.

A customer may submit requests to multiple firms to compare quotes. In a **competitive bidding** process, each supplier receives an identical RFQ and is asked to submit a price quote. All bids are "blind," so communication between buyer and sellers remains strictly confidential. After all quotes have been received, they are reviewed. Each supplier is evaluated based on its ability to fulfill the terms of the RFQ at an acceptable price. All things being equal, the supplier that can meet the RFQ criteria at the lowest cost will be chosen. A good purchasing representative will consider not only cost, but also the reputation or track record of a supplier when making a final sourcing decision.

As part of the competitive bidding process, a company's purchasing department often engages in some degree of negotiation with suppliers. A **negotiated price** is the result of a back-and-forth discussion between a buyer and seller regarding the final price of a product or service. Purchasers attempt to trim costs from a bid to obtain a lower price, while sellers try to protect their profit margins. Price negotiation may occur face-to-face or online, through a variety of commercial Web portals. And negotiation is not limited to the business-to-business marketplace, because consumers may also negotiate prices. Negotiation is a common practice when buying a new car or home.

Global Pricing

It used to be that transportation expense and limited access to global communications kept pricing information fairly contained within national borders. The globalization of commerce and travel has led to consumers who are more aware of prices in multiple nations. And the Internet has made it simple to acquire a product or service from almost anywhere in the world. Almost every firm is affected, because although one firm may not engage in multinational operations, other firms can export their products into the firm's home market. Increased competition and downward pressure on prices are the result.

At the same time, there is also opportunity in the global market. Consumers differ from country to country. Brands are different. Products are different. The price of an item in one country could be more than twice as much as in another country. Marketers who recognize and act on market differences customize prices based on individual regional, national, or local characteristics. Prices should be set recognizing the product costs, customer demand, brand equity, and the power of distributors in each market.

As in the United States, legal requirements also impact global pricing strategies. Marketers must set prices, taking into account limitations imposed by possible quotas or tariffs. **Quotas** are limits on the amount of a product that can be imported into a country. Limiting product supply may create the opportunity to raise prices if the product is in high demand, but it also constrains revenue. A **tariff** is a schedule of duties (or fees) applied to goods and services from foreign countries. When a tariff is imposed on a product, the net effect is to increase the product's price, and marketers must take this into account. **Antidumping laws** in some countries are activated when the government perceives that a price has been set too low in an attempt to harm local manufacturers or producers. Quotas, tariffs, fines, and other penalties may result if a firm is found guilty of dumping.

Currency exchange rates specify the price of one currency in terms of the price of another. Currencies flow freely on the global capital market, and their values are constantly changing. Even though a marketer may have taken great care in setting the price for a product, a fluctuation in currency exchange may have the net effect of raising (or lowering) the product's price overnight. There is nothing a marketer can do to influence exchange rates, but when pricing opportunity (or risk) is presented due to a currency fluctuation, the marketer must act quickly.

Pricing Strategy (pp. 142–146)

 DEFINED A **pricing strategy** *identifies what a business will charge for its products or services.*

 EXPLAINED
Pricing Strategy

A pricing strategy includes all activities that convey and enhance the value of a purchase. As already discussed, a price must convey a product's value to customers. It also needs to be fair, or consumers will defect to competitors. There are dimensions to pricing strategy that go beyond the traditional notion of a "price" however. Each of the following is also an example of a pricing strategy:

- Offering a discount when a customer pays within 30 days
- Giving a new-car buyer a trade-in value for his or her old vehicle
- Earning points for purchases when using a retailer's credit card

None of these examples change the literal "price" of the product. The quoted or sticker price remains unchanged. But they all have an impact on the perceived value the customer is receiving and, as a result, are part of pricing strategy.

Pricing objectives are goals that keep marketing actions in alignment with overall business objectives. Any marketing strategy or tactic that influences price or perceived customer value should meet the firm's pricing objectives. Different pricing objectives include the following:

- **Profitability**—to maximize profit or to achieve a target profit level
- **Volume**—to maximize volume or market share
- **Meeting competition**—to remove price as a differentiator by matching competitor prices
- **Prestige**—to create an image of exclusiveness and quality by setting a high price

 APPLIED
Pricing Strategy

Should the price for a product be set above, equal to, or below its competition? When setting prices, marketers follow a stepwise process:

1. Develop pricing objectives.
2. Estimate demand.
3. Determine costs.
4. Evaluate the pricing environment.
5. Choose a pricing strategy.
6. Develop pricing tactics.

Steps 1 through 4 have already been discussed in this chapter. Step 5 involves choosing the pricing strategy that is most appropriate, given the product or service. Strategies vary depending on the newness of the product, as well as where it will be sold. In Step 6, a company implements its strategy and monitors the results.

EXAMPLE **PRICING STRATEGY**

Many of us enjoy a really tasty hamburger. But not all hamburgers are created (or priced) equal. Restaurants charge different prices for their burgers, according to the unique characteristics of their products and their pricing objectives. Here are some examples:

- **Profitability**—Applebee's sells a cheeseburger for about $7.00. It is not the cheapest burger, nor the most expensive, but it is sold at a price adequate enough to cover costs and earn a little profit.
- **Volume**—White Castle sells cheeseburgers for about 70 cents. This low price is designed to maximize sales volume—and encourage you to buy a sack full of cheeseburgers!

- **Meeting competition**—Both McDonald's and Burger King sell cheeseburgers for around $1.00. Because their cheeseburgers are basic, prices are essentially equal, and marketing emphasis shifts to promotions, for example, movie tie-ins or kid's meal prizes.
- **Prestige**—A Burger Royale at the DB Bistro Moderne in New York City sells for $32. It is a sirloin burger stuffed with short ribs and foie gras (maybe the restaurant will add a slice of cheese gratis). The ingredients are high quality, but customers are also paying for the prestige of a burger prepared by some of New York's top chefs.[10]

PHOTO: Joao Virissimo

>> END EXAMPLE

New Product and Service Pricing Strategies

Suppose that you are planning to introduce a totally new product into the marketplace. Perhaps it is an amazing innovation that offers customers surprising benefits they simply will not be able to find anywhere else. The fixed and variable costs for this product are known to you, but what price should you charge? There is probably a segment of customers who are eager to obtain the product at almost any price, or who will certainly pay a premium for it. At the same time, there is another group who like the product, but are unwilling to pay a higher price. This segment will try the product only if it is sold at a low price, which reduces their risk of purchase.

A **skimming price** is set above the marketplace price for similar products or services, usually with the objective of maximizing revenue or profit. Much like a farmer might skim cream from a pail of milk, this strategy attempts to skim out of the market those customers who are willing to pay a higher price. Early adopters who want the latest and greatest technology will pay more for a new product when it is first introduced, even though prices may fall dramatically 12 to 18 months later. Using a skimming price is only feasible when the new product or service has clear, meaningful advantages over alternatives in the market. The main advantage of a skimming price is that it "does not leave money on the table" and it earns the maximum possible margin for the company on each product sold.

When a **penetration price** is used, the product or service is offered at a low price compared to its competition. Although a product may be sufficiently appealing to command a higher

price, and therefore is a candidate for a skimming strategy, a marketer might prefer to set a low price so as to quickly generate sales volume, market segment penetration, and production scale. According to the **experience curve** theory, costs to manufacture a product will decline as volume increases. This is because when manufacturing is done at higher volumes, companies are able to buy their inputs in larger, cheaper quantities. They also become more skilled and efficient in their manufacturing processes. As a result, even though margins and profits may be slight at first, they should increase over time as costs fall. The firm also gains from brand recognition as a top-selling product in its category. Table 12.4 outlines when a skimming or a penetration price is most appropriate.[11]

Most products and services are not breakthrough, market-changing innovations. Instead, they are incremental improvements to existing products or line extensions under already well-known brand names. Skimming or penetration pricing strategies can be appropriate, but marketers must fully understand consumer perceptions of the product and its pricing power. Marketers should also keep in mind that competitors will react to whatever pricing strategy is employed and attempt to capitalize on vulnerabilities.

EXAMPLE NEW PRODUCT AND SERVICE PRICING STRATEGIES

Every day, ballpoint pens are used by millions of people. The basic design of each pen is similar and includes a barrel, ink cartridge, and pocket clip. Simple versions employ a cap to keep ink fresh, while others are spring activated by a push button. For some customers, ballpoint pens are merely a means to an end: a way to write a school paper or a quick note. For other customers, they might be a high-involvement specialty product, and convey an image of prestige or exclusiveness based on the

Table 12.4 Proper Uses of Skimming and Penetration Pricing

Use a skimming price when...	Use a penetration price when...
• The product performs better than alternatives.	• Demand is very elastic.
• Early adopters will value the product highly.	• Producing higher quantities can reduce costs.
• Demand is initially inelastic.	• The threat of competitor imitation is strong.
• A company cannot meet expected demand.	• No segment is willing to pay a higher price.
• The goal is to position the product as high quality.	• A low price may prevent competitors from entering the market.
• A company wants to avoid a price war.	

brand of pen or its heritage. As a result, marketers of ballpoint pens follow different pricing strategies:

- The BIC brand uses a penetration pricing strategy to generate high sales volume. BIC targets a large segment of consumers who view ballpoint pens as purely functional, disposable devices. A package of 12 BIC pens might sell for $3 to $4 (or as little as 12 cents per pen).
- Mont Blanc targets a smaller group of customers who are highly involved with their pens and view them as fashion items or exclusive collectibles. The brand uses a skimming pricing strategy because its buyers will pay a premium for top quality and craftsmanship. Mont Blanc rollerballs can run $300, or more than 2,000 times the price of a disposable pen.[12]

PHOTO: Dusan Zidar

>> END EXAMPLE

Online and Storefront Pricing Strategies

Before the Internet emerged as another place for customers to buy (or sell) products, people bought the majority of their goods and services through traditional retail channels like grocery stores, mass merchandisers, or other "brick and mortar" businesses. **Storefront pricing** (also called offline pricing) refers to prices established for products or services sold through these kinds of traditional sales channels.

Today, the Internet is an important part of global commerce, with players like Amazon.com becoming a major force in online retailing. **Online pricing** is the process of setting prices for products or services sold over the Internet or through an electronic medium. When developing a pricing strategy, depending on its distribution methods, a firm may use online pricing, offline pricing, or a combination of both.

The Internet's primary effect on pricing strategy has been in the area of **cost transparency**, which is the ability of consumers to understand a firm's true costs. Information about prices is readily abundant, easy to find, and free to anyone with a computer and Internet connectivity. A seller's costs and profit margins become more transparent to its customers. In the past, if you wanted to understand the true cost of a product or whether a price was fair, you had to visit many different storefront locations to collect pricing data. Few customers had the time or willingness to do this. Internet pricing sites like Priceline.com will provide this information quickly and for free. Table 12.5 displays price differences for contact lenses sold both online and offline.[13]

From the marketer's perspective, although cost transparency may be good for consumers' pocketbooks, it also makes online pricing more difficult. Cost transparency has four effects on pricing strategy:[14]

- It erodes high margins because consumers have a better understanding of product costs.
- It can turn products and services into commodities that can be sold only at a common market price.
- It may weaken customer loyalty to brands (if margins are perceived as unfair).
- It can create a perception of price unfairness (if customers feel they are paying too much).

Although marketers can never put the Internet genie back into the bottle, there are strategies marketers can deploy to offset the impact of online cost transparency. A company may use **price lining** (also called **tiered pricing** or **versioning**) to create different prices for different products and services. This technique is commonly used by telecommunications companies that offer various plans at different price points based on customer needs. **Dynamic pricing** (or **"smart" pricing**) is the practice of varying prices based on market conditions, differences in the cost to serve customers, or in the value customers place on a product. When airlines charge a higher fare to business travelers who attempt to book a flight at the last minute, they are leveraging the power of dynamic pricing. Marketers should be cautious in setting dynamic prices, because customers may feel they have been treated unfairly or could even bring accusations of price discrimination.

Auction Pricing Strategies

"Going once...going twice...sold!" is the phrase we commonly associate with **auctions**, in which buyers and sellers engage in an adjudicated process of offer and counteroffer until a price acceptable to both parties is reached. A **forward auction** happens when a buyer puts forth what he or she is seeking to purchase and sellers respond in kind with bids (or prices). Forward auctions end when a bid that is high enough for the seller and low enough for the buyer is reached. In contrast, a **reverse auction** takes place when a buyer communicates not only his or her specifications for the product or service, but also an exact price he or she is willing to pay. If one or more companies are willing to accept the buyer's price, then the reverse auction is complete.

Until recently, the auction process has been used most often in business-to-business contexts. Online auction sites, such as eBay.com, have popularized the notion of negotiating prices in the business-to-consumer and consumer-to-consumer realms.

Table 12.5 Online and Storefront Pricing Comparisons for Contact Lenses			
	Average All Lenses	Average Spherical	Average Specialty
All online	$ 87.92	$ 65.51	$ 119.85
All offline	$ 107.95	$ 81.89	$ 146.36
Offline premium	$ 20.03	$ 16.38	$ 26.51

Many customers no longer accept the sticker price and expect that they will be able to negotiate. Respected brands, unique products, and store location (screen placement) can help protect margins. However, new competitors and more powerful price comparison sites are popping up on a daily basis, so marketers must be prepared to negotiate without giving up too much profit.

It is critical for marketers conducting online auctions or price negotiations with customers to understand the **incremental cost** leading to an online sale. These costs include not only the wholesale costs of the product or service, but also the expected clickthrough fees paid to platforms. **Clickthrough fees** are the amount one online entity charges another online entity for passing along a Web user who clicks an ad or link. On price-comparison sites, these fees range from 40 cents to as much as $1.50, or more. Knowing the incremental cost helps marketers more accurately gauge their potential profitability during an auction and establish a price "floor," which tells them when to stop or decline a sale.

EXAMPLE   AUCTION PRICING STRATEGIES

Many consumers view eBay and similar auction services available at Yahoo!, Amazon.com, or Google as the modern-day alternative to classified ads, flea markets, or plain old word of mouth. You do not need to be a corporation with a multimillion dollar marketing budget to be a retailer. Just make your sales pitch on eBay and see who turns up!

eBay has become the world's most popular online auction site, selling over $60 billion worth of gross merchandise volume through its marketplace channels. One of the main selling points for eBay, or for any online auction, is that it keeps prices low by "cutting out the middleman" and encouraging negotiation. Buyers and sellers are able to interact one-on-one without the need for additional markups (except for commissions or listing fees charged by the site). Dedicated shoppers use strategies like sniping, where they hold off making a bid until the last seconds before an auction expires. Professional snipers even install software such as Auction Sentry or HammerSnipe on their PCs to let them monitor multiple auctions simultaneously and bid more quickly.[15]

PHOTO: Dmitriy Shironosov

>> END EXAMPLE

Portfolio Pricing Strategies

As defined in Chapter 11, a product portfolio is the collection of all products and services offered by a company. When a company owns a large portfolio of products, pricing decisions focus on whether to charge a similar price across brands or to vary a price according to brand and product type. For example, Samsung sells LCD, plasma, and DLP (digital light projection) televisions under a variety of subbrand names (such as Series 6). Should all of these products be priced in a similar fashion? Should some have higher percentage margins than others? Should all products within a related product line follow a line pricing strategy?

Each product line usually has a **price ceiling**, which is the price below which all products in that line will be priced. A product line also might have a **price floor**, which is the price above which all products within a line will be priced. The price ceiling and floor create a price range for the product line, and individual products are priced anywhere between the two bounds. Over time, price ranges come to be associated with brand names. If a marketer sets a price outside the brand's normal price range, either higher or lower, the product's value may be suspect. The brand's image must be broad enough to accommodate this kind of stretch in its price range. The following diagram illustrates how different products may be priced within a brand's price floor and ceiling.

FIGURE 12.3   Price Ceiling, Price Floor, and Their Effects on Product Pricing

Although there is a degree of overlap in pricing between some products, all prices remain within the price range for the entire product line. They do not exceed the boundaries established by the price ceiling and floor. The same principles apply to portfolios that include multiple product lines and brands. In the illustration, simply replace "Product 1" with "Product Line A" or "Brand X."

As with the majority of pricing questions, a sound portfolio pricing strategy begins with an understanding of customer wants, needs, and willingness to pay. Marketers should then overlay individual product performance compared to competition. If portfolio pricing is not properly managed, then the firm will risk product cannibalization (due to excessive overlaps in price) or erosion in brand equity.

Price Adjustment Strategies

A quoted or sticker price is not necessarily the final price that a customer pays. In some cases, marketers may choose to reduce prices due to competitive pressures, cost advantages, or product improvements. The most straightforward method is to cut the selling price, but once a price is lowered, it may be tough to raise it again. As an alternative, marketers employ several price adjustment strategies to lower the actual price paid by customers, while leaving the MSRP intact:

- **Cash discount**—Customers paying in cash are given a percentage or fixed amount off the quoted price.
- **Quantity discount**—Buying a larger quantity of an item results in a discount per item purchased.
- **Trade-in**—A customer is given cash value for an item in trade toward the new purchase.
- **Rebate**—A manufacturer makes a cash payment back to a customer who has purchased their product at full price.

Reducing prices too often can lead to damaging **price wars** with other firms. Suppose one firm reduces the price of its products. A competitor may react by lowering its prices in turn. Then, the first company may be tempted to reduce price even further. A price war happens when two firms become locked in a downward spiral of constantly reducing prices in reaction to each other. No one wins a price war because if it continues long enough, it will eventually wipe out everyone's profits.

EXAMPLE   PRICE ADJUSTMENT STRATEGIES

In 2007, pizza restaurants had a tough year. Foreign demand for dairy products sent cheese prices skyrocketing, and droughts in the United States propelled flour prices to all-time highs.

In the past, product quality and customer service drove market share. With more customers looking for discounts in today's tighter economy, pizza retailers are using low prices as the primary tool to win more business. Combined with higher ingredient costs, price wars among pizza makers are squeezing profit margins.

To avoid the negative consequences of price competition, pizza makers are looking for new ways to maximize revenue and reduce cost. Technology is an answer for some, and more stores are giving customers the option of ordering online or by cell-phone texting. Operators say that check averages for online orders are 10% higher because the Web allows customers to discover items they did not know about. A Papa John's in Louisville, KY, even uses a computer-controlled oven that does not burn at full power until a sufficient number of orders are received.[16]

PHOTO: Hywit Dimyadi

>> END EXAMPLE

▼**Visual** Summary

Chapter 12 Summary

Pricing is perhaps the most dynamic element of the marketing mix because it is constantly changing in reaction to competitive pressures and marketplace shifts. At the most fundamental level, prices depend on marketplace structure, costs, demand, and price elasticity. Once these factors are understood, marketers overlay pricing practices such as legal or bidding requirements. Final pricing strategies are then developed based on the nature of the product (new or existing), where it will be sold (online, offline, or in an auction), its role in a portfolio, and the need to make pricing adjustments.

Establishing Prices pp. 135–139

assign

The price of a good or service is determined by what a consumer is willing to pay for a product or service and what a merchant is willing to accept.

Pricing Practices pp. 140–142

factors

Variables such as bidding processes, market forces, and legal requirements must be taken into account when determining prices.

Pricing Strategy pp. 142–146

objective

Once the marketers know the variables associated with their setting of a price, they create a price that achieves the business objectives.

Capstone **Exercise** p. 149

▼Chapter Key Terms

Establishing **Prices** (pp. 135–139)

A **price** *is the exchange value of a product or service in the* *marketplace.* (p. 135) **Opening Example** (p. 135) **Example:** **Cost-based Pricing** (p. 137)

Key Terms (pp. 135–139)

Break-even point is the volume or price at which a company's revenue for a product exactly equals its fixed cost. **(p. 137)**

Contribution margin is the difference between a product's price and its variable cost. **(p. 137)**

Cost-based pricing establishes a price based on the cost to manufacture a product or deliver a service. **(p. 136) Example: Cost-based Pricing (p. 137)**

Cost-plus pricing adds a fixed amount to the cost of each product or service sufficient to earn a desired profit. **(p. 137)**

Demand curve (or demand schedule) charts the projected sales for a product or service for any price customers are willing to pay. **(p. 138) Example: Demand and Price Elasticity (pp. 138–139)**

Elastic refers to the situation in which price elasticity is greater than one or when demand is highly responsive to a change in price. **(p. 139) Example: Demand and Price Elasticity (pp. 138–139)**

Fair prices are those consumers perceive as offering good value and meeting personal and social norms. **(p. 135)**

Fixed costs (or overhead) are costs that are incurred regardless of any production or sales. **(p. 136)**

Inelastic refers to the situation in which price elasticity is less than one or when demand is relatively nonresponsive to a change in price. **(p. 139)**

Market structure refers to the type of marketplace situation the company faces: monopoly, oligopoly, monopolistic competition, or pure competition. **(p. 136)**

Markup is a percentage or fixed amount added to the cost of a product or service. **(p. 137) Example: Cost-Based Pricing (pp. 137–138)**

Monopolistic competition refers to a market composed of firms with somewhat differentiated products and limited pricing power sufficient to influence the price of their own products to a degree. **(p. 136)**

Monopoly refers to a market composed of a single firm with pricing power sufficient to set the marketplace price for all products or services. **(p. 136)**

Oligopoly refers to a market composed of a small group of firms that share pricing power sufficient to set the marketplace price for their products or services. **(p. 136)**

Price elasticity is the measure of a percentage change in quantity demanded for a product, relative to a percentage change in its price. **(p. 139) Example: Demand and Price Elasticity (pp. 138–139)**

Price–quality ratio is the ratio between the price of a product and its perceived quality. **(p. 136)**

Pricing power is the ability of a firm to establish a higher price than its competitors without losing significant market share. **(p. 136) Example: Cost-based Pricing (pp. 137–138)**

Profit margin is the difference between the price of a product and its total cost per unit. **(p. 136)**

Pure competition refers to a market composed of a large number of firms that together lack sufficient pricing power to influence the market price for their products. **(p. 136)**

Total cost is the sum of fixed and variable costs. **(p. 136)**

Variable costs are costs directly attributable to the production of a product or the delivery of a service. **(p. 136)**

Pricing Practices (pp. 139–142)

Pricing practices *are considerations (such as legal requirements or* *bidding practices) that must be taken into account when establishing a* *price for a product or service.* (p. 139) **Example: Legal** **Requirements** (p. 141)

Key Terms (pp. 140–142)

Antidumping laws are laws designed to prevent predatory pricing. **(p. 142)**

Antitrust law is a catchall phrase for federal legislation meant to prohibit anticompetitive actions on the part of manufacturers, wholesalers, or resellers. **(p. 140) Example: Legal Requirements (p. 141)**

Bait-and-switch pricing occurs when a firm advertises a low price on a desirable product but, in an attempt to trade customers up to more expensive items, it does not make a good faith effort to carry sufficient quantities of that product. **(p. 141)**

Competitive bidding involves suppliers in a bid process that receive identical RFQs and then return quotes in secret to the buyer. **(p. 141)**

Currency exchange rates are variable rates that specify the price of one currency in terms of the price of another. **(p. 142)**

Deceptive pricing occurs when a price is meant to intentionally mislead or deceive customers. **(p. 141)**

Loss-leader pricing involves the sale of items below cost to drive floor traffic. **(p. 141)**

Negotiated price is the result of a back-and-forth discussion between a buyer and seller regarding the final price of a product or service. **(p. 141)**

Odd-even pricing is a practice that sets prices at fractional numbers, instead of whole ones. **(p. 140)**

Predatory pricing occurs when a firm sells its products at a low price to drive competitors out of the market. **(p. 140)**

Price bundling occurs when two or more items are priced at a single, combined price instead of individually. **(p. 140)**

Price discrimination occurs when a firm injures competition by charging different prices to different members of its distribution channel. **(p. 140)**

Price fixing occurs when two or more companies discuss prices in an effort to raise the market price for their products. **(p. 140) Example: Legal Requirements (p. 141)**

Promotional pricing is the strategy of using price as a promotional tool to drive customer awareness and sales. **(p. 141)**

Request for quote (RFQ) is a document a buyer sends to a potential supplier that outlines the criteria for the goods or services to be purchased. **(p. 141)**

Quotas are limits on the amount of a product that can be imported into a country. **(p. 142)**

Quotation is a supplier's response to an RFQ from a potential customer. **(p. 141)**

Sticker price (MSRP [manufacturer's suggested retail price]) is the quoted or official price for a product. **(p. 141)**

Tariff is a schedule of duties (or fees) applied to goods and services from foreign countries. **(p. 142)**

Pricing Strategies (pp. 142–146)

Pricing strategy *identifies what a business will charge for its products* *and services.* (p. 142) **Example: Pricing Strategies (pp. 142–143)** **Example: New Product and Service Pricing Strategies** **(pp. 143–144) Example: Price Adjustment Strategies (p. 146)**

Key Terms (pp. 142–146)

Auctions are markets in which buyers and sellers engage in a process of offer and counteroffer until a price acceptable to both parties is reached. **(p. 144) Example: Auction Pricing Strategies (p. 145)**

Cash discount is a percentage or fixed amount off the quoted price of an item, and is given when a customer pays in cash. **(p. 146)**

Clickthrough fees are the amount one online entity charges another online entity for passing along a Web user who clicks an ad or link. **(p. 145) Example: Auction Pricing Strategies (p. 145)**

Cost transparency is the ability of consumers to understand a product's actual cost. **(p. 144)**

Dynamic pricing (or "smart" pricing) is the practice of varying prices based on marketplace conditions. **(p. 144)**

Experience curve is an economic model that presumes costs will decline as production volume increases. **(p. 143)**

Forward auction is a market in which a buyer states what he or she is seeking to purchase and sellers respond in kind with bids (or prices). **(p. 144)** **Example: Auction Pricing Strategies (p. 145)**

Incremental cost is the additional cost to produce or sell one more product or service. **(p. 145)**

Online pricing is the process of setting prices for products or services sold over the Internet or through an electronic medium. **(p. 144)** **Example: Auction Pricing Strategies (p. 145)**

Penetration price is a price that is set low to maximize volume and market share. **(p. 143)** **Example: New Product and Service Pricing Strategies (pp. 143–144)**

Price ceiling is the price all products in a product line must be priced below. **(p. 145)**

Price floor is the price above which all products in a product line must be priced. **(p. 145)**

Price lining (or tiered pricing, versioning) is a strategy used to create different prices for different, but related, products or services. **(p. 144)**

Price wars occur when businesses cut prices to take sales from competitors. **(p. 146)** **Example: Price Adjustment Strategies (p. 146)**

Pricing objectives are goals that keep marketing actions in alignment with overall business objectives. **(p. 142)**

Quantity discount is a discount per item purchased that is given to customers buying a larger quantity of a product. **(p. 146)**

Rebate is a cash payment made back to a customer who has purchased his or her products at full price. **(p. 146)**

Reverse auction is a market in which a buyer states what he or she is seeking to purchase, as well as the price he or she is willing to pay. **(p. 144)** **Example: Auction Pricing Strategies (p. 145)**

Skimming price is a price that is set high in order to maximize revenue and profit. **(p. 143)** **Example: New Product and Service Pricing Strategies (pp. 143–144)**

Storefront pricing (also called offline pricing) refers to prices established for products or services sold through traditional sales channels like grocery stores, mass merchandisers, or other "brick and mortar" businesses. **(p. 144)**

Trade-in is the cash value given to a customer when he or she offers his or her own product in trade toward a new purchase. **(p. 146)**

▼Capstone Exercise

Pricing—the focus of this chapter—is an area of marketing that people tend to overlook. Pricing is a key factor in a business's success and failure.

The Internet has had a major impact on pricing strategies. The nature of the Internet allows customers to comparison shop across many vendors. It changes the geographical boundaries of shopping because buyers can compare local retail prices against a large Internet company. The Internet "levels the playing field" for buyers and provides them with more choices.

1. The exercise is to comparison shop for a specific product locally and on the Internet. Compare the prices and, depending on the product, explain why sometimes you would buy it online and why sometimes you would not. What factors influence you one way or the other? Are the prices on the Internet much less after you factor in shipping costs?

▼Application Exercises

Complete the following exercises:

1. Take a trip to your local grocery store and pick an aisle filled with items you enjoy, such as cereal or potato chips. Note the product types, brands, and prices. Which items are priced the highest? Which items are priced the lowest? Which are on sale? What is the price range for this category of products? Develop some hypotheses about why marketers chose their various pricing strategies. (*Note*: Any kind of store will work for this exercise—clothing, drug, furniture.)

2. Oil and petroleum are essential to the manufacture and use of many products and services. When oil prices increase, which products and services are most affected? Will marketers be able to raise prices, or will they need to lower them? Are there nonprice strategies marketers use to combat the rising price of oil? Be prepared to discuss your ideas in class.

3. Product price bundling has become a popular pricing strategy. Review and compare the current pricing strategies your local cable provider uses and those DirectTV (www.directtv.com) uses. Do the companies make the most of product price bundling? What suggestions could you offer to improve their competitive positions against one another?

4. Look at Rolex watches: www.rolex.com/en. What pricing strategy is being employed? What message does this pricing strategy send to potential consumers?

chapter 13

Part 1   Explaining (Chapters 1, 2, 3, 4)
Part 2   Creating (Chapters 5, 6, 7, 8)
Part 3   Strategizing (Chapters 9, 10)

Part 4   **Managing (Chapters 11, 12, 13, 14, 15)**
Part 5   Integrating (Chapters 16, 17)

Supply Chain and Distribution Strategies

Chapter Overview After a product has been created and priced, the next step is to determine how it will be made available to customers for purchase. This chapter deals with physical distribution, or the transportation, storage, and sale of products to consumers or businesses. It describes various forms of marketing channels and channel strategies. Logistics, transportation, warehousing, retailing, and wholesaling are also discussed as important aspects of the distribution process.

▼ Chapter **Outline**

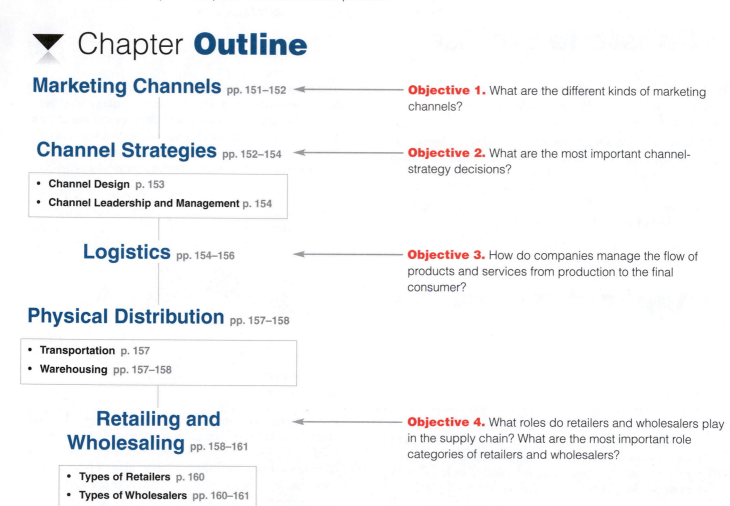

MARKETING CHANNELS (pp. 151–152)

> ▼ **DEFINED** *A **marketing channel** is a network of all parties involved in moving products or services from producers to consumers or business customers.*

▼ **EXPLAINED**

Marketing Channels

Imagine that you have moved into a new apartment and you need to shop for furniture. Perhaps you decide to stop in at the IKEA store, where a variety of affordable, Swedish-designed home products are available. Your shopping experience (although imaginary) is made possible through the power of **distribution**, which is the process of delivering products and services to customers. Distribution is an essential part of marketing because without it, products aren't available for customers to buy and profits are lost.

Several different businesses participate in the movement of products from production to the point of sale. A marketing channel includes all of the parties involved in the distribution process. Channels may consist of one or more members, each performing roles in producing, collecting, sorting, transporting, promoting, pricing, and selling products or services to customers. Important functions performed by marketing channels include the following[1]:

- Gathering information about customers, competition, and the marketing environment
- Developing communications to stimulate purchasing
- Reaching agreements on price and other applicable terms
- Placing orders with manufacturers
- Storing and transporting products through the marketing channel
- Providing credit and other purchasing options to customers
- Overseeing the actual sale of products or services to consumers or businesses

▼ **APPLIED**

Marketing Channels

The simplest form of a marketing channel is a **direct channel** (or **zero-level channel**), where the same member both produces and distributes a product or service. An **indirect channel** involves one or more intermediaries between producer and consumer. The role of intermediaries is to improve the overall efficiency and effectiveness of the marketing channel. Types of intermediaries include the following:

- Wholesalers—firms that acquire large quantities of products from manufacturers and then sort, store, and resell them to retailers or businesses.
- Retailers—all channel members who are involved in selling products or services to consumers.
- Agents—people who facilitate the exchange of products but do not take title (i.e., purchase) anything that they sell.
- Facilitators—people who assist in the distribution of products and services but do not take title or negotiate sales.

Marketing channels are expensive. Costs due to marketing channels can account for 30% to 50% of the ultimate selling price of a product.[2] Marketers accept these added costs due to the **contact efficiency** channels can provide. Consider the hypothetical

At midnight on July 21, 2007, the final installment of the Harry Potter series of books, *Harry Potter and the Deathly Hallows*, went on sale in bookstores around the world. Anticipation among fans was palpable; some stood in line for hours so they could be among the first to own a copy. A year earlier, in 2006, the book's publisher, Scholastic, began distribution plans for 12 million copies—a record number of books for a first printing. To keep the book from slipping out in advance of the official release date, every copy had to arrive in customers' hands as close to 12:01 a.m., July 21, 2007 as possible. Given the enormity of the task, and the book's importance to its readers, Scholastic worked with printers, trucking companies, warehouses, and retailers to make Harry's final bow a complete success. If all the trucks delivering the books were lined up end to end, they would have stretched for 15 miles. The publisher used GPS (Global Positioning System) trackers on every truck to prevent shipments from getting lost. Upon receiving the books, Barnes & Noble.com separated copies according to zip code. A complicated formula was used to calculate exactly when to release a copy to the post office or UPS to guarantee simultaneous arrival across the United States.[3]

example shown in Figure 13.1. The example assumes that there are six consumers who want to purchase six different items from six different manufacturers. Figure 13.2 shows the effect of adding one retailer as a channel intermediary between these two groups.

FIGURE 13.1   **Manufacturer-to-Customer Channel**

FIGURE 13.2   **Manufacturer-to-Retailer-to-Customer Channel**

In our simple example, the number of contacts is reduced by 67% (or (36 – 12) / 36) as the retailer collects the various products from producers and then resells them to consumers. Considering the huge number of exchanges between manufacturers and consumers every day, it's almost impossible to imagine a world without marketing channels.

EXAMPLE   **MARKETING CHANNELS**

Have you ever wondered how a bottle of Listerine mouthwash ends up in your local drugstore or grocery store? Every bottle travels through a series of manufacturing and distribution partners that work together to form a marketing channel:

- Warner-Lambert, the maker of Listerine, purchases eucalyptol, synthetic alcohol, sorbitol, menthol, citric acid, and

other ingredients. These are transported to Warner-Lambert's manufacturing and distribution facility, where they are mixed together to create Listerine mouthwash.
- The product is bottled, capped, labeled, and then put in large boxes called "shippers." The shippers are organized into pallets, which are then transported to the distribution center where they will remain for about two to four weeks.
- When Warner-Lambert receives an order from a retailer (such as a drugstore), the order is screened to ensure that it can be filled. Software calculates the price for the order and how much product is already in stock. If there is a shortage, additional production is scheduled.
- When the order can be filled, pallets are transported by forklift to the appropriate shipping door. Trucks are loaded with the product, and those trucks depart for the customer's warehouse.
- The trucks are unloaded at the customer's warehouse where the Listerine is stored for as long as three weeks until it is needed.
- When one of the retailer's stores begins running low on Listerine, that store requests a shipment of additional product from the warehouse. Another software program optimizes delivery schedules for all of the retailer's stores that are requesting product, and boxes of Listerine are shipped.
- Trucks unload their cargo of Listerine at each of the destination stores, where staffers place bottles on shelves.[4]

PHOTO: EuToch

>> END EXAMPLE

Channel Strategies (pp. 152–154)

▼ **DEFINED** A **channel strategy** *describes the levels, organization, and distribution intensity of a marketing channel.*

▼ **EXPLAINED**

Channel Strategies

Smart marketers don't just distribute products and services; they conduct their business according to a clearly defined **channel strategy**. When formulating a channel strategy, marketers have to make the following three decisions:

1. **How many levels of intermediaries will be used?** A channel could distribute directly to customers or involve one or more intermediaries.
2. **How will the channel be organized?** All channel members could be owned by the same firm or associated with each other in some way.
3. **What will be the intensity of distribution?** There could be many points of distribution within geographic areas, or only a few.

Each kind of channel requires a separate channel strategy. If a company sells its products through stand-alone stores, online, and through catalogs, then three channel strategies are needed. The nature of the product or service, customer characteristics, competitive actions, and the business environment all influence channel strategy.

▼ **APPLIED**
Channel Strategies

As mentioned earlier, marketers must decide on the correct number of intermediaries for the channel. A zero-level, or direct channel, is quite "short," because a producer sells directly to its consumers (B2C) or to its business customers (B2B). One benefit of a direct channel is that it gives the manufacturer greater control over every step in the distribution process. On the other hand, indirect channels leverage the growing importance of retailers. Stores like The Home Depot, Best Buy, and Bed Bath & Beyond are increasingly "where customers go first" for hardware, home electronics, and housewares. Producers realize benefits such as the performance of transportation, storage, return, and transaction functions from indirect channels.

Channel organization defines how channel members will work together and the role each one should play. Three methods for channel organization are as follows:

- **Conventional**—Under a conventionally organized channel, each member works independently of the others, buying and selling products or services. The channel is self-regulating according to market forces.
- **Vertical Marketing System (VMS)**—A VMS exists when a firm takes on the role of another channel member, either through acquisition or by developing its own distribution capabilities. For instance, a manufacturer could vertically integrate by acquiring its own wholesale or retail business. As a result, the channel becomes more efficient due to reductions in conflict, sharing of information and resources among channel members, and greater collective-bargaining power.
- **Horizontal**—Channels are organized horizontally when two or more channel members at the same level (e.g., two or more wholesalers, two or more retailers) form an alliance. The firms may be related or unrelated in function, but they share resources and services as a means to improve channel performance.

Distribution intensity is the final decision marketers must make when developing a channel strategy. Intensity describes the number of outlets or locations where a product will be sold. Products with higher intensity are sold at many locations within a geographic area, and are therefore easily obtained. Convenience products usually follow an **intensive distribution** strategy and are sold through a large number of outlets, so they are readily available. In contrast, shopping products often employ a more **selective distribution** strategy. Consumers are willing to exert a bit more time and effort to buy blue jeans or PCs, so these kinds of shopping products are distributed more selectively, through retailers like Best Buy or independent computer stores. Many luxury or high-ticket items use **exclusive distribution**, where retailers or wholesalers are given exclusive rights to sell a product. This level of intensity is frequently used to maintain a perception of exclusivity and prestige for these products.

EXAMPLE **CHANNEL STRATEGY**

When Hyundai decided to offer its customers a 10-year warranty on its products, it also had to begin planning for a decade-long period when repair parts might be needed to fulfill this promise.
PHOTO: Jamzol

>> **END EXAMPLE**

Channel Design

The process of channel design always begins with an understanding of the target customer. Because the purpose of marketing channels is to delight customers, all channel decisions must be aligned with a customer's desires. Once customer desires are fully understood, marketers determine what kinds of channels are required. Figure 13.3 illustrates various kinds of business-to-consumer (B2C) and business-to-business (B2B) channels.[5]

Online sales and distribution channels have opened up new opportunities for marketers. Until the late 1970s, all transactions were conducted offline, and happened at physical brick-and-mortar locations. Today, many B2B and B2C sales are online and take place in a virtual "mouse click" universe. As a result, part of channel design strategy involves a decision between "bricks and clicks," or how to achieve the balance between offline and online distribution.

Dual distribution (or **multichannel distribution**) is the use of two or more types of distribution channels. The main reason for using multiple channels is to better satisfy customer wants and needs. One segment of customers may like to shop in retail stores, while another segment will only order and purchase online. Dual distribution can also reduce overall distribution costs and offer a more customized shopping experience.

The next step is to establish objectives for all channel members. If the goal is to maximize channel efficiency, the optimal design minimizes lot size, shortens wait time, provides maximum convenience, limits product variety, and provides limited services. But if the goal is to offer customers more choice and shopping flexibility, a different and more expensive design is needed.

The final step is to weigh all elements of the decision—channel types, objectives, intermediaries, online versus offline—and select an optimal channel design. Regardless of the channel design, smart marketing practice always builds distribution channels based on customer insights, and not solely on company objectives.

Channel Leadership and Management

Smoothly operating channels depend on relationships among people. Manufacturers, wholesalers, retailers, agents, and facilitators often are independent entities, each with their own strategic goals and profit targets (see Figure 13.3). On occasion, their interests conflict; such conflicts can negatively affect how smoothly the entire channel functions.

- **Channel conflict** refers to situations in which there is a disagreement among two or more parties in a distribution channel. For instance, a retailer may think that a wholesaler's terms and conditions are unreasonable.
- **Vertical conflict** occurs between two channel members at different levels. A wholesaler's argument with a manufacturer over access to a popular item is an example of vertical conflict.
- **Horizontal conflict** involves channel members at the same level, such as two retailers arguing over sales territories.
- **Multichannel conflict** refers to conflicts among multiple channel types. A manufacturer selling products through its own Web site might experience conflict with its independent brick-and-mortar retailers over pricing strategy.

A **channel leader** (also called a channel captain) is a firm with sufficient power over other channel members to take a leadership role, enforcing norms and processes. A strong leader who can establish and enforce "rules of engagement" for the channel is also a leader who can reduce conflict. Manufacturers have traditionally been channel leaders due to their ownership of powerful brands, desirable products, and access to customer information. However, retailers are increasingly taking on leadership roles because of the number of customers they influence and the increasing sophistication of their marketing approach.[6]

Marketers who successfully manage their distribution channels carefully select their channel partners on the basis of expertise and ability to cooperate. These successful marketers also work to motivate members to achieve shared objectives for the entire channel, often through training and financial incentives. The performance of channel participants is also carefully measured according to stated objectives, such as volume, profitability, and market share. Underperforming members are removed from the channel and replaced.

Logistics (pp. 154–156)

> ▼ **DEFINED** **Logistics** *is the coordination of all activities related to the transportation or delivery of products and services that occur within the boundaries of a single business or organization.*

▼ **EXPLAINED**

Logistics

Logistics is about getting several things right. Products and services must reach the right customers, in the right place, at the right time, in the right quantities, at the right price, and with the right level of service. **Logistics** involves the coordination of a single company's every activity that influences the flow of products or services from production to final customer. Production forecasting, information

---

FIGURE 13.3 Business-to-Consumer and Business-to-Business Channels

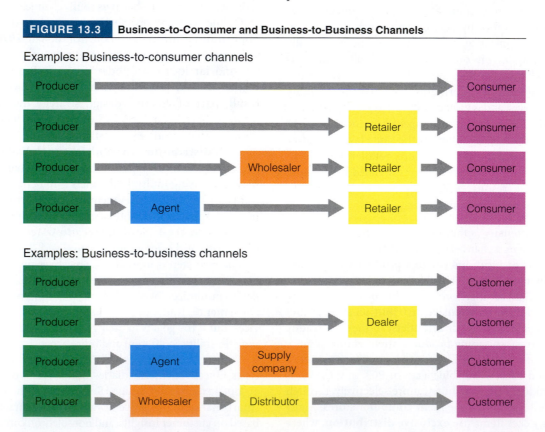

Examples: Business-to-consumer channels

Examples: Business-to-business channels

FIGURE 13.4   Supply Chains

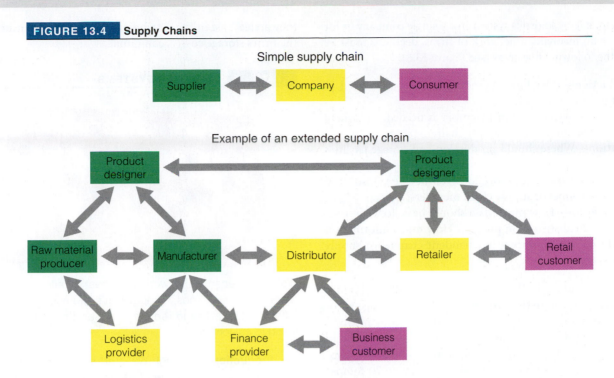

systems, purchasing, inventory management, warehousing, and transportation are all aspects of logistics.

Supply chain management broadens the concept of logistics to include all firms or organizations, both inside and outside a company, that impact the distribution process. Finance, new product development, and customer service operations also fall under the definition of supply chain management. Some supply chains are simple, involving only a few players; others are more complex, spanning every distribution activity from raw materials to retailing as demonstrated in Figure 13.4.[7]

▼ **APPLIED**

Logistics

Logistics involves the management of three flows of products and information. There are three main types of logistics (see Figure 13.5):

- **Outbound logistics** controls the movement of products from points of production (factories or service delivery points) to consumers.
- **Inbound logistics** deals with the flow of products or services from suppliers to manufacturers or service providers.

- **Reverse logistics** addresses the methods consumers use to send products backward through a channel for return or repair. For instance, Estée Lauder created a $250-million product line from returned cosmetics, which were then sold in discount stores and in developing countries.[8]

Marketing specialists called **logistics managers**, or supply chain managers, are responsible for coordinating the activities of all members of a company's distribution channel. Well-managed logistics and supply chains have several benefits. By coordinating activities among channel members, they can reduce distribution costs, which leads to higher profits and potentially lower prices for customers. Such well-managed chains may also result in improved customer service as a result of improved information flows, faster delivery, and easier product returns.

Different segments of customers are looking for different things from a distribution channel. One segment may value low prices, and so a logistics manager will focus on minimizing delivery costs. Another segment may want exceptional service, which means added cost to hire and train qualified customer service personnel. A central part of the logistics manager's role is to satisfy customer demands, yet at the same time maximize channel profit, by making trade-offs such as these between cost and service.

FIGURE 13.5   Logistics[9]

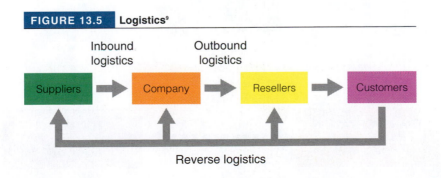

When managing logistics systems for a single company or for a supply chain involving a network of firms, decisions must be made in the following five areas (see Figure 13.6):[10]

- **Production**—What kind of products should be produced, in what quantities, and when?
- **Inventory**—What level of inventory is needed, and where should it be stored in the supply chain?
- **Location**—Where should production and storage facilities be located? Where should products be sold?
- **Transportation**—How should inventory be transported between channel or supply chain members?
- **Information**—How much data should be collected at each point in the distribution process? How much information should be shared among independent channel or supply chain members?

Instead of handling its logistics systems internally, a firm may hire a **third-party logistics company (3PL)** to manage all or part of its distribution network. At least 70% of companies worldwide are using a 3PL for one or more key supply chain tasks. For example, UPS Supply Chain Solutions operates a two-million square-foot campus that services more than 70 companies.[11] Third-party logistics firms help marketers save money by performing functions more efficiently, giving them access to more sophisticated distribution networks, and allowing them to focus on their core business. Some 3PLs even handle product returns or manage repair centers for their clients.

Holding inventory for long periods of time is expensive due to storage and maintenance costs. As a result, manufacturers and retailers look for ways to minimize the time they actually have possession of physical inventory. Minimizing possession time keeps carrying costs as low as possible and maximizes production capability or the use of manufacturers' and retailers' sales floors. Initially developed and implemented by Toyota, **just-in-time** inventory management is a technique in which goods are delivered within a predefined time "window." This time slot corresponds to exactly when the goods are needed, so

they arrive "just in time" to be used or sold, thus ensuring that the firm's storage costs are minimal.

EXAMPLE   LOGISTICS SYSTEMS

Wal-Mart became the world's largest retailer by promising "Every Day Low Prices." Its logistics systems are aligned in the following five areas to reduce costs and pass those savings along to customers:[12]

- **Production**—Although Wal-Mart is a mass-market retailer, it manufactures some of its own products by partnering with low-cost global suppliers.
- **Inventory**—Wal-Mart stores follow a "big box" format, allowing the company to combine a store and warehouse in one location, and to gain operating efficiencies by doing so.
- **Location and Transportation**—Sites for large distribution centers (DCs) are identified, and then Wal-Mart stores are located near DCs. Supply chain costs, such as transportation, are minimized as a result.
- **Information**—Wal-Mart's electronic data interchange (EDI) systems automate ordering and payment processes with its suppliers, thereby reducing costs and improving order accuracy.

PHOTO: Infomages

>> **END EXAMPLE**

FIGURE 13.6   **Logistics Decisions**

PRODUCTION
What, how, and when to produce

INVENTORY
How much to make and how much to store

INFORMATION
The basics for making these decisions

TRANSPORTATION
How and when to move product

LOCATION
Where best to do what activity

Physical Distribution (pp.157–158)

> **DEFINED** **Physical distribution** *(or freight transportation) is the process of carrying goods to customers.*

 EXPLAINED

Physical Distribution

A basic function of marketing channels is to facilitate the movement of products from point A to point B. **Physical distribution** (or freight transportation) deals with the transport and storage of everything from raw materials to finished goods. This is perhaps the most fundamental role channels play in marketing, because products must eventually end up in the hands of customers for consumption to take place.

Another way to think about distribution is as a subset of logistics. Distribution focuses on outbound logistics by managing the movement of physical products from point of manufacture to customers. Products are transported from location to location and often stored for periods of time before the journey ends. Transportation services, such as air carriers, railroads, and trucking companies, physically move products, while warehouses handle product storage and manage product inventory. The term **inventory** refers to a store of goods awaiting transport or shipping. Because holding inventory can be expensive, marketers try to keep inventory quantities low, but still large enough to satisfy customer demand. Distribution planners coordinate these activities, balancing costs with the need for quick delivery and customer service.

▼ **APPLIED**

Physical Distribution

Best-in-class distribution is not a solo activity; each channel member does not act independently and according to his or her own interests. It is a group performance, with participants acting in a manner that benefits themselves as well as the whole distribution network. Three parties are involved in the distribution process:

- **Shippers** who own the goods being distributed. Bobs Candies acts as a shipper when it sends candy canes from its factories in Albany, GA to retailers on the West Coast.
- **Consignees** who receive the distributed goods. In the case of Bobs Candies, its consignees are food and candy resellers who take delivery of the candy canes in time for the holiday season.
- **Carriers** who physically transport the goods from shippers to consignees. Like most consumer products, the majority of Bobs Candies are shipped by truck from its factory.[13]

For carriers to take physical possession of the goods, shippers must have the correct quantities of products ready to ship at the appointed time. Consignees rely on carriers to deliver their shipments efficiently and on schedule. In turn, shippers depend on both carriers and consignees to transport products and to make the actual sales.

Transportation

Each year, U.S. companies spend more than hundreds of billions of dollars on the physical transportation of goods. Transportation can employ a range of methods, or modes. **Intermodal** distribution strategies use more than one kind of transportation mode for a product. For instance, physical distribution is also referred to as freight transportation because more than 70% of all transport is by truck at some point in the distribution process.[14] The major modes of carrier transportation include the following:

- **Trucks**—The most popular form of transport, trucks are a relatively quick and affordable means of transportation. Truck transport is slower than air transport, however, and the cost of highway transportation fluctuates due to fuel costs and the availability of skilled drivers.
- **Air**—Airplanes are a the fastest mode of transport, but they are also expensive. In addition, destinations can be somewhat limited in rural areas if airport facilities are not available.
- **Rail**—Although slower than other methods, rail transport is attractive due to its low cost. Rail is usually reserved for bulk goods or large items that do not need to be delivered quickly. Distribution points are restricted to destinations connected by rail lines.
- **Water**—Transport by water, usually on large cargo ships, is cost effective, but slow. Like rail travel, water shipping has limits. Goods can be transported by water only to locations with navigable waterways and docks.

Pipelines are another transportation mode suitable for liquids such as oil or natural gas. Although **electronic transport** is fast, flexible, and efficient, it can be used only for data (e.g., music, pictures, or text) and is, therefore, not suitable for physical distribution.[15]

When deciding which mode (or modes) of transportation to use, marketers consider several factors, among them each mode's advantages and disadvantages, rising fuel costs, more complicated global supply chains, and limited supplies of trucks or drivers at certain times of the year. To manage the complexity of transportation decisions, some companies install **transportation management systems** (**TMS**), which are software packages that automate shipping processes. A TMS can make recommendations on everything from carrier selection to scheduling. In spite of initial prices ranging from $50,000 to as much as $1 million, cost savings from these systems often allow firms to recoup their upfront investment within one year.[16]

Warehousing

A **warehouse** is a physical facility used primarily for the storage of goods held in anticipation of sale or transfer within the marketing channel.[17] Most businesses or retailers don't require large quantities of products all at one time, so it's more cost-effective to store items at warehouses and then ship items to their ultimate destination in smaller, more frequent orders. Warehouses help other distribution channel members by **breaking bulk**, or reducing large product shipments into smaller ones more suitable for individual retailers or companies. Another function warehouses serve is to **create assortments** of products from the wide variety they carry. When one truck carries an assortment of five orders to a single destination, five different trucks no longer have to make the same trip.[18]

Inventory management is the focus of efficient warehousing operations. Carrying too much inventory is wasteful, because the storage space could be used for more profitable items. However, having too little inventory on hand is a missed opportunity. Inventory levels vary based on time of year, the type of industry being serviced, and customer demand. Items are tracked within a warehouse and throughout the distribution process by using **stock-keeping unit** (**SKU**) numbers, which serve as identification codes that are unique for each product.

A large warehouse may also be called a **distribution center**. As mentioned earlier in this chapter, Wal-Mart locates its stores near its own centralized distribution centers to minimize transportation costs. Distribution network planning determines the number and locations of warehouses or distribution centers a company needs. Some key questions to answer when developing a warehouse or distribution center strategy are as follows:

- How many warehouses or distribution centers do you need?
- Where should they be located?
- How much inventory should be stocked at each one?
- Which customers should each warehouse or distribution center service?
- How often should shipments be made to each customer?
- What additional services should be provided?[19]

Some warehouses or distribution centers use **RFID** (**radio frequency identification**) tags to track the movement of goods electronically. An RFID tag carries an electronic chip and an antenna, which sends the precise location of each item to a computer. Using RFID, marketers can follow a product all the way from production to shipment. A study by Kurt Salmon Associates estimates that RFID can reduce the amount of time needed to track inventory by as much as 90%.[20]

Bar codes (or **barcodes**) are another form of identification used to monitor inventory. Every product carries a bar code with unique numerical identifiers that can be scanned within a warehouse to confirm the product's storage location, to ensure its correct destination when being shipped, or to record its final sale at checkout. Retail bar codes specify a product's **Universal Product Code** (or **UPC**), which is a series of numbers uniquely identifying that product.

More sophisticated supply chains use **cross-docking** to minimize inventory holding costs and improve delivery time. Goods that are cross-docked are never warehoused at all, but are simply unloaded at a distribution center, immediately sorted by destination, and then reloaded onto trucks for dispatch.

EXAMPLE   PHYSICAL DISTRIBUTION

As one of America's largest retailers, Sears, Roebuck and Co. manages physical distribution for three major categories of products:

- **Seasonal products**, such as snowblowers or lawn mowers, which must be fully stocked during times of peak demand
- **Fast-moving products** like home improvement or DIY items, which must arrive at and depart from the distribution centers quickly
- **Slow-moving products** such as washing machines and dryers, which can be transported more slowly and economically

In addition to sales through its brick-and-mortar stores, the company also makes six million deliveries directly to customers' homes.

Cross-docking helps Sears keep its inventory moving efficiently. For example, when a truckload of high-definition TVs arrives at one of Sears' regional distribution centers, the load is broken down and single TVs are then loaded onto trucks headed for different stores or homes across the United States.[21]

PHOTO: Baloncici

>> END EXAMPLE

Retailing and Wholesaling (pp. 158–161)

 DEFINED **Retailing** *involves the sale of products or services to consumers.* **Wholesaling** *is the sorting, storing, and reselling of products to retailers or businesses.*

 EXPLAINED

Retailing and Wholesaling

Most consumers buy products such as bread, pillowcases, or music downloads from a **retailer**. A supermarket, department store, or Internet music site is a called a retailer because it sells its wares to end consumers. Retailing is the last step in a business-to-consumer distribution channel. Business-to-business transactions are not considered retailing because the ultimate customer in such transactions is an organization, not an individual.

In contrast, the customer of a **wholesaler** is a retailer or a business. Wholesalers service companies, institutions, and governments. As a marketing tactic, some companies call themselves "wholesale" clubs, or promote that they offer "wholesale" pricing. However, because these firms do sell to consumers, they are actually retailers, not wholesalers.

Retailing and wholesaling may be conducted either online or offline. The U.S. Census Bureau estimated total retail sales for 2007 at more than $4 billion. E-commerce retail sales for 2007 were estimated at $136.4 billion, an increase of approximately 19% over 2006.[22]

▼ APPLIED
Retailing and Wholesaling

As with any aspect of marketing, retailing and wholesaling begin with an understanding of the company's target customers. Marketers then develop a retailing or wholesaling strategy that is aligned with customers' wants and needs. For example, a retailing strategy is defined along the following six dimensions:

- **Merchandise**—What categories of products will be sold? What level of quality? What breadth of selection? Will any particular brand names be emphasized?
- **Promotion**—How will the store be positioned? What forms of media will be used (e.g., broadcast, print, Internet)? How often will price promotions be employed?
- **Location**—Where will the store be located? Will there be multiple locations? What distribution channels will be used? Will an online channel be supported?
- **Atmosphere**—What will the store environment be like? What colors and materials will be used? Will music be played? Will there be wide or narrow aisles?
- **Pricing**—In general, will prices be higher, lower, or equal to the competition? How often will sales be allowed? Will prices be negotiable? Will credit be available?

FIGURE 13.7   **Retailing Strategy Dimensions**

- **Customer service**—What level of customer service should be offered (e.g., self-service, full-service)? What will be the store's return policy? How much training will salespeople require?

All retailers find their own set of answers to these questions. Wal-Mart and Target are both mass merchandisers, but Wal-Mart competes primarily on price, while Target focuses on branded merchandise and atmosphere. Wholesalers must also arrive at a similar kind of strategy, although some dimensions will receive less emphasis or take a different form. For example, store atmosphere is not relevant for wholesalers because they do not maintain retail locations. It is also likely that promotional tactics will emphasize trade ads or visits by sales representatives over mass media advertising.

EXAMPLE   **RETAILING**

Known for its innovative approach to cosmetics retailing, Sephora operates more than 750 stores on three continents. Most cosmetics have traditionally been sold in department stores, alongside furniture, electronics, and hardware. Sephora has built a niche for itself as a specialty retailer, similar to chains like Ikea, Best Buy, or The Home Depot. Sephora offers customers a unique shopping experience by focusing its retailing strategy on innovation, exclusivity, and customer service. The following are key points in that strategy:

- **Merchandise**—Sephora carries exclusive product brands, such as Benefit Cosmetics, Stila, Philosophy, and Perricone MD, that aren't widely available. As Bare Escentuals CEO Leslie Blodgett said, "Sephora is a trailblazer . . . it takes brands that seemingly no one else will and turns them into stars."
- **Promotion**—Unlike department stores, Sephora doesn't invest heavily in advertising, but relies on positive customer experiences to generate favorable word-of-mouth promotion.
- **Location**—Sephora attempts to secure high-traffic locations in cities or malls. Such locations draw people into the stores. There is a Sephora store on the Champs-Elysées in Paris and on Fifth Avenue in New York City.
- **Atmosphere**—The concept for Sephora stores is perhaps its greatest innovation. Products are displayed in an open-sell environment without glass cases, so shoppers can touch, compare, and sample the items. Each store's distinctive black-and-white decorating scheme

draws attention to the colorful product packages that are on display.

- **Pricing**—Prices are generally on par with department stores, but Sephora attempts to deliver better value through product selection, store atmosphere, and customer service. Coaches are even trained to create made-to-order products for customers by mixing cosmetics to match individual color and skin tones.
- **Customer service**—Sephora invests heavily in employee training, so that its salespeople become "beauty coaches" who provide detailed information and assistance to customers.

As of 2007, Sephora continues to open new stores and improve its operating margin, with double-digit sales growth on a same-store basis in the United States for the seventh consecutive year.[23]

PHOTO: Kulish Viktoriia

>> END EXAMPLE

Types of Retailers

Retailing is one of the largest industries in the United States, accounting for approximately 10% of our gross national product.[24] Some of the largest categories of retailers are motor vehicle and parts dealers, general merchandise stores, food and beverage stores, gasoline stations, and building material and garden equipment supplies dealers.[25] Major retailers are classified by type, with each one performing a different function (see Table 13.1).[26]

Types of Wholesalers

Wholesalers sell a variety of products, from components essential for the manufacture of finished goods (e.g., bicycle seats) to supplies used to conduct everyday business activities (e.g., paper clips). Some wholesalers specialize in a particular category of products, while others sell a broad range. Wholesalers perform essential functions in distribution channels. They store goods until consumers need them. They simplify product, payment, and information flows between producers and customers. They inject capital into businesses by providing cash in advance of product sales to customers. They may even assume responsibility for technical support and order processing, thereby making life easier for manufacturers.[27]

There are two major kinds of wholesalers. **Independent intermediaries** conduct business with many different manufacturers and customers. They work primarily with small- to medium-sized resellers and come in a variety of forms, as shown in Table 13.2.

Manufacturer-owned intermediaries work for a single manufacturer. As a form of a vertically integrated channel, manufacturer-owned intermediaries create efficiencies for large firms. A **sales branch** maintains inventory for a company in different geographic areas. On the other hand, **sales offices** carry no inventory, but instead provide selling services for specific geographies. A **manufacturer's showroom** is a facility where a firm's products are permanently on display for customers to view. Any purchases are then fulfilled from distribution centers or warehouses.[28]

Table 13.1 Categories of Retailers

Retailer Type	Description	Example
Specialty store	Offers a narrow product line within a specialized category	The Sharper Image, The Limited, Sports Authority
Department store	Offers several product lines across multiple categories	Sears, JC Penney, Nordstrom
Supermarket	Large stores that offer food and household products at low prices	Ralphs, Kroger, Jewel
Convenience store	Small stores that offer convenience products and are often open 24 hours a day	7-Eleven, Circle K
Discount store	Focuses on low-priced merchandise	Wal-Mart, Family Dollar
Off-price retailer	Offers leftover goods, overruns, or irregular merchandise at prices below normal retail	Marshalls, TJ Maxx
Superstore	Large stores that offer a wide range of products and services, or "category killers," which concentrate a broad assortment of products within a specific category	Meijer, Staples, The Home Depot
Online retailer	Retail store that sells products or services over the Internet	Amazon.com, Flowers.com

Table 13.2 Categories of Wholesalers

	Wholesaler Type	Description
Merchant Wholesalers	Cash-and-carry wholesaler	Provide products for small businesses that buy at the wholesaler's location and self-transport
	Truck jobbers	Deliver food and tobacco items to retailers
	Drop shippers	Fill retail orders for products drop-shipped from manufacturers
	Mail-order wholesalers	Catalog, mail-order, or telephone wholesalers
	Rack jobbers	Handle displays, inventory, and merchandise for retailers
Merchandise Agents and Brokers	Manufacturer's agents	Independent salespeople who carry several lines of noncompeting products
	Selling agents	Handle all marketing functions for small manufacturers
	Commission merchants	Wholesalers who receive commissions on sales price of products
	Merchandise brokers	Work as brokers in markets with large numbers or small buyers and sellers

▼**Visual** Summary

Chapter 13 Summary

Marketers deliver products to consumers and businesses through the use of distribution channels. A company may choose to employ one or more channel types, depending on the requirements of its customers. A channel's number of levels, organization, and distribution intensity determine its strategy. Logistics and supply chain management are employed to oversee the transportation and warehousing of products. Retailing and warehousing complete the distribution chain by buying, storing, and selling products to end consumers, businesses, or resellers.

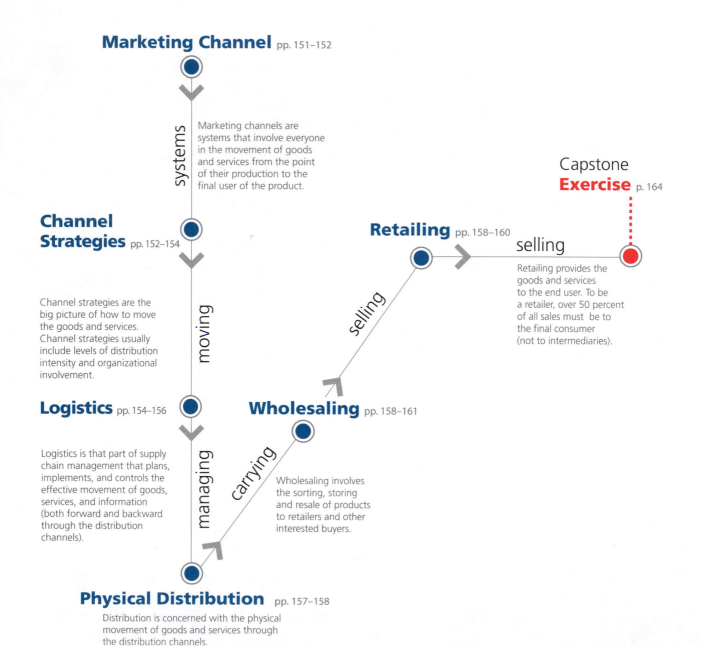

Marketing Channel pp. 151–152

Marketing channels are systems that involve everyone in the movement of goods and services from the point of their production to the final user of the product.

Channel Strategies pp. 152–154

Channel strategies are the big picture of how to move the goods and services. Channel strategies usually include levels of distribution intensity and organizational involvement.

Logistics pp. 154–156

Logistics is that part of supply chain management that plans, implements, and controls the effective movement of goods, services, and information (both forward and backward through the distribution channels).

Physical Distribution pp. 157–158

Distribution is concerned with the physical movement of goods and services through the distribution channels.

Wholesaling pp. 158–161

Wholesaling involves the sorting, storing and resale of products to retailers and other interested buyers.

Retailing pp. 158–160

Retailing provides the goods and services to the end user. To be a retailer, over 50 percent of all sales must be to the final consumer (not to intermediaries).

Capstone **Exercise** p. 164

▼Chapter Key Terms

Marketing Channels (pp. 151–152)

*A **marketing channel** is a network of all parties involved in moving products or services from producers to consumers or business customers. (p. 151)* **Opening Example (p. 151)**
Example: Marketing Channels (p. 152)

Key Terms (pp. 151–152)

Contact efficiency is the efficiency gained in terms of a reduction in the number of contacts required through the use of channel intermediaries. **(p. 151)**

Direct channel is a single channel member that produces and distributes a product or service. **(p. 151)**

Distribution is the process of delivering products and services to customers. **(p. 151)** **Example: Marketing Channels (p. 152)**

Indirect channel is a channel involving one or more intermediaries between producer and customer. **(p. 151)**

Channel Strategies (pp. 152–154)

*A **channel strategy** describes the levels, organization, and distribution intensity of a marketing channel. (p. 152)*
Example: Channel Strategy (p. 153)

Key Terms (pp. 153–154)

Channel conflict occurs when two or more channel members disagree. **(p. 154)**

Channel leader is a firm with sufficient power over other channel members to take a leadership role in the channel. **(p. 154)**

Distribution intensity determines the number of outlets or locations where a product will be sold. **(p. 153)**

Dual distribution is the use of two or more types of distribution. **(p. 153)**

Exclusive distribution refers to the distribution of products in only a few locations. **(p. 153)**

Horizontal conflict occurs between channel members at the same level in a channel (e.g., two retailers). **(p. 154)**

Intensive distribution refers to the distribution of products in a relatively large number of locations. **(p. 153)**

Multichannel conflict refers to conflict between different types of channels. **(p. 154)**

Selective distribution refers to the distribution of products in relatively few locations. **(p. 153)**

Vertical conflict refers to conflict between channel members at different levels in a channel (e.g., a wholesaler and a retailer). **(p. 154)**

Vertical Marketing System (VMS) is a channel that is vertically integrated based on acquisition or formal agreement, or by a firm developing its own distribution capabilities. **(p. 153)**

Logistics (pp. 154–156)

***Logistics** is the coordination of all activities related to the transportation or delivery of products and services that occur within the boundaries of a single business or organization. (p. 154)* **Example: Logistics Systems (p. 156)**

Key Terms (pp. 155–156)

Inbound logistics controls the flow of products or services from suppliers to manufacturers or service providers. **(p. 155)**

Logistics manager is a person responsible for coordinating the activities of all members of a company's distribution channel. **(p. 155)**

Outbound logistics controls the movement of products from points of production (factories or service delivery points) to consumers. **(p. 155)**

Reverse logistics addresses the methods consumers use to send products backward through a channel for return or repair. **(p. 155)**

Supply chain management is the management of all firms or organizations, both inside and outside a company, that impact the distribution process. **(p. 155)** **Example: Logistics Systems (p. 156)**

Third-party logistics company (3PL) manages all or part of another company's supply chain logistics. **(p. 156)**

Physical Distribution (pp. 157–158)

*ial distribution** (or freight transportation) is the process of carrying goods to customers. (p. 157)* **Opening Example (p. 151)**
Example: Physical Distribution (p. 158)

Key Terms (pp. 157–158)

Bar codes are unique product identification codes used to monitor inventory. **(p. 158)**

Breaking bulk refers to the process of reducing large product shipments into smaller ones that are more suitable for individual retailers or companies. **(p. 158)**

Carrier is the entity that physically transports goods from shipper to consignee. **(p. 157)**

Consignee is the receiver of goods being distributed. **(p. 157)**

Creating assortments is the process of collecting an assortment of products into a single shipment to a destination. **(p. 158)**

Cross-docking is a warehousing technique that minimizes holding costs by unloading products at a warehouse or distribution center and then reloading them almost immediately for transport. **(p. 158)** **Example: Physical Distribution (p. 158)**

Distribution center (DC) is a large warehouse used to store a company's products. **(p. 158)** **Example: Physical Distribution (p. 158)**

Electronic transport is a transportation mode used for electronic media. **(p. 157)**

Intermodal is a distribution strategy that uses more than one kind of transportation mode. **(p. 157)**

Inventory is a store of goods awaiting transport or shipping. **(p. 157)** **Example: Physical Distribution (p. 158)**

Pipeline is a transportation mode used for liquids such as oil or natural gas. **(p. 157)**

RFID (radio frequency identification) is an electronic chip and an antenna that can identify the precise physical location of a product. **(p. 158)**

Shipper is the owner of goods being distributed. **(p. 157)**

Stock-keeping unit (SKU) is a unique identification number used to track and organize products. **(p. 158)**

Transportation management systems (TMS) are software programs used to automate the shipping process. **(p. 157)**

Universal Product Code (or UPC) is the standard format for retail bar codes. **(p. 158)**

Warehouse is a physical facility used primarily for the storage of goods held in anticipation of sale or transfer within the marketing channel. **(p. 157)** **Example: Marketing Channels (p. 152) Example: Physical Distribution (p. 158)**

Retailing and Wholesaling (pp. 158–161)

Retailing *involves the sale of products or services to consumers.* (p. 158) **Opening Example** (p. 151) **Example: Marketing Channels** (p. 152) **Example: Retailing** (p. 159)

Wholesaling *involves the sorting, storing, and reselling of products to retailers or businesses.* (p. 158) **Example: Marketing Channels** (p. 152)

Key Terms (pp. 159–161)

Cash-and-carry wholesaler provides products for small businesses that buy at the wholesaler's location and self-transport. **(p. 161)**

Commission merchant is a wholesaler who receives commissions on the sales price of products. **(p. 161)**

Convenience store is a small store that offers convenience products and often is open 24 hours a day. **(p. 160)**

Department store is a store that offers several product lines across multiple categories. **(p. 160)** **Example: Retailing** (p. 159)

Discount store is a store focused on selling low-priced merchandise. **(p. 160)**

Drop shipper fills retail orders for products drop-shipped from a manufacturer. **(p. 161)**

Independent intermediary conducts business with many different manufacturers and customers. **(p. 160)**

Mail-order wholesaler is a catalog, mail-order, or telephone wholesaler. **(p. 161)**

Manufacturer-owned intermediary provides wholesaling services for a single manufacturer. **(p. 160)**

Manufacturer's agent is an independent salesperson who carries several lines of noncompeting products. **(p. 161)**

Manufacturer's showroom is a facility where a firm's products are permanently on display. **(p. 160)**

Merchandise broker works as broker in markets with large numbers of small buyers and sellers. **(p. 161)**

Off-price retailer is a store that offers leftover goods, overruns, or irregular merchandise at prices below normal retail. **(p. 160)**

Online retailer is a retail company that sells products or services over the Internet. **(p. 160)**

Rack jobber handles displays, inventory, and merchandise for a retailer. **(p. 161)**

Sales branch maintains inventory for a company in a geographic area. **(p. 160)**

Sales office provides selling services for a company in a geographic area. **(p. 160)**

Selling agent handles all marketing functions for a small manufacturer. **(p. 161)**

Specialty store offers a narrow product line within a specialized category. **(p. 160)**

Supermarket is a large store that offers food and household products at low prices. **(p. 160)**

Superstore is a large store that offers a wide range of products and services, or offers a "category killer" that concentrates on a deep assortment of products within a specific category. **(p. 160)**

Truck jobber delivers food and tobacco items to retailers. **(p. 161)**

▼Capstone Exercise

As a knowledgeable marketing consultant specializing in distribution channel design, you have recently signed the following three new clients:

- The first client has designed a new kitchen utensil—a potato peeler that is far superior to anything currently on the market. The problem is that the peeler will retail for $8.00, while the majority of peelers currently on the market sell for $2.00.
- The second client sells specialized software that greatly improves how trucking companies manage the maintenance of their vehicles. The software costs $75,000 per system.
- The third company makes salsa that has a wonderful taste.

Design a channel strategy for each of these clients. To do that, you must answer the following questions:

1. Who are your target customers?

2. What functions do the intermediaries need to perform?

3. What is the added value of your choice?

4. How many levels of intermediaries do you need? (Each must make a profit.)

5. What is your distribution intensity: intensive, exclusive, or selective?

▼Application Exercises

Complete the following exercises:

1. In 2007, Amazon.com was the largest Internet retailer in the United States. It sells a wide range of products, including books, toys, sporting goods, and motorcycle accessories. (If you aren't aware of the kinds of products Amazon.com carries, please visit its Web site and take a few minutes to familiarize yourself.) Customers place orders through the Web site and their products are shipped to them as soon as the next day.

   When thinking about Amazon.com, consider the following questions:

   • When a customer orders a product on Amazon.com, what is the typical distribution channel used to fulfill the order? Do you think Amazon.com has a warehouse? What inventory management systems does it use?
   • If an order is expedited for next-day delivery, would the channel structure change? Why does Amazon.com charge more for faster delivery?
   • If a product must be returned, what does the reverse channel look like? How is the return processed?

2. Office supply stores such as Staples or Office Depot serve a variety of business-to-business and business-to-consumer market segments. The product needs and shopping habits of each segment vary substantially. Consider the type of distribution channel an office supply store would need to satisfy the following types of customers:

   • A large business customer who is purchasing supplies for a multistory office building.
   • A real estate agent who needs paper, pens, and other items for their one-room home office.
   • A retailer who operates a chain of stores within a regional area, such as a city or state, who wants to set up a yearly contract to supply all of its operations.
   • Online customers who want to purchase items on the Internet, and then pick them up at a brick-and-mortar store.

3. Visit a local discount store (e.g., Wal-Mart, Target) and a local off-price store (e.g., T.J. Maxx, Stein Mart). Examine the product mix and pricing strategies of both stores. Who would you say is the target market of each retailer? Why?

4. Describe the major types of wholesalers located in your community and give an example of each.

chapter 14

Part 1   Explaining (Chapters 1, 2, 3, 4)
Part 2   Creating (Chapters 5, 6, 7, 8)
Part 3   Strategizing (Chapters 9, 10)

Part 4   Managing (Chapters 11, 12, 13, 14, 15)
Part 5   Integrating (Chapters 16, 17)

Consumer-Influence Strategies

Chapter Overview How can a company use marketing communication to build relationships with customers? This chapter introduces consumer-influence strategies and outlines the marketing communication process. The chapter also discusses how marketers use integrated marketing communications campaigns to connect with consumers through advertising, public relations, sales promotion, and sponsorship.

▼ Chapter **Outline**

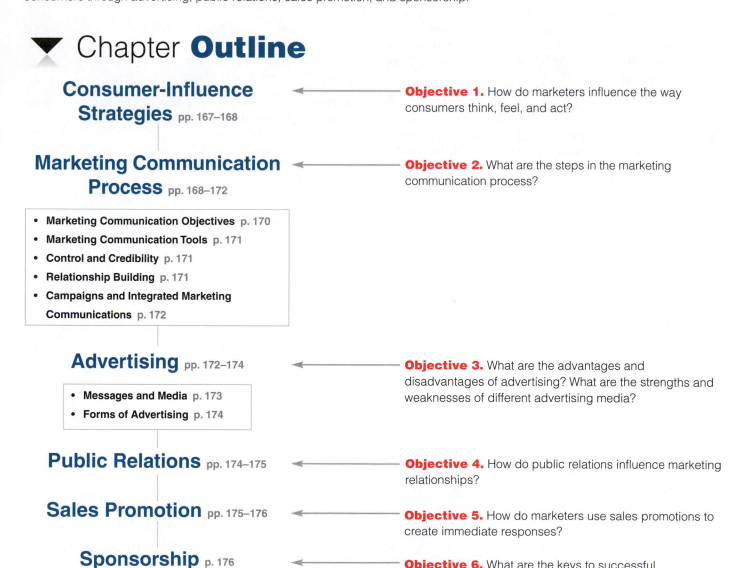

Consumer-Influence Strategies pp. 167–168

Objective 1. How do marketers influence the way consumers think, feel, and act?

Marketing Communication Process pp. 168–172

Objective 2. What are the steps in the marketing communication process?

- **Marketing Communication Objectives** p. 170
- **Marketing Communication Tools** p. 171
- **Control and Credibility** p. 171
- **Relationship Building** p. 171
- **Campaigns and Integrated Marketing Communications** p. 172

Advertising pp. 172–174

Objective 3. What are the advantages and disadvantages of advertising? What are the strengths and weaknesses of different advertising media?

- **Messages and Media** p. 173
- **Forms of Advertising** p. 174

Public Relations pp. 174–175

Objective 4. How do public relations influence marketing relationships?

Sales Promotion pp. 175–176

Objective 5. How do marketers use sales promotions to create immediate responses?

Sponsorship p. 176

Objective 6. What are the keys to successful sponsorship?

CONSUMER-INFLUENCE STRATEGIES (pp. 167–168)

> ▼ **DEFINED** **Consumer-influence strategies** *are strategies for engaging consumers and influencing how they think, feel, and act toward a brand or market offering through the use of marketing communication.*

Consumer-Influence Strategies

Developing, pricing, and distributing a product or service will get it into the market, but how do consumers find out about it? This is where consumer-influence strategies play a vital role. Whether the communication is an exciting Super Bowl commercial or an informative magazine ad, the idea is to call attention to a particular offering and influence consumers' thoughts, feelings, and actions toward it. Because of competing messages and other distractions, however, getting and keeping the audience's attention long enough to convey a message—the first step toward influence—can be a real challenge.

Consumer-influence strategies can add value for consumers and marketers alike. However, if the consumer sees little or no value in what is being communicated, or the results deliver little or no return on the marketer's investment, the strategy will not be effective.

Consumer-Influence Strategies

As you know from your own experience, companies are constantly trying to influence consumers through a variety of marketing communications. In addition to companies, organizations and people also develop consumer-influence strategies for marketing purposes. For example, New York State uses print advertising, television commercials, and its tourism Web site, iloveny.com, to get people to visit New York. Consumer-influence strategies apply to individuals buying for themselves or for a household as well as to individuals buying for a business, governmental agency, or nonprofit group. See Figure 14.1 for the steps on creating a consumer-influence strategy.

New Dove Firming. As tested on real curves.

Dove's "Campaign for Real Beauty" has put a fresh face on skincare advertising and reenergized a decades-old brand. Rather than focusing on supermodels, Dove's magazine, television, billboard, and online ads for soaps, creams, and body washes showcase the beauty of real women of all ages, sizes, and shapes. Unilever, Dove's parent company, has also invited consumers to share their thoughts about beauty on the campaign's Web site and create their own television commercials using the "real beauty" theme. The campaign not only won awards for creativity and effectiveness, it also helped Dove increase its worldwide market share and launch profitable new products.

PHOTO: The New York Times

FIGURE 14.1 | **Developing a Consumer-Influence Strategy**

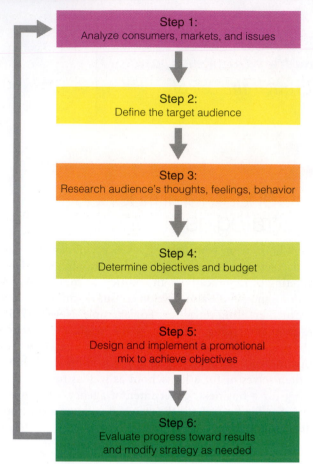

Step 1:
Analyze consumers, markets, and issues

Step 2:
Define the target audience

Step 3:
Research audience's thoughts, feelings, behavior

Step 4:
Determine objectives and budget

Step 5:
Design and implement a promotional mix to achieve objectives

Step 6:
Evaluate progress toward results and modify strategy as needed

EXAMPLE | **CONSUMER-INFLUENCE STRATEGIES**

As shown in Figure 14.1, there are six steps to developing a consumer-influence strategy:

1. *Analyze consumers, markets, and issues.* This will reveal opportunities for reaching more customers or making more sales. It will also uncover threats, such as aggressive competition, that could threaten the strategy's success. For example, Harley-Davidson observed that many motor-cycle owners, particularly younger owners, were customizing their bikes to look like the stripped-down models of the 1940s. Because the average age of Harley buyers is about

47, the company recognized an opportunity to expand market share by attracting younger buyers.[2]

2. *Define the target audience.* Harley decided its target audience would be motorcycle buyers under the age of 35.

3. *Research audience's thoughts, feelings, and behavior.* Harley learned that the target audience felt nostalgic for the authentic look of stripped-down motorcycle models.

4. *Determine the objectives and the budget.* A marketer might want to boost brand awareness or improve competitive standing, for example, with a corresponding budget invest-ment. Harley set awareness and sales objectives for the new Dark Custom motorcycle line it designed for younger riders. It also established an appropriate budget for com-municating with the target audience.

5. *Design and implement a promotional mix to achieve the objectives.* The **promotional mix** is the specific combi-nation of communication tools selected for a particular influence strategy. The exact choice of media and mes-sages will depend on market analyses, audience research, and the competitive situation. With its ad agen-cies, Harley decided on television, Internet, print, and direct-mail ads, along with special events and public relations.

6. *Evaluate progress toward results and modify strategy as needed.* Once Harley implemented its influence strategy, it regularly researched awareness of and attitudes toward Dark Custom bikes. It also monitored weekly, monthly, and quarterly sales to determine whether it was moving toward achieving its sales objective.

PHOTO: Ljupco Smokovski

>> END EXAMPLE

Marketing Communication Process (pp. 168–172)

 DEFINED *The* **marketing communication process** *is the way in which a sender encodes a marketing idea and conveys it through message and medium so receivers can decode and understand it, and then respond with feedback.*

▼ **EXPLAINED**
Marketing Communication Process

Marketing communication, the heart of every consumer-influence strategy, requires two parties. The sender initiates the process by *encoding* a marketing idea, which is translating the meaning into a *message* (for example, by using language, graphics, and music) to be conveyed through a *medium* that serves as channel to convey the idea. By *decoding*, the receiver interprets the sender's message to understand its meaning. Then, the receiver completes the process by providing the sender with *feedback*—a reaction to the message (see Figure 14.2).

Feedback may take the form of a purchase, a comment on a product blog, a phone call to the company, or a consumer-created commercial for the marketer's brand.

Noise is anything that might distort, block, or otherwise prevent the message from being properly encoded, sent, decoded, received, and/or comprehended. Competing messages represent noise, for instance, which is why the Chinese government limited billboard and airport advertising by marketers who were not official sponsors during the Beijing Olympics. This cleared the way for messages from official sponsors, such as McDonald's and Panasonic, to be noticed and received by visitors to the Olympic games.[4]

EXAMPLE | MARKETING COMMUNICATION PROCESS

H.J. Heinz has invited consumers to create and submit 30-second commercials that express their passion for the company's market-leading ketchup. The company announced the contests online and on its product labels. "The most powerful vehicle for us to communicate with consumers is our own bottle," explained the ketchup brand manager. Feedback came in the form of thousands of video entries that consumers viewed more than 10 million times on TopThisTV.com and YouTube. Then, the company selected 10 finalists and posted a message asking consumers to choose their favorite. Tens of thousands of consumers responded by clicking to view and vote. Heinz gave the winner $57,000 and aired the winning commercial on national television.[3]

PHOTO: Dirk Herzog

>> END EXAMPLE

▼ **APPLIED**

Marketing Communication Process

In traditional models of the communication process, the marketer is the sender and the consumer is the receiver. However, today's empowered consumer frequently acts as sender in initiating communication with a marketer. A consumer might encode a message (such as a question about a product's warranty) and choose a medium (such as an e-mail) to reach the marketer. After decoding the message, the marketer would use feedback to respond in an appropriate way, such as e-mailing a copy of the product warranty.

FIGURE 14.2   The Marketing Communication Process

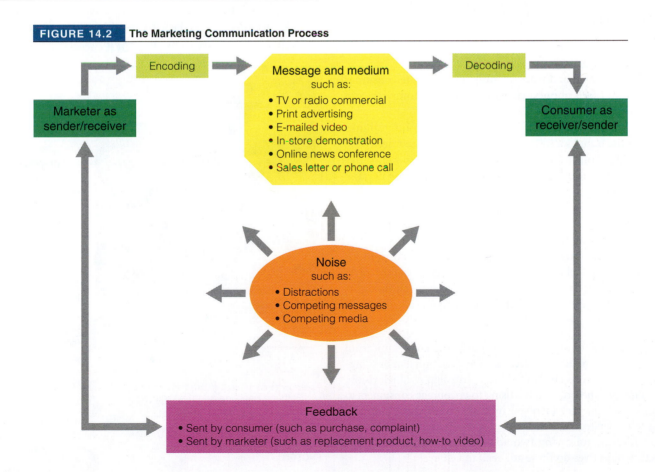

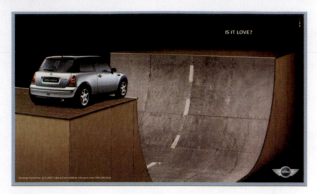

IS IT LOVE?

Mini Cooper uses print, television, and online advertising to influence how consumers think and feel about its car. Showing a Mini poised to plunge into a half-pipe helps consumers imagine that the experience of driving a Mini is as exciting as extreme sports.

PHOTO: Courtesy of BMW Worldwide.

>> END EXAMPLE

Marketing Communication Objectives

The overall goal of marketing communication is to influence the thoughts, feelings, or behavior of the target audience. Rather than trying for a one-time purchase, most companies aim to promote long-term brand loyalty. To do this, based on where the target audience is in the decision-making process, marketers set the following objectives:

- Help the consumer recognize a need (influence how the consumer thinks about a problem or need).
- Build awareness and interest (influence how the consumer thinks and feels about a category, brand, or company, and encourage the consumer to find out more).
- Inform about benefits (influence how the consumer thinks about the brand's ability to satisfy the recognized need).
- Persuade about value (influence how the consumer thinks and feels about the brand's competitive superiority in satisfying needs).
- Stimulate action (influence the consumer to take the next step toward buying, such as forming an intention to buy or placing an order for that brand).
- Reinforce the buying decision (influence the consumer's thoughts and feelings about having purchased that brand).
- Remind about brand (influence the consumer's thoughts about the brand's value and encourage trial or repeat purchasing).

Nonprofit organizations also set marketing communication objectives, such as building awareness of a social problem or bringing in donations. A recent United Way campaign used television, print, billboard, and online advertising to encourage consumers to take three actions: get involved in their communities, donate money to the United Way, and volunteer their time for local causes.

Consider the following two ads and compare them. What marketing objectives do these ads seek to achieve?

This is a good example of reminder advertising. **What makes it work**?

The Pepsi brand and logo are particularly prominent.

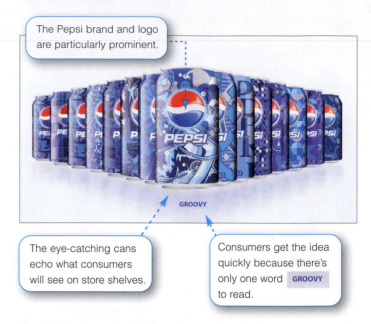

GROOVY

The eye-catching cans echo what consumers will see on store shelves.

Consumers get the idea quickly because there's only one word **GROOVY** to read.

This ad is intended to inform executives—the target audience—about Credit Suisse's benefits. **What makes it work**?

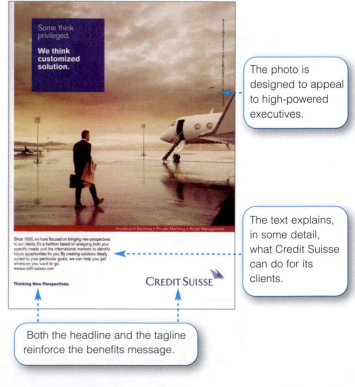

The photo is designed to appeal to high-powered executives.

The text explains, in some detail, what Credit Suisse can do for its clients.

Both the headline and the tagline reinforce the benefits message.

Marketing Communication Tools

The promotional mix for a consumer-influence strategy will include at least one of these marketing communication tools:

- Advertising
- Public relations
- Sales promotion
- Sponsorship
- Personal selling
- Direct marketing

The first four tools are explored later in this chapter; the last two are discussed in Chapter 15.

Control and Credibility

It is important to note that the marketer does not have complete control over these marketing communication tools. Although a company can control the creation and placement of ads, it cannot control how competitors react and whether consumers embrace or ignore the ads. Consumers may turn the page if they see a magazine ad or change channels if they see a television commercial. On the other hand, consumers often talk about ads and e-mail videos of commercials to friends.

Similarly, a company can control the creation and delivery of discount coupons. However, except for setting expiration dates, it cannot control whether or when consumers redeem coupons. As shown in Figure 14.3, public relations is even less controllable. Once a company has contacted reporters or bloggers, it cannot control what they do with the information, or whether they use any or all of it. The marketer has the least control over **word of mouth**, consumers communicating with each other about a brand, marketing offer, or marketing message. In fact, when people talk, write, e-mail, blog, or otherwise communicate about a brand or an offer, they may change, distort, or exaggerate the original message.

Word of mouth is influential because friends, relatives, neighbors, and colleagues are seen as more credible sources of information than company-controlled sources. Are you more likely to buy a new product if you hear about it from a friend who likes it, or if you see it featured on the company's Web site? Consumers also see outside experts and reporters as credible because they are more objective than company-controlled sources. Many marketers seek to stimulate word of mouth through **viral marketing**, activities that encourage consumers to electronically share a company's marketing message with friends.

Adidas has been running hard to catch Nike, the market leader in athletic shoes. Its Basketball is a Brotherhood campaign, which focused on Adidas basketball shoes, included viral marketing as well as print, television, and online advertising. Adidas invited consumers to sign up via text message to receive recorded voice messages from an NBA star, for example, Tim Duncan of the San Antonio Spurs. The messages sent consumers to a Web site where they could personalize and download ringtones featuring the voices of NBA players. The novelty prompted many consumers to talk about Adidas and forward the Web site address so their friends could mix their own ringtones.[5]

PHOTO: Dan Thomas Brostrom

>> END EXAMPLE

Relationship Building

For maximum impact, the tools used in a consumer-influence strategy should be selected with two-way communication in mind. Starting a dialogue with consumers helps the marketer better understand and respond to the target audience's needs and behaviors. Keeping the dialogue going strengthens the marketer's relationship with the target audience and has a positive effect on the audience's thoughts, feelings, and actions, which leads to higher brand loyalty and sales. Many small businesses build relationships by sending birthday cards to customers, calling to check on product satisfaction, or sending e-mails with special offers.

In the earlier viral marketing example, Adidas wanted only to get consumers talking about its brand and its unique basketball-star ringtones, not to make an immediate sale. Feedback, such as the number of consumers who signed up to receive messages and the number who mixed personalized ringtones, told Adidas whether it was reaching its target audience and

FIGURE 14.3 Company Control over Marketing Communications

whether its message was of interest. Other messages in other media were designed to motivate consumers to actually buy Adidas products.

Campaigns and Integrated Marketing Communications

With a **campaign**, a company seeks to influence its target audience over time, using a consistent communication theme and varying message creativity and delivery. The purpose is to connect with the target audience in different ways during the campaign period, increasing the likelihood that consumers will notice, comprehend, and act on the messages. Despite the many possible ways to reach out to audiences, marketers must carefully weigh the cost of multiple marketing activities against the expected outcome. As a result, a campaign may last for a few weeks or as long as a few years, depending on the objectives, the budget, the competition, and the target audience's response.

A successful campaign requires **integrated marketing communications**, the careful coordination of every communication contact for message consistency across all media. Conflicting messages can confuse and influence consumers in ways that the marketer never intended. The overall impact is much stronger when the content and the look or sound of every message are consistent with the brand's image and the campaign's objectives.

EXAMPLE INTEGRATED MARKETING COMMUNICATIONS

One Geico campaign features a wise-cracking gecko, while another features modern-day cavemen. Both campaigns highlight the insurance company's key benefit of saving customers money. Using a variety of media and creative interpretations enables Geico to target audiences that respond to different versions of the core money-saving message. All the messages—whether they air on television or radio, appear in print or on billboards, arrive in the mailbox, or flash across the computer screen—use the humorous, irreverent tone that sets Geico apart from competitors. Even the company's wildlife conservancy efforts reinforce the association of the gecko with the Geico brand. With an annual communications budget that tops $500 million, Geico is aiming to increase market share and soon become the third-largest U.S. insurance company.[6]

Companies can use a campaign to *pull* a product through the marketing channel by getting consumers to ask retailers and wholesalers for it—a **pull strategy**. In a **push strategy**, the campaign targets retailers and wholesalers, and encourages them to order the product and *push* it through the channel to consumers (see Figure 14.4). Marketers often combine pull and push through communications that are coordinated to induce timely responses from intermediaries and consumers. Chicago-based USG, which makes building products, uses both push and pull. Its pull strategy targets builders and contractors using

magazine and online advertising to encourage purchasing; its push strategy targets building-supply stores using viral marketing and print advertising to encourage retail support.[7] As with any strategy, marketers must continually monitor results to determine what is working and what is not working, and then make changes as needed.

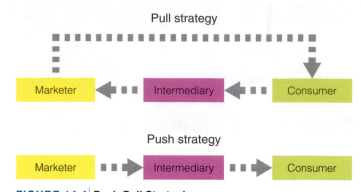

FIGURE 14.4 | **Push-Pull Strategies**

PHOTO: Ryan J. Lane/Courtesy of www.istockphoto.com

>> END EXAMPLE

Advertising (pp. 172–174)

 DEFINED **Advertising** *is the paid, nonpersonal communication of a marketing message by an identified sponsor through mass media.*

▼ **EXPLAINED**

Advertising

As the advertising definition states, advertising is distinguished from other communication tools in the following four ways:

1. **Paid message**—The marketer pays to have the marketing message delivered.
2. **Nonpersonal communication**—Advertising is not delivered personally.
3. **Identified sponsor**—A marketer (a company or another sponsor) is behind every advertising message, even if the only identification is a logo, such as the Nike swoosh.
4. **Mass media**—The message is delivered through media that reach people in large numbers.

Table 14.1 classifies advertising according to target audience.

Advertising has several advantages and disadvantages. It can alert members of the target audience to products with benefits that will satisfy their needs, let them know when and where offerings are available, suggest how to compare competing products or brands, and provide entertainment. As a consumer, you may have been entertained, surprised, informed, touched, or motivated by advertising in some way. However, you may also view some advertising as intrusive, offensive, irritating, irrelevant, overly aggressive, or even misleading.

Table 14.1 Classifying Advertising by Target Audience

Type of Advertising	Target Audience
Consumer	People who buy for personal or household use
Industrial	People who buy on behalf of a business
Trade	People who work for retailers, wholesalers, or other intermediaries
Professional	People who are professional practitioners, such as doctors, lawyers, and accountants

For marketers, advertising can be a cost-effective, creative way to communicate with groups of people, educate the audience about a product or category, and help initiate or maintain a dialogue with the audience. Because advertising is nonpersonal and delivered through mass media, potential disadvantages are that the audience may not notice the message, may misinterpret it, or may react differently from how the marketer expected.

 ▼ **APPLIED**

Advertising

Advertising is big business: Worldwide, companies spend an estimated $449 billion on advertising every year.[8] Procter & Gamble, which makes Tide detergent, Pampers diapers, and hundreds of other household products, spends more than $3.5 billion annually on U.S. television, magazine, newspaper, and online advertising.[9] Determining exactly how much to invest in advertising to get the desired sales results can be tricky, because consumer purchasing can be affected by competitors' actions, economic conditions, and other factors besides advertising. Like many (but not all) companies, Procter & Gamble hires advertising agencies to plan and implement ad campaigns for every brand, including researching the audiences, creating the messages, choosing the media, placing the ads, and researching the results.

Advertising influences consumers through the following AIDA model:

- **A**wareness—Draw attention to the message visually and verbally.
- **I**nterest—Provide information to get the audience interested.
- **D**esire—Create desire for the product or service.
- **A**ction—Encourage the audience to take a specific action, such as making a purchase.

Messages and Media

What idea will each message convey, and how will it express that idea? Messages that discuss the brand's benefits or competitive superiority are intended to influence how the audience thinks about the brand. Such messages convey the unique selling proposition (USP), which was introduced in Chapter 9. From an advertising perspective, the USP is the point of differentiation that "sells" the brand in a positive way that the target audience values and believes. The USP for Geico insurance is that it saves consumers money. To get the audience thinking about this benefit, Geico's ads ask, "How much could you save?"

Advertising messages that use emotional appeals such as love, friendship, fear, or guilt are intended to influence how the audience feels. Cesar sells dog food through ads that appeal to the consumer's love for a pet: "I promise to always be there when you wake." The nonprofit Ad Council and the U.S. Army aim to reduce high school dropout levels through ads that appeal to friendship: "Help a friend graduate."

How a message is creatively presented depends on the medium in which it will appear. Therefore, before marketers start to create any messages, they must make several decisions about selecting and using media. What media do members of the target audience use and prefer? What creative opportunities does each medium offer? How, when, where, and how often should the message be delivered, given the available budget for a campaign?

EXAMPLE ADVERTISING

General Motors designed its "Built to last, built to love" campaign to make consumers aware of the redesigned Chevy Malibu, get them interested in visiting a dealership, create a desire to own a Malibu, and sell more Malibus during the model year. The promotional mix combined television advertising, interactive online advertising, and magazine advertising, plus sponsorship of the Lo Nuestro Latin Music Awards, publicity from bloggers' test drives, exhibits at auto shows, and personal selling by Chevy dealers. The first ads attracted attention by showing the new car and using the slogan: "The car you can't ignore." The next ads created interest with quotes from independent experts praising the car. Finally, GM advertised specific details to build desire and bring buyers into dealerships. The result: Consumers developed more positive perceptions of the new Malibu, and the car's sales accelerated.[10]

PHOTO: Kalim

>> END EXAMPLE

Forms of Advertising

Traditional examples of advertising include television, radio, newspapers, magazines, direct mail, billboards, e-mail, and Web sites. Increasingly, marketers are including other forms of advertising in their consumer-influence campaigns. **Place-based advertising** is advertising that reaches people outside the home—where they work, play, or shop. Frito-Lay, Unilever, and other companies use place-based advertising on Wal-Mart TV to reach shoppers who walk by the screens in Wal-Mart's U.S. stores.[11] **Specialty advertising** is advertising in which the marketer gives away small items (such as T-shirts or mugs) bearing its name or logo to keep the audience thinking of the brand and feeling good about it. For more about media refer to Chapter 16.

Public Relations (pp. 174–175)

 DEFINED **Public relations** *is two-way communication designed to improve mutual understanding and positively influence relationships between the marketer and its internal and external publics.*

 EXPLAINED

Public Relations

The target audiences of public relations—the **publics**—are people inside or outside the company who have a "stake" in what it does. These publics include customers, stockholders, employees, suppliers, distributors, government officials, industry groups, community members, reporters, and others who may influence or be influenced by the marketer in some way.

The objectives of public relations are as follows:

- To gauge what various publics think and feel about the marketer's brands and about business issues
- To establish a dialogue about various publics' interests and concerns
- To enhance the marketer's image
- To build or rebuild trust and goodwill
- To build a solid foundation for ongoing marketing efforts

▼ **APPLIED**

Public Relations

A marketer can use **corporate public relations** to evaluate and shape or reshape long-term public opinion of the company. The focus is on polishing the company's image over time, rather than on achieving an immediate marketing objective. Sometimes companies spotlight their involvement with causes or organizations that are important to its publics, the way McDonald's communicates its support of the Ronald McDonald House Charities. Similarly, The Home Depot builds goodwill through its connection with Habitat for Humanity in many communities.

In contrast, **marketing public relations** seeks to achieve specific marketing objectives by targeting consumers with product-focused messages. For example, Kraft Foods has six Oscar Mayer Wienermobiles touring the country, to introduce new products and reinforce brand awareness. One of the most visible forms of marketing public relations is **product placement**, in which the company arranges for its brand or product to appear in a movie or another entertainment vehicle. Cisco Systems' video-conferencing products have appeared on *CSI* episodes; branded Coca-Cola cups have been prominently featured on *American Idol*. Integrating a product into a movie, television program, videogame, concert tour, or stage show sends a more subtle message about the brand and its desirability than does marketer-controlled advertising.

Note that **publicity**, generating unpaid, positive media coverage about a company or its products, is only one part of public relations and can be used for either corporate or marketing purposes. Table 14.2 shows some of the most common techniques used for publicity purposes.

One of the major functions of public relations is to prepare the company for effective two-way communication during crises caused by natural disasters, criminal activity, product recalls, or other problems. What a company says and does during such difficult situations will affect its image, reputation, and relationships. Despite the very real potential for damage, a crisis can also be an opportunity to demonstrate genuine concern for the safety and welfare of employees, customers, and other publics.

Table 14.2 Commonly Used Publicity Techniques	
Technique	**Use**
News release	Printed, electronic, or video information about a product or the company delivered to media for news purposes
Media kit	General information about the company, personnel, products, history, and activities delivered to media as background for news
News conference	A meeting with media representatives to publicly communicate company or product news and answer questions
Public appearance	Live appearances by company or celebrity spokespeople to call attention to a brand, product, issue, or cause

Mattel faced a serious crisis when the paints on some of its toys imported from China were found to contain dangerous levels of lead. Even before the company and the U.S. government completed their investigations, Mattel's CEO decided to recall millions of toys, increase supplier scrutiny, and expand safety testing. The CEO also publicly apologized to consumers, retailers, legislators, and business leaders, seeking to regain their trust by highlighting Mattel's actions to head off future problems. "When my children tell me to trust them," the CEO told a Chamber of Commerce meeting, "I tell them, 'deeds, not words.' That's never been more true for us at Mattel than in recent months."[12]

PHOTO: Comstock Complete

>> END EXAMPLE

Sales Promotion (pp. 175–176)

 DEFINED Sales promotion *is marketer-controlled communication to stimulate immediate audience response by enhancing the value of an offering for a limited time.*

 EXPLAINED

Sales Promotion

Sales promotion achieves short-term marketing objectives by getting the target audience to take action right away. It does this by adding to the product's value for a brief time. Depending on the audience, the added value may be anything from a free sample or a prize to a coupon or a rebate. Consumers get the message that they must act now because the extra value is available for a limited period only. Fast response and marketer control over the message are only two advantages of sales promotion. Another is accountability: marketers can quickly and easily measure consumer response by counting how many samples have been given away or how many coupons have been redeemed.

In contrast, communication tools such as advertising and public relations influence consumers over a longer period. It takes time to build brand loyalty and strengthen relationships by influencing how consumers think, feel, and act. And because so many factors play a role in stimulating purchases, it is difficult to measure the direct effect of advertising and public relations on sales. Therefore, the short-term, measurable influence of sales promotion is a good complement to the long-term influence of other communication tools.

The target audience for sales promotion may be consumers or the trade (retailers and wholesalers). **Consumer sales promotion** aims to get consumers (including business customers) to try a

product or buy it again. **Trade sales promotion** aims to get retail and wholesale buyers to buy an existing product, stock a new product, or feature a particular product; it can also encourage retail and wholesale salespeople to push a certain product.

▼ **APPLIED**

Sales Promotion

Companies can use a variety of consumer sales promotion techniques, including the following:

- **Coupons** encourage consumers to try a new product or keep buying an existing product at a limited-time discount.
- **Samples and trial offers** allow consumers to try and evaluate a good or service for free or at a low price.
- **Refunds and rebates** return some or all of the purchase price to the buyer to encourage product trial or repurchase.
- **Loyalty programs** reward consumers for repeat purchases of a product or brand.
- **Contests and sweepstakes** offer prizes to build excitement and involve customers in a brand-related activity.
- **Premiums** give buyers free (or low-cost) items in the product package, in the store, or by mail, to encourage buying.
- **Point-of-purchase displays** draw shoppers' attention to particular products with eye-catching in-store displays.

The Arby's fast-food chain frequently uses coupons to bring consumers into its restaurants and boost sales of specific menu items. Now Arby's is reaching out to a wider audience by delivering coupons by cell phone. Instead of handing a printed coupon to the cashier, the consumer shows the coupon on his or her cell phone screen. According to the vice president of marketing, "Arby's does a lot of couponing in newspaper and direct mail, so it was a natural transition to do a mobile couponing offer. We look for alternative media opportunities to reach different audiences and we felt that mobile was the perfect way to reach a younger audience."[13]

PHOTO: Juanmonino/Courtesy of www.istockphoto.com

>> END EXAMPLE

Trade sales promotion techniques include the following:

- **Trade show exhibits** showcase products to many buyers during industry events.
- **Trade allowances** reward retailers or wholesalers with discounts or payments for promoting a product to consumers.
- **Co-operative advertising allowances** pay part of the cost for wholesalers and retailers that include a product in their local advertising.

- **Sales contests** reward salespeople for meeting or exceeding sales goals.
- **Training** improves the trade's product knowledge and sales skills.

Sales promotion can be fun and engaging, but it can also be controversial. Pharmaceutical companies have invested billions of dollars in consumer coupons, free samples, and payments to doctors for attending product-training courses. Critics worry that these promotions will prompt consumers to ask doctors for unneeded or inappropriate drugs. They also worry that doctors will be swayed to prescribe drugs unnecessarily or prefer the promoted drugs over other alternatives. In response, some states have restricted pharmaceutical sales promotions targeting doctors. And the Pharmaceutical Research and Manufacturers of America, an industry group, has adopted voluntary guidelines limiting payments and gifts to doctors.[14]

Sponsorship (p. 176)

 DEFINED Sponsorship *is a way of publicly associating a brand with an event or activity that the company supports financially.*

 EXPLAINED

Sponsorship

Sponsorship links a brand with an event or activity that interests its target audience. Whereas advertising conveys a specific message and sales promotion sparks immediate action, sponsorship influences brand awareness, attitudes, and feelings. According to a senior marketer at the British cell phone company Vodafone, "The emotional connection with people is what is valuable."[15] The positive thoughts and feelings provoked by sponsorship lay the groundwork for making the sale using other tools in the promotional mix. Sponsorship can also target internal audiences, building pride in the company and using event attendance to reward employees.

The key to successful sponsorship is to choose an event or activity that reaches the right audience, is important to that audience, and has a natural connection with the brand. Depending on the brand and the audience, the company can sponsor anything from a sports event, museum exhibit, or rock concert to an entertainment convention, charity fundraiser, or special online event. McDonald's reaches out to young men by sponsoring the Midnight Gamers Championships, because this tournament is a natural fit with the target audience and the chain's promotion of its late-night hours.[16]

EXAMPLE SPONSORSHIP

Anheuser-Busch InBev links its Budweiser brand with the excitement of NASCAR racing by sponsoring Kasey Kahne's car, as well as the Budweiser Shootout at Daytona. It sponsors Bud Light Bleachers at Chicago's Wrigley Field to link the brand with major league baseball. And it reaches nearly 100 million viewers every winter as one of the long-time sponsors of the Super Bowl (and a major advertiser during the game). The goal is to have fans who attend the events and fans who watch on television associate the brand with their enjoyment of sports.[17]

PHOTO: Robert Byron/Courtesy of www.istockphoto.com

>> END EXAMPLE

 APPLIED

Sponsorship

Companies around the world spend an estimated $38 billion yearly on sponsorship. Adidas, for instance, is investing hundreds of millions of dollars over 10 years to sponsor the German national soccer team, among other sports-related sponsorships. But how does a company evaluate its return on investment from a sponsorship? A company uses the following elements for such evaluations:

- **Exposure**—Determine how many people were exposed to the brand (reach) and how many times they were exposed (frequency) during the event.
- **Efficiency**—Compare the cost of this reach and frequency with the cost of using other communication tools.
- **Reaction**—Research changes in audience brand awareness, attitudes, emotions, and purchase intentions to see whether the sponsorship had a positive effect on the audience. Get feedback from many publics for a well-rounded picture of the reaction.
- **Image**—Analyze whether the sponsorship enhanced the company's or the brand's image. Sponsoring a major event like the Super Bowl, or even a community activity such as a local health fair, can pay off in long-term goodwill, prestige, and preference.
- **Synergy**—Evaluate whether the promotional mix would be as effective in influencing the audience if the sponsorship ended. Sponsorship should work in concert with the promotional mix to increase the overall audience impact.

▼**Visual** Summary

Part 1 Explaining (Chapters 1, 2, 3, 4)	**Part 4** **Managing (Chapters 11, 12, 13, 14, 15)**
Part 2 Creating (Chapters 5, 6, 7, 8)	**Part 5** Integrating (Chapters 16, 17)
Part 3 Strategizing (Chapters 9, 10)	

Chapter 14 Summary

Marketers use consumer-influence strategies to shape how their target audiences think, feel, and act toward their brands. Allowing for two-way communication can strengthen the relationship between the marketer and its target audience. In an effective consumer-influence strategy, the promotional mix of advertising, public relations, sales promotion, sponsorship, personal selling, and/or direct marketing must be integrated for message consistency across all media.

Consumer-Influence Strategies pp. 167–168

Consumer-influence strategies are an organization's mix of communications tools (such as advertising, personal selling, sales promotion, etc.) that act as the communications arm of the company or organization.

tools

Marketing Communications Process pp. 168–172

The marketing communications process is where a company or organization (message source) decides which message will best be understood by its audience (encoding); then the company selects a communications vehicle that the audience sees (medium). The audience (or receiver of the message) must decode the message. It is imperative that the company or organization understands how its message is being decoded by the audience.

shapes

Advertising pp. 172–174

Advertising is typically the most often used IMC variable. It is the paid, nonpersonal communication of a message by a sponsor.

message

create

Public Relations pp. 174–175

Public relations is another IMC variable. It can be personal or nonpersonal (i.e., through press releases). Its function is to create a positive impression of the company (or an issue) to both internal and external publics.

Sales Promotions pp. 175–176

Sales promotions are used to stimulate, or promote sales. They are typically executed in the short term.

promote

Sponsorships p. 176

Sponsorships are a form of promotions and are used to associate brand names with events or activities.

associate

Capstone Exercise p. 179

▼Chapter Key Terms

Consumer-Influence Strategies (pp. 167–168)

Consumer-influence strategies *are strategies for engaging consumers and influencing how they think, feel, and act toward a brand or market offering through the use of marketing communication.* *(p. 167)* **Opening Example** **(p. 167)** **Example: Consumer-Influence Strategies** **(p. 168)**

Key Terms (p. 168)

Promotional mix is the specific combination of communication tools selected for a particular influence strategy. **(p. 168)** **Example: Consumer-Influence Strategies** **(p. 168)**

Marketing Communication Process (pp. 168–172)

Marketing communication process *is the way a sender encodes a marketing idea and conveys it through message and medium so receivers can decode and understand it, and then respond with feedback.* *(p. 168)* **Example: Marketing Communication Process** **(p. 169)**

Key Terms (pp. 169–172)

Campaign is how a company seeks to influence its target audience over time, using a consistent communication theme and varying message creativity and delivery. **(p. 172)**

Integrated marketing communication is the careful coordination of every communication contact for message consistency across all media. **(p. 172)** **Example: Integrated Marketing Communications (p. 172)**

Noise is anything that might distort, block, or otherwise prevent a message from being properly encoded, sent, decoded, received, and/or comprehended. **(p. 169)**

Pull strategy aims to have consumers ask retailers and wholesalers for a product, thus pulling it through the marketing channel. **(p. 172)**

Push strategy aims to have retailers and wholesalers order the product and push it through the channel to consumers. **(p. 172)**

Viral marketing stimulates word of mouth through activities that encourage consumers to electronically share a company's marketing message with friends. **(p. 171)** **Example: Word of Mouth (p. 171)**

Word of mouth is communication between consumers about a brand, marketing offer, or marketing message. **(p. 171)** **Example: Word of Mouth (p. 171)**

Advertising (pp. 172–174)

Advertising *is the paid, nonpersonal communication of a marketing message by an identified sponsor through mass media.* *(p. 172)* **Example: Advertising (p. 173)**

Key Terms (p. 174)

Place-based advertising is advertising that reaches people outside the home, where they work, play, or shop. **(p. 174)**

Specialty advertising is advertising in which the marketer gives away small items bearing its name or logo to keep the audience thinking of the brand and feeling good about it. **(p. 174)**

Public Relations (pp. 174–175)

Public relations *is two-way communication to improve mutual understanding and positively influence relationships between the marketer and its internal and external publics.* *(p. 174)* **Example: Public Relations (p. 175)**

Key Terms (p. 174)

Corporate public relations is how management evaluates and shapes or reshapes long-term public opinion of the company. **(p. 174)** **Example: Public Relations (p. 174)**

Marketing public relations is how marketers seek to achieve specific marketing objectives by targeting consumers with product-focused messages. **(p. 174)**

Product placement is an arrangement in which the company has its brand or product appear in a movie or another entertainment vehicle. **(p. 174)**

Publics are the target audiences of public relations; the people inside or outside the company who have a "stake" in what it does. **(p. 174)**

Publicity is generating unpaid, positive media coverage about a company or its products. **(p. 174)**

Sales Promotion (pp. 175–176)

Sales promotion *is marketer-controlled communication to stimulate immediate audience response by enhancing the value of an offering for a limited time.* *(p. 175)* **Example: Sales Promotion (p. 175)**

Key Terms (p. 175)

Consumer sales promotion aims to get consumers (including business customers) to try a product or buy it again. **(p. 175)** **Example: Sales Promotion (p. 175)**

Trade sales promotion aims to get retail and wholesale buyers to buy an existing product, stock a new product, feature a particular product, or encourage salespeople to push a certain product. **(p. 175)**

Sponsorship (p. 176)

Sponsorship *is a way of publicly associating a brand with an event or activity that the company supports financially.* *(p. 176)* **Example: Sponsorship (p. 176)**

▼ Capstone Exercise

The creative aspect of any message must be consistent with the campaign's marketing communication objectives. Using a consumer magazine of your choice, select five ads and identify the communication objective of each. Be prepared to explain your reasoning in class.

▼ Application Exercises

Complete the following exercises:

1. Jot down or photograph all the marketing efforts you notice on campus for two hours, including advertising and sponsorship. Are you the target audience for every message you saw or heard? Did you notice messages from competing companies? Which media and messages particularly attracted your attention, and why? Can you think of another unique way to influence students on campus?

2. Walk through a nearby shopping center and identify as many forms of consumer sales promotions as you can. Which forms are most common? Select two from different marketers to analyze. What is the added value for each one, and what specific action does each try to encourage? How do you think these marketers will track the results of their sales promotions?

3. Marketers can choose from two basic promotion mix strategies—push or pull promotion. First, describe each strategy. Larger companies typically use a combination of both strategies. Find two examples of companies that are successfully using both promotion mix strategies. Describe what they are doing and why you believe it is successful.

4. Many supermarkets will give you coupons based on what you purchase. What type of promotion is this, and do you believe it to be effective?

chapter **15**

Part 1 Explaining (Chapters 1, 2, 3, 4)
Part 2 Creating (Chapters 5, 6, 7, 8)
Part 3 Strategizing (Chapters 9, 10)

Part 4 **Managing (Chapters 11, 12, 13, 14, 15)**
Part 5 Integrating (Chapters 16, 17)

Personal Selling and Direct Marketing Strategies

Chapter Overview This chapter establishes personal selling and direct marketing as powerful targeted elements of the marketing mix. The central concepts of personal selling will be covered, including a detailed discussion of the pros and cons of personal selling, the selling process, sales management, and sales channels. In addition, the key elements of direct marketing will be covered.

Chapter **Outline**

PERSONAL SELLING (pp. 181–182)

> ▼ **DEFINED** **Personal selling** *is when a representative of a company interacts directly with a consumer to provide information to help the consumer make a buying decision about a product or service.*

▼ **EXPLAINED**

Personal Selling

Personal selling is one of the oldest and most effective forms of marketing communication. What makes it so effective is that a salesperson provides detailed information to a customer or prospect (a potential customer) about a product or service in a one-on-one situation.

Personal selling is targeted, is individual, and can be highly effective in consumer and business-to-business marketing. However, personal selling may not be cost-effective or appropriate for all businesses.

Personal selling can take place in person in a variety of locations, such as the following:

- A retail environment, for example, store, bank, or a dealership
- A business environment, for example, client office, sales office, real estate site, or job site
- A nonbusiness environment, for example, trade-show, event, fair, golf course, restaurant, or new home site
- A customer's or prospect's home, for example, door-to-door selling or personal consultation
- On the phone
- Online

▼ **APPLIED**

Personal Selling

Personal selling can be one element or part of a total marketing mix. Personal selling offers some advantages over other marketing options, including the following:

- **Development of personal relationships**—With personal selling, the relationship with the salesperson can influence a customer's or prospect's decision.
- **Ability to engage in consultative selling**—When salespeople are not trying to sell products or services, but are focused on solving their customer's or prospect's problem, it is called **consultative selling**. Consultative relationships are more likely to be long-term relationships that are mutually beneficial.
- **Ability to better target consumers**—With personal selling, companies can train their salespeople to focus on the most desirable customers and prospects.

There are also some weaknesses associated with personal selling. Selling costs are high and include compensation, management, support, motivation, and recognition to retain salespeople. **Turnover**, the percentage of the sales force that leaves a company in one year, has real costs, including hiring and training new

Richard Santulli, CEO of NetJets, a company that specializes in fractional jet ownership, once telephoned a prospective customer who was worried that he would never be important to NetJets. The prospect told him, "You guys are big and successful, and I'm just a little guy." Richard said that it was 12:10 p.m., and that he was getting married at 1:00 p.m. that day. As he spoke, his wife-to-be was yelling at him to get off the phone. Richard said, "I insisted that I give you a call to show you we do care." The prospect has been a customer since 1998—and a happy one.

PHOTO: USTIN

salespeople, as well as opportunity costs related to sales that were not realized while one or more salespeople were not in place. Further, a customer's personal relationship with a salesperson may extend beyond the company. In some cases, a salesperson may "take the customer with" him or her when moving to a different company.

Personal selling is best used in the following situations:

- When the company employs a "push" strategy, such as with new products and services like financial services and cell phones
- When the product or service is complex, for example, high-end electronics and real estate
- When the product or service is purchased infrequently, such as home appliances and furniture
- When the product or service is expensive, such as engagement rings, homes, and cars
- When the product or service has a long consideration period, such as home-improvement services
- When the product or service is customized, for example, monogrammed products
- When post-purchase service is required, such as cars and service agreements
- When negotiation is required, such as with the purchase of cars and professional services

Although personal selling can be extremely effective, it is not always appropriate. When a product or service has a low-ticket value, such as groceries, or when many small customers make up the target audience, such as fast food, personal selling is not cost effective.

EXAMPLE PERSONAL SELLING

Doris Christopher, who saw the need for professional-quality kitchen tools in kitchens across America, started Pampered Chef in 1980. Pampered Chef uses over 60,000 Independent Consultants worldwide who sell their products in living rooms through personal demonstrations. Pampered Chef consultants are often part-time workers who sell to make additional money. They make a commission on their sales and receive bonus merchandise from the company, based on their sales. The company has over $700 million in sales annually.

PHOTO: Antonios

>> END EXAMPLE

Personal Selling Process (pp. 182–184)

 DEFINED The **personal selling process** *is the practice used by salespeople to identify, research, and approach potential customers to sell products and services.*

 EXPLAINED
Personal Selling Process

The process of personal selling is creative, because every prospect is unique. This process is fast-paced and demanding, yet extremely rewarding financially, professionally, and personally. That's why so many people are involved in personal selling. According to the U.S. Bureau of Labor Statistics, over 15 million people in the United States were employed in sales and related occupations as of 2006. By 2016, employment in the field is expected to exceed 17 million, which represents a growth rate of over 7%.[2]

 APPLIED
Personal Selling Process

As distinctive as each contact is, there is a standard selling process that virtually every company uses when training and managing their salespeople. The process has been proven effective over the years. Although each particular company may use unique terms, descriptions, or requirements, the general process is widely accepted, and this process consists of seven steps.[3] Each step is designed to help identify qualified prospects (also called leads) and understand their needs. When a salesperson truly understands the problems that the prospect needs to solve, then they can provide a solution. The seven steps in the personal selling process are discussed in the following sections.

Step 1: Prospecting and Qualifying

Because salespeople cannot physically interact with every consumer, they start by identifying which consumers have the greatest need for the product or service. This process, called **prospecting**, includes researching multiple sources to find potential customers or prospects.

There are several compiled lists that salespeople can use for prospecting. These lists are available from many sources, including Web sites such as www.hoovers.com, www.infousa.com, and www.usadata.com. Another source of business prospects is professional social networks such as www.linkedin.com, www.ryze.com, www.biznik.com, and www.womanowned.com. Using these sites, professionals can network online with people they already know, and they can request "introductions" to people they want to know. Professional social networking is a fast, efficient way to establish a connection with people to whom salespeople might not otherwise have access.

Cold calling, or contacting a prospect with whom one does not have a previous relationship, is another way for a salesperson to identify potential customers. Salespeople will often cold call people they have identified from one of the lists or through professional social networking. A cold call helps the salesperson **qualify** the prospect (that is, determine whether the prospect has the potential to become a customer) by asking questions about the prospect's interest in the product or service, their current provider, or the timing of their current contract and current pricing.

Step 2: Preapproach

Once a qualified prospect is identified, the salesperson must conduct in-depth research about the prospect; for business prospects, this includes identifying key decision makers, company business strategy, financial performance, current business practices, current providers, and current relationships. It's critical that a salesperson has as much detailed information as possible about a prospect. While lists are helpful during the prospecting and qualifying step, more detailed research is required during the preapproach step. Sources such as *Standard & Poor's 500 Directory*, Dun and Bradstreet's *Million Dollar Directory*, www.hoovers.com, www.lexisnexis.com, local and national business publications, industry publications, and a company's Web site are ideal places to build knowledge of the prospect and its business challenges, financial situation, and credit history.

A salesperson may also find information about a prospect in his or her company's CRM system. Here, the salesperson can learn whether there has been previous contact with the prospect, and if so, the timing of the contact, the response, the key decision makers, and the reasons for not purchasing at that time.

Information can also come from informal sources, such as noncompetitive salespeople who have done business with the prospect or other professionals in the industry. Insights into the company's culture, the communication style of key decision makers, and personal and professional relationships can provide valuable details about the prospect.

The objective of the preapproach step is for the salesperson to learn as much as possible about the prospect. For business prospects, this includes identifying the prospect's business needs and challenges and determining how to help solve the problem and add value to the prospect's business. This step also includes identifying the correct person in the organization with whom to make initial contact, as well as identify other key decision makers and key influencers who will have an impact on the final purchasing decision.

Step 3: Approach

After a prospect has been qualified and research has been conducted to identify specific needs, the salesperson is ready to approach the prospect and schedule or conduct a sales call. A successful approach includes a professional introduction, building rapport with the prospect, and establishing how the salesperson can deliver value to the prospect. The approach is a critical step in the selling process because this is when the prospect decides whether he or she is interested in hearing the sales presentation.

Step 4: Sales Presentation

This is the step during which the salesperson's research all comes together. It is the opportunity for the salesperson to make the case for how the product or service will meet the prospect's needs. There are several key elements that should be covered by the salesperson during this step.

Build rapport. Whether the sales presentation is in person, on the phone, or online, building rapport is critical. To help build rapport with the prospect, the salesperson might include a short introductory dialogue about a nonbusiness issue, such as the weather, a local sports team, or a current holiday. This helps break the ice and gives the salesperson an opportunity to learn something personal about the prospect to help build a relationship.

Make a general benefit statement. Throughout the sales presentation, the salesperson should skillfully ask questions to validate the challenge facing the prospect. A, one that broadly addresses the prospect's need and offers an all-encompassing solution, can be effective at the beginning of a sales presentation. For instance, a foodservice sales representative may make the following general benefit statement when delivering a sales presentation to a restaurant owner: "I have an idea that will help you increase your guest check average. Is that something that would be of interest to you?" The combination of the benefit statement and the question provides the salesperson an opportunity to involve the prospect in the dialogue and validate the direction of the sales presentation.

Make a specific benefit statement. In the sales presentation, the salesperson should ask the prospect questions to continue to gather information. The salesperson should also make a **specific benefit statement** that describes precisely how the product or service will help meet the prospect's needs. An example of a specific benefit statement is, "You mentioned that only about 10% of your guest checks include desserts. Would you be interested in increasing it to 25%?" This specific benefit statement allows the salesperson to present an entire line of high-end desserts instead of selling just one product and gives the restaurant owner an opportunity to meet his business objectives.

Step 5: Overcome Objections

Reasons the prospect won't buy the product or service, or objections, should be anticipated based on the research conducted during the preapproach step. Some common objections relate to price, quality, timing, and existing contracts. The salesperson should ask questions to clearly understand the prospect's objections and then demonstrate how the company can meet the objections. For example, if the restaurant owner objects to buying the high-end desserts because he feels they are too expensive, the salesperson might say, "If I could prove that these high-end desserts would increase your guest check average by at least 10%, would you be willing to give them a try?" Supporting information such as testimonials, references, and case studies can help salespeople successfully overcome objections.

Step 6: Close the Sale

After the salesperson has answered all objections, it's time to ask for the order—it's time to **close** the sale. Because a salesperson is constantly engaged in the process of delivering value to the prospect, it should not be a huge leap to ask for the sale. For example, the foodservice salesperson could ask for the sale by saying, "So, I'll add a case each of the chocolate cake, carrot cake, apple pie, and banana cream pie for next week's delivery. I'll stop by next Wednesday after the delivery to review the new line and go over some selling tips with your wait staff." Or, the salesperson can use the prospect's objection to help close the sale. If, for instance, the restaurant owner's objection related to price, the salesperson might say, "If I'm able to give you introductory pricing on your first order, will you be willing to add the items to your order today?"

Sometimes it is important for the salesperson to create a sense of urgency for the prospect to act. In this case, the salesperson might say, "I'm able to give you an introductory price on your initial order, but that pricing is only available until Wednesday. Can I add those items to your order today?"

No matter what the situation, the close is a critical part of the selling process. As part of the close, the salesperson should always reinforce the decision. For example, the foodservice salesperson might say something like, "You are making a smart business decision by adding these desserts to your menu. I'm confident you'll see the benefits as your guest check average increases."

Step 7: Follow-up

After the sale is closed, the salesperson needs to follow up with activities that include placing the order, arranging delivery, getting signatures on a contract, arranging service teams, finalizing purchase terms, arranging for credit checks, and collecting payment. In addition, a salesperson should always follow up personally with the customer to ensure that everything is going smoothly.

In the foodservice example, the salesperson should go the extra mile to call the restaurant owner to confirm the delivery and set up a time to meet with the wait staff to review the new line of desserts. Also, the salesperson may want to stop into the restaurant during his or her free time to order one of the desserts to see how the wait staff presents the desserts and how restaurant patrons are responding. This follow-up will help the salesperson better understand the restaurant owner's business and provide insight for additional opportunities.

EXAMPLE   PERSONAL SELLING PROCESS

At Pitney Bowes, a global provider of physical and digital mailing products and services, sales representatives and drivers rely on vital customer and inventory information available on their mobile devices. They can, for example, get information about their next sales call, ensure they have the proper parts and inventory within their vans, and access client sales and service histories. Sales reps and drivers are able to make more calls in a day because they spend less time on each call.[4]

PHOTO: Galina Barskkaya

>> END EXAMPLE

Sales Management
(pp. 184–185)

 DEFINED **Sales management** *is the process of planning, implementing, and controlling the personal selling function.*[5]

 EXPLAINED

Sales Management

Because sales are the lifeblood of every company, good sales management is a requirement for success. Sales management clearly communicates company objectives, strategies, and product information so the salespeople can communicate with customers. A **sales manager** is responsible for overseeing the selling function. Sales managers organize, motivate, and lead salespeople, thereby ensuring that sales targets or objectives are met. A sales manager usually supervises a group of salespeople. If the company is large, it may also have sales managers for different product lines or divisions, or perhaps for certain geographical areas, such as a part of a city, state, or country. Many companies also have a vice president of sales, who manages all of the sales managers and is ultimately responsible for meeting the company's sales objectives.

 APPLIED

Sales Management

Effective sales managers provide leadership, which, in turn, outlines priorities and direction to salespeople. Sales managers are constantly looking for ways to reduce nonselling functions, such as paperwork and internal meetings, so salespeople have more time to focus on selling activities, such as meeting with customers and prospects.

Sales managers use an organizational structure to help provide accountability and increase salesperson productivity. Although all sales forces are not structured exactly the same, some general functions are used by most selling organizations. Sales managers may oversee different types of salespeople. Salespeople who are physically located inside the office and rarely, if ever, have face-to-face contact with customers or prospects are called **inside sales**. Salespeople who spend the majority of their time outside the office meeting with customers and prospects are called **outside sales**. Sales managers may exclusively use one type of sales force or combine the two types, based on the company's sales strategy and financial structure. An inside sales force is usually less expensive because it does not generate travel costs. However, an outside sales force has the benefit of developing face-to-face relationships, which are critical to the selling process.

Some key sales roles include order taker, customer service representative, technical or product specialist, sales representative, sales support, and new business development. All of these roles can be performed either as inside or outside sales functions.

EXAMPLE   SALES MANAGEMENT

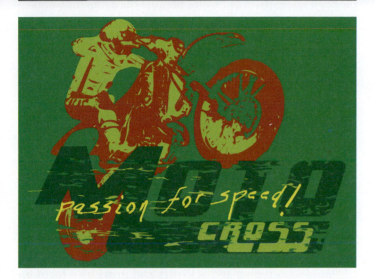

Rebecca Herwick, CEO of Harley Davidson licensee Global Products, knew her sales strategy wasn't working when seven of her nine sales representatives walked out during August 2006. Herwick had been using independent sales reps to sell her products, everything from Harley Davidson–branded bandanas to coffee mugs, to over 800 Harley dealerships nationwide. The independent sales reps were selling other product lines that didn't compete with her products, but she still felt like her company wasn't getting the attention it deserved. Rather than hiring a dedicated but expensive internal sales staff, she learned to better manage her independent sales reps. She laid down ground rules, including new commission rates, new requirements for customer visits, and customer feedback surveys to help assess sales representative performance. The changes are paying off. Sales are up, and more important, customers have noticed a difference in attention and service.[6]

PHOTO: Daniel Rosales

>> END EXAMPLE

Sales Management Process (pp. 185–187)

 DEFINED The **sales management process** *is a comprehensive approach that sales managers use to determine the size and type of the sales force and how they will hire, recruit, manage, motivate and evaluate the performance of the individual salespeople.*

 **EXPLAINED**

Sales Management Process

The size and structure of a company's sales force is established as part of the sales management process. Many companies use the sales management process the same way they use the selling process—to plan, implement, and control the selling function. Although the individual steps may have different names or terms in different companies and settings, the general approach is widely accepted.

 APPLIED

Sales Management Process

The sales management process has four major steps, and the vice president of sales and/or sales managers conducts this process throughout a company.[7] The process provides the blueprint to manage salespeople and deliver results.

Step 1: Setting Sales Force Objectives

Sales force objectives are sales goals that reflect the company's objectives. These objectives express exactly what the sales force needs to accomplish and by when. One example of a sales force objective is as follows: "Increase sales of Pinnacle Performance Software in the United States to $3 million by 2010." This objective is used as the framework for every sales manager and salesperson in the company. The vice president of sales and the sales managers determine how much of the $3 million each sales manager will deliver and by when. The goals for each sales manager are then broken down among the manager's salespeople by month, week, and even day, so that everyone involved in the selling function knows what is expected of them and by when.

Objectives also help sales managers develop even more specific goals for each salesperson in terms of how many sales should be generated from each existing customer, how many sales should come from new customers, and how many new business calls must be made to meet the overall sales objective. The specific sales objectives then become the basis of sales staff compensation.

Step 2: Developing the Sales Force Strategy

The sales force strategy is the approach that sales management uses to meet a company's sales objectives. To develop this strategy, the sales managers must determine how many salespeople and what type of sales positions are needed to meet sales objectives. These people and positions must then be organized in the most efficient manner possible.

For example, Pinnacle Performance Software Company might organize its sales people in one of several ways:

- **Organize by geography.** This approach ensures there is coverage in all key geographic areas. This so-called geographic, or territory, strategy is common because it is among the most cost-efficient approaches in that it minimizes the amount of time salespeople spend traveling between calls.

- **Organize by product line.** This means that each salesperson specializes in selling a particular product or product line. This strategy is effective in putting the focus on individual products or product lines, but it can be difficult and expensive to implement because it means that each salesperson might have to travel to various geographic areas to meet with customers or prospects. This approach may also require that some customers or prospects have multiple salespeople calling on them from the same company.
- **Organize by industry.** This means that each salesperson calls on companies in one industry, such as retail, financial services, or pharmaceuticals. This strategy is successful when products or services are complex and have different applications in different industries. Here, salespeople have the opportunity to learn from each customer and apply this knowledge to help others in the industry.
- **Organize by key accounts.** This strategy recognizes that the major customers of a product or service are the most important, so those customers should receive dedicated personal-selling resources. The key account strategy can be used alone, or it can be supplemented with any of the strategies mentioned earlier. For instance, Pinnacle Performance Software Company may have some salespeople dedicated to calling on key accounts, while the balance of its sales force may be organized by territory, product line, or industry.

Step 3: Recruiting, Compensating, Training, and Motivating the Sales Force

Recruiting and hiring the right salespeople is one of the most important activities a sales manager can perform. The salesperson is an ambassador for the company and, in many cases, the customer's exclusive point of contact with the company. A salesperson can make the difference between success and failure in meeting both the customer's and his or her company's objectives. Most companies therefore make a significant investment in training, managing, motivating, and recognizing salespeople.

Salespeople must possess specific characteristics, such as good personal skills, good listening skills, the ability to work independently, the ability to work as part of a team, the ability to manage a budget, and the ability to resolve problems in a timely manner. They must also have the ability to identify and research a qualified prospect, the ability to close a sale, the ability to follow up, and the drive and passion to move forward, even when everything is not going smoothly.

There is no ironclad method for hiring the right sales people. Some companies administer tests to see whether sales candidates have the characteristics and skills they want. Other companies use an extensive interviewing process in which sales candidates meet with several people inside the company and accompany existing staff on sales calls.

In most companies, the sales function is built on a **pay-for-performance compensation strategy**. This strategy means that a large part or all of a salesperson's income is based on the amount of sales or profit he or she delivers to his or her

company in a given time frame. When this is the case, salespeople are paid on **commission**. Commission is a percentage of the sales or profit the salesperson generates. In some companies, a salesperson may earn commission, plus an incentive or bonus for sales or profit delivered over a stated goal. A bonus may be an additional commission rate, a set dollar amount, a trip, a gift card, or some other incentive to make a goal. In many companies, there is no limit to how much money a salesperson can make, because the company wants to sell as much of its products and services as possible.

The opportunity of unlimited income potential is attractive to salespeople. However, it is difficult to maintain energy, excitement, and commitment to selling, especially when sales are slow. And, many salespeople are not based in the company's main office—instead, they are based in a local office, or they work out of their homes. In such cases, it's especially important that sales managers keep salespeople informed, educated, and motivated.

Training is critical for salespeople to be successful. There are several types of training. Usually, sales management provides a combination of types of training for salespeople on an ongoing basis. The types of training include the following:

- Product training is information about the features and benefits of specific products or product lines.
- Sales training includes information about the company, product offering, and activities and provides a focus on developing skills, such as listening skills, selling skills, and closing skills. Sales training also includes technical training regarding the company's systems, such as CRM or account-management tools.
- Personal-development training includes exposure to areas that help prepare salespeople to advance to the next level. This can include topics such as management training and leadership skills.

Sales meetings are the traditional method to train salespeople. A sales meeting allows salespeople to meet their peers; all salespeople hear the company message at the same time and feel the energy of the meeting. In addition, technology plays a significant role in all types of sales training, with webinars, podcasts, video conferences, audio conferences, on-demand training videos, Web-based knowledge centers, and video games. Sales managers know that in-person meetings with technology-based training can be a powerful combination.

Motivating the sales force is key in any company. Money and incentives can be motivating for salespeople, but they are usually short-term motivators. Great sales managers realize that it takes more than money and prizes to motivate and engage salespeople. Rather, motivating a sales force requires constant communication and recognition. Communication keeps an organization on track by maintaining the focus on goals and providing updates about successes. Communication can involve a combination of in-person conversations, telephone calls, and e-mails. Incentives, such as those mentioned earlier, can help build excitement to meet short-term goals. However, it is recognition that best motivates and retains salespeople. Many companies have recognition programs that highlight high achievers in a variety of areas. For instance, in addition to recognizing sales achievements, many companies also recognize salespeople who have provided extraordinary customer service, supported other employees, or otherwise gone above and beyond the call of duty. Recognition programs may include rewards such as a being invited to a recognition dinner, receiving a check and/or a plaque, or becoming a member of a performance "club."

Step 4: Evaluating the Sales Force

The last step in the sales-management process—evaluating the sales force—links back to the first step in the process. A sales manager starts with the objectives. It is then the job of the manager to allocate how much of the sales objective each salesperson must deliver and establish metrics by which to evaluate performance. Once the objectives and metrics are established, regular reports must be made available to all salespeople so that they can track their performance against these objectives. Regular meetings between the sales manager and the salesperson can help keep performance on track. Coaching by the sales manager can help the sales person correct or improve in any area necessary.

Some companies also include customer feedback as part of the process to evaluate their salespeople. In these cases, the company issues a survey (by mail, by phone, or online) and gathers feedback about the performance of the company and the salesperson. Customer feedback can be a valuable additional source of information with which to evaluate a salesperson.

Evaluation is an ongoing process. Formal evaluations usually take place on a regular basis, such as monthly, quarterly, or annually. New objectives for the upcoming time period are established, based on each salesperson's performance.

EXAMPLE   **EVALUATING THE SALES FORCE**

MetLife Auto & Home Insurance's "Best of the Best" program has one aspect that makes it uniquely successful. Specifically, front-line employees, all of whom are volunteers, manage this program. It is truly a bottom-up recognition program, which is the way upper management wants it. Marge Rody, the vice president of customer service operations, says, "We really wanted it to be peer recognition in local offices and let local recognition champions create the program. It can't be top-down." Since 2003, when the program began, employee satisfaction scores have increased from 3.89 to 4.43 on a 1 to 5 scale, customer satisfaction and

retention rates have increased, and the number of justified customer complaints fell.[8]

PHOTO: Alexander Raths

>> END EXAMPLE

Direct Marketing (pp. 187–190)

 DEFINED **Direct marketing** *is any communication addressed to a consumer that is designed to generate a response.*

▼ EXPLAINED

Direct Marketing

Direct marketing is an interactive process that uses communication that is addressed to an individual consumer to generate an action or response from that consumer. The desired response could be an order, a request for further information, or a visit to a store or other place of business to purchase a product.[9] Direct marketing is considered interactive because the consumer actually interacts with the marketer as a direct result of the marketing communication.

Direct marketing is sometimes referred to as "one-to-one" marketing because marketers can target the communication and even personalize the message to each individual. Direct marketing can employ this high degree of targeting because it involves the use of consumer databases. This type of database may include demographic information, such as name, address, income, age, gender, number of children in the household, home ownership status, and prior purchases of specific products or services. Some consumer databases also include psychographic information, such as hobbies, travel preferences, personal aspirations, or perceptions of certain products, services, brands, or stores. Direct marketers use the information in such databases to target specific messages to specific consumers at specific times to increase the likelihood of getting the desired response. Marketers can create their own proprietary databases of customer information based on previous inquiries, transactions (such as frequent purchasers), and surveys; this type of database is called a **house file**. Alternatively, marketers can rent consumer information from companies that collect and maintain databases. These rented lists are called **outside lists**, and they can be used alone or in conjunction with a house file.

▼ APPLIED

Direct Marketing

The key benefits of direct marketing are as follows:

- **Targeting**—As previously discussed, direct marketing allows marketers to deliver their message only to those consumers that meet their target audience characteristics.
- **Measurability**—Direct marketing is trackable and measurable. Marketers can calculate a true ROI (return on investment) based on the consumer responses.

- **Testing**—With direct marketing, marketers can test offers, creative approaches and responsiveness of specific customer segments. Testing makes it possible to fine-tune a company's marketing efforts before launching a full campaign.
- **High ROI**—The Direct Marketing Association reports that, on average, direct marketing generates a return on investment of $11.69, compared to $5.24 for nondirect marketing expenditures.[10]

On the other hand, the key weaknesses of direct marketing include the following:

- **Expense**—The cost per contact (that is, the cost to reach each consumer) is usually higher for direct marketing than for other media. Paper, printing, and postage have a significant impact on the costs for printed direct marketing. Although the upfront cost of direct marketing is high, the return on the investment is high and helps offset the expense.
- **Response rates**—Direct marketing usually yields a response rate of 1–5%. That means that 95–99% of the consumers who receive a particular direct marketing communication do not respond to it.
- **Lack of general brand awareness**—When companies use direct marketing alone, consumers who do not receive the direct marketing may not be aware of the brand or product.

Direct marketing should be considered as part of the marketing mix when one or more of the following conditions holds true:

- The product or service is used only by a clearly defined segment or portion of consumers.
- The product or service purchase is time sensitive.
- The product or service is available in a particular geographic location.
- The marketer wants to reach previous purchasers of the product or service to encourage a repeat purchase or trial of a related product.
- The marketer wants to make an offer to a select group of consumers.

Direct marketing includes catalogs, direct mail, direct-response TV and radio, infomercials, and the Internet. Direct marketing has evolved significantly over the years. What started with a flyer sent to customers about products in the nineteenth century has developed into sophisticated and customized communications to consumers on the Internet, via mobile phones, and even on video game consoles. Technology has become a major force behind the evolution of direct marketing with over 1.4 billion people around the world who use the Internet. The diversity of direct marketing is discussed in the following sections.[11]

Mail Order

In 1872, Aaron Montgomery Ward and two partners created a one-page flyer that listed their merchandise with prices, hoping to generate some interest in their retail store.[12] But it was Richard Sears, who in 1888 published a flyer to advertise his watches and jewelry, who truly revolutionized the direct marketing business.

Sears promised his customers that "we warrant every American watch sold by us, with fair usage, an accurate time keeper for six years—during which time, under our written guarantee we are compelled to keep it in perfect order free of charge."[13] It was the promise of satisfaction guaranteed that changed the face of mail-order marketing.

Today, mail order includes two types of marketing—catalogs and direct mail. The term **mail order** describes "the business of selling merchandise through the mail."[14]

Catalogs

Catalogs are a common marketing strategy for many marketers, such as Pottery Barn, Neiman Marcus, Staples, J. Crew, and PC Mall. Over 19 billion catalogs are distributed annually.[15] They provide marketers an opportunity to showcase a large selection of their product and service offerings to their target audience. In the current multichannel environment, marketers want to make it easy and convenient for consumers to buy their goods and services. Most catalogers thus offer consumers different ways to respond by including a phone number, Web address, and street address of the closest store or stores (if the marketer has retail stores) in their catalogs.

Catalogs are an effective element in the marketing mix because they are targeted, can generate high returns per catalog mailed, and can be accurately measured for the sales and profit they generate. However, catalogs are extremely expensive to print and mail; costs range from $0.50 to over $3.00 or more per catalog mailed, depending on, for example, the number of pages, quantity printed, and paper quality. In addition, it can be difficult to track the impact of a catalog on sales obtained via other channels, such as the Internet or retail stores.

Direct Mail

Direct mail differs from a catalog because it does not showcase an entire assortment of products. Instead, direct mail usually involves only a pamphlet or flyer that focuses on a specific product or service. Direct mail may also include a postcard, letter, brochure, or product sample. Charities, political groups, retail stores, and packaged goods companies are major users of direct mail. Some Internet companies such as Netflix also use direct mail to drive traffic to their Web sites.

Although there are many variations of direct mail, all successful direct mail campaigns include three major elements:

- **Offer**—A compelling offer should be apparent to the recipient. An offer is usually promotional in nature to provide incentive for the recipient to respond. Examples of common offers are "Save 20%," "Free shipping," or "Buy One, Get One Free."
- **Mailing list**—When conducting a direct-mail campaign, identifying targets is as important as crafting the message. The mailing list should include only those consumers who have the highest likelihood of responding. For example, if Wal-Mart wants to mail coupons for baby products, the mailing list should include only those households with children under the age of one that are located within a five-mile radius of each store.

- **Call to action**—A **call to action** describes the response the company wants to elicit from the consumer. Examples of a call to action are the following: "Call 800-555-5555 to make an appointment," "Visit www.si.com and order today," or "Visit your nearest Lexus dealership." The call to action should be clear and easy to act on.

Direct mail can be an effective medium because it is targeted. However, like catalogs, direct mail can be an expensive option due to the cost of paper, printing, and postage.

EXAMPLE | **DIRECT MAIL**

The United States Postal Service is going green. On its Web site, www. usps.com, it lists tips for marketers to adopt greener mail practices, including using water-based inks and recycled materials, letting consumers easily opt out of mailings, and encouraging consumers to recycle mailings after reading them.[16]

PHOTO: Joy Brown

>> END EXAMPLE

Telemarketing

Telemarketing is direct marketing conducted over the phone. Telemarketing is one of the most intrusive forms of direct marketing because the consumer must listen to the marketer's message at the time the marketer chooses, not when the consumer chooses (except in the case of telemarketing messages left on voice mail). Examples of marketers that often rely on telemarketing to consumers include charities, political parties, financial services, and retailers.

Telemarketing can be an effective part of a marketer's media mix because it provides a real-time personal conversation with a consumer. However, because of consumer perceptions of telemarketers calling at inconvenient times and using unscrupulous selling techniques, some marketers avoid telemarketing as part of their marketing mix. Telemarketing is also an expensive form of marketing because the costs include staff, telecommunication, database and software. Because there are so many capital investments required to conduct telemarketing, many businesses and organizations hire telemarketing companies to conduct calls to consumers on their behalf. In addition, legislation that was passed in 2003 and updated in 2008 established the national **Do Not Call Registry**, which prohibits telemarketers from calling any phone number registered with the Federal Trade Commission.

Direct-Response Advertising

Direct-response advertising is a direct marketing approach that includes a specific offer and call to action for the consumer to immediately contact the marketer to purchase or inquire about the product. The Internet has become the medium of choice for many direct-response advertisers.

However, direct-response ads can also be found in magazines, newspaper, radio, and television.

DRTV (direct-response TV) includes any kind of television commercial or home shopping television show that advertises a product or service and allows the viewer to purchase the product or service directly. Companies such as QVC and Home Shopping Network made DRTV mainstream. Newer forms of DRTV are emerging that can deliver targeted television commercials based on selected criteria and provide a personalized call to action.

DRTV blends portions of direct response and television by including the call-to-action aspect of direct response and the visual element of television. DRTV requires an investment in production and media. When produced and targeted properly, DRTV can be a strong part of a marketing mix or a stand-alone marketing effort.

Infomercials, television shows that are a combination of an information session and a commercial, are considered direct-response marketing when they include a method for viewers to purchase the product or service directly. Infomercials can be as short as 3 minutes, as long as 30 minutes, and sometimes longer. The growth of cable television has provided a significant amount of programming time, which has appealed to producers of infomercials. Once the flagship of entrepreneurs and some unscrupulous marketers, infomercials have come of age; they now generate $91 billion in sales annually.[17] Major marketers such as VW, American Airlines, and Proctor & Gamble successfully use this format to drive consumer response.

Infomercials are effective because they are targeted based on the television or radio stations on which they are airing. In addition, they give marketers an opportunity to describe and demonstrate the features and benefits of a product or service. Infomercials are well suited for new product introductions as well as complex products because the format provides more selling time than a traditional 30-second commercial. However, producing infomercials can be expensive.

Internet

The Internet is an ideal direct-marketing medium. It is quickly evolving to offer unique, personalized experiences for users and targeted audiences for marketers. The different kinds of online direct-marketing opportunities continue to expand, based on technological advancements and consumer behavior.

E-mail has evolved from an approach of "blasting" a message to all customers in a company's e-mail database to sophisticated **life cycle marketing** with e-mail messages targeted specifically to individual consumers as each progresses through a specific life stage or life cycle (such as pregnancy to birth for baby products' marketers). Some companies use **dynamic imaging** to systematically populate individual e-mails with products targeted specifically to each consumer, based on behavior patterns and inventory.

Personalized experiences, including Web pages and offers, are also being developed and tested by several companies. The use of personalized URLs (PURLs) and landing pages (the page on which you land when you enter a URL or Web site address) allows a marketer to create a completely customized Internet experience in the form of a "mini Web site" that is personalized with the consumer's name, relevant information, and product or content that is appropriate to his or her interests. For instance, if a consumer, who is named Sarah Morrison, receives a direct mail piece or e-mail that includes a call to action to visit www.sarahmorrison.abccompany.com, and the landing page includes customized information and an offer, the response rate can increase significantly.[18] PURLs are not yet widely tested, so a cutting-edge marketer can use this marketing approach to target their message in a new way.

Consumer Privacy

The nature of direct marketing is that it involves personal and targeted communications from marketers to consumers. Some marketers have abused this relationship by sending too much "junk" mail, calling consumers at dinner time, and sending unsolicited e-mails. Because of this, the Direct Marketing Association, which has more than 3,600 members (including the majority of companies on the *Fortune* 100 list), has established a **Do Not Mail List** for consumers who do not want to receive direct marketing. In addition, in 2007, the group created the Commitment to Consumer Choice, which requires that member companies notify consumers of the opportunity to modify or eliminate future mail solicitations.[19]

Various laws also require that companies must clearly inform consumers of their **privacy policy**, which includes their policy on renting their list of customer names, physical addresses, and e-mail addresses. To this end, most companies post their privacy policy on their Web site.

When illegitimate marketers began sending millions of unsolicited, misleading, and inappropriate e-mails, Congress passed the **CAN-SPAM Act of 2003** (Controlling the Assault of Non-Solicited Pornography and Marketing Act). This law has the following requirements regarding Internet marketers:

- It bans false or misleading e-mail header information, such as in the "To" and "From" fields.
- It prohibits deceptive e-mail subject lines.
- It requires that e-mails provide recipients with opt-out methods.
- It requires that commercial e-mail be identified as an advertisement and include the sender's valid physical postal address.

The CAN-SPAM Act specifies significant fines, including banning advertising, for any violators.[20]

▼**Visual** Summary

Chapter 15 Summary

The power of targeted marketing is demonstrated in personal selling and direct marketing. Using methods ranging from salespeople to catalogs, direct mail, e-mail, and even mobile marketing, marketers can get their brand message directly to those consumers that are most likely to respond to it. Personal selling and direct marketing can be effective marketing channels when used alone or as part of an integrated marketing plan.

Personal Selling pp. 181–182

Personal selling involves the face-to-face communication with consumers/customers in order to make sure the buyer's needs and wants are satisfied.

Personal Selling Process
pp. 182–184

The personal selling process is a system developed by organizations to allow salespeople to identify, research, and approach prospects.

Sales Management
pp. 184–185

Sales management allows a company to designate an individual, or individuals who will be in charge of the sales process of planning, implementing, and executing a sales plan.

Sales Management Process pp. 185–187

The sales management process is used by sales managers to determine their sales needs; to identify and hire salespeople who fill those needs; and to recruit, motivate, evaluate, and manage individual sales personnel.

Direct Marketing pp. 187–190

Direct marketing and in this case, direct selling is a system developed to allow companies to go directly to their consumers to make a sale, by passing traditional retailing centers of distribution. Direct marketing is designed to elicit an immediate and measurable response from consumer targets.

Capstone
Exercise p. 193

▼Chapter Key Terms

Personal Selling (pp. 181–182)

Personal selling *is when a representative of a company interacts directly with a consumer to provide information to help the consumer make a buying decision about a product or service.* (p. 181) **Example: Personal Selling (p. 182) Opening Example (p. 181)**

Key Terms (p. 181)

Consultative selling is when salespeople focus on solving their customer's or prospect's problems, rather than focus on selling products or services. **(p. 181)**

Turnover is the percentage of the sales force that leaves a company in one year. **(p. 181)**

Personal Selling Process (pp. 182–184)

Personal selling process *is the practice salespeople us to identify, research, and approach potential customers to sell products and services.* (p. 182) **Example: Personal Selling Process (p. 184)**

Key Terms (pp. 182–184)

Close is the part of the selling process in which the salesperson asks for an order. **(p. 184)**

Cold calling is the act of contacting a prospect with whom the salesperson does not have a previous relationship, in order to identify potential customers. **(p. 183)**

General benefit statement is a broad claim about the value a product or service can deliver to a prospect. **(p. 183)**

Prospecting is the process of researching multiple sources to find potential customers or prospects. **(p. 182)**

Qualify is the process of determining whether a prospect has the potential to become a customer. **(p. 183)**

Specific benefit statement is a precise claim about the value a product or service can deliver to a prospect. **(p. 183)**

Sales Management (pp. 184–185)

Sales management *is the process of planning, implementing, and controlling the personal selling function.* (p. 184) **Example: Sales Management (p. 185)**

Key Terms (pp. 184–185)

Inside sales are members of the sales team who reside inside the office or company location and rarely, if ever, have face-to-face contact with customers or prospects. **(p. 184)**

Outside sales are salespeople who meet face-to-face with customers and prospects. **(p. 184) Example: Sales Management (p. 185)**

Sales manager is the person responsible for organizing, motivating, and leading a team of salespeople and is also responsible for meeting the company's sales objectives. **(p. 184) Example: Sales Management (p. 185)**

Sales Management Process (pp. 185–187)

Sales management process *is the method used by companies to plan, implement, and control the selling function.* (p. 185) **Example: Evaluating the Sales Force (p. 187)**

Key Terms (p. 186)

Commission is the part of or all of a salesperson's income that is based on the amount of sales or profit delivered in a given time frame. **(p. 186)**

Pay-for-performance compensation strategy is the compensation system in which salespeople are paid based on the amount of sales or profits they deliver to the company. **(p. 186)**

Direct Marketing (pp. 187–190)

Direct marketing *is any communication addressed to a consumer that is designed to generate a response.* (p. 187) **Example: Direct Mail (p. 189)**

Key Terms (pp. 187–190)

Call to action is the response that a marketer wants a consumer to take as a result of receiving a direct-mail communication. **(p. 189)**

CAN-SPAM Act of 2003 (Controlling the Assault of Non-Solicited Pornography and Marketing Act) is the law that requires e-mail marketers to abide by certain requirements when e-mailing consumers. **(p. 190)**

Catalog is a printed direct-mail piece that showcases an assortment of products or services offered by a company. **(p. 188)**

Direct mail is a printed advertisement in the form of a postcard, letter, brochure, or product sample that is sent to consumers who are on a targeted mailing list. **(p. 188) Example: Direct Mail (p. 189)**

Direct-response advertising is a direct marketing approach that includes a specific offer and call to action for the consumer to immediately contact the marketer to purchase or inquire about the product. **(p. 189)**

Do Not Call Registry is a list of consumers who do not want to receive phone calls from telemarketers. Consumers can contact the Federal Trade Commission to be added to the Do Not Call Registry. **(p. 189)**

Do Not Mail List is the list of consumers who do not want to receive direct mail. Consumers can contact the Direct Marketing Association to be added to the Do Not Mail List. **(p. 190)**

DRTV (direct-response TV) is any kind of television commercial or home shopping television show that advertises a product or service and allows the viewer to purchase it directly. **(p. 189)**

Dynamic imaging is the process of systematically populating individual e-mails with products targeted specifically to each consumer, based on specific criteria such as behavior patterns, inventory, and other criteria. **(p. 189)**

House file is a proprietary database of customer information collected from transactions, inquiries, or surveys from the company. **(p. 187)**

Infomercial is a television show that is a combination of an information session and a commercial. **(p. 189)**

Life cycle marketing is a series of targeted messages to customers and prospects based on their experience during a sequence of events that takes place during a specific stage in life. **(p. 189)**

Mail order is the term that describes the business of selling merchandise through the mail. **(p. 188)**

Outside lists consist of consumer information compiled by an outside company and rented to a marketer. **(p. 187)**

Telemarketing is a phone call placed to a specific consumer to offer products or services for sale. **(p. 189)**

Privacy policy is a company's practice as it relates to renting customer information to other companies. **(p. 190)**

▼Capstone Exercise

During this chapter, we read about the various techniques of personal selling. One issue to explore further is when to use a direct sales force and how to compensate them.

A direct sales force is generally used when the product or service is expensive and/or complex and the customer needs "hand-holding." Direct sales forces are not efficient, from a financial point of view, for low-margin products.

Once you have made a decision to use a direct sales force, then the next decision is how to compensate the sales force. Compensation strategies are usually not well understood, but are critical to a sales program's success.

A well-designed compensation plan encourages the right behaviors (the ones you want) on the part of the sales reps. The compensation plan should be tied to your business objectives. There are two more things to keep in mind when designing compensation plan: Does the proposed compensation plan link rewards to desired performance of management goals? Does the compensation provide incentives as well as negative reinforcements? (This is commonly called the "carrot and stick.")

Other concepts to be aware of include the difference between inside and outside salespeople and between base compensation and commission. And finally, be aware of a SPIFF, which is a small, immediate bonus for a sale. A SPIFF is used to give small but immediate compensation for selling a product that the company wants to emphasize. Research these items before answering the exercise.

1. Your task is to think about the business issues in designing a sales compensation plan for a salesperson who works for Chicago Bridge & Iron Company N.V., an engineering and construction company that builds power plants. Their Web site address is http://www.cbi.com/.

2. How would you structure the plan? What issues would you consider when determining what to pay the salespeople? When and how should the territory be structured?

3. What other incentives would you include, if any, and why?

▼Application Exercises

Complete the following exercises:

1. Choose two students to participate in a role-playing exercise. One student will play the part of the salesperson selling luxury watches in a high-end department store. The other student will play the role of the consumer. Students will use the following situation information. How does the salesperson use the steps in the selling process to sell the watch?

   • **Salesperson**
     • Needs to sell a Rolex watch to make his or her sales quota for the day.
     • Wants to sell a Rolex watch rather than a different brand because he or she can earn a bonus.
     • Wants to establish an ongoing relationship with the consumer so he or she can ask for a referral.

   • **Consumer**
     • Does not necessarily want to buy a Rolex watch.
     • Wants to see what other watches are available in a lower price range.
     • Will refer his or her friend to this salesperson if he or she gets good service and good advice.

2. If you were starting a retail business that sold all-natural baked goods, which of the marketing options discussed in this chapter would you use, and why? Which marketing options would you choose not to use, and why?

3. Choose a company that sells products or services through more than one sales channel. Identify all of the sales channels the company uses. Discuss why you think the company uses these sales channels.

The **Media Mix**

Chapter Overview The previous chapter explained how companies develop selling strategies for products, services, pricing, distribution, and communications. Personal selling strategies also were discussed. This chapter explains how to integrate diverse forms of communication and personal selling through use of the media mix. The chapter begins by describing the current media environment, and then continues with explaining the advantages and disadvantages of various types of media. The process for media selection (planning and buying) is explained, as well as techniques used to optimize media.

▼ Chapter **Outline**

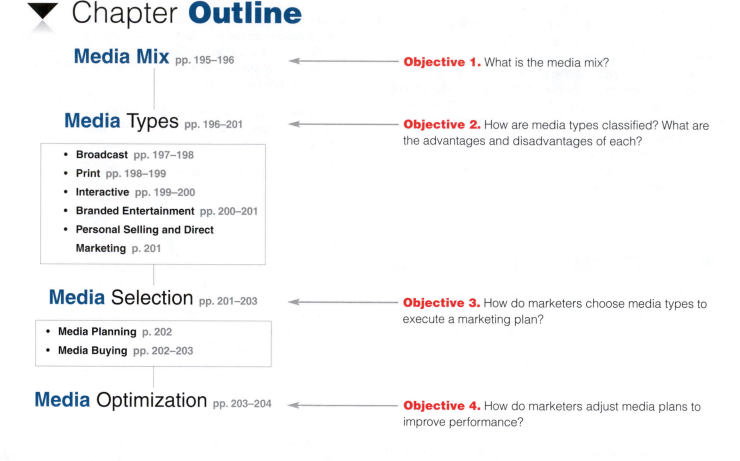

Media Mix pp. 195–196 ← **Objective 1.** What is the media mix?

Media Types pp. 196–201 ← **Objective 2.** How are media types classified? What are the advantages and disadvantages of each?

- **Broadcast** pp. 197–198
- **Print** pp. 198–199
- **Interactive** pp. 199–200
- **Branded Entertainment** pp. 200–201
- **Personal Selling and Direct Marketing** p. 201

Media Selection pp. 201–203 ← **Objective 3.** How do marketers choose media types to execute a marketing plan?

- **Media Planning** p. 202
- **Media Buying** pp. 202–203

Media Optimization pp. 203–204 ← **Objective 4.** How do marketers adjust media plans to improve performance?

MEDIA MIX (pp. 195–196)

>  **DEFINED** *The **media mix** is the selection of media used for an advertising campaign as well as the budget allocated to each medium.*

(pp. 195–196)

▼ **EXPLAINED**

Media Mix

Written or verbal communications are frequently organized according to the following: who, what, where, when, and how. Integrating marketing communications can be thought of in a similar way. Consumer influence and personal selling strategies determine what messages will be communicated, to whom, and how. Media strategy integrates these elements by deciding where and when advertising will appear.

Advertising media (or **"media"**) refers to the collection of channels (physical or electronic) used to carry marketing communications. Many of the terms applied to media are based on transportation-related metaphors. Media is said to "carry" messages, types of media are called "vehicles," and messages are "delivered" to recipients. In the not-too-distant past, communication direction was strictly one-way, from businesses or large organizations to consumers. New technology has enabled **consumer-generated media (CGM)**, such as blogs or video Web sites, that allow ordinary people to create and send their own messages.

The combination of media vehicles used for an ad campaign, along with their individual budget levels, is called the **media mix**. Marketers use a mix of media because no single vehicle is suitable for every customer segment, message, or occasion. According to TNS Media Intelligence, advertising spending on media in the United States in 2007 was almost $150 billion.[1] Television, print, and newspapers made up the largest portions of the overall media mix, with growth in these areas coming from innovations in digital and online content.

▼ **APPLIED**

Media Mix

Our media environment is constantly evolving. Thirty years ago, media options were relatively limited. Network television dominated the American media landscape, along with print, including newspapers and magazines, radio, and outdoor advertising such as billboards. In the twenty-first century, television will still play a role in the media mix, but new forms of communication are rapidly changing the number and variety of choices available to consumers. As evidence, consider the complexity of an average American's media habits:[2]

- We spend more than 3,000 hours a year consuming some form of media.
- Over 1,500 hours are spent watching television (including broadcast, cable, and satellite).
- Over 900 hours are spent listening to the radio.
- Almost 200 hours are spent on the Internet.
- About 175 hours are spent reading newspapers.
- Over 100 hours are spent reading magazines or books.
- Over 80 hours are spent playing video games.

Bringing new meaning to the phrase "captive audience," the media firm Captivate specializes in place-based advertising like video terminals in elevators. Are you bored with watching floor numbers change? Just watch a minute of programming on Captivate, which mixes snippets of news and entertainment content with paid ads. The company has installed more than 8,200 digital, wireless screens in buildings in 23 major North American markets. Captivate screens deliver almost 55 million impressions (or ad views) per month, and reach the often hard-to-find, college-educated business professional. Every time they ride the elevator, 88% of riders watch the Captivate programming, and over half report increased interest in a product or service they saw advertised.[3]
PHOTO: Losevsky Pavel

To make things even more complicated, some consumers are using multiple types of media at the same time. Potential customers could be watching TV, using their cell phones, and surfing the Internet simultaneously.

New technology is also having an impact on the ways people use media. Computers and the Internet have created revolutionary forms of media. **Interactive media** (sometimes called **digital media**) is a broad term used to refer to electronic methods of communication where users have the ability to directly shape, interact with, or respond to media. **Search marketing** includes techniques such as paying for inclusion in specific search results on megasites like Google and Yahoo! **Mobile advertising** refers to advertisements delivered over portable communication devices such as mobile phones and PDA.

Growing personal control over media, a broader range of media choices, and the introduction of ever-advancing technology will result in quite different media mixes. As consumers migrate away from traditional media vehicles like TV or radio, digital media is predicted to capture a larger portion of the future mix (see Figure 16.1).[4]

Although our media choices are increasing, our ability to pay attention remains limited because no one has found a way add hours to a day. To communicate effectively, marketers need to create innovative media strategies that deliver relevant messages to us whenever we're prepared to receive them.

FIGURE 16.1

Past Media Mix

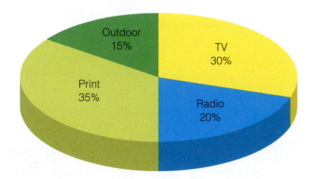

Outdoor 15%
TV 30%
Print 35%
Radio 20%

Future Media Mix

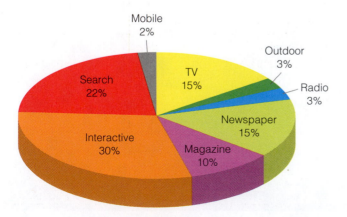

Mobile 2%
Search 22%
Interactive 30%
TV 15%
Outdoor 3%
Radio 3%
Newspaper 15%
Magazine 10%

EXAMPLE   MEDIA MIX

The Israel Ministry of Tourism conducted an advertising campaign with the objective of increasing awareness of Israel as a potential holiday destination among British travelers. With the assistance of the London-based Total Media Group, the Ministry developed a broad-based media mix for the campaign, including the following:

- **TV**—A television ad campaign ran for one month, reaching 75% of the target audience in key regions.
- **Outdoor**—Large-format posters were placed in the London Underground, along with colorful signs on cabs.
- **Newspapers**—Ads were run in national newspaper supplements and specialist press publications.
- **Interactive**—Online advertising contained links to drive traffic to the Israeli tourism Web site.

By combining awareness-building media, for example, television, outdoor, and newspapers, with more information-intensive media, for example, interactive, the advertising creative and media mix substantially increased the number of visitors to Israel from the UK during the campaign period.[5]

PHOTO: Nathan Chor

>> END EXAMPLE

Media Types (pp. 196–201)

> **DEFINED** A **media type** (or **media vehicle**) *is a form of media used for marketing communications, including types such as broadcast, print, interactive, branded entertainment, and social networks.*

▼ **EXPLAINED**

Media Types

Media come in different types because people are different. Your favorite way to spend an evening might be on the couch in front of the TV. Perhaps you like to relax by striving for a high score on your PlayStation or Xbox. Maybe you love to settle in with satellite radio for a night filled with jazz or classical music. Whether you're a television fanatic, a gamer, or a music aficionado, there's a type of media that's just right for you.

There are numerous ways to classify media types. One way is according to whether people are directly involved in delivering a message. **Personal media** refers to direct, one-to-one communication between individuals. Marketing pitches from retail salespeople or telemarketers are examples of personal media. In contrast, messages delivered by **nonpersonal media** do not involve personal contact between sender and receiver. Examples of nonpersonal media are ads shown on TV or published in glossy magazines. Marketers group types of media into a few broad categories:

- **Broadcast**—Includes network TV, cable TV, and radio
- **Print**—Includes newspapers, magazines, and direct mail
- **Out-of-home (OOH)**—Includes display advertising such as billboards, signs, and posters
- **Interactive**—Includes media such as e-mail, Web advertising, and Web sites
- **Branded entertainment**—Incorporates brand messages into entertainment venues like movies or TV shows

Marketers also categorize media according to whether the messages conveyed are paid for by a sponsor. **Paid advertising (or media)** refers to messages delivered to an audience on behalf of a company, organization, or individual in return for payment. In 2007, the largest U.S. advertisers were Proctor & Gamble, AT&T, and Verizon, with each spending between $2 and $3 billion dollars on media.[6]

In the case of **unpaid advertising (or media)**, there is no payment in return for sending messages. Word of mouth (WOM), or stories carried in the official news media about products or services are examples of unpaid advertising. In addition to the media types already mentioned, personal selling and direct marketing should also be included in any discussion of media strategy. In combination with nonpersonal media forms, personal selling and direct marketing communicate messages to potential customers as part of an overall IMC strategy.

 APPLIED

Media Types

With so many types of media from which to choose, how do marketers decide which ones to use? **Media efficiency** measures how inexpensively a media vehicle is able to communicate with a particular customer segment. Because media budgets are not infinite, marketers weigh efficiency very carefully. More efficient forms of media are less expensive, but less able to finely target niche demographic or behavioral segments.

The main way media companies earn revenue is by selling advertising, so they have an incentive to fill up their time slots and ad space. In some instances, a particular type of media becomes **cluttered**, with too many competing ads fighting for attention. Marketers prefer media with little or no clutter because their advertisements do not have to work as hard to stand out.

Media impact is a qualitative assessment as to the value of a message exposed in a particular medium. For example, consumers may view an ad in the *New York Times* as having more credibility than if it appeared in the *Weekly World News*. Marketing research companies also collect measures of **media engagement**, which evaluate how attentively audiences read, watch, or listen to media.

Two TV shows may deliver audiences of equal size, but viewers of one show may be significantly more engaged and involved in their experience than viewers of another show.

Product or service characteristics are also taken into account. Does the product need to be demonstrated for consumers to understand what it does? If so, then visual media like television or online advertising is required. Are customers located in a fairly tight geographic area? If so, then local newspapers or local radio would be a great solution. Each type has relative advantages and disadvantages that are weighed when developing a media mix.[7]

Broadcast

For decades, broadcast was the media type of choice among U.S. advertisers. Broadcast sends messages to large numbers of people extremely quickly, at a fraction of the cost of other media. Today, broadcast still has appeal for marketers, but interactive spending is growing in response to shifts in media-usage patterns. The two traditional forms of broadcast are television and radio.

Network television for example, CBS, NBC, ABC, and FOX, refers to the broadcast of programming and paid advertising through a nationwide series of affiliate TV stations. Although network TV commands the majority of broadcast spending, **cable television**, for example, CNN, MTV, and HGTV, is gaining strength. Unlike network television, which started by broadcasting over free public airwaves, cable TV networks have used cables or satellite dishes to deliver their signals. Some cable networks are funded by paid ads, while others charge viewers a fee to watch.

Among all types of media, television has the greatest ability to deliver audiences en masse. **Reach** measures the number of people who could potentially receive an ad through a particular media vehicle. It can be expressed as a raw number of individuals or as a percentage of a target audience. An **impression** is a single delivery of an advertising message. Another way to think about television is that it offers high reach, because it can generate a huge number of impressions. Nielsen Media reports television and radio **ratings** that are the percentage of the total available audience watching a TV show or tuned in to a radio program.[8]

Television is also attractive to marketers because it serves up big audiences at a low cost per viewer. **CPM (or cost-per-thousand)** is a metric that calculates the cost for any media vehicle to deliver one thousand impressions among a group of target customers. To calculate CPM, all a marketer needs to know is total media cost and the number of impressions. Cost is then divided by impressions converted into thousands.

EXAMPLE   COST PER THOUSAND

An advertising campaign costs $4,000 and generates 120,000 impressions. The CPM can be calculated using the following formula:[9]

$$\text{Cost per Thousand (CPM)} = \frac{\text{Advertising}}{(\text{Impressions Generated}/1,000)}$$

$$= \frac{\$4,000}{(120,000/1,000)}$$

$$= \frac{\$4,000}{120} = \$33.33$$

>> END EXAMPLE

TV is perhaps the only kind of media that can deliver sight, sound, and motion in a highly dramatic manner. (Just think about the last exciting ad you saw on a high-definition widescreen television!)

Despite its strengths, television has a few disadvantages. In addition to concerns over declining viewership, marketers balk at the high costs associated with television advertising. Production expenses on a polished TV commercial will often run into millions of dollars. When media purchases are added into the equation, the total cost for an effective national ad campaign can easily top $100 million. In addition, TV is a better choice for marketers targeting broad population groups, such as adults aged 18–54. As targets become smaller and more narrowly defined, the efficiency of television is lost.

Growth in the use of DVRs (digital video recorders) also poses a threat to television advertising. **Time-shifting** is the practice of recording a television program at one time to replay it at another. Research shows that during playback, 53% of viewers with DVRs skip over the commercials, which is troubling to networks with business models based on advertising.[10]

In contrast with television, radio is a low-cost medium. Media rates to advertise on radio stations are much lower than for network or cable television. Network and cable signals may cover an entire country, but radio broadcasts are mostly confined to the geographic reach of a station's signal transmitter. Radio ads are also purchased to target specific local or regional areas. It should therefore come as no surprise that local businesses like automotive dealers or restaurants use significant amounts of radio advertising.

Radio also does an excellent job of targeting audiences with specific interests. Programming ranges across diverse genres such as music, talk, sports, and news. Even within the music format, listeners can find almost any kind of channel they want, from hip-hop to classical music. This ability to target audiences is why marketers who segment customers based on their lifestyles or interests find radio appealing.

A major disadvantage to radio is that advertising messages cannot include visuals. The entire ad must succeed, or fail, based on a virtual "theatre of the mind" where consumers imagine products or services based solely on what they hear. This poses a creative challenge for many ad agencies, but radio ads have a significant impact on listeners when done well. Because they involve only the sense of hearing, radio ads may also leave a more fleeting impression on listeners. This problem is compounded because our attention is usually divided while listening to radio. Most of us are doing something else, such as driving a car or cooking, while tuned in.

As digital media increases in popularity, spending on broadcast-station-based terrestrial radio will continue to decline. However, this does not mean that radio will disappear. Both television and radio are looking for new ways to distribute their programming content. Some TV networks and radio stations are broadcasting or streaming shows online to laptops or mobile devices. For a small fee, ABC lets viewers watch episodes of *Lost* on the Web at any time or any location. Satellite radio is a fairly recent addition to the media landscape and uses space-based satellites to broadcast instead of local antennas. As their listener base increases, satellite radio companies may begin to offer limited on-air advertising opportunities to marketers.

Print

Magazines and newspapers are the two most frequently used forms of print advertising. Posters, flyers, signs, and other printed communications are included under the heading of "print," but are used by marketers much less frequently.

There are thousands of magazines published in the United States every year. You can find a magazine devoted to almost any interest or hobby imaginable. If you're a news junkie, you can read *Time Magazine* or *The Week*. If you love pets, then perhaps you should check out *Pet Fancy*. Are you a high school science teacher? *Science Teacher* magazine might be right for you. Companies selling products or services related to occupations, lifestyles, or interests use magazines because they can pinpoint their target audiences. For instance, it would be efficient and effective for a business manufacturing yoga mats to run ads in *Yoga* magazine.

Magazines also have a degree of credibility and prestige, due in part to their ability to reproduce high-quality images. As any reader of *GQ* or *Vogue* will testify, there is no medium with ads as beautiful as those found in glossy magazines. The credibility of such magazines is further enhanced by the professionally written stories and editorials they contain. Magazines also have fairly long lives; monthlies may be kept around and read for 30 days or longer.

The number of published and distributed copies of a magazine is called its **circulation**. A magazine's circulation can be thought of a measure of its readership, or reach. The long life span of magazines creates a pass-along effect, where a single issue might have multiple readers. Copies of magazines that you might read in a doctor's office are an example of a single issue "passing along" from one patient to another.

One disadvantage to magazines is their high CPM relative to other types of media. Marketers justify the added expense of magazines based on their ability to deliver specific target audiences, their credibility, and their longer life spans. **Lead time** is the amount of preparation time a media type requires before an advertisement can be run. Four-color magazines require longer lead times than television or newspapers, and the position, for example, front cover or back cover, of an ad in a particular issue is usually not guaranteed.

EXAMPLE   MEDIA TYPES

Grape juice sales have been falling due to rising competition and parents' concerns over beverages with high sugar content. Marketers for Welch's brand noticed that traditional media plans emphasizing TV ad with pictures of smiling, happy kids weren't as effective as in the past. Welch's revamped its entire message and media strategy.

Instead of emotional appeals, new ads emphasize the fact that Welch's has twice the antioxidant power of orange juice. With a total budget of $10 million, and the need to provide consumers with an information-intensive message, a breakthrough approach to media was also needed. Special print ads with "Peel 'n Taste" strips attached appeared in magazines such as *People* and *Cookie*, inviting readers to experience Welch's bold flavor. After peeling back the strip and then licking it, consumers were able to read about the juice's health benefits. News coverage for the innovative ad included stories in *The Wall Street Journal* and on *Good Morning America*, and dramatically expanded the campaign's reach. Best of all, during the campaign period, sales of Welch's grape juice increased 10%.[11]

PHOTO: David P. Smith

>> **END EXAMPLE**

Local newspapers focus the bulk of their coverage on a city or regional area, like the *Chicago Tribune* or *Miami Herald*. Messages that are relevant to specific geographic areas, like ads for 24-hour sales at a neighborhood furniture store, are well suited to local papers. Similar to magazines, ads in newspapers are surrounded by independently written stories that may lend credibility to their marketing messages. Newspapers also have more advertising flexibility than magazines because they usually publish on a daily basis. Compared with television, local papers are a somewhat less-expensive media option, but this advantage can be offset by their limited geographic coverage. Purchasing ad space in enough local papers to reach large cities or the entire nation would quickly become very costly. For instance, to fully cover a city like Seattle, an advertiser might need to purchase ad space in over a dozen local papers. Papers like *USA Today* or the *Wall Street Journal* are distributed nationwide, thus allowing marketers to reach the whole United States with a single media buy. Readership of national newspapers tends to be more upscale, for example, businesspeople and travelers. They offer the same advantages of timeliness and credibility as local newspapers, but their overall audience numbers are small when compared with television or other types of media.

A major drawback to using newspapers as part of a media mix is their declining readership. Fewer people are reading newspapers, as evidenced in a study by the Pew Research Center for the People & the Press. In 2008, only 34% of people reported reading a newspaper the previous day, down 6% from just two years prior.[12]

Web readership is increasing, but there are not yet sufficient numbers of online readers to offset declines in printed newspapers. To offset weaker ad sales, publishers are creating online versions of their papers as new outlets for content. Over the next decade, advertising spending on newspaper sites is expected to grow to $10 billion.[13]

Compared with a magazine, the average newspaper has a very short life. Readers may be exposed to an ad for only a single day before a paper is consigned to the recycle bin. As a result, opportunities for pass-along readership are limited. Image reproduction quality is also relatively poor. To keep newspaper prices low, publishers use less expensive paper and most ads are printed in black and white.

Out-of-Home

Media channels aren't limited to delivering messages into our homes or into our hands. Because people are often in transit at some point during the day, marketers place brief advertising messages along people's travel routes. **Out-of-home (OOH)** media is a term that covers the following three main types of media:[14]

- **Outdoor boards** are large ad display panels, usually near highways or other heavily trafficked locations.
- **Posters** are smaller than outdoor boards and are frequently used at bus or train stops.
- **Transit advertising** appears on buses, trains, in air terminals, in taxis, and wherever people are being transported from one place to another.

Out-of-home is an extremely popular type of media among advertisers, with spending exceeding $8 billion annually. This is due in part to the implementation of new OOH technology like digital billboards, which can rotate ad messages, generating 10 times the advertising revenue of a static board.[15] As an example of applying new technology to outdoor advertising, Nike installed an electronic billboard in New York's Times Square that displayed a tennis shoe that passersby could modify by using their cell phones. **Frequency** is the number of times an individual is exposed to an advertising message by a media vehicle. Frequency can be increased in two ways: through scheduling, which is running a TV ad multiple times during the same program, or through the characteristics of the media itself. One advantage of out-of-home media is that it can result in high message frequency among people who often travel the same route past an outdoor board or transit ad.

Marketers use out-of-home media when they have a short message that needs to be exposed to a broad audience. Out-of-home media does an excellent job of delivering sheer numbers of impressions at a low CPM. It is also a good choice for messages that have a geographic component, like an ad sited along a highway that says: "For a great meal, exit here!" The OOH media environment is fairly uncluttered, compared with magazines or television. And marketers have total control over the location of their messages; they choose the size, site, and duration of their advertising. Some boards are even movable, allowing expanded market coverage.

Although its CPM is low, out-of-home advertising can have significant out-of-pocket costs. In a top national market, the monthly cost for outdoor boards can add up to millions of dollars. The time for passerby to process messages is also fleeting, so advertising copy must be kept to a minimum. If you need a lot of words to explain your product or service, then outdoor is not the most appropriate medium.

Interactive

Interactive media is certainly the new media "kid on the block," with broadband penetration in the United States estimated at 48.3% (or 139.4 million people).[16] Definitions and categories of interactive media change almost daily, but some of the most frequently recognized types are as follows:

- **Banner advertising**—The placement of advertisements (called banners) onto various Web sites that link to the sponsor's Web page.

- **Classified advertising**—The online version of traditional classified ads.
- **Search marketing**—The optimization of Web site keywords and marketing agreements with search engines to drive traffic to Web sites.
- **Mobile advertising**—Refers to advertisements delivered over portable communication devices such as mobile phones and PDA.
- **Gaming**—Is the online and offline inclusion of advertising and brand names into games.
- **User-generated content**—Like social networks, such as Facebook or MySpace, user blogs, and filesharing, such as Flickr or Snapfish, are sources of both word-of-mouth communications and advertising.

Digital media spending topped $21 billion in 2007,[17] propelled mainly by display ads, search, and online classifieds.[18] One of the most attractive aspects of interactive media for marketers is the ability to target Web users based on their previous behavior, interests, or other factors. To give a simple example, a search of Google for "refrigerators" might serve up a banner ad for a GE freezer along with the results. CPM per contact can also be fairly low, and the message result can be immediate. Unlike ads in any other form of media, customers can interact directly with ads, clicking or texting in response to a sponsor's messages. This characteristic adds another level of accountability for interactive media, which is vital for marketers who must prove a return on investment from their advertising campaigns.

Social networks, such as Facebook and MySpace, connect people with common interests and those who are looking to make friends online. These sites are growing in popularity, and marketers are experimenting with their advertising potential. Electronic publishing, such as blogs, e-magazines, and e-books, are also emerging marketing opportunities. Marketers are even exploring virtual worlds, such as SecondLife or CyWorld, where users have avatars that act as cyberspace "selves" who work, play, and interact online. Advertisements may be placed or virtual market tests conducted in these new media environments.

Interactive media also has some limitations. Penetration of interactive media is growing, but large portions of the U.S. population are not yet online. Research has shown that on the question of television or Internet advertising, the answer is not "either/or," but "both." There are parts of the population who can be reached only through the Web. And there are others who can be reached only by using traditional media communications. Campaigns have been proven to be more effective when using combinations of media instead of using one type exclusively.

Marketers need to adopt a completely different perspective when thinking about interactive media. For the most part, consumers are in control of the communication process. At any given time, consumers' personal interests dictate when and where they will end up on the Web. Most advertisements are not so much "transmitted" in an interactive world as they are "found." In addition, surfers are only a click away from any ad they find offensive or boring.

EXAMPLE   **INTERACTIVE MEDIA**

The United States Air Force stages recruiting events at state fairs and other locations around the country. At many of these events, real fighter jets are often available for attendees to touch, and thus increase excitement about the Air Force. But once a potential recruit leaves an event, how does the USAF maintain that excitement and interest? One way is through the use of mobile media. Event attendees can download 17 different types of USAF-related content to their cell phones, including videos, wallpaper, and ringtones. Signs at events display SMS short codes, which can be sent as phone text messages to unlock videos detailing specific careers in the Air Force. Quick response (QR/2D) code messaging is also possible, whereby attendees with phones containing special software may scan a bar code granting them access to USAF promotional material. Event staffers are also on hand to provide visitors with training in the use of these advanced features, if needed. For prospects who will not or cannot attend formal events, the USAF also places a variety of ads on mobile sites from channels such as *MTV* and *Comedy Central*, which direct viewers to resources offering additional content.[19]

PHOTO: Tebnad

>> END EXAMPLE

Branded Entertainment

The integration of brands or brand messages into entertainment media, for example, films, television, novels, and songs, is called **branded entertainment**, or product placement. Well-known examples of this practice are *American Idol*, which has branded Coke, Target, and Ford Motor Company, and the James Bond film series, which has branded Aston-Martin, Omega, and Bollinger. In 2006 alone, the list of films containing placements for Heineken beer included *The Departed*, *V for Vendetta*, *Madea's Family Reunion*, *Eight Below*, and *Phat Girls*.[20]

Branded entertainment can deliver large numbers of impressions, but is generally viewed as a complement to other forms of media. Brand insertions into films or TV shows are relatively brief and experienced in the context of a story, like a main character wearing Armani or using an Ericsson cell phone. As a result, branded entertainment is well suited for brands that already have mass awareness, so marketers don't need to worry if audiences understand a product's basic purpose. But exposure in entertainment lends an aura of prestige or credibility, especially if a well-known movie, music, or TV star is using the product. In addition, many audience members might prefer to avoid advertising, but will sit for two hours watching a movie embedded with brands. Product placements are immune to DVR or TiVo as well, because viewers may zip past ads, but they would never skip their recorded programs.

Like television advertising, branded entertainment ventures have low CPM but often carry high initial costs. Studios and publishers are quite aware of the value of product placements, and the price for brand involvement is rising. These prices are inflated as marketers bid against each other for the right to appear in the hottest properties. In the majority of instances, onscreen brand impressions are fleeting, so the impact of audience exposures may be questionable. Even the most savvy media maven can't accurately predict the success or failure of a film, song, book, or TV show. Branded entertainment is partially a "roll of the dice" because marketers have to guess a year or more in advance which are the special properties that audiences, listeners, and readers will embrace.

EXAMPLE   BRANDED ENTERTAINMENT

Even branded entertainment can become a cluttered media environment. In the 2001 film *Driven*, Brandchannel identified 102 different brand or product placements. These included both paid and unpaid brand exposures, which can be frustrating for those companies who invested significant dollars to be part of the movie. Brands represented in this movie included KoolAid, Marlboro, Snapple, and Nextel.

In part, this was due to the film's storyline about racing, which naturally contains a large number of brand identifications. Unfortunately for everyone involved, the film only grossed $54.7 million on a production budget of $94 million.[21]

PHOTO: Konstantin Sutyagin

>> END EXAMPLE

Personal Selling and Direct Marketing

The effectiveness of any mass media advertising campaign can be greatly increased through the use of personal selling and direct marketing. As discussed in Chapter 15, personal selling involves marketing messages delivered face-to-face, from sales people to customers. The impact of a mass-media campaign is multiplied when salespeople are able to clarify and build on its basic message at point of sale. With personal selling, communication with prospects is customizable on the spot. Questions can be answered, products demonstrated, or additional information provided.

On a CPM basis, however, personal selling is expensive because its reach is extremely limited. Training is required to ensure that salespeople have the knowledge needed to deliver the right messages, which increases the total cost for the campaign. The quality of personal selling also varies; it depends on an individual salesperson's personality, knowledge, and selling ability.

Direct marketing is another useful complement to broader-reach media. Similar to personal selling, direct marketing is highly targeted, because each recipient is preselected based on his or her product usage, demographics, interests, or geography.

Marketers leverage the wider audience of mass media like broadcast or even print, and then reinforce the impact of this advertising with specific target audiences via direct marketing.

Media Selection (pp. 201–204)

> ▼ **DEFINED** **Media selection** *refers to the process of choosing which media types to use, when, where, and for what duration in order to execute a media plan.*

▼ **EXPLAINED**

Media Selection

Marketing communication campaigns involve the definition of a target customer, specification of communication objectives, development of a creative strategy, and media selection. While earlier chapters covered the first parts of this list, the remainder of this chapter focuses on media selection, implementation, and measurement. Marketers follow a stepwise process to select, implement, and measure advertising media (see Figure 16.2).

The process starts by establishing a media budget and media objectives. A media budget is a subset of the marketing communications budget, which also includes funds for nonmedia activities such as sales force support and public relations. In turn, the marketing communications budget is a portion of the company's overall marketing budget. The **media budget** specifies the total amount a firm will spend on all types of advertising media.

As a first step, along with the media budget, an understanding of **media objectives** is required. A media objective is a clear, unambiguous statement as to what media selection and implementation will achieve. This statement should convey, in as much detail as possible, what the media will accomplish and when. Some examples of media objectives are as follows:[22]

- Within the $10 million budget, create national awareness for our product before the end of the year.
- During the launch period, reach 80% of target customers an average of five times, and reach 50% of target customers an average of three or more times.
- Sustain product awareness by reaching 30% of target customers at least once a month.

Media budgets and media objectives are interrelated, because it would be impossible to fully achieve an objective without sufficient funding. The optimal way to set budgets is by using a **task-and-objective** approach, and by allocating dollars sufficient to attain media objectives. In reality, many firms have limited budgets, and simply decide to use an easily calculated method, for example, a percentage of sales revenue, or to spend whatever they can afford.

▼ **APPLIED**

Media Selection

Marketing decisions should be based on an in-depth understanding of the customer, and media is no exception. The next step in the media-selection process is to build a detailed profile

FIGURE 16.2   Media Selection

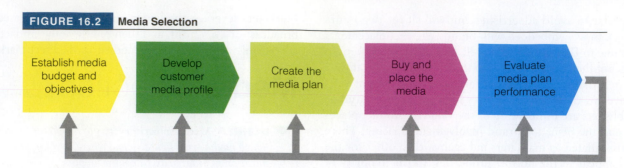

of the target customers and their media habits. This profile will include data on the following characteristics of target customers:

- **Demographics**—Who are they?
- **Geographic location**—Where do they live?
- **Media consumption habits**—What types of media do they consume? At what times of day?
- **Lifestyles and interests**—How do they live? What are their likes and dislikes?

Marketers use these profiles to guide their media-selection decisions. A hypothetical profile may suggest that a target customer is a heavy user of print media, an occasional user of interactive, and never listens to radio. The target may also live on the West Coast of the United States and make product purchases twice a month. All of these findings will have implications for media strategy.

Once the media objectives have been established, the media budget has been set, and the target customer media profile has been developed, then media planning can begin. **Media planning** involves the creation of a **media plan**, which is a document that describes how an advertiser plans to spend its media budget to reach its objectives. A media plan specifies the types and amounts of media to be used, the timing of media, and the geographic concentration—national, regional, or local.

The media plan is implemented through media buying and placement. **Media buying** is the negotiation and purchase of media. These purchases should correspond to the direction as given in the media plan. **Placement** is the implementation of the media plan via the purchased media vehicles. Ads must be sent (or trafficked) to media companies in time for them to run as scheduled. As the plan and buying are implemented in real time, their performance is monitored and evaluated. Realtime conclusions and insights from the plan are fed back into the process for continuous improvement.

Media Planning

Media planning is a complicated activity; it requires advertisers to balance many different inputs. For a large advertiser, the planning department of the company's advertising agency writes the media plans. A **media planner** has extensive knowledge about media vehicles and expertise in formulating media plans. Planners consider several issues when building a media plan.

When formulating a plan, media planners take into account not only the suitability of each media, but how different types could work together to deliver the advertising message. The impact of a message viewed on television is multiplied when heard on the radio or seen on a billboard. Working with creative teams, planners also look for ways to combine or link media vehicles. For instance, TV ads sometimes contain Web addresses directing customers to

the Internet or to 800 numbers to call to obtain additional product information or make purchases. Some advertisers include special codes in magazine ads that readers can scan with Webcams or enter into cell phones to unlock additional online content.

Gross Rating Points (GRPs) are a way for planners to approximate the impact of media decisions. A GRP is the product of reach multiplied by frequency. For example, if an ad is scheduled to air two times in a single TV show (frequency), where the show has a 5.0 rating (reach), the plan will result in 10 GRPs. Demographics are always specified for GRPs (like ratings among adults aged 25–54).

A **media flowchart** (or **media footprint**) is a visual representation of the media plan. Expressed in worksheet or project software, the flowchart is essentially a calendar with time periods as columns and media types as rows. Whenever the plan dictates a media vehicle should be used, the column and row intersection contains estimated GRPs and a budget allocated to that media type. Multiple levels of geography may be shown on a single footprint or separately. The footprint allows planners to view at a glance the complete media plan. An example of a media flowchart for a women's athletic shoe brand can be seen in Figure 16.3.[23]

Media Buying

Based on the media plan, a group of agency experts called **media buyers** negotiate and purchase media properties. All media is sold on an open market, with media companies trying to sell their properties for top dollar and advertisers looking to scoop up the best deals. Media prices vary, according to marketplace demand and the skill of negotiators on both sides of the table.

The bulk of network television is sold in an **upfront market**, which is a long-lead marketplace where TV networks and advertisers negotiate media prices for the fourth quarter of the current year, plus the first three quarters of the following year. In an upfront market, advertisers commit to purchase media and, in return, the networks set aside ad time for their upcoming programs. Advertisers can usually lock in the best pricing and programming by participating in an upfront market, but their ability to cancel or sell off any commitments is limited. Ads that are not purchased in advance via an upfront market, but are secured on a quarterly basis, are called **scatter buys**. Although scatter buys can be less efficient, media buyers can use them to react to changes in the marketplace and they allow greater spending flexibility.

Magazines, newspapers, radio, and out-of-home are purchased on the basis of **rate cards**, which are officially published prices for different types of media. Rate cards are often negotiable, and with the merger of large media companies, packages featuring a single price for combined offline and online media buys are increasingly common.

FIGURE 16.3   Media Flowchart

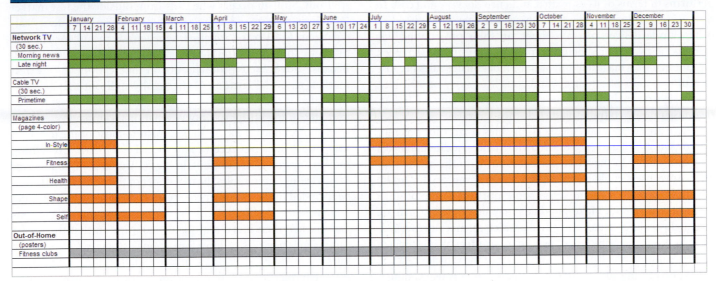

Internet advertising is usually priced on a CPM basis, and prices vary according to the size and type of ad. Advertisements could take many forms, such as banners or interstitial ads (also called "pop-ups"). Search advertising operates differently, with advertisers paying search engines or directories only after Web surfers have clicked their ad or link.

After media has been purchased, the advertising agency or marketing firm must deliver ads to the various media companies for broadcast, publication, or posting. The procedure for getting finished ads to the correct media firms is called **ad trafficking** because ads are "routed" on their way to implementation. For a list of strategic questions in media selection, see Table 16.1.

Media Optimization (pp. 203–204)

▼ **DEFINED** *Media optimization is the adjustment of media plans to maximize their performance.*

▼ **EXPLAINED**

Media Optimization

When a media plan is developed, it is based on the estimated performance of each broadcast program, magazine, newspaper, outdoor board, Web site, or any other media vehicle that it contains.

Table 16.1 Strategic Questions in Media Selection

Issue	Strategic Questions (Examples)	Impact
Reach versus frequency	Should the plan maximize the number of customer impressions (reach), the number of times each customer is communicated with (frequency), or both?	Maximizing reach will require heavy investments in mass media, such as broadcast; maximizing frequency may more heavily employ vehicles with less reach.
Scheduling	Should the plan be continuous, where advertising is running constantly? Should the plan involve a flight, where advertising is running for only brief periods? Should the plan be some combination of the two?	Continuous plans can be expensive, but are well suited to products or services in demand year-round, for example, food, beverages, and telecommunications. Flights are less expensive and are good for products that are more seasonal, for example, Halloween costumes and snow blowers, or for brand-reminder advertising.
Geography	Should the plan cover the entire world? A single country? Regions within a country? Cities or localities?	A plan could have national, regional, or local coverage, or combinations of any of the three. The media plan's geographic coverage is determined by the location of target customers.
Product type	How frequently is the product purchased? How much information do customers need?	Products that are used frequently require more continuous media. Ones that are information intensive suggest plans that employ print, interactive, or direct media.
Media cost	What does this media type cost? What is its CPM to deliver the target audience?	All issues are weighed in relation to media cost. A media type may be effective in terms of achieving objectives, but highly inefficient. It may also be efficient, but does a poor job of reaching the target audience.

A **media audit** measures how well each selected media vehicle performs in terms of its estimated audience delivery and cost. In the real world, some media will achieve their target levels, while others underdeliver, or overdeliver, on their projections. For instance, a TV ad could be preempted by a special news report. Or an issue of a magazine might have blockbuster sales because of a movie star's photo or a scandalous lead story on its cover. Audit reports include metrics such as GRPs delivered, CPM, response rates, Web traffic, and click-through rates.

There are several ways media companies correct for preemption or significant audience underperformance. Additional media may be credited to the advertiser's account with the media supplier. Advertisers could use this extra media inventory for future advertising, or they might claim some portion of the original amount as a refund. **Make-good** ads may be offered, which are essentially replacements for any media which did not run as scheduled. Some media vehicles come with **guarantees** that estimated audience numbers will be achieved, or part of the vehicle's cost will be retuned to the advertiser. Guaranteed media is usually more expensive, because the media supplier is accepting financial risk.

Although actions by media companies are one way to bolster media plan implementation, marketers also make changes on their own. **Media optimization** is the process of adjusting media plans to improve their performance. Advertisers review the media audit reports and, whenever possible, reallocate media weight away from weak properties and toward strong ones. Optimization can take place on many levels, such as overall spend-by-media category, for example, radio versus Outdoor, or by individual media vehicles, for example, a particular radio station versus a particular outdoor board. Marketers also optimize media by changing plans in reaction to marketplace conditions. Competitive actions and economic conditions may lead to a plan adjustment. For instance, if a competitor increases advertising spending in a geographic region, a firm may reallocate its own media dollars to this area to blunt the attack.

▼ **APPLIED**

Media Optimization

Media planning and buying is very complex, with many interrelated components. As a result, the task of optimizing a full-blown media plan can be incredibly daunting. **Modeling** is a tool that many large advertisers use to guide their media planning and plan optimization. In an advertising context, economic modeling decomposes the impact of individual media vehicles on a target variable such as sales. For example, an econometric model would calculate how the amount of money spent in each category of media influences product sales.

Live test markets are sometimes used to conduct a "test run" of a proposed national media plan. Geographic markets are selected where the plan will be implemented on a limited basis. Products are manufactured, priced, and distributed into the test market, so that as the media runs, advertisers are able to track actual sales in response to the campaign. Any market chosen should have a range of media channels, demographics, purchase behavior, and other characteristics that reflect the media profile of the broader geography to be used in the overall plan as much as possible.

In addition, advertisers consider the potential for spill-in or spill-out. **Spill-in** occurs when ads from outside the test market "spill into" the area, which may confuse reach and frequency calculations. **Spill-out** happens whenever ads meant for the test market "spill out" and touch people in adjacent markets. Because advertised products are available only in the test market, potential customers affected by spill-out may become frustrated if they attempt to make a purchase. As a result, they may ignore any future roll-out of a national campaign.

A control market has a profile similar to those of the test markets, but it does not receive any special treatment. Everything remains "normal," or constant, in the control market, so in terms of marketing, it resembles the remainder of the nontest markets to be included in the overall media plan. If metrics such as product awareness or sales increase in test markets more than in the control market, then it is a reasonable assumption that the media campaign is having a positive impact on customers. Conversely, if sales fall in test markets or are unchanged, then the creative strategy, media plan, or both should be revised before implementation.

EXAMPLE   MEDIA OPTIMIZATION

In 2003, Ford launched the newest version of its best-selling F-150 pickup truck. During a six-month launch period, the media plan targeted males, aged 25–54. The media plan included heavy television advertising, magazines such *Car & Driver* or *Western Horsemen*, as well as online advertising. A relatively new form of advertising at the time, digital roadblocks, was also employed. Digital roadblocks are ads automatically served to visitors at Web portals like AOL.com, Yahoo!.com, or MSN.com. To understand the effectiveness and efficiency of its media choices, Ford conducted a study to model the impact and net cost of each media type. The study found the following:

- Although TV was expensive, it bolstered the overall performance of the other media channels.
- At half the cost of television, magazines could deliver a similar impact on purchase intent.
- Digital roadblocks were very efficient in terms of cost-per-person influenced.

Extending the impact of suggested media changes from sales to revenues, the study estimated that optimization of the F-150 media plan would lead to a significant incremental profit for Ford.[24]

PHOTO: Marek Slusarczyk

>> END EXAMPLE

▼**Visual** Summary

Part 1   Explaining (Chapters 1, 2, 3, 4)
Part 2   Creating (Chapters 5, 6, 7, 8)
Part 3   Strategizing (Chapters 9, 10)

Part 4   Managing (Chapters 11, 12, 13, 14, 15)
Part 5   Integrating (Chapters 16, 17)

Chapter 16 Summary

Marketers communicate advertising messages through a variety of media channels. Media mixes reflect how companies allocate their spending across different types of media. Potential media vehicles include broadcast, for example, television or radio; print, for example, magazines and newspapers; and out-of-home and interactive. Comprehensive media strategies also take into account the impact of personal selling and direct marketing. Media plans specify the media vehicles to be used as well as scheduling, geographic, and cost considerations. Plans are implemented through the purchase and placement of media. Measurement and optimization of media plans complete the process, thus improving current performance and providing insight for future campaigns.

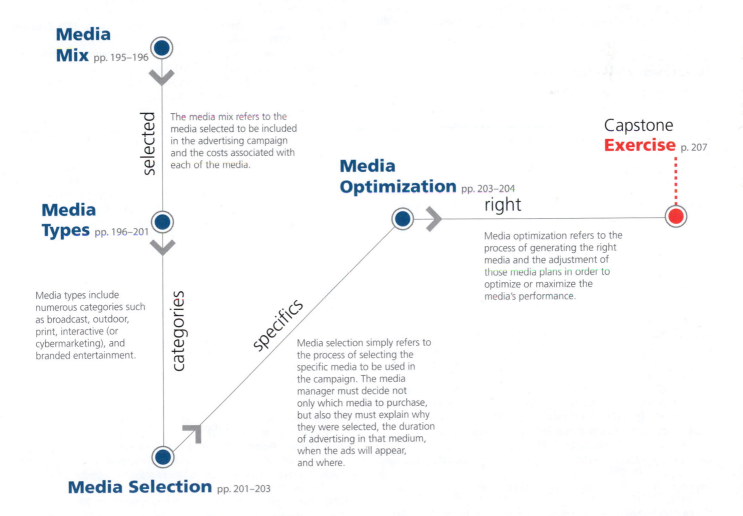

Media Mix pp. 195–196

selected

The media mix refers to the media selected to be included in the advertising campaign and the costs associated with each of the media.

Media Types pp. 196–201

categories

Media types include numerous categories such as broadcast, outdoor, print, interactive (or cybermarketing), and branded entertainment.

Media Selection pp. 201–203

specifics

Media selection simply refers to the process of selecting the specific media to be used in the campaign. The media manager must decide not only which media to purchase, but also they must explain why they were selected, the duration of advertising in that medium, when the ads will appear, and where.

Media Optimization pp. 203–204

right

Media optimization refers to the process of generating the right media and the adjustment of those media plans in order to optimize or maximize the media's performance.

Capstone **Exercise** p. 207

▼Chapter Key Terms

Media Mix (pp. 195–196)

Media mix refers to the selection of media used for an advertising campaign as well as the budget allocated to each medium. (p. 196)
Opening Example (p. 195) Example: Media Mix (p. 196)

Key Terms (pp. 195–196)

Advertising media (or "media") is the collection of mediums (physical or electronic) used to carry marketing communications. **(p. 195)** (Opening Example) **Example: Media Mix (p. 196)**

Consumer-generated media (CGM), such as blogs or video Web sites, allow ordinary people to create and send their own messages. **(p. 195)**

Interactive media (sometimes called **digital media**) is a broad term used to refer to electronic methods of communication where users have the ability to directly shape, interact with, or respond to media. **(p. 196) Example: Media Mix (p. 196)**

Mobile advertising refers to advertisements delivered over portable communication devices. **(p. 196) Example: Media Mix (p. 196)**

Search marketing includes techniques such as paying for inclusion in specific search results on search engines. **(p. 196) Example: Media Mix (p. 196)**

Media Types (pp. 196–202)

Media type (or media vehicle) refers to a form of media used for marketing communications, including types such as broadcast, print, interactive, branded entertainment, and social networks. (p. 196) **Example: Media Types (p. 198)**

Key Terms (pp. 196–202)

Banner advertising is the placement of advertisements (called banners) onto various Web sites that link to the sponsor's Web page. **(p. 199)**

Branded entertainment is the integration of brands or brand messages into entertainment media, for example, films, television, novels, and songs. **(p. 197) Example: Branded Entertainment (p. 201)**

Broadcast media include network TV, cable TV, and radio. **(p. 197)**

Cable television refers to TV broadcasts using cables or satellite dishes. **(p. 197) Example: Media Types (p. 198)**

Circulation is the number of published and distributed copies of a magazine. **(p. 198)**

Classified advertising is the online version of traditional classified ads. **(p. 200)**

Clutter is a qualitative assessment of the degree to which a particular media vehicle contains too many ads competing for attention. **(p. 197) Example: Branded Entertainment (p. 201)**

CPM (or cost-per-thousand) is a metric that calculates the cost for any media vehicle to deliver one thousand impressions among a group of target customers. **(p. 197)**

Frequency is the number of times an individual is exposed to an advertising message by a media vehicle. **(p. 199)**

Gaming includes the online and offline inclusion of advertising and brand names into games. **(p. 200)**

Impression refers to the single delivery of an advertising message by a media vehicle. **(p. 197)**

Interactive include electronic media such as e-mail, Web advertising, and Web sites. **(p. 197) Example: Interactive Media (p. 200)**

Lead time is the amount of preparation time a media type requires before an advertisement can be run. **(p. 198)**

Media efficiency measures how inexpensively a media vehicle is able to communicate with a particular customer segment. **(p. 197)**

Media engagement evaluates how attentively audiences read, watch, or listen to a particular media vehicle. **(p. 197)**

Media impact is a qualitative assessment as to the value of a message exposed in a particular medium. **(p. 197)**

Network television refers to the broadcast of programming and paid advertising through a nationwide series of affiliate TV stations. **(p. 197)**

Nonpersonal media refers to media that does not involve personal contact between sender and receiver. **(p. 197)**

Out-of-Home (OOH), or display, advertising includes media types that are encountered outside the home, such as billboards, signs, and posters. **(p. 199)**

Outdoor boards are large ad display panels, usually near highways or other heavily trafficked locations. **(p. 199)**

Paid advertising (or media) refers to messages delivered to an audience on behalf of a company, organization, or individual in return for payment. **(p. 197) Example: Media Types (p. 198)**

Personal media refers to direct, one-to-one communication between individuals. **(p. 197)**

Posters are smaller than outdoor boards and are frequently used at bus or train stops. **(p. 199)**

Print media include newspapers, magazines, and direct mail. **(p. 197) Example: Media Types (p. 198)**

Ratings are the percentage of the total available audience watching a TV show or tuned in to a radio program. **(p. 197)**

Reach is a measure of the number of people who could potentially receive an ad through a particular media vehicle. **(p. 197)**

Social networks, such as Facebook and MySpace, connect people with common interests and those who are looking to make friends online. **(p. 200)**

Time-shifting is the practice of recording a television program at one time to replay it at another. **(p. 198)**

Transit advertising appears on buses, trains, air terminals, taxis, and wherever people are being transported from one place to another. **(p. 199)**

Unpaid advertising (or media) is the delivery of messages without payment in return. **(p. 197) Example: Media Types (p. 198)**

User-generated content such as social networks, for example, Facebook or MySpace, user blogs, and filesharing, for example, Flickr and Snapfish, are sources of word-of-mouth communications and advertising. **(p. 200)**

Media Selection (pp. 201–204)

Media selection refers to the process of choosing which media types to use, when, where, and for what duration in order to execute a media plan. (p. 201)

Key Terms (pp. 202–204)

Ad trafficking is the procedure for delivering finished ads to the correct media firms for placement. **(p. 203)**

Gross Rating Points (GRPs) are a way for planners to approximate the impact of media decisions and are the product of reach multiplied by frequency. **(p. 202)**

Media buyers negotiate and purchase media properties according to the media plan. **(p. 202)**

Media buying is the negotiation and purchase of media. **(p. 202)**

Media budgets specify the total amount a firm will spend on all types of advertising media. **(p. 201)**

Media flowcharts (or media footprints) are visual representations of the media plan. **(p. 202)**

Media objectives are clear, unambiguous statements as to what media selection and implementation will achieve. **(p. 201)**

Media plans specify the types and amounts of media to be used, the timing of media, and the geographic concentration (national, regional, or local). **(p. 202)**

Media planners create media plans based on their extensive knowledge about media vehicles and expertise. **(p. 202)**

Media planning involves the creation of a media plan, which is a document that describes how an advertiser plans to spend its media budget to reach its objectives. **(p. 202)**

Placement is the implementation of the media plan via the purchased media vehicles. **(p. 202)**

Rate cards are officially published prices for different types of media. **(p. 202)**

Scatter buys are ads that are not purchased in advance via an upfront market, but are secured on a quarterly basis. **(p. 202)**

Task-and-objective is an approach to media budgeting that allocates dollars sufficient to attain media objectives. **(p. 201)**

Upfront markets are long-lead marketplaces where TV networks and advertisers negotiate media prices for the fourth quarter of the current year plus the first three quarters of the following year. **(p. 202)**

Media Optimization (pp. 203–206)

Media optimization *is the adjustment of media plans to maximize their performance.* *(p. 203)* **Example: Media Optimization (p. 204)**

Key Terms (p. 204)

Guarantees are promises made by media companies that estimated audience numbers will be achieved, or part of the cost of advertising will be retuned to the advertiser. **(p. 204)**

Make-goods are ads given by media companies as replacements for any media that did not run as scheduled. **(p. 204)**

Media audits measure how well each selected media vehicle performs in terms of its estimated audience delivery and cost. **(p. 204)**

Media optimization is the process of adjusting media plans to improve their performance. **(p. 204)** **Example: Media Optimization (p. 204)**

Modeling is a tool that many large advertisers use to guide their media planning and plan optimization. **(p. 204)**

Spill-in occurs when ads from outside a test market "spill into" the test market area. **(p. 204)**

Spill-out happens whenever ads meant for a test market "spill out" and touch people in adjacent markets. **(p. 204)**

▼Capstone Exercise

This chapter deals with the media mix. A critical aspect of this mix is the choice of which media one will use, which is commonly known as media planning.

There are several media choices and, of course, you have to decide which ones are best, based on what is the right choice to reach your target customer. The following list includes many of the available choices:

Traditional Media

Broadcast: TV, cable, radio
Print: Newspaper, magazine
Outdoor: Billboards, buses, signs

Alternative Media

Direct response
Campaigns
Sponsorships, Nonprofit tie-in
Internet, Web E-commerce

Most publications offer media kits that try to convince potential advertisers to buy space in their publications. You can find an example at http://mediakit.businessweek.com/. Depending on their product and target customer, why would an advertiser choose *BusinessWeek* to place its advertisements?

A source for Magazine Audience Estimates can be found at http://www.mediamark.com/PDF/Spring%202008%20Pocketpiece.pdf.

Your library may have access to www.srds.com, which has significant information on media rates and planning data.

Your assignment is to plan a promotion campaign for a product of your choice, based on a document like the one found at the following URL as a guide:

http://www.cmo.vermont.gov/resources/documents/AGuidetoDevelopingaMediaPlan_000.pdf

▼Application Exercises

Complete the following exercises:

1. What is the main difference between reach and frequency? Write a definition of each.

2. How is public relations different from advertising and sales promotion?

3. What are the advantages and disadvantages of the various types of media?

4. What form of media do you believe would be best for reaching a 70-year-old retired schoolteacher? For reaching a 12-year-old girl?

The **Marketing Mix**

Chapter Overview The concept of the marketing mix was introduced in Chapter 1. The marketing plan was introduced in Chapter 10, and each of the primary elements of the marketing mix, represented through marketing planning, was profiled in Chapters 11–15. This chapter is designed to explore how the marketing mix is constructed, managed, and modeled. Contemporary marketing-mix classifications are introduced and the concept of optimizing elements of the marketing mix is discussed.

▼ Chapter **Outline**

Marketing Mix pp. 209–210

Objective 1. What choices do marketers make to achieve their sales goals?

Marketing-Mix Strategies pp. 210–213

- **Within the Marketing Mix** p. 212
- **Beyond the 4 Ps** p. 213

Objective 2. How do marketers select a particular marketing mix to achieve their sales goals?

Marketing-Mix Models pp. 213–215

Objective 3. How do marketers measure the effects of each component in a marketing program?

208

MARKETING MIX (pp. 209–210)

> ▼ **DEFINED** A **marketing mix** *is a group of marketing variables that a business controls with the intent of implementing a marketing strategy directed at a specific target market.*

Marketing Mix

The concept of a marketing mix was originally discussed in the 1950s and included 12 categories of marketing variables that were deemed important to a marketing plan:[1]

- **Product planning**—Which products to offer and where to sell them
- **Pricing**—Product price and margin structure
- **Branding**—How the product will be branded and if any intellectual property will be involved
- **Channels of distribution**—How to move the product from manufacturer to consumer
- **Personal selling**—Extent to which personal selling will be utilized
- **Advertising**—Product image, type of advertising, and how much will be spent
- **Promotions**—Role and type of promotion to be used
- **Packaging**—Labeling and package design
- **Display**—Location and type of point-of-sale display
- **Servicing**—Type of after-sales service
- **Physical handling**—Warehousing, inventory control, and transportation
- **Fact finding and analysis**—Securing and analyzing marketing information

The 12 categories were later organized into what is now referred to as the **4 Ps**: product, price, place, and promotion.[2]

The 4 Ps remain the most common classification of a marketing mix. It is important to think of the 4 Ps from a managerial perspective because they help organize business activities. Businesses must be sure that they are marketing the right *product* to the right *person* through the right *promotion* at the right *price* in the right *place* at the right *time*.

Each of the 4 Ps influences the other elements of the marketing mix. A failure in one marketing-mix variable could undermine good choices made with the other marketing-mix variables. Consider a manufacturer of backpacks that are targeted at typical college students and their options (see Table 17.1).

It is essential to understand the marketing objectives and the needs and wants of target segments. It is important to select a target that can deliver the necessary sales volume, revenue, and profitability.

▼ **APPLIED**
Marketing Mix

In practice, businesses make decisions about marketing-mix variables either by reacting to changes in the market, strategically changing position to achieve better financial results, or by default when not responding to market changes. While many businesses organize themselves to manage elements of the 4 Ps, the businesses that practice a marketing orientation actually must consider more than the 4 Ps. Broadening the definition of the marketing mix to include elements beyond the 4 Ps is discussed later in this chapter, and factors such as employees, customers, and processes are often considered when developing marketing-mix strategies.

H&R Block, formed in 1955 as a tax-preparation and bookkeeping business, currently operates out of over 13,800 offices in the United States, Canada, the United Kingdom, and Australia. H&R Block became famous in the late 1980s with its "Rapid Refund" service that allowed its customers who filed their taxes electronically to receive refunds much more quickly than through the mail. H&R Block is known as tax professionals, but they wanted to appeal to younger individuals by creating a marketing mix that includes various types of social media. H&R Block is active on Second Life, MySpace, Facebook, YouTube, and Twitter and uses these sites to communicate with customers and manage the company image. Some examples of social media activities by H&R Block include using Twitter to respond to consumer questions, comments, or concerns and the Me & My Super Sweet Refund competition that includes video submissions on YouTube on how consumers might spend refunds. Another social media activity is Ask a Professional nights in digital shops in Second Life.[3]
PHOTO: Comstock Images

Table 17.1 Options for a Backpack Manufacturer Targeting College Students		
Marketing-Mix Element	It would be more desirable to market:	As opposed to marketing:
Product	A stylish and functional backpack	A high-fashion designer backpack that emphasizes appearance over function
Price	An affordable price	A high price
Place	Through mass merchandisers, bookstores, and moderately priced retailers	Through exclusive designer boutiques
Promotion	Through direct-mail, word-of-mouth, and point-of-sale material	Through invitation-only events and high-gloss magazine advertisements in magazines that target affluent readers

Marketing-Mix
Strategies (pp. 210–213)

 DEFINED **Marketing-mix strategy** *is the logic that guides the selection of a particular marketing mix to achieve marketing objectives.*

 **EXPLAINED**
Marketing-Mix Strategies

While there are many marketing-mix possibilities for any marketing situation, certain marketing mixes are more desirable than others for some of the following reasons:

- Ability to achieve business and marketing objectives
- Time available to fulfill objectives
- Resources, human and financial, available to fulfill objectives
- Influence of market factors, such as competition and consumer interest
- Consistency with business mission and vision
- Level of risk and exposure to business

The most effective marketing-mix strategies consider those factors mentioned previously as well as how each marketing-mix element interacts with the other elements.

Once a marketing-mix decision has been made, it is important to monitor market performance and the target market to determine if changes need to be made. A variety of changes could occur that would require a reevaluation of marketing-mix strategies:

- Competitors could enter or leave the market or reposition themselves.
- New products or services could be offered in the market.
- The market could grow or shrink.
- Target consumers could change their attitudes.
- New trends could emerge.
- Technology could evolve or change the cost structure for products or services.
- New distribution channels could emerge or evolve.

Consider the U.S. market for sport utility vehicles. The segment grew rapidly throughout the 1990s and into 2007 before gas prices increased and the economy declined rapidly. Many automakers dedicated a large share of their manufacturing capacity to sport utility vehicles, as opposed to sedans. In addition, many of the product decisions also involved a slow adoption of alternative propulsion systems such as hybrid technology. Pricing decisions reflected the perception of strong product demand and margins were used to subsidize product development of other vehicles. Fewer incentives were offered for sport utilities, as opposed to other vehicles such as small cars. Considerable promotional investment was dedicated to communicating a new sport utility vehicle launch, as opposed to other vehicles. A large volume of sport utility vehicles were built and distributed through the dealer networks.

When the market changed, significant marketing-mix decisions needed to be made relative to sport utility vehicles. Fewer sport utility vehicles were produced, but that reduced overall margins for all vehicles. Therefore, less money was available for product development, unless money was diverted from other parts of the business. Promotional dollars were severely reduced from sport utility vehicles to support other vehicle types, such as small cars, which saw a significant increase in demand. Many sport utility vehicles were in the distribution pipeline and automotive dealers and manufacturers had to discount prices and offer special financing to help reduce inventory. The result is structural change among companies and suppliers in the automotive sector that will take several years to adjust. In the meantime, careful decisions must be made regarding the marketing mix for sport utility vehicles.

 APPLIED
Marketing-Mix Strategies

Businesses are constantly reevaluating and recreating marketing-mix strategies. A change of business objectives or marketing objectives are common reasons to reconsider a marketing-mix strategy. Business acquisitions of brands, such as common with packaged-goods companies, change brand portfolios and may require repositioning or retargeting existing brands through new marketing-mix strategies. Sometimes market conditions change and new marketing-mix strategies need to be developed. In other cases, the existing marketing-mix strategies are not effective. Examples of marketing-mix strategies with the underlying marketing situation are considered next.

Situation 1: Managing products with different targets within the same product portfolio requires an understanding of how each product contributes to portfolio performance.

EXAMPLE | MARKETING-MIX STRATEGIES: SITUATION 1

Cadillac, founded in 1902 and historically one of General Motors' most prestigious brands, has experienced a sales renaissance over the past decade with edgy high-performance products. The Cadillac product portfolio consists of sedans (CTS, DTS, and STS), a crossover (SRX), a sport utility (Escalade), and a sports car (XLR). There are some variations within the portfolio, including different engine sizes and a V-series premium performance version of most of the vehicles. Although the CTS and XLR-V both weigh just over 3,800 pounds, there are many differences, including the marketing-mix strategies for each vehicle.[4]

Targets—The XLR-V is targeted at high-income individuals, including entertainers and professional athletes. The XLR-V targets tend to also consider vehicles like the BMW M6 and the Mercedes SL55 AMG. The CTS, rather than the XLR-V, is targeted in the entry luxury segment that is more expensive than most vehicles, but includes a much wider target range of individuals, particularly those who are trendy and younger and who might typically purchase non-American brands. CTS targets often consider a variety of other entry luxury brands, including Mercedes C-Class, Audi A4, BMW 3-Series, and Saab 9-3.

Pricing—The CTS and XVR-V represent both ends of the price range of the product portfolio. The CTS starts around $34,000, and the XLR-V starts above $100,000.

Product—The XLR-V is a 2-seat, 443-horsepower coupe based on the Chevrolet Corvette manufacturing platform. The CTS is a midsize sport sedan that shares a platform with the Saab 9–3 and Chevrolet Malibu.

Place—Both the CTS and the XLR-V are sold through the Cadillac dealer network. The XLR-V is sold in limited volumes and not all dealers have them in stock. The XLR-V is often used as a "halo" vehicle, one that is used to create interest in other vehicles and increase showroom traffic.

Promotion—Both vehicles are shown in national television advertising as part of the entire Cadillac portfolio. The CTS

also has its own television advertisement, along with content for most media channels. The XLR is primarily featured in more targeted print advertising. Both the CTS and the XLR-V have their own microsites within the Cadillac Web site. Both models reflect Cadillac's performance luxury positioning, but in the context of their respective market segments. Virtual re-creations of the XLR-V have even been added to Xbox Live's Project Gotham Racing 3.

PHOTO: Konovalikov Andrey

>> END EXAMPLE

Situation 2: Using alternative media to build emotional connections with people across the globe requires an understanding of how different media types work together and how different people throughout the world use media.

EXAMPLE | MARKETING-MIX STRATEGIES: SITUATION 2

Fiskars is one of the oldest companies in the world and was founded in 1649 in Finland. Fiskars began as an ironworks and expanded through the centuries to manufacture a wide range of consumer and industrial products, ranging from cutlery to steam engines. Fiskars employs 4,300 people across the globe and operates four manufacturing divisions: garden, housewares, outdoor recreation, and craft. Fiskars Orange®, products with an iconic orange color, has become ubiquitous with almost 900 million orange-handled scissors sold. Fiskars manages a marketing mix that incorporates a significant amount of word-of-mouth marketing and social networking, including viral marketing, online videos, and blogs. The Fiskars marketing mix focuses on creating an emotional connection with its customers. Project Orange Thumb[SM] provides community garden groups with plants, tools, materials, and grants needed for beautification and education. Fiskars has also created "Fiskateers," a social network ambassador program, for its most loyal customers that has increased loyalty, online interaction, and sales.[5]

PHOTO: Vrjoyner

>> END EXAMPLE

Situation 3: Introducing a new product to an established market segment through a unique positioning requires a thorough understanding of market competitors and their products, as well as the wants and needs of the market.

EXAMPLE | MARKETING-MIX STRATEGIES: SITUATION 3

Axe, owned by the consumer products company Unilever, is a brand of male grooming products that includes Axe Body Spray, Axe Dry, Shower Gel, and Deodorant Stick. Axe was launched in the United States in 2003 with an award-winning

advertising campaign that was targeted at males aged 18–24 with the message that the more men spray, the more likely they are to get the girl. The advertising campaign has drawn some criticism as being sexist, degrading, and encouraging sexual promiscuity. Initially, Axe's marketing mix utilized a Web presence prior to launching traditional television communication. The decision to utilize Web initiatives was based on the idea that the target segment would like to learn about products such as Axe in an environment to which they are more accustomed, such as the Web.[6]

PHOTO: Tomasz Trojanowski

>> **END EXAMPLE**

Situation 4: Repositioning an established brand for a different target audience requires understanding the wants and needs of the new targets, which products they currently are purchasing, and what other substitute products are important to the target.

EXAMPLE | **MARKETING-MIX STRATEGIES: SITUATION 4**

Godiva Chocolatier, an 80-year-old company founded in Brussels, Belgium, produces and sells a wide range of premium chocolates as well as coffee and liqueur through its 450 global stores. Owned by Campbell Soup Company for 30 years, Godiva was sold in 2007 to the Turkish company Yildiz Holding. The iconic gold boxes are brand cues Godiva uses to support its relationship with consumers. Those customers are increasingly younger than from the previous decade. The typical target is now 25- to 35-year-olds. Godiva made a strategic decision several years ago to broaden its appeal to younger consumers with a marketing campaign resembling fashion advertisements. One advertisement for Godiva's Limited Edition Truffles featured Victoria's Secret model Frankie Rayder, and appealed to women's "inner divas." Other promotion includes advertising in magazines such as *Vogue*, *Harper's*, and *Vanity Fair*. While Godiva chocolates are typically more expensive than average chocolate, Godiva's target tends to consider a group of premium chocolates in addition to Godiva. Chocoladefabriken Lindt & Sprüngli A.G, known mainly for its Ghirardelli brand; See's Candies, Inc.; Ferrero USA Inc., known mainly for its Ferrero Rocher brand; Lake Champlain Chocolates; and Scharffen Berger are all considered premium brands and influence Godiva's marketing planning. Godiva does not limit its competition to other premium chocolate brands. Other Godiva competitors include champagne and flowers. Godiva chocolates

are available in Godiva retail stores and online, and now can be purchased through a new mobile application for BlackBerry that uses an individual's stored contact list.[7]

PHOTO: Ronald Sumners

>> **END EXAMPLE**

Within the Marketing Mix

While various marketing-mix combinations must be evaluated to select an overall strategy, it is also essential to consider how to address each marketing-mix element. Some examples include the following:

- Product
  - Does the target like the products or services offered?
  - Do the products or services meet the needs of the target?
  - How satisfied is the target with the quality of the products or services?
  - Are there any foreseeable changes in requirements of the target?
  - Is there a way to track target requirements?
  - At what stages of the product life cycle are the products and services?
  - How profitable are the products or services being sold to the target?
  - Is there another target that might be more viable and profitable than the current choice?

- Price
  - What are your manufacturing costs (fixed and variable), and at what level of sales volume do you need to produce and sell to cover your costs?
  - What do your competitors charge for their products and services?
  - What is your target willing to pay for your products and services?

- Place
  - If selling to consumers, will wholesalers, retailers, direct-to-consumers, or some combination be used?
  - If selling to businesses, will middlemen or an in-house sales force be used?

- Promotion
  - What type of media does the target view?
  - What is the message to be conveyed, and which media is most appropriate to communicate that message to the target?
  - What is the target's level of awareness, familiarity, opinion, and level of consideration for each competitive brand?
  - What advertising, sales promotion, direct marketing, personal selling, and public relations opportunities exist with the target?

Based on the responses to these types of questions, specific marketing-mix choices can be made. While pricing can be established based solely on the required profit for a given product or service, there are broader implications that should be considered. A change in pricing typically has an impact on other elements of the mix. Pricing involves understanding what influences value perceptions in a category. The components of brand value include the following:[8]

- Price
- Product features
- Channel features
- Brand equity

Promotions are yet another dynamic component of the marketing mix. There are a variety of promotion options. These include the following:[9]

- **Price promotion**—Short-term price reductions and coupons
- **In-store advertising**—On-shelf advertisements, in-store radio, shopping cart advertisements
- **Packaging**—Package promotions, design, marketing tie-ins
- **Product placement**—In-store samples, secondary product displays

Promotional efforts can contribute to incremental purchases and profitable customer response. Product and place, the remaining mix elements, also influence the other elements of the mix. The product is perceived by customers as a result of where the product is available, how it is priced, and how it is promoted, relative to other products in the category.[10]

Beyond the 4 Ps

The 4 Ps were developed in the manufacturing economy of the 1960s when large consumer goods firms were serving mass markets.[11] The 4 Ps were intended to refer to the combination of elements that a business controls to satisfy customers, and each element was considered both distinct and interdependent.[12] In the contemporary environment, market segmentation, targeting, and positioning are practiced and entities other than manufacturing businesses practice marketing. In view of this environment, concepts such as relationship marketing and the marketing strategies of not-for-profit businesses, places, and events create the need for a broader perspective on the elements of the marketing mix. There are many contemporary perspectives that challenge the sufficiency of the 4 Ps as the only marketing-mix framework. These include Booms and Bitner's 7 Ps and Kotler's 4 Cs.

Primarily responding to the growth of service businesses, Booms and Bitner proposed 3 additional Ps to add to the traditional 4 Ps to create a **7 Ps** classification. The additional 3 Ps include the following:[13]

- **People**—The role that people play in satisfying the customer
- **Physical evidence**—The environment of the service
- **Process**—The way the service is delivered

An example of an important marketing mix that includes people involves employee attitudes toward their business's brand. Employees can either enhance brand image or undermine brand image through their actions or inaction. Research

by Market & Opinion Research, Ltd. claims that 30% of employees in the United Kingdom are brand neutral and a further 22% are brand saboteurs. The remaining 48% are considered brand champions and will spread the brand message. One-third of all employees would talk positively about the brand if asked, and 15% claim they would talk positively about the brand spontaneously.[14] This provides an opportunity to differentiate not only on the traditional marketing mix, but also on another P—people. With an entire organization focused on the brand, such differentiation can be possible. Without such a focus, a brand's marketing investment is undermined.

Kotler challenged the relevancy of the 4 Ps from a buyer perspective. Considering the traditional 4 Ps, which Kotler views to be a seller's model, Kotler proposes the **4 Cs**. The variables include the following:[15]

- Customer value
- Cost
- Convenience
- Communication

Customer value takes the place of product from the traditional classification. Cost to the customer replaces price decisions. Convenience replaces place. Communication takes the place of the promotion mix. Kotler bases these recommendations on the idea that customer relations is more important that customer acquisition.[16]

The appropriateness of the various marketing-mix perspectives should be considered in the context of how businesses relate to their customers, which is typically through transactional methods, relational methods, or some combination of the two. Current marketing practice remains mainly transactional, which fits with the traditional perspective of the marketing mix.[17]

However, as companies increasingly focus on customer retention and strong supply-chain management, marketers are increasing their use of technology. In addition, increased competition and consumerism are influencing more demanding consumer expectations.[18] The result is the need to increasingly consider relational marketing perspectives such as those offered by the 7 Ps and 4 Cs marketing-mix classifications.

Marketing-Mix
Models (pp. 213–215)

 DEFINED **Marketing-mix models** *evaluate the contribution that each component of a marketing program makes to changes in market performance.*

 EXPLAINED

Marketing-Mix Models

Marketing-mix models began as a result of increasingly available scanner data—data obtained from checkout scanners at supermarkets and other retail stores—and has grown in its use among many different industries. Marketing activities can be tracked on databases with statistical modeling as a measurement tool. Scanner data or other sales data can be compared with sales price and volume. Overlaying performance data with marketing events, such as the launch of a new television advertising campaign or direct mail, can assist with developing marketing-mix models (see Figure 17.1).[19]

FIGURE 17.1 | Contribution to Sales

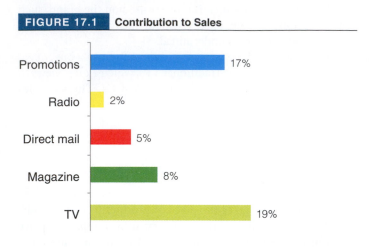

- Promotions: 17%
- Radio: 2%
- Direct mail: 5%
- Magazine: 8%
- TV: 19%

Baseline data is developed from historical information to predict what sales performance might occur without any changes in marketing activity. The accumulated effect of advertising, public relations, brand usage, and experiences such as testimonials and word-of-mouth is considered to be the brand's baseline.[20] Sales-lift models, based on those things that contribute to incremental sales, can be developed from considering the various marketing-mix elements as defined for a particular business. The costs for specific marketing-mix elements are also factored into an analysis. The variables are processed through a software package that maximizes marketing-mix elements with respect to particular financial outcomes. The result is an optimized marketing plan. **Marketing-mix optimization** involves assigning portions of the marketing budget to each marketing-mix element so as to maximize revenues or profits.

An example of an optimized marketing mix that relates media and promotions to sales performance follows:

FIGURE 17.2 | Optimized Marketing Mix

Using the example in Figure 17.1, TV has the greatest contribution to total sales, and, assuming similar media costs across channels, money that might have been allocated to other media such as radio and magazine could be re-directed to television. Alternatively, if an optimum level of spending for television can be determined, then excess funding can be redirected to the next-most-efficient medium of magazines or possibly promotions, provided brand image is not degraded.

There are a variety of applications of marketing-mix models. They can be used to measure the impact of temporary price adjustments, coupons, and displays, as well as to forecast future brand sales.

▼ APPLIED
Marketing-Mix Models

Marketing activities are under constant pressure to demonstrate the benefits derived from the marketing budget. Companies in the consumer packaged-goods sector were the first to adopt marketing-mix models, which are now used in many business sectors. Implementing a marketing-mix model often requires moving from "gut" decisions to a more structured approach to decision making.

There can be challenges to developing marketing-mix models, such as the following:

- Establishing buy-in throughout organizations for using marketing modeling
- Determining a way to optimize nontraditional marketing activities such as events, product placement, and social media
- Creating a balance between creativity and a strict interpretation of marketing-mix model output

EXAMPLE MARKETING-MIX MODELS

The Home Depot, the world's largest home-improvement retailer and the second-largest retailer in the United States, uses a proprietary computer model to relate specific promotions and advertisements to sales performance. Because of this information, The Home Depot can increase various types of marketing activity in specific markets, such as increasing direct-mail offers for product discounts in New York relative to the rest of the country, while using different marketing activity such as special financing offers in other regions, based on consumer behavior. The Home Depot believes that this information creates a competitive advantage.[21]

PHOTO: Pavel Kosek

>> END EXAMPLE

Effective implementation of marketing-mix models can provide strategic advantages relative to competitors, including efficient use of marketing funds across different media.

EXAMPLE   **EXAMPLE: MARKETING-MIX MODELS**

In late 2003, Miller Brewing announced a major shift in its marketing strategy based on a marketing-mix assessment. Miller determined the relative contribution that public relations (PR), advertising, sales promotion, and other marketing variables had on its product sales. The conclusion was that PR was much more effective, when cost is considered, than

other marketing activities. Miller identified that PR accounted for 4% of incremental sales. This can be contrasted to a 17% contribution for TV advertising at a significantly higher cost. The ratio was the basis for reallocating marketing dollars away from TV advertising and toward PR.[22]

PHOTO: Svry

>> END EXAMPLE

▼**Visual** Summary

Chapter 17 Summary ◄

Marketing mix is a group of marketing variables that a business controls with the intent of implementing a marketing strategy directed at a specific target market. The most common classification of the marketing mix is referred to as the 4 Ps, consisting of product, price, place, and promotion. There are many contemporary perspectives that challenge the sufficiency of the 4 Ps as the only marketing-mix framework, including the 7 Ps and 4 Cs. The 7 Ps, often referred to as the service marketing mix, adds people, physical evidence, and process. The 4 Cs, a marketing-mix perspective that considers the buyer's perspective over the seller's perspective, consists of customer value, cost, convenience, and communication.

Marketing-mix models evaluate the contribution that each component of a marketing program makes to changes in market performance. There are a variety of applications of marketing-mix models. They can be used to measure the impact of temporary price adjustments, coupons, and displays, as well as to forecast future brand sales.

There can be challenges to developing marketing-mix models, such as the following:
- Establishing buy-in throughout the organization for using marketing modeling
- Determining a way to optimize nontraditional marketing activities such as events, product placement, and social media
- Creating a balance between creativity and a strict interpretation of marketing-model output

Effective implementation of marketing-mix models can provide strategic advantages relative to competitors, including efficient use of marketing funds across different media.

Marketing Mix pp. 209–210

variables

The marketing mix is typically represented by four variables (product, place, price, and promotion) that are controllable by the marketing manager.

Marketing-Mix Strategy

pp. 210–213

selecting

A marketing mix strategy refers to the process of selecting the correct marketing mix for the company's target market.

Marketing-Mix Models pp. 213–215

project

Marketing-mix models are used to help project and track the effectiveness of the marketing-mix strategy.

Capstone **Exercise** p. 217

▼Chapter Key Terms

Marketing Mix (pp. 209–210)

Marketing mix is a is a group of marketing variables that a business controls with the intent of implementing a marketing strategy directed at a specific target market. (p. 209) **Opening Example** (p. 209)

Marketing-Mix Strategies (pp. 210–213)

Marketing-mix strategy is the logic that guides the selection of a particular marketing mix to achieve marketing objectives. (p. 210) **Example: Marketing-Mix Strategy: Situations 1, 2, 3 (p. 211) Situation 4 (p. 212)**

Key Terms (p. 209–213)

4 Cs are a classification of a marketing mix that includes customer value, cost, convenience, and communication. **(p. 213)**

4 Ps are the most common classification of a marketing mix and consist of product, price, place, and promotion. **(p. 209) Example: Marketing-Mix Strategy: Situation 1 (p. 211)**

7 Ps are a classification of a marketing mix that includes product, price, place, promotion, people, physical evidence, and process. **(p. 213) Example: Marketing-Mix Strategy: Situation 4 (p. 212)**

Marketing-Mix Models (pp. 213–215)

Marketing-mix models evaluate the contribution that each component of a marketing program makes to changes in market performance. (p. 213) **Example: Marketing-Mix Models (pp. 214–215)**

Key Terms (p. 214)

Marketing-mix optimization involves assigning portions of the marketing budget to each marketing-mix element so as to maximize revenues or profits. **(p. 214)**

▼Capstone Exercise

1. ACME manufacturing has traditionally spent very little on marketing activities. Recently, ACME invented several new products and has greatly expanded its portfolio. ACME has decided to increase its marketing expenditures and plans to implement marketing-mix modeling. Explain marketing-mix modeling and describe the potential benefits that ACME could realize.

▼Application Exercises

Complete the following exercises:

1. GE is planning to launch a new collection of kitchen appliances. Discuss how marketing-mix models might help GE with their product launch in a two-page paper.

2. Develop a marketing-mix strategy using the 7 Ps for a product of your choice.

3. Consider Wal-Mart (www.walmart.com) and Amazon (www.amazon.com). In what ways do these two companies compete? Compare them using the variables of the marketing mix. Specifically, look at how both companies market their music offerings. Which do you believe has the upper hand? Why?

Interior Views LLC

Marketing Plan — August, 2006

This sample marketing plan has been made available to users of *Marketing Plan Pro*, marketing planning software published by Palo Alto Software. Our sample plans were developed by existing companies or new business start-ups as research instruments to determine target market viability, explore marketing strategies, or prepare funding proposals. Names, locations and numbers may have been changed, and substantial portions of text may have been omitted to preserve confidentiality and protect proprietary information.

You are welcome to use this plan as a starting point to create your own, but you do not have permission to reproduce, publish, distribute or even copy this plan as it exists here.

Requests for reprints, academic use, and other dissemination of this sample plan should be addressed to the marketing department of Palo Alto Software.

Copyright Palo Alto Software, Inc., 1999-2006 Confidentiality Agreement

The undersigned reader acknowledges that the information provided by _____ in this marketing plan is confidential; therefore, reader agrees not to disclose it without the express written permission of _____.

It is acknowledged by reader that information to be furnished in this marketing plan is in all respects confidential in nature, other than information which is in the public domain through other means and that any disclosure or use of same by reader, may cause serious harm or damage to _____.

Upon request, this document is to be immediately returned to _____.

Signature

Name (typed or printed)

Date

This is a marketing plan. It does not imply an offering of securities.

Table of Contents

1.0 Executive Summary

Interior Views is a retail home decorator fabrics and complementary home accessories and services concept that is now in its third year. This destination store offers the advantages of providing fabrics specifically designed for home decorator use in fabric widths of 54 inches and greater. Over 900 fabrics are available on the floor at any time with more than 3,000 sample fabrics for custom "cut" orders. Customers see, touch, feel, and take the fabric to their home as they work through their purchase decision.

Market research indicates a specific and growing need in the area for the products and services Interior Views offers in the market it serves. The market strategy will be based on a cost effective approach to reach this clearly defined target market. The three-phase approach will utilize resources to create awareness of the store and encourage customers to benefit from the convenience and services it offers. Interior Views will focus on its selection, accessibility of product, design services, and competitive pricing.

The marketing objective is to actively support continued growth and profitability through effective implementation of the strategy.

2.0 Situation Analysis

Interior Views is a retail store heading into its third year of operation. The store has been well received, and marketing is now critical to its continued success and future profitability. The store offers the most extensive selection of in-stock decorator fabrics as well as a resource for special ordered fabrics. The basic market need is to offer a good selection of decorator fabrics at reasonable prices, for the "do-it-yourself" and the "buy-it-yourself" customers, through a personalized retail store that offers excellent service, design assistance, and inspiration for people to redecorate their homes.

2.1 Market Needs

Interior Views is providing its customers the opportunity to create a home environment to express who they are. They have the choice to select their fabric and go whatever direction they choose — to fabric it themselves or have it done for them. They have the opportunity to actively participate in the design, look, and feel of their home. They desire their home to be personal, unique, and tasteful as well as communicate a message about what is important to them. We seek to fulfill the following benefits that we know are important to our customers.

- **Selection** - A wide choice of current and tasteful decorator fabrics.
- **Accessibility** - The buyer can walk out of the store with the fabric they need to begin their project.
- **Customer Design Services** - Employees have a design background to make them a resource for the customer. This enables customers to benefit from suggestions regarding the selection of their fabric and related products in a manner to complement their design choice.
- **Competitive Pricing** - All products will be competitively priced in comparison to stores in the Portland, Oregon market (best price comparison) and other channels of distribution, such as catalog sales.

2.2 The Market

We possess good information about our market and know a great deal about the common attributes of our most prized and loyal customers. We will leverage this information to better understand who we serve, their specific needs, and how we can better communicate with them.

Table: Market Analysis

Market Analysis

Potential Customers	Growth	2006	2007	2008	2009	2010	CAGR
Country Club Women	25%	73,500	91,875	114,844	143,555	179,444	25.00%
Boomers in Transition	20%	28,500	34,200	41,040	49,248	59,098	20.00%
Professional Youngsters	18%	23,000	27,140	32,025	37,790	44,592	18.00%
Home Builders	12%	18,000	20,160	22,579	25,288	28,323	12.00%
Total	21.48%	143,000	173,375	210,488	255,881	311,457	21.48%

Market Analysis (Pie)

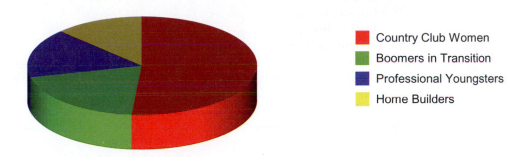

Legend:
- Country Club Women
- Boomers in Transition
- Professional Youngsters
- Home Builders

2.2.1 Market Demographics

The profile of the Interior Views customer consists of the following geographic, demographic, psychographic, and behavior factors:

Geographics

- Our immediate geographic market is the Boise area, with a population of 168,300.
- A 50-mile geographic area is in need of our products and services.
- The total targeted area population is estimated at 568,800.

Demographics

- Female.
- Married.
- Have children, but not necessarily at home.
- Have attended college.
- A combined annual income in excess of $50,000.
- Age range of 35 to 55 years, with a median age of 42.
- Owns their home, townhouse and/or condominium valued at over $125,000.
- If they work out of the home, it's by choice in a professional/business setting.
- Belong to one or more business, social and/or athletic organizations, which may include:
  - Downtown Athletic Club.
  - Boise Country Club.
  - Junior League of Boise.
  - American Business Women's Association.

We know the following regarding the profile of the typical resident of Boise:

- 67% have lived in Boise for 7 years or more.
- 23% are between the ages of 35 and 44.
- 40% have completed some college.
- 24% are managers, professionals and/or owners of a business.
- 53% are married.
- 65% have no children living at home.
- 56% own their residence.

Psychographics:

- The appearance of her home is a priority.
- Entertaining and showing her home is important.
- She perceives herself as creative, tasteful and able, but seeks validation and support regarding her decorating ideas and choices.
- She reads one or more of the following magazines:
  - Martha Stewart Living.
  - Country Living.
  - Home.
  - House Beautiful.
  - Country Home.
  - Metropolitan Home.
  - Traditional Homes.
  - Victoria.
  - Architectural Digest.
  - Elle Decor.

Behaviors

- She takes pride in having an active role in decorating their home.
- Her home is a form of communicating "who she is" to others.
- Comparisons within social groups are made on an ongoing basis, but rarely discussed.

Table: Market Demographics

Market Demographics

Market Segments	Age	Annual Income	Average Sale	Focus	Characteristic
Country Club Women	35-60	80000	High	Social and High Profile	-
Boomers in Transition	50-60	Varies	High	Time and Security	-
Professional Youngsters	25-35	50000	Moderate	Image and Climbing	-
Home Builders	30-45	60000	High	Image and Security	-

2.2.2 Market Trends

The home textile market, considered to include sheets, towels, draperies, carpets, blankets, and uphol-stery, accounts for 37% of all textile output. The trade publication "*Home Textiles Today*" estimates the size of the U.S. home textiles market at the wholesale level, excluding carpets, to be between $6.5 billion to $7 billion annually. The industry is expected to realize a steady increase over the next few years.

The industry is driven by the number of "household formations" which is expected to continue through the first years of the new millennium. This is primarily due to the solid growth in the number of single-parent and non-family households. This growth also comes from baby boomers needing bigger houses to accommodate growing and extended families and, as people get older, they are buying homes rather than renting to realize tax and equity building benefits. Favorable mortgage rates will also enable others to invest in their existing home.

The "do-it-yourself" (DIY) market continues to grow and closely parallels the professional home-improvement market. DIY market growth is attributed to an increased presence of products, the personal satisfaction experienced, and the cost savings customers realize. A portion of the do-it-yourself market is the "buy-it-yourself" (BIY) market. Consumers are buying the product and arranging for someone else to do the fabrication and/or installation. This is more expensive then the do-it-yourself approach, but less costly than buying finished products from other sources. It also provides similar feelings of creativity, pride, and individuality associated with direct creative involvement. This sense of "participation" in home decorating is an important factor for many of these committed customers.

Market Analysis (Trends)

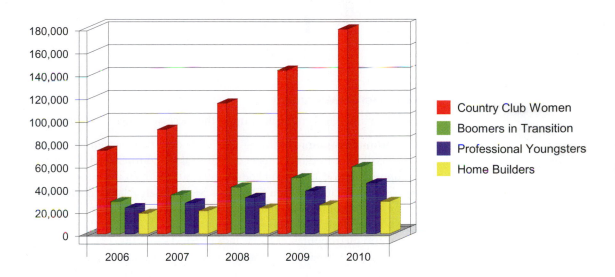

2.2.3 Market Growth

The publication, *American Demographics*, projected the number of U.S. households will grow by 16% between 1995 and the year 2010, an increase from 98.5 million to 115 million. Of the households comprised of people from 35 to 44 years old, almost half are married couples with children under the age of 18. Based on research by *American Demographics*, households in the 45 to 65 age range were estimated to grow to 34 million by the year 2000. These households will increase another 32 percent to 45 million in 2010 as baby boomers add to this peak-earning and spending age group. With approximately 46.2% of the nation's 93.3 million dwellings built before 1960, many of these homeowners are also expected to update. These factors contribute to an increased need for home decorator fabrics for window treatment, upholstering, pillows, bedding, and other fabric accessory needs. This demand is expected to be complemented by the growth in the Boise market. The majority of homeowners spend a large percentage of their disposable income on home goods within two years after buying a new house. Therefore, positive trends in new housing activity represents growth and opportunity for home textiles.

One important factor is that married couples in the 35 to 65 age range represent a growth segment and enjoy larger incomes than other family structures. They enjoy the choice to spend their disposable income on life's amenities. They may demonstrate "cocooning" by making their home a more comfortable and attractive haven. They choose to spend resources here rather than on vacations and other discretionary options. This group represents a larger sub-segment of the target market.

Market Analysis (C.A.G.R)

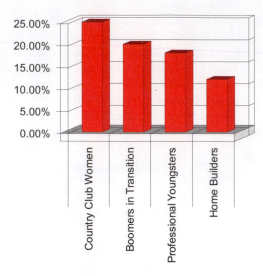

2.2.4 Macroenvironment

The following trends and issues impact the success of Interior Views.

- **National economic health** — The store does better when the country experiences "good times" regardless of its direct impact on the local economy. Sales decrease when the stock market falls. An upbeat State of the Union address correlates with an increase in sales.
- **New home construction activity** — More closely related to what is taking place in our local economy, new home construction has a significant impact on sales across all product lines.
- **Shifts in design trends** — Major changes in design trends increase sales. The Boise market lags behind metropolitan design trends by 6 to 12 months. This offers a buying advantage for the store, offering a preview of what is coming and how we should adjust our in-stock inventory.

2.3 The Company

Interior Views is a retail home decorator fabrics and complementary home accessories and services concept. This destination store offers the advantages of providing fabrics specifically designed for home decorator use in fabric widths of 54 inches and greater. Over 900 fabrics are available on the floor at any time with more than 3,000 sample fabrics for custom "cut" orders. Customers see, touch, feel, and take the fabric to their home as they work through their purchase decision.

Judy Wilson, the owner, is the one primarily responsible for marketing activities. This is in addition to her other responsibilities, and she does depend on some outside resources for mailing (Donna at Postal Connection) and some graphic design work. Judy does delegate responsibilities to Julie Hanson to assist with television advertising. Julie and the other staff members are also responsible for at least one special event throughout the year.

2.3.1 Mission

Interior Views LLC is a store for discerning, quality-conscious buyers of decorator fabrics and complementary home accessories and furniture. The store celebrates the home through the color and texture of fabric. The experience informs, inspires, and shows people how to transform their home into a unique and personalized expression of themselves. Interior Views seeks to encourage people to imagine what can be, and help make their vision a reality.

2.3.2 Product Offering

Our primary points of differentiation offer these qualities:

- The most extensive access to in-stock, first quality decorator fabrics within 100 miles of our primary geographic market and offered at affordable prices.

- The largest selection of special-order fabrics, with arrangements to have most of those products shipped to the store within 10 days of placing the order.
- Personal assistance from a design-oriented staff that is qualified and capable of meeting the needs of discerning customers with high expectations.
- Complementary product offering, including hard-covering window treatment, hardware, home accessories, made-to-order upholstered furniture, and antiques that are designed, selected, and displayed in a way to emphasize the use of fabric in home design.

Interior Views will qualify for the most attractive retail discount through these suppliers, offering greater profit margins and more competitive pricing for bolt purchases in quantities of 50 to 60 yards, or in half of that yardage with a "cutting fee" that increases cost per yard by an average of 50 cents. The primary product lines will include fabrics from the following textile sources:

- Robert Allen Fabrics
- Fabricut
- Waverly Fabrics
- Spectrum
- Art Mark
- Covington
- P/Kaufmann

Complementary accessories, including fabric trims, drapery hardware, and hard-covering window treatments, are supplied from the following sources:

- Hunter Douglas — Hard-window coverings.
- Kirsh — Rods and selected window hardware and accessories.
- Conso — Trims and Fabric Accessories.
- Petersen-Arne — Trims and Accessories.
- Graber — Selected window hardware.
- Grumman — Threads.

2.3.3 Positioning

For the person creating a personalized and unique impression of her home, Interior Views is the best local source for selection and price points of the fabric, customer-oriented design services, and a variety of other home accessory and furniture products. Customers will be impressed with, and return for, the great in-stock selection, value-oriented pricing, and excellent customer service. Unlike JoAnn's, Warehouse Fabric, or catalogs, Interior Views is a pleasant and tasteful resource that encourages everyone in the process of decorating their home. Unlike employing an interior decorator, Interior Views allows the individual to participate in their design choices to the extent they choose, and realize greater value for the dollars they invest.

2.3.4 SWOT Summary

The following SWOT analysis captures the key strengths and weaknesses within the company, and describes the opportunities and threats facing Interior Views.

2.3.4.1 Strengths

- Strong relationships with suppliers that offer credit arrangements, flexibility, and response to special product requirements.
- Excellent and stable staff, offering personalized customer service.
- Great retail space that offers flexibility with a positive and attractive atmosphere.
- Strong merchandising and product presentation.
- Good referral relationships with complementary vendors, local realtors, and some designers.
- In-store complementary products through "The Window Seat" and "Antique Bureau" add interest, stability and revenue.
- High customer loyalty among repeat and high-dollar purchase customers.

2.3.4.2 Weaknesses

- Access to capital.
- Cash flow continues to be unpredictable.
- Owners are still climbing the "retail experience curve."
- Location is not in a heavily traveled, traditional retail area.
- Challenges of the seasonality of the business.

2.3.4.3 Opportunities

- Growing market with a significant percentage of our target market still not knowing we exist.
- Continuing opportunity through strategic alliances for referrals and marketing activities.
- Benefiting from high levels of new home construction.
- Changes in design trends can initiate updating and therefore sales.
- Increasing sales opportunities beyond our "100-mile" target area.
- Internet potential for selling products to other markets.

2.3.4.4 Threats

- Competition from a national store; or a store with greater financing or product resources could enter the market.
- Catalog resources, including Calico Corners and Pottery Barn, are aggressively priced with comparable products.
- Continued price pressure, reducing contribution margins.
- Dramatic changes in design, including fabric colors and styles, creates obsolete or less profitable inventory.

2.3.5 Historical Results

The following tables shows estimated industry revenue as well as estimated market share, expenses and net margin for Interior Views.

Table: Historical Data

Historical Data			
Variable	**2003**	**2004**	**2005**
Industry Revenue	$1,305,000	$1,650,000	$2,062,500
Company Market Share	11%	12%	13%
Company Revenue	$143,550	$198,000	$257,813
Industry Variable Costs	$717,750	$750,000	$1,179,750
Company Variable Costs	$78,953	$90,000	$147,505
Industry Gross Contribution Margin	$587,250	$900,000	$882,750
Company Gross Contribution Margin	$64,597	$108,000	$110,308
Marketing Expenses	$1,150	$12,560	$15,920
Company Net Contribution Margin	$63,447	$95,440	$94,388

2.4 Competition

Competition in the area of decorator fabric comes from three general categories: traditional fabric retail stores, catalog sales, and discounters. The other local fabric retailers are direct competition, but we have seen strong indirect competition from catalog sales and discounters.

2.4.1 Direct Competition

Retail Stores

Current local competition includes the following:

- **House of Fabrics** — Nationwide recognition and buying power of numerous types of dated fabric with strong product availability. This store has experienced financial difficulty in recent years and has closed several locations throughout the country.
- **Warehouse Fabrics** — Locally owned, offering low-cost products with a wide selection of discontinued fabrics and only a limited number of "current" fabrics. This warehouse concept offers marginal customer service with what many "upper end" customers consider to be an "undesirable" shopping environment.
- **JoAnn's** — Nationwide chain with strong buying power. They have a broad fabric selection for clothing with a limited number of in-store decorator fabrics available. Their primary target markets are the clothing seamstress, with an increasing emphasis on craft items.
- **Interior Designers** — Interior designers make profit off mark up of fabric in addition to their hourly services charges. Their costs per yard are typically higher since they do not benefit from retail or volume discounts. Therefore, their costs to their customer is often two to four times higher than the price per yard from Interior Views.
- **Website Providers** — Fabric sales over the Web are limited at this time, and this will be a source of competition for the future to watch. Currently, there is no measurable impact on our market through competitive websites.

Table: Growth and Share Analysis

Growth and Share			
Competitor	**Price**	**Growth Rate**	**Market Share**
House of Fabrics	$80	5%	18%
Warehouse Fabrics	$75	8%	23%
JoAnn's Fabrics	$80	6%	16%
Interior Designers - Combined	$205	12%	25%
Interior Views	$135	25%	29%
Average	$115.00	11.20%	22.20%
Total	$575.00	56.00%	111.00%

Competitor by Growth and Share

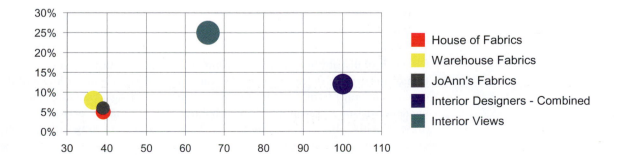

Table: Competitive Analysis

Competitive Analysis

	#1	#2	#3	#4	#5
Competitor	House of Fabrics	Warehouse Fabrics	JoAnn's	Interior Designers	Interior Views
Product and/or Service	House of Fabrics	Warehouse Fabrics	JoAnn's	Interior Designers	Interior Views
Quality	7	8	6	2	6
Selection	6	7	3	1	8
Price	5	8	2	2	8
Other	0	0	0	0	0
Location and Physical Appearance	House of Fabrics	Warehouse Fabrics	JoAnn's	Interior Designers	Interior Views
Visibility	8	7	8	3	6
Convenience Factors	6	6	6	3	8
Other	0	0	0	0	0
Added Value Factors	House of Fabrics	Warehouse Fabrics	JoAnn's	Interior Designers	Interior Views
Pre and Post Sales Service	5	4	5	8	9
Experience	4	4	4	7	7
Expertise	6	5	6	9	8
Reputation	2	8	6	8	8
Image	3	3	3	6	8
Stability	0	0	0	0	0
Strategic Alliances	0	0	0	0	0
Other	0	0	0	0	0
Other Marketing Activities	House of Fabrics	Warehouse Fabrics	JoAnn's	Interior Designers	Interior Views
Established Sales Channels	6	6	4	3	6
Advertising	6	7	4	5	7
Post-purchase Support	4	4	8	9	7
Incentives	4	5	2	1	8
Loyalty Components	6	5	2	1	8
Other	0	0	0	0	0
Total	78	87	69	68	112

2.4.2 Indirect Competition

Catalog Competitors

An increasing level of competition is anticipated from catalog sales. Recent trends, such as those demonstrated in the well established but evolving catalog *Pottery Barn*, indicates increased interest in offering decorator fabric, window designs, and other home decorating products through this increasingly popular channel of distribution. Catalog sources do not offer customers the option to see, touch, and have the fabric in their homes. Price is the most significant competitive factor this product source presents. The most aggressive catalog competitor is *Calico Corners* followed by *Pottery Barn* and other home-accessory-based providers.

Discounters

Channels of distribution continue to shift in favor of discounters, who account for a significant portion of the growth in the industry. As consumers experience lower levels of disposable income, discounters leverage frequent store promotions to entice frugal, value-oriented consumers. One of the biggest criticism of discounters is their failure to offer a quality service experience and their failure to present inviting displays to promote sales. These discounters, along with specialty store chains, present one of the most severe competitive threats for individually-owned specialty stores. This is partially due to extensive promotional efforts, price advantages, and established relationships with their vendors. One example of these discounters is the "home improvement" chains, such as Home Base. This aggressive retailer has adopted a strategy to include complete decorator departments in their metropolitan stores. Currently existing in the Los Angeles market, this strategy is anticipated to be introduced into the Seattle area and other select metropolitan markets within the year. Although the Boise Home Base store sells basic curtain rod hardware and other hard cover window treatment, there are no known plans at this time for the Boise Home Base store to implement this in the foreseeable future. This will be an important issue to monitor for competitive purposes.

3.0 Marketing Strategy

This plan will further Interior Views' financial and marketing objectives:

Financial objectives: create sales growth of 12%, reduce existing credit line, and increase the average dollar amount per transaction

Marketing objectives: increase visibility of store for potential customers, and better retain existing customers

3.1 Value Proposition

Interior Views sells more than fabric, we sell a personalized and unique vision for your home. Interior Views helps you revive your home and your living experience.

3.2 Critical Issues

Interior Views is still in the "speculative" stage as a retail store. Its critical issues are:

- Relatively slow annual sales growth. With admirable results through the first 30 months of operation, the market continues to hold promise, but, as learned through the first two years of operation, it is still smaller that what it should be to support a store of this kind.
- Continue to take a fiscally-conservative approach; downscale when necessary and modify our business model based on market response.

3.3 Financial Objectives

1. A growth rate in sales of 12% for the year 2005, to total in excess of $341,200 in total revenues.
2. An average sales per business day (305 days per year) in excess of $1,000.
3. Reduce the existing credit line by a minimum of $26,400.

3.4 Marketing Objectives

1. Maintain a gross margin of 45% each month.
2. Generate an average of $1,000 of sales each business day each month.
3. Experience a $5,000 increase in quarterly sales with each newsletter.
4. Realize an annual growth rate of approximately 25% in the year 2000.

3.5 Target Market Strategy

The target markets are separated into four segments; "Country Club Women," "Boomers in Transition," "Professional Youngsters" and "Home Builders." The primary marketing opportunity is selling to these well defined and accessible target market segments that focuses on investing discretionary income in these areas:

Country Club Women — The most dominant segment of the four is comprised of women in the age range of 35 to 50. They are married, have a combined income of greater than $80,000, own at least one home or condominium, and are socially active at and away from home. They are members of the Boise Country Club, The Downtown Athletic Club, the Junior League of Boise, AAUW, and/or the Doctor Wives Auxiliary. They have discretionary income, and their home and how it looks is a priority. The appearance of where they live communicates who they are and what is important to them. This group represents the largest collection of "Martha Stewart Wanna Be's," with their profile echoing readers of *Martha Stewart Living* magazine, based on the current demographics described in the *Martha Stewart Living Media Kit* .

Boomers in Transition — This group, typically ranging in age from 50 to 65, is going through a positive and planned life transition. They are changing homes (either building or moving) or remodeling due to empty nest syndrome, retirement plans, general downsizing desires, or to just get closer to the golf course. Their surprisingly high level of discretionary income is first spent on travel, with decorating their home a close second. The woman of the couple is the decision maker, and often does not always include the husband in the selection or purchase process.

Professional Youngsters — Couples between the ages of 25 and 35 establishing their first "adult" household fall into this group. They both work, earn in excess of $50,000 annually, and now want to invest in their home. They seek to enjoy their home and communicate a "successful" image and message to their contemporaries. They buy big when they have received a promotion, a bonus, or an inheritance.

Home Builders — People in the building process, typically ranging in age from 40 to 60, are prime candidates for Interior Views.

3.6 Messaging

Interior Views can help you create the personalized and unique vision you have for your home, with the best local source for fabric selection and price, customer-oriented design services, and a variety of other home accessory and furniture products. Revive your home today!

3.6.1 Branding

Our name is our brand. "Interior Views" represents our mission of celebrating the home through the color and texture of fabric. The brand invokes the fact that the home should be a unique and personalized expression of the person living there. The home is a "view" of the home's owner. The word "view" also evokes the vision of what a home owner wants their home to be.

In addition to our name, our logo reflects the architectural quality of the work that we do. Our products are more than just decoration, they enhance and reflect the home itself.

Table: Target Market Messaging

Target Market Messaging	
Market Segments	**Messaging**
Country Club Women	Make your home new again
Boomers in Transition	It's time for a new look
Professional Youngsters	It's your first home - make it yours
Home Builders	Presentation is everything

3.7 Strategy Pyramids

The single objective is to position Interior Views as the premier source for home decorator fabrics in the Greater Boise area, commanding a majority of the market share within three years. The marketing strategy will seek to first create customer awareness regarding the products and services offered, develop that customer base, establish connections with targeted markets and work toward building customer loyalty and referrals.

Interior Views' four main marketing strategies are:

1. Increased awareness and image.
2. Leveraging existing customer base.
3. Cross selling.
4. New home construction promotion.

The following Strategy Pyramid charts shows the specific tactics and programs planned to achieve each planned strategy.

Strategy Pyramid: Increase Awareness/Image

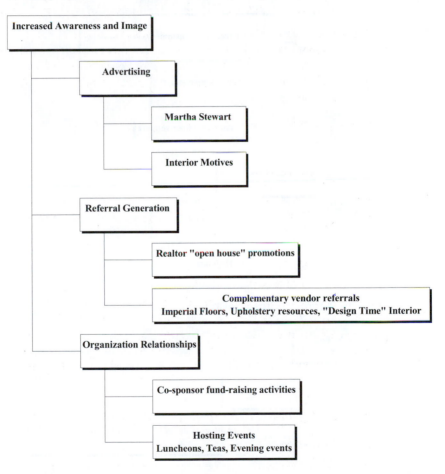

Strategy Pyramid: Leveraging Existing Customer Base

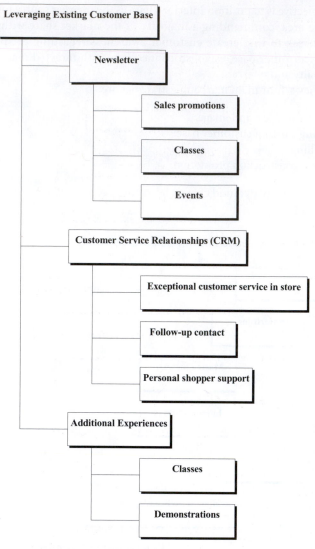

Leveraging Existing Customer Base

Newsletter

Sales promotions

Classes

Events

Customer Service Relationships (CRM)

Exceptional customer service in store

Follow-up contact

Personal shopper support

Additional Experiences

Classes

Demonstrations

Strategy Pyramid: Cross Selling

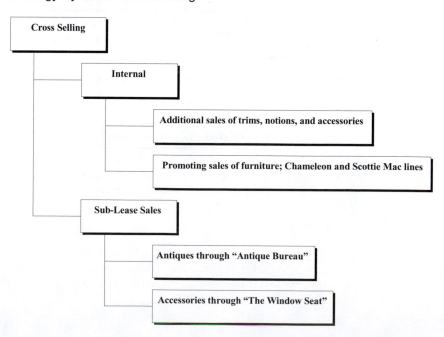

Cross Selling

Internal

Additional sales of trims, notions, and accessories

Promoting sales of furniture; Chameleon and Scottie Mac lines

Sub-Lease Sales

Antiques through "Antique Bureau"

Accessories through "The Window Seat"

Strategy Pyramid: New Home Construction Promotion

```
┌─────────────────────────────────┐
│ New Home Construction Promotion  │
└─────────────────────────────────┘
      │
      │   ┌────────────────────────────┐
      ├───│ Connecting with "Suppliers" │
      │   └────────────────────────────┘
      │         │
      │         │   ┌──────────────────────────────────┐
      │         ├───│ Realtors gift certificate program │
      │         │   └──────────────────────────────────┘
      │         │
      │         │   ┌──────────────────────────────────┐
      │         ├───│ Builders design support services  │
      │         │   └──────────────────────────────────┘
      │         │
      │         │   ┌──────────────────────────────────────┐
      │         └───│ Loan Officers gift certificate program │
      │             └──────────────────────────────────────┘
      │
      │   ┌────────────────────────────┐
      └───│ Connecting with "Customers" │
          └────────────────────────────┘
                │
                │   ┌─────────────────────────────────────────┐
                ├───│ Subscription and use of "newcomers" report │
                │   └─────────────────────────────────────────┘
                │
                │   ┌─────────────────────────────────────────┐
                └───│ Chamber of Commerce new members update    │
                    └─────────────────────────────────────────┘
```

4.0 Marketing Mix

In brief, our marketing mix is comprised of these approaches to pricing, distribution, advertising and promotion, and customer service.

Pricing — A keystone pricing formula plus $3.00 will be applied for most fabrics. The goal is to have price points within 5% of the list price of Calico Corners' retail prices. This insures competitive pricing and strong margins.

Distribution — All product is distributed through the retail store. The store does receive phone orders from established customers and we will be developing a website.

Advertising and Promotion — The most successful advertising has been through the Boise Herald and through ads on "Martha Stewart" and "Interior Motives" television shows. The quarterly newsletter has also proven to be an excellent method to connect with the existing customer base, now with a mailing list of 4,300 people.

Customer Service —Excellent, personalized, fun, one-of-a-kind customer service is essential. This is perhaps the only attribute that cannot be duplicated by any competitor.

4.1 Product Marketing

Our products enable our customers to experience support, gather ideas and options, and accomplish their decorating goals. They will be able to create a look that is truly unique to their home. They will not be able to do this in the same way through any other resource.

4.2 Pricing

Product pricing is based on offering high value to our customers compared to most price points in the market. Value is determined based on the best quality available, convenience, and timeliness in acquiring the product. We will consistently be below the price points offered through interior designers and consistently above prices offered through the warehouse/seconds retail stores, but we will offer better quality and selection.

4.3 Promotion

Our most successful advertising and promotion in the past has been through the following:

- **Newspaper Advertisements** - Boise Herald.
- **Television Advertisements** - "Martha Stewart" and "Interior Motives" television shows.
- **Quarterly Newsletter and Postcard** - A direct mail, 4-page newsletter distributed to the customer mailing list generated from people completing the "register" sign up in the store. The mailing list now totals more than 4,300 people.
- **In Store Classes** - "How to" classes, most of which are free, have been successful because of the traffic and sales they generate after the class. Typically 90 minutes in length and most held on Saturday, these are "the most popular classes:
  - "Pillow Talk" - Pillow fabrication.
  - "Speaking of Slip Covers" - Slip cover presentation and discussion.
  - "Shades of the Season" - Window treatment options with fabric.

4.3.1 Advertising

Expand newspaper advertisements to surrounding towns, and buy two half-page ads every month. Continue television ads.

Table: Advertising Milestones

Milestones					
Advertising	**Start Date**	**End Date**	**Budget**	**Manager**	**Department**
Television Campaign 1	1/1/2006	1/30/2006	$780	Julie	New
Television Campaign 2	9/1/2006	12/31/2007	$3,120	Julie	New
Total Advertising Budget			$3,900		

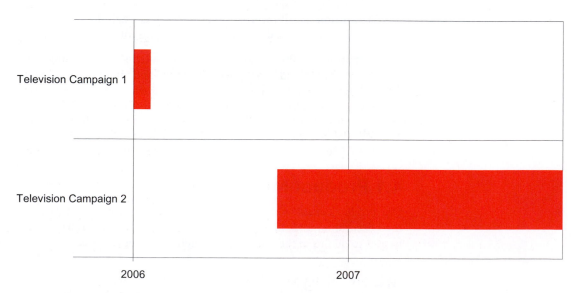

Advertising Milestones

4.3.2 Public Relations

Our public relations plan is to pitch a twice-monthly column in the "Home" section of the local paper, covering our in-store classes, with profiles of our customers and their redecorated rooms. Readers will see how our classes directly relate to individual decorating projects.

Table: PR Milestones

Milestones					
PR	**Start Date**	**End Date**	**Budget**	**Manager**	**Department**
Event: Realtor Promotion	2/1/2006	2/28/2006	$400	Julie	Home Bldrs
Event: Junior League	5/1/2006	5/31/2006	$400	Kandi	New
Event: For the Arts	9/1/2006	9/30/2006	$400	Pat	New
Event: Relief Nursery	11/1/2006	11/25/2006	$400	Jo	New
Total PR Budget			$1,600		

4.3.3 Direct Marketing

Improve the quality of the newsletter, increase the number of one-time customers who sign up for it, and offer an email-newsletter option to catch the more tech-savvy customers.

Table: Direct Marketing Milestones

Milestones					
Direct Marketing	**Start Date**	**End Date**	**Budget**	**Manager**	**Department**
Newsletter Q1	12/1/2005	1/2/2006	$1,350	Judy	Existing
Newsletter Q2	2/15/2006	3/15/2006	$1,400	Judy	Existing
Newsletter Q3	6/1/2006	6/30/2006	$1,450	Judy	Existing
Newsletter Q4	9/1/2006	9/30/2006	$1,500	Judy	Existing
Postcard	11/15/2006	12/5/2006	$750	Judy	Existing
Total Direct Marketing Budget			$6,450		

4.4 Web Plan

Interior Views is a retailer of home decorator fabrics and complementary home accessories now in its fourth year. This destination store offers the advantages of providing fabrics specifically designed for home decorator use. Over 1,000 fabrics are available on the floor at any time with more than 8,000 sample fabrics for custom orders. The goal of this Web plan is to extend the reach of the store to others outside the area and add to the revenue base.

Interior Views currently has a website but has not given it the attention or focus needed to assess its marketing potential. The site offers basic functions and we consider it to be a crude version of what we can imagine it will become through a site redesign that will produce revenue and enhance the image of the business.

Market research indicates a specific and growing need in the area for the products and services Interior Views offers in the market it serves and there are indications that Web sales will play an increasing role in connecting customers with sellers. The most significant challenge is that the core target customer, women between the ages of 35 and 50, are some of the least likely of groups to shop on the Web. Shopping for decorator fabric presents an additional challenge.

The online marketing objective is to actively support continued growth and profitability of Interior Views through effective implementation of the strategy. The online marketing and sales strategy will be based on a cost effective approach to reach additional customers over the Web to generate attention and revenue for the business. The Web target groups will include the more Web-savvy younger customer base that the store currently serves (women between the ages of 25 and 35) and out-of-area potential customers that are already shopping on the Web for the products Interior Views offers. The website will focus on its selection, competitive pricing, and customer service to differentiate itself among other Internet options.

Interior Views' website is for the person who wants her home to be an individual expression of who she is. Unlike other online fabric sites, Interior Views will provide these customers with first quality decorator fabric selections and complementary products to decorate their homes, as well as intelligent and helpful customer service and support for each sale. Interior Views is a pleasant and tasteful resource that encourages everyone in the process of decorating their home, allows the individual to participate in their design choices to the extent they choose, and offers greater value for the dollars they invest.

4.4.1 Website Goals

Our website will generate revenue through initiating product sales to the targeted audience that we would not have realized through the retail store. It will be measured on the basis of revenue generated each month compared to our stated objective. On a secondary basis, we will also measure and track traffic to the site and document what activities that traffic contributes to the other objectives of the site, including sales leads and information dissemination.

Objectives

- Increase revenues through Web-based sales by $2,400 per month with a 5% growth rate thereafter.
- Enhancing "information channels" with the established customer base to provide additional options to receive information from the store.
- Meet the needs of customers outside the immediate serving area through Web accessibility.

Future Development

The objectives of the site redesign will include:

- Increased speed.
- Enhanced navigation.
- Additional products added to the decorator fabric selections including "Oval Office Iron" hardware and select home accessories.

4.4.2 Website Marketing Strategy

Our website strategy will be to reach these key groups listed in order of importance based on their expected use and purchases from the site.

- **Professional Youngsters** - Expected to be the most likely of the targeted segments to use this resource because of their relatively high Internet use compared to the other segments. This group should offer the greatest online revenue opportunity.
- **Outsiders** - Comprised of people outside the area with Internet access that have come in contact with the physical store or learned of it though a referral or promotion. This group, most commonly located in rural areas of the Western U.S. and Hawaii, are expected to be a small but faithful sector of buyers.
- **Online Fabric Shoppers** - Most often find the site through search engines and these online decorator fabric shoppers are browsing multiple sites for a best buy or access to discontinued and hard-to-find fabric. They hold potential, but are typically the most work for the lowest return.
- **Internet Learners** - Represents all of the targeted segments that are just beginning to become familiar with the site and will increase their use of the Internet over time. Revenue expectations from this group are low at this point and it is viewed as an investment in the future.

The online strategy supports the objective to position Interior Views as a preferred source for home decorator fabrics on the Web as we maintain the position of being considered the premier source in the geographic area of the store. The online sales strategy seek to first, inform visitors about the site, and create a positive awareness regarding the products offered; second, provide successful purchasing experiences, and establish connections with targeted markets; and third, work toward building customer loyalty and referrals.

The online sales approach will accomplish these four objectives:

1. Increased overall awareness and image.
2. Meet the online interests and needs of the existing customer base.
3. Expand the total out-of-area customer population.
4. Exploit upsell and cross-sell opportunities.

Strategy #1 - Increasing Awareness and Image
Informing those not yet aware of what Interior Views offers.

- Search engine presence.
- Leveraging the newsletter and mailing programs.

Strategy #2 - Leveraging Existing Internet-Savvy Customers
Our best sales in the future will come from our current customer base.

- Newsletter information.
- Web-only promotions.

Strategy #3 - Upselling and Cross-selling Activities
Increasing the average dollar amount per transaction.

- Additional and complementary fabric.
- Other product sales:
  - Additional sales of trims, notions, and accessories.
- Promoting sales of furniture.

4.4.3 Development Requirements

Once we have determined the general look and navigation of the new site, we will accomplish the following tasks:

- Define initial site layout and general design characteristics;
- Fabric selection for site, and;
- Product selection including decisions about "Oval Office Iron" and lighting products.

Front End

We currently have the basic elements of the site in place at www.fabric-online.com. It possesses some of the functional compontents that we want to keep including:

- A URL that is not ideal, but tollerable.
- Identifiable home page.
- The ability to select and view the most popular fabrics.
- Newsletter access.
- Contact information.

A sign redesign is desperately needed to attract additional traffic, support easier and quicker navigation, and hopefully result in increased sales. We are not satisfied with these components of the site:

- Graphic design characteristics - the look and feel of the site is dated and "amateurish."
- Speed - the site is slow in areas where we can speed the process.
- Basic navigation through the site - a consistent method to move throughout the site.
- The addition of other products including "Oval Office Iron" hardware and select home accessories.

Back End

Our back-end features should include the following:

1. Web hosting with 98% uptime through the local provider.
2. Statistics to determine page views, unique users, banner impressions, sponsorship impressions and clickthroughs.
3. The ability to enable visitors to gain easy access to product information, visuals, newsletter information, and a robust email system.

Resource Requirements

The site has been, and will continue to be, supported through a local Internet provider and the consultant that we have been working with. We have found that experience to be relatively economical and he has been highly responsive to our need. Employees do not have the expertise to do much more than respond to emails and check the status of the site, so this has been a good complement to what time and resource limitations impose.

The monthly budget, including Internet access, is $65.00 in addition to hourly consulting rates for redesign work and fabric scanning.

Table: Pay-per-click ROAS

Pay-Per-Click ROAS

Network	Monthly Cost	Clicks	Leads Generated	Orders	Monthly Revenue	ROAS	Cost-per-click	Cost-per-lead
Google	$2,000	4000	100	30	$3,000	150%	$0.50	$20.00
Yahoo!	$1,250	2000	45	14	$1,400	112%	$0.63	$27.78
Total	3250	6000	145	44	4400	131%	$0.56	$23.89

Table: Website Milestones

Milestones

Web Development	Start Date	End Date	Budget	Manager	Department
Site Redesign Plan	1/1/2006	1/15/2006	$0	Julie	Marketing
Source Designers	1/1/2006	1/15/2006	$0	Julie	Marketing
Other	1/1/2006	1/15/2006	$0	Julie	Marketing
Total Web Development Budget			$0		

4.5 Service

The first goal is to recognize everyone as they come into the store. If they are a repeat customer, they are referred to by name. If they are a new customer, they are asked, "How did you hear about us?" Help is always available and never invasive. The store is staffed to be able to dedicate time and energy to customers that want assistance when they need it. The store is designed so a customer can sit as long as they want to look at books, fabric samples, and review the resources in the store. Their children are also welcome, with a television, VCR, and toys available in the childrens' area in clear view of the resource center. We provide service in a way that no other competitive retail store can touch. It is one of our greatest assets and points of differentiation. Insight, ideas, inspiration, and fun is the goal. Repeat, high dollar purchases from loyal customers is the desired end product.

4.6 Implementation Schedule

The following identifies the key activities that are critical to our marketing plan. It is important to accomplish each one on time and on budget.

Table: Milestones

Milestones					
Advertising	**Start Date**	**End Date**	**Budget**	**Manager**	**Department**
Television Campaign 1	1/1/2006	1/30/2006	$780	Julie	New
Television Campaign 2	9/1/2006	12/31/2007	$3,120	Julie	New
Total Advertising Budget			$3,900		
PR	Start Date	End Date	Budget	Manager	Department
Event: Realtor Promotion	2/1/2006	5/28/2006	$400	Julie	Home Bldrs
Event: Junior League	5/1/2006	5/31/2006	$400	Kandi	New
Event: For the Arts	9/1/2006	9/30/2006	$400	Pat	New
Event: Relief Nursery	11/1/2006	11/25/2006	$400	Jo	New
Total PR Budget			$1,600		
Direct Marketing	Start Date	End Date	Budget	Manager	Department
Newsletter Q1	12/1/2005	1/2/2006	$1,350	Judy	Existing
Newsletter Q2	2/15/2006	3/15/2006	$1,400	Judy	Existing
Newsletter Q3	6/1/2006	6/30/2006	$1,450	Judy	Existing
Newsletter Q4	9/1/2006	9/30/2006	$1,500	Judy	Existing
Postcard	11/15/2006	12/5/2006	$750	Judy	Existing
Total Direct Marketing Budget			$6,450		
Web Development	Start Date	End Date	Budget	Manager	Department
Site Redesign Plan	1/1/2006	1/15/2006	$0	Julie	Marketing
Source Designers	1/1/2006	1/15/2006	$0	Julie	Marketing
Other	1/1/2006	1/15/2006	$0	Julie	Marketing
Total Web Development Budget			$0		
Other	Start Date	End Date	Budget	Manager	Department
Misc.	1/1/2003	1/15/2003	$0	ABC	Department
Other	1/1/2003	1/15/2003	$0	ABC	Department
Total Other Budget			$0		
Totals			$11,950		

5.0 Financials

Our marketing strategy is based on becoming the resource of choice for people looking for decorator fabrics, do-it-yourself, and buy-it-yourself resources to create a look in their home. Our marketing strategy is based on superior performance in the following areas:

- Product selection.
- Product quality.
- Customer service.

Our marketing strategy will create awareness, interest, and appeal from our target market for what Interior Views offers our customers.

This section will offer a financial overview of Interior Views as it relates to our marketing activities. We will address break-even information, sales forecasts, expense forecasts, and how those link to our marketing strategy.

5.1 Break-even Analysis

The break-even analysis below illustrates the number of single sales, or units, that we must realize to break even. This is based on average sale and costs per transaction.

Table: Fixed Costs

Fixed Costs	
Cost	
Utilities	$400
Web Site Hosting	$200
Recuring Marketing Expenses	$1,200
Payroll	$6,000
Rent	$1,500
Total Fixed Costs	$9,300

Table: Break-even Analysis

Break-even Analysis	
Monthly Revenue Break-even	$20,427
Assumptions:	
Average Percent Variable Cost	54%
Estimated Monthly Fixed Cost	$9,300

Break-even Analysis

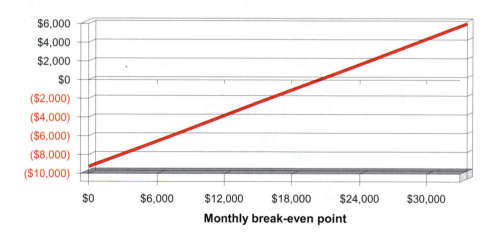

Monthly break-even point

Break-even point = where line intersects with 0

5.2 Sales Forecast

The sales forecast is broken down into the four main revenue streams; direct sales, Web sales, consignment sales, and sub-lease revenues. The sales forecast for the upcoming year is based on a 25% growth rate. This is a slower growth rate than what was experienced in previous years at 33%, and also less than what is expected for future sales, estimated to be approximately 28%. These projections appear attainable and take the increasing base into consideration. Future growth rates are based on percentage increases as follows:

- Direct Sales 20% growth rate per year.
- Web Sales 50% growth rate per year.
- Consignment Sales 20% growth rate per year.
- Sub-lease Revenues 10% growth rate per year.

Table: Sales Forecast

Sales Forecast	2006	2007	2008	2009	2010
Sales					
Direct Sales	$322,000	$386,400	$463,700	$556,400	$667,700
Web Sales	$12,500	$18,750	$28,125	$42,190	$63,280
Consignment Sales	$1,360	$1,632	$1,960	$2,350	$2,820
Sub-Lease Revenue	$5,340	$5,600	$6,165	$6,780	$7,460
Total Sales	$341,200	$412,382	$499,950	$607,720	$741,260
Direct Cost of Sales	2006	2007	2008	2009	2010
Direct Sales	$178,850	$214,000	$255,500	$307,000	$370,000
Web Sales	$6,875	$10,400	$12,000	$18,000	$20,000
Consignment Sales	$71	$85	$102	$123	$150
Sub-Lease Revenue	$60	$66	$73	$80	$88
Subtotal Direct Cost of Sales	$185,856	$224,551	$267,675	$325,203	$390,238

Sales Monthly

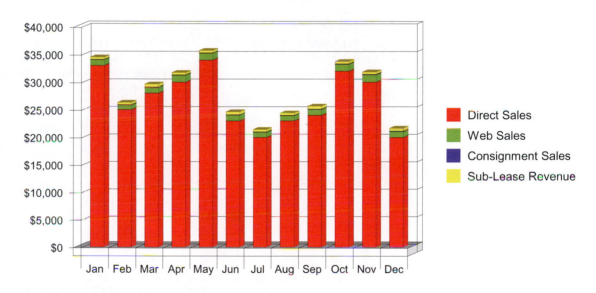

5.2.1 Sales by Manager

Fabric sales account for approximately 74% of total sales. The remaining sales result from complementary products sales, including trims, tassels, pillows, drapery rods and hardware, books, and upholstered furniture.

Table: Sales Breakdown by Manager

Sales by: Manager	2006	2007	2008	2009	2010
Sales					
Drapery Weight	$53,633	$65,351	$79,298	$96,470	$117,762
Upholstery Weight	$26,815	$32,675	$39,649	$48,235	$58,881
Mixed	$100,566	$122,533	$148,683	$180,882	$220,803
Special Order	$67,040	$81,688	$99,122	$120,588	$147,202
Other	$93,146	$110,135	$133,198	$161,545	$196,612
Total	$341,200	$412,382	$499,950	$607,720	$741,260
Average	$68,240	$82,476	$99,990	$121,544	$148,252

Sales Breakdown by Manager Monthly

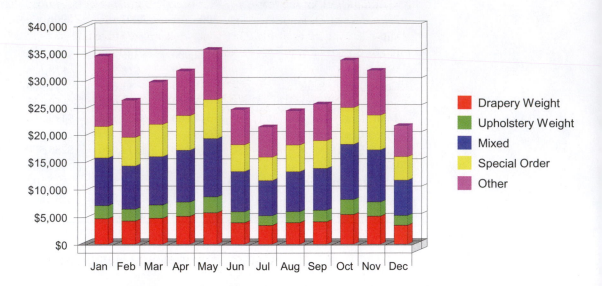

5.2.2 Sales by Segment

Consignment sales account for a relatively small portion of total sales and are primarily supported to create a better feel and look for the store. This is an area that does provide useful information feedback regarding other possible product sales the store may want to sell in the future.

Table: Sales Breakdown by Segment

Sales by: Segment					
	2006	**2007**	**2008**	**2009**	**2010**
Sales					
"The Window Seat"	$11,732	$14,295	$17,346	$21,103	$25,760
Antiques	$26,815	$32,675	$39,675	$48,235	$58,881
Other	$302,653	$365,412	$442,929	$538,382	$656,619
Total	$341,200	$412,382	$499,950	$607,720	$741,260
Average	$113,733	$137,461	$166,650	$202,573	$247,087

Sales Breakdown by Segment Monthly

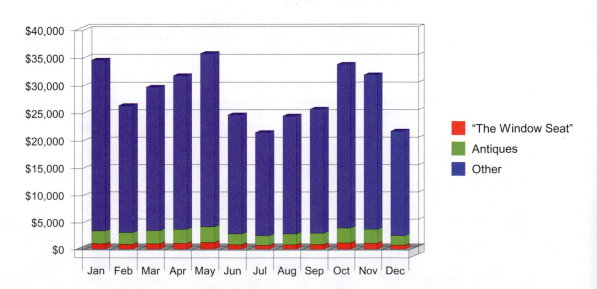

5.2.3 Sales by Region

The Antique Bureau sub-leases approximately 450 square feet. This store offers a selection of authentic antiques. It attracts additional customers and provides revenue for space that is currently unused. Two additional areas are available. The "conference room" space is available for special events, and the second office is available for an interior designer to sub-lease.

Table: Sales Breakdown by Region

Sales by: Region					
	2006	**2007**	**2008**	**2009**	**2010**
Sales					
The Antique Bureau	$4,320	$4,750	$5,225	$5,750	$6,325
Event/Sale Revenue	$840	$925	$1,020	$1,120	$1,230
Other	$336,040	$406,707	$493,705	$600,850	$733,705
Total	$341,200	$412,382	$499,950	$607,720	$741,260
Average	$113,733	$137,461	$166,650	$202,573	$247,087

Sales Breakdown by Region Monthly

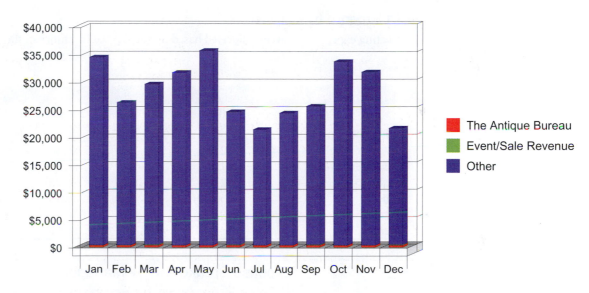

5.3 Expense Forecast

Marketing expenses are to be budgeted at approximately 5% of total sales. Expenses are tracked in the major marketing categories of television advertisements, newspaper advertisements, the newsletter and postcard mailings, Web marketing support, printed promotional materials, public relations, and other.

Table: Marketing Expense Budget

Marketing Expense Budget	2006	2007	2008	2009	2010
Television Ads	$3,900	$4,600	$5,620	$6,740	$8,200
Newspaper Ads	$1,800	$2,160	$2,592	$3,110	$3,800
Newsletter/Postcard	$6,450	$7,700	$9,200	$11,150	$13,400
Printed Promotional Materials	$960	$1,150	$1,380	$1,660	$2,000
Web Marketing/Support	$1,500	$1,950	$2,535	$3,295	$4,300
Public Relations	$240	$345	$415	$500	$600
Promotional Events	$1,700	$1,950	$2,300	$2,800	$3,400
Website Expenses	$2,400	$2,600	$2,800	$3,000	$3,000
Other	$400	$480	$575	$700	$850
Total Sales and Marketing Expenses	$19,350	$22,935	$27,417	$32,955	$39,550
Percent of Sales	5.67%	5.56%	5.48%	5.42%	5.34%

Monthly Expense Budget

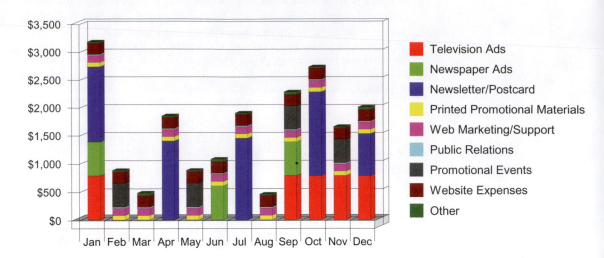

5.3.1 Expense by Manager

Marketing expenses are evenly allocated based on the type of inventory in the store.

Table: Expense Breakdown by Manager

Expenses by Manager					
	2006	**2007**	**2008**	**2009**	**2010**
Expenses					
Drapery Weight	$2,546	$3,268	$3,965	$4,824	$5,888
Upholstery Weight	$1,265	$1,634	$1,982	$2,412	$2,944
Mixed	$2,230	$5,100	$6,400	$8,000	$9,000
Other	$13,309	$12,933	$15,070	$17,719	$21,718
Total	$19,350	$22,935	$27,417	$32,955	$39,550
Average	$4,838	$5,734	$6,854	$8,239	$9,888

Expense Breakdown by Manager Monthly

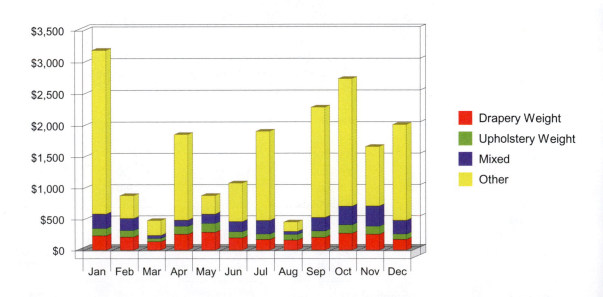

5.3.2 Expense by Segment

Fixtures and in-store improvements are important for us to track and allow us to better understand how we are using the space allocated.

Table: Expense Breakdown by Segment

Expenses by Segment					
	2006	2007	2008	2009	2010
Expenses					
Fabric Racks	$1,200	$1,400	$1,500	$1,600	$1,700
Office Furniture	$600	$800	$900	$1,000	$1,100
Leasehold Improvements	$1,000	$1,200	$1,400	$1,600	$1,800
Other	$16,550	$19,535	$23,617	$28,755	$34,950
Total	$19,350	$22,935	$27,417	$32,955	$39,550
Average	$4,838	$5,734	$6,854	$8,239	$9,888

Expense Breakdown by Segment Monthly

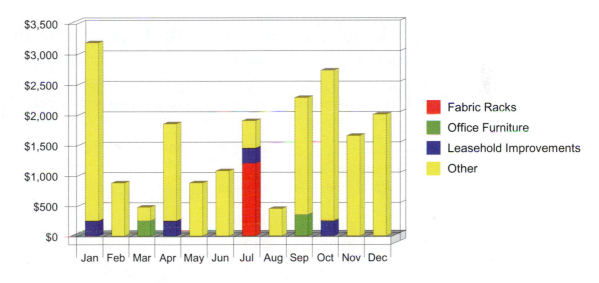

5.3.3 Expense by Region

Supplies are one of the more controllable expenses and will be important to monitor as we grow.

Table: Expense Breakdown by Region

Expenses by Region					
	2006	2007	2008	2009	2010
Expenses					
Office Supplies	$420	$480	$540	$600	$660
Fabrication Supplies	$300	$340	$380	$420	$460
Other	$18,630	$22,115	$26,497	$31,935	$38,430
Total	$19,350	$22,935	$27,417	$32,955	$39,550
Average	$6,450	$7,645	$9,139	$10,985	$13,183

Expense Breakdown by Region Monthly

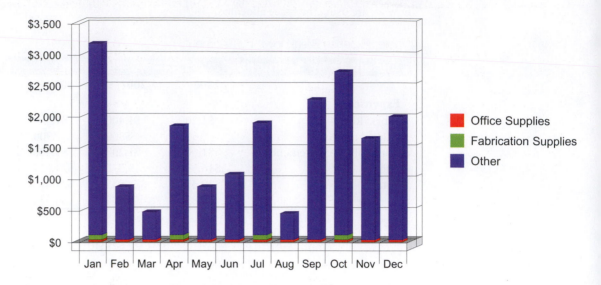

5.4 Linking Expenses to Strategy and Tactics

Our marketing expenses are allocated based on this prioritized approach:

1. Invest in our current customer base - 60%.
2. Invest in prospective customers that match our known profile - 30%.
3. Invest in creating greater awareness in the community - 10%.

Sales vs. Expenses Monthly

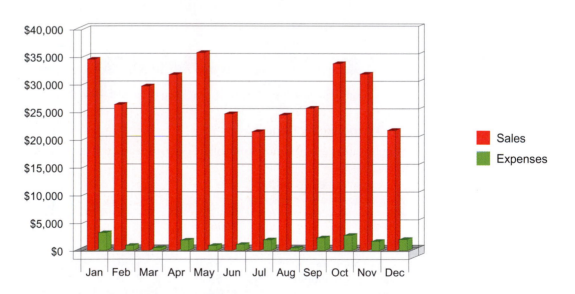

5.5 Contribution Margin

A key component of our marketing plan is to try and keep gross margins at or above 45%.

Table: Contribution Margin

Contribution Margin

	2006	2007	2008	2009	2010
Sales	$341,200	$412,382	$499,950	$607,720	$741,260
Direct Costs of Goods	$185,856	$224,551	$267,675	$325,203	$390,238
Cost of Goods Sold	$185,856	$224,551	$267,675	$325,203	$390,238
Gross Margin	$155,344	$187,831	$232,275	$282,517	$351,022
Gross Margin %	45.53%	45.55%	46.46%	46.49%	47.35%
Marketing Expense Budget	2006	2007	2008	2009	2010
Television Ads	$3,900	$4,600	$5,620	$6,740	$8,200
Newspaper Ads	$1,800	$2,160	$2,592	$3,110	$3,800
Newsletter/Postcard	$6,450	$7,700	$9,200	$11,150	$13,400
Printed Promotional Materials	$960	$1,150	$1,380	$1,660	$2,000
Web Marketing/Support	$1,500	$1,950	$2,535	$3,295	$4,300
Public Relations	$240	$345	$415	$500	$600
Promotional Events	$1,700	$1,950	$2,300	$2,800	$3,400
Website Expenses	$2,400	$2,600	$2,800	$3,000	$3,000
Other	$400	$480	$575	$700	$850
Total Sales and Marketing Expenses	$19,350	$22,935	$27,417	$32,955	$39,550
Percent of Sales	5.67%	5.56%	5.48%	5.42%	5.34%
Contribution Margin	$135,994	$164,896	$204,858	$249,562	$311,472
Contribution Margin / Sales	39.86%	39.99%	40.98%	41.07%	42.02%

Contribution Margin Monthly

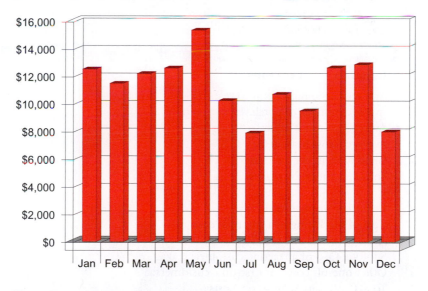

6.0 Controls

The following will enable us to keep on track. If we fail in any of these areas, we will need to reevaluate our business model:

- Gross margins at or above 45%.
- Month-to-month annual comparisons indicate an increase of 20% or greater.
- Do not depend on the credit line to meet cash requirements.
- Continue to pay down the credit line at a minimum of $24,000 per year.

6.1 Implementation

We will manage implementation by having a weekly milestones meeting with the entire staff to make sure that we are on track with our milestones and re-adjust our goals as we gather new data.

Once a quarter, we will review this marketing plan to ensure that we stay focused on our marketing strategy and that we are not distracted by opportunities simply because they are different than what we are currently pursuing.

Table: ROI Calculator

Return On Investment (ROI)	Television	Events	Online Advertising	Radio
Campaign Details				
Total Impressions	200,000	300	6,000	75,000
Total Program Cost	$15,000.00	$800.00	$3,250.00	$4,000.00
Response Rate	0.75%	15.00%	5.00%	1.00%
Conversion Rate	30.00%	40.00%	3.00%	20.00%
Average Customer Purchase	$85.00	$124.00	$800.00	$65.00
Response				
Total Responders	1,500	45	300	750
Total Buyers	450	18	9	150
Revenue Generated	$38,250.00	$2,232.00	$7,200.00	$9,750.00
Costs				
Cost per Response	$10.00	$17.78	$10.83	$5.33
Cost per Sale	$33.33	$44.44	$361.11	$26.67
Total Campaign Profit	$23,250.00	$1,432.00	$3,950.00	$5,750.00
Marketing ROI	155.00%	179.00%	121.54%	143.75%

Table: Customer Lifetime Value

Customer Lifetime Value		
Customer Purchase Forecast:		
Average Customer Lifetime (years):		5
Average number of purchases per year:		2
Average purchase value:		$100.00
Average Gross Margin %:	70%	
Gross Margin per purchase		$70.00
Total Customer Purchases:		$700.00
Customer Acquisition Costs:		
Cost of marketing to a potential customer:		$5.00
Average conversion rate:	4%	
Subtotal Cost of attracting customer:		$125.00
Other one-off costs for first-time customers:		$0.00
Total Customer Acquisition Costs:		$125.00
Unadjusted Customer Lifetime Value:		$575.00
Adjusted Customer Lifetime Value:		
Discount Rate:	8%	
Net Present Value of Customer Lifetime Value:		$391.34

6.2 Keys to Success

- Maintain gross margins in excess of 45%.
- Retain customers to generate repeat purchases and referrals.
- Generate average sales in excess of $1,000 per business day.

6.3 Market Research

- Initial Question Results — The staff notes customer responses to the "How did you hear about us?" question. We attempt to correlate that with our advertising and promotional activities and referral-generation programs.
- Store Suggestions — The store suggestion box is another method to gain additional information from customers. Some of the most productive questions are:
  - What suggestion do you have to improve the store?
  - Why did you visit the store today?
  - What other products or services would you like to have available in the store?
  - Competitive Shopping — We continually shop other stores. We visit each store in our market at least once each quarter for competitive information, we visit stores in the Seattle and Portland markets for merchandising and buying insight, and we subscribe to every catalog we know that has decorator fabrics as any part of their product line.

6.4 Contingency Planning

Difficulties and Risks

- Slow sales resulting in less-than-projected cash flow.
- Unexpected and excessive cost increases compared to the forecasted sales.
- Overly aggressive and debilitating actions by competitors.
- A parallel entry by a new competitor.

Worst case risks might include:

- Determining the business cannot support itself on an ongoing basis.
- Having to liquidate the inventory to pay back the bank loan.
- Locating a tenant to occupy the leased space for the duration of the five year lease.
- Losing the assets of the investors used for collateral.
- Dealing with the financial, business, and personal devastation of the store's failure.

6.5 CRM Plans

Our best sales in the future will come from our current customer base. In order to build this customer base, we need to provide exceptional customer service when they visit the store, have regular follow-up correspondence to thank them for their business (as well as to notify them of special promotions, etc.), and to provide personal shopper support so that each visit to the store meets their needs.

In order to keep track of these activities, we will need to create a spreadsheet showing follow-up correspondence with customers and what, if any, feedback we have received from them. At least quarterly, we will plan to meet and discuss if we are, in fact, retaining our current customers and whether that base has grown, or what changes may need to be made.

Appendix Table: Sales Forecast

Sales Forecast

Sales		Jan	Feb	Mar	Apr	May	Jun	Jul	Aug	Sep	Oct	Nov	Dec
Direct Sales	0%	$33,000	$25,000	$28,000	$30,000	$34,000	$23,000	$20,000	$23,000	$24,000	$32,000	$30,000	$20,000
Web Sales	0%	$1,000	$800	$1,000	$1,200	$1,200	$1,000	$900	$900	$1,000	$1,200	$1,300	$1,000
Consignment Sales	0%	$100	$100	$110	$120	$110	$100	$100	$100	$120	$130	$140	$130
Sub-Lease Revenue	0%	$405	$405	$525	$405	$405	$525	$405	$405	$525	$405	$405	$525
Total Sales		$34,505	$26,305	$29,635	$31,725	$35,715	$24,625	$21,405	$24,405	$25,645	$33,735	$31,845	$21,655
Direct Cost of Sales		Jan	Feb	Mar	Apr	May	Jun	Jul	Aug	Sep	Oct	Nov	Dec
Direct Sales		$18,250	$13,500	$16,400	$16,600	$18,800	$12,750	$11,100	$12,750	$13,300	$17,700	$16,600	$11,100
Web Sales		$550	$440	$550	$660	$660	$550	$495	$495	$550	$660	$715	$550
Consignment Sales		$5	$5	$6	$6	$6	$5	$5	$5	$6	$7	$8	$7
Sub-Lease Revenue		$5	$5	$5	$5	$5	$5	$5	$5	$5	$5	$5	$5
Subtotal Direct Cost of Sales		$18,810	$13,950	$16,961	$17,271	$19,471	$13,310	$11,605	$13,255	$13,861	$18,372	$17,328	$11,662

Appendix Table: Sales Breakdown by Manager

Sales by: Manager

Sales	Jan	Feb	Mar	Apr	May	Jun	Jul	Aug	Sep	Oct	Nov	Dec
Drapery Weight	16%	$4,638	$4,209	$4,722	$5,076	$5,714	$3,921	$3,425	$3,905	$4,084	$5,398	$5,095	$3,446
Upholstery Weight	8%	$2,319	$2,104	$2,361	$2,538	$2,857	$1,960	$1,712	$1,952	$2,042	$2,699	$2,548	$1,723
Mixed	30%	$8,696	$7,892	$8,855	$9,518	$10,715	$7,352	$6,422	$7,322	$7,658	$10,121	$9,554	$6,461
Special Order	20%	$5,797	$5,261	$5,903	$6,345	$7,143	$4,901	$4,281	$4,881	$5,105	$6,747	$6,369	$4,307
Other		$13,055	$6,839	$7,794	$8,248	$9,286	$6,491	$5,565	$6,345	$6,756	$8,770	$8,279	$5,718
Total		$34,505	$26,305	$29,635	$31,725	$35,715	$24,625	$21,405	$24,405	$25,645	$33,735	$31,845	$21,655
Average		$6,901	$5,261	$5,927	$6,345	$7,143	$4,925	$4,281	$4,881	$5,129	$6,747	$6,369	$4,331

Appendix Table: Sales Breakdown by Segment

Sales by: Segment

Sales	Jan	Feb	Mar	Apr	May	Jun	Jul	Aug	Sep	Oct	Nov	Dec
"The Window Seat"	$1,014	$921	$1,033	$1,110	$1,250	$858	$749	$854	$893	$1,181	$1,115	$754
Antiques	$2,319	$2,104	$2,361	$2,538	$2,857	$1,960	$1,712	$1,952	$2,042	$2,699	$2,548	$1,723
Other	$31,172	$23,280	$26,241	$28,077	$31,608	$21,807	$18,944	$21,599	$22,710	$29,855	$28,182	$19,178
Total	$34,505	$26,305	$29,635	$31,725	$35,715	$24,625	$21,405	$24,405	$25,645	$33,735	$31,845	$21,655
Average	$11,502	$8,768	$9,878	$10,575	$11,905	$8,208	$7,135	$8,135	$8,548	$11,245	$10,615	$7,218

Appendix Table: Sales Breakdown by Region

Sales by: Region

Sales	Jan	Feb	Mar	Apr	May	Jun	Jul	Aug	Sep	Oct	Nov	Dec
The Antique Bureau	$360	$360	$360	$360	$360	$360	$360	$360	$360	$360	$360	$360
Event/Sale Revenue	$45	$45	$120	$45	$45	$120	$45	$45	$120	$45	$45	$120
Other	$34,100	$25,900	$29,155	$31,320	$35,310	$24,145	$21,000	$24,000	$25,165	$33,330	$31,440	$21,175
Total	$34,505	$26,305	$29,635	$31,725	$35,715	$24,625	$21,405	$24,405	$25,645	$33,735	$31,845	$21,655
Average	$11,502	$8,768	$9,878	$10,575	$11,905	$8,208	$7,135	$8,135	$8,548	$11,245	$10,615	$7,218

Appendix Table: Marketing Expense Budget

Marketing Expense Budget

Budget	Jan	Feb	Mar	Apr	May	Jun	Jul	Aug	Sep	Oct	Nov	Dec
Television Ads	$780	$0	$0	$0	$0	$0	$0	$0	$780	$780	$780	$780
Newspaper Ads	$600	$0	$0	$0	$0	$600	$0	$0	$600	$0	$0	$0
Newsletter/Postcard	$1,350	$0	$0	$1,400	$0	$0	$1,450	$0	$0	$1,500	$0	$750
Printed Promotional Materials	$80	$80	$80	$80	$80	$80	$80	$80	$80	$80	$80	$80
Web Marketing/Support	$125	$125	$125	$125	$125	$125	$125	$125	$125	$125	$125	$125
Public Relations	$20	$20	$20	$20	$20	$20	$20	$20	$20	$20	$20	$20
Promotional Events	$0	$425	$0	$0	$425	$0	$0	$0	$425	$0	$425	$0
Website Expenses	$200	$200	$200	$200	$200	$200	$200	$200	$200	$200	$200	$200
Other	$25	$25	$50	$25	$25	$50	$25	$25	$50	$25	$25	$50
Total Sales and Marketing Expenses	$3,180	$875	$475	$1,850	$875	$1,075	$1,900	$450	$2,280	$2,730	$1,655	$2,005
Percent of Sales	9.22%	3.33%	1.60%	5.83%	2.45%	4.37%	8.88%	1.84%	8.89%	8.09%	5.20%	9.26%

Appendix Table: Expense Breakdown by Manager

Expenses by Manager

Expenses	Jan	Feb	Mar	Apr	May	Jun	Jul	Aug	Sep	Oct	Nov	Dec
Drapery Weight	$232	$210	$136	$254	$286	$196	$171	$160	$204	$270	$255	$172
Upholstery Weight	$116	$105	$50	$127	$143	$98	$86	$90	$102	$135	$127	$86
Mixed	$235	$195	$50	$100	$150	$165	$220	$50	$220	$300	$325	$220
Other	$2,597	$365	$239	$1,369	$296	$616	$1,423	$150	$1,754	$2,025	$948	$1,527
Total	$3,180	$875	$475	$1,850	$875	$1,075	$1,900	$450	$2,280	$2,730	$1,655	$2,005
Average	$795	$219	$119	$463	$219	$69	$475	$113	$570	$683	$414	$501

Appendix Table: Expense Breakdown by Segment

Expenses by Segment

Expenses	Jan	Feb	Mar	Apr	May	Jun	Jul	Aug	Sep	Oct	Nov	Dec
Fabric Racks	$0	$0	$0	$0	$0	$0	$1,200	$0	$0	$0	$0	$0
Office Furniture	$0	$0	$250	$0	$0	$0	$0	$0	$350	$0	$0	$0
Leasehold Improvements	$250	$0	$0	$250	$0	$0	$250	$0	$0	$250	$0	$0
Other	$2,930	$875	$225	$1,600	$875	$1,075	$450	$450	$1,930	$2,480	$1,655	$2,005
Total	$3,180	$875	$475	$1,850	$875	$1,075	$1,900	$450	$2,280	$2,730	$1,655	$2,005
Average	$795	$219	$119	$463	$219	$269	$475	$113	$570	$683	$414	$501

Appendix Table: Expense Breakdown by Region

Expenses by Region

Expenses	Jan	Feb	Mar	Apr	May	Jun	Jul	Aug	Sep	Oct	Nov	Dec
Office Supplies	$35	$35	$35	$35	$35	$35	$35	$35	$35	$35	$35	$35
Fabrication Supplies	$75	$0	$0	$75	$0	$0	$75	$0	$0	$75	$0	$0
Other	$3,070	$840	$440	$1,740	$840	$1,040	$1,790	$415	$2,245	$2,620	$1,620	$1,970
Total	$3,180	$875	$475	$1,850	$875	$1,075	$1,900	$450	$2,280	$2,730	$1,655	$2,005
Average	$1,060	$292	$158	$617	$292	$358	$633	$150	$760	$910	$552	$668

Table Appendix Table: Contribution Margin

Contribution Margin

	Jan	Feb	Mar	Apr	May	Jun	Jul	Aug	Sep	Oct	Nov	Dec
Sales	$34,505	$26,305	$29,635	$31,725	$35,715	$24,625	$21,405	$24,405	$25,645	$33,735	$31,845	$21,655
Direct Costs of Goods	$18,810	$13,950	$16,961	$17,271	$19,471	$13,310	$11,605	$13,255	$13,861	$18,372	$17,328	$11,662
Cost of Goods Sold	$18,810	$13,950	$16,961	$17,271	$19,471	$13,310	$11,605	$13,255	$13,861	$18,372	$17,328	$11,662
Gross Margin	$15,695	$12,355	$12,674	$14,454	$16,244	$11,315	$9,800	$11,150	$11,784	$15,363	$14,517	$9,993
Gross Margin %	45.49%	46.97%	42.77%	45.56%	45.48%	45.95%	45.78%	45.69%	45.95%	45.54%	45.59%	46.15%
Marketing Expense Budget	Jan	Feb	Mar	Apr	May	Jun	Jul	Aug	Sep	Oct	Nov	Dec
Television Ads	$780	$0	$0	$0	$0	$0	$0	$0	$780	$780	$780	$780
Newspaper Ads	$600	$0	$0	$0	$0	$600	$0	$0	$600	$0	$0	$0
Newsletter/Postcard	$1,350	$0	$0	$1,400	$0	$0	$1,450	$0	$0	$1,500	$0	$750
Printed Promotional Materials	$80	$80	$80	$80	$80	$80	$80	$80	$80	$80	$80	$80
Web Marketing/Support	$125	$125	$125	$125	$125	$125	$125	$125	$125	$125	$125	$125
Public Relations	$20	$20	$20	$20	$20	$20	$20	$20	$20	$20	$20	$20
Promotional Events	$0	$425	$0	$0	$425	$0	$0	$0	$425	$0	$425	$0
Website Expenses	$200	$200	$200	$200	$200	$200	$200	$200	$200	$200	$200	$200
Other	$25	$25	$50	$25	$25	$50	$25	$25	$50	$25	$25	$50
Total Sales and Marketing Expenses	$3,180	$875	$475	$1,850	$875	$1,075	$1,900	$450	$2,280	$2,730	$1,655	$2,005
Percent of Sales	9.22%	3.33%	1.60%	5.83%	2.45%	4.37%	8.88%	1.84%	8.89%	8.09%	5.20%	9.26%
Contribution Margin	$12,515	$11,480	$12,199	$12,604	$15,369	$10,240	$7,900	$10,700	$9,504	$12,633	$12,862	$7,988
Contribution Margin / Sales	36.27%	43.64%	41.16%	39.73%	43.03%	41.58%	36.91%	43.84%	37.06%	37.45%	40.39%	36.89%

● Notes

▼ CHAPTER 1

1. http://www.marketingpower.com (accessed September 9, 2008); http://www.the-cma.org (accessed September 11, 2008).
2. "Social Marketing Do's and Don'ts," *Adweek*, October 8, 2007; http://www.facebook.com (accessed September 10, 2008).
3. http://www.reuters.com/article/pressRelease/idUS156332+09-Jun-2008+MW20080609 (accessed September 12, 2008).
4. http://www.llbean.com/customerService/aboutLLBean/background.html?nav=ln (accessed September 23, 2008).
5. http://www.reuters.com/article/pressRelease/idUS122196+27-Feb-2008+BW20080227 (accessed September 17, 2008); M. McCarthy, "Vegas Goes Back to Naughty Roots," *USA Today*, April 11, 2005, http://www.usatoday.com (accessed September 14, 2008).
6. http://adage.com/century/timeline/index.html (accessed August 15, 2008).
7. Ibid.
8. Ibid.
9. R. Jaroslovsky, review of *Birth of a Salesman*, by Walter A. Friedman, *Wall Street Journal*, "More Than a Shoeshine and a Smile," June 8, 2004.
10. Ibid.
11. "Consumer Interest in Socially Responsible Companies Rising, Survey Finds," July 16, 2007, http://www.greenbiz.com/news/2007/07/16/consumer-interest-socially-responsible-companies-rising-survey-finds (accessed December 16, 2008).
12. Peter F. Drucker, *Innovation and Entrepreneurship: Practice and Principle* (New York, HarperBusiness, 1985).

▼ CHAPTER 2

1. P. McGreevy, "State Bans Trans Fat," *LA Times*, July 26, 2008; T. Lueck and K. Severson, "New York Bans Most Trans Fats in Restaurants," *New York Times*, December 6, 2006.
2. http://www.marketingpower.com (accessed August 5, 2008).
3. M. Porter, *Competitive Strategy* (The Free Press: New York, 1980).
4. http://www.orioncoat.com/anti-microbial-fluorplate-examples (accessed September 5, 2008); "Making Hospitals Pay for Their Mistakes," *New York Times*, December 19, 2007; "Kline Report on Smart Coatings Cites Immediate Opportunities in Antimicrobial Coatings, Cool Paint, and Smart Glass," *PRNewswire,* November 19, 2007.
5. J. Matras, "2009 VW Jetta TDI Diesel Adds Low Emissions to Fuel Economy for 50-State Availability," *Automotive Examiner*, August 19, 2008, http://www.examiner.com (accessed September 16, 2008).
6. http://www.marketingpower.com (accessed August 5, 2008).
7. http://www.selig.uga.edu/forecast/GBEC/GBEC0703Q.pdf (accessed August 5, 2008).
8. Ibid.
9. http://www.marketingpower.com (accessed August 5, 2008).
10. Ibid.
11. Ibid.
12. P. Robinson, C. Faris, and Y. Wind, *Industrial Buying and Creative Marketing* (Boston: Allyn & Bacon, 1967).
13. Ibid.
14. http://www.neopathhealth.com (accessed August 6, 2008).

▼ CHAPTER 3

1. http://www.wholefoods.com (accessed August 22, 2008).
2. http://www.marketingpower.com (accessed August 22, 2008).
3. http://www.teva.com (accessed September 10, 2008).

4. R. S. Kaplan and D. P. Norton, "The Balanced Scorecard – Measures That Drive Performance," *Harvard Business Review* (January/February 1992): 71–79.
5. http://www.balancedscorecard.org/BSCResources/AbouttheBalancedScorecard/tabid/55/Default.aspx (accessed August 21, 2008).
6. E. Wilson, "Swimsuit for the Olympics Is a New Skin for the Big Dip," *New York Times*, February 13, 2008, http://www.nytimes.com (accessed August 15, 2008).
7. http://www.marketingpower.com (accessed August 22, 2008).

▼ CHAPTER 4

1. Organization for Economic Cooperation and Development, *OECD Factbook 2008* (Paris: OECD, 2008), http://miranda.sourceoecd.org/pdf/factbook2008/302008011e-02-01-01.pdf (accessed September 2, 2008).
2. J. Schmid, "Product Recalls Rise; Analysts Recommend Better Relations with China," *Milwaukee Journal Sentinel*, July 25, 2008.
3. M. Earls, "Advertising to the Herd: How Understanding Our True Nature Challenges the Ways We Think about Advertising and Market Research," *International Journal of Market Research* 45, no. 3 (2003): 313; http://accountplanning.net/Central/Downloads/Earls_Herd.pdf (accessed September 2, 2008).
4. G. Teague, *Culture Smart! – USA* (Great Britain: Kuperard, 2004).
5. "Wazzup Bud?" *Ad Focus – Supplement to the Financial Mail*, May 18, 2001, http://free.financialmail.co.za/report/adfocus2001/adfocuseditorial/9ddbcomm.pdf (accessed September 2, 2008).
6. Advertising Age, *Digital Marketing & Media Fact Pack* (Chicago: Crain Communications).
7. P. Kotler and G. Armstrong, *Principles of Marketing* (Upper Saddle River: Prentice Hall, 2007).
8. R. Markin, "Consumerism: Militant Consumer Behavior," *Business and Society* 12, no. 1 (Fall 1971): 5.
9. "Industry Flayed on Safety Attitude," *Automotive News* 75, no. 5891 (August 28, 2000): 56.
10. "Eight Basic Consumer Rights," *Choice.com.au*, http://www.choice.com.au/viewArticle.aspx?id=100736&catId=100528&tid=100008 (accessed August 30, 2008).
11. R. Markin, "Consumerism: Militant Consumer Behavior," *Business and Society* 12, no. 1 (Fall 1971): 5.
12. R. Innes, "A Theory of Consumer Boycotts under Symmetric Information and Imperfect Competition," *Economic Journal* 116 (2): 511, http://www.res.org.uk/society/mediabriefings/pdfs/2006/apr06/innes.asp (accessed September 1, 2008).
13. W. Davidson, D. Worrel, and A. El-Jelly, "Influencing Managers to Change Unpopular Corporate Behavior Through Boycotts and Divestitures," *Business and Society* 34, no. 2: 192.
14. L. Miller, "Products to Break the Chemical Habit and Get Eco-Friendly," *New York Times*, July 19, 2007, http://www.nytimes.com/2007/07/19/business/media/19adco.html (accessed September 2, 2008).
15. Hoovers, "Method Products Company Description," 2008, http://www.hoovers.com/method-products/—ID__155282—/free-co-profile.xhtml (accessed September 2, 2008).
16. Method Products, "Company Information—What We're For," http://www.methodhome.com (accessed September 2, 2008).
17. The LOHAS Consumer Trends Database™, Natural Marketing Institute, 2007, http://www.nmisolutions.com/lohasd_segment.html (accessed September 2, 2008).
18. "US: Consumers Buying Green Despite Economic Woes," *Just-Food.com*, April 30, 2008, http://www.just-food.com/article.aspx?id=102186&lk=s (accessed August 30, 2008).

19. B. Cummings, "Despite Economic Dip, Organic Food Sales Soar," *Brandweek*, June 9, 2008, 6.

20. J. Edwards, "Accountability in the Consumer Movement," *Consumer Policy Review* 16, no. 1 (Jan/Feb 2006): 20.

21. M. Solomon, G. Marshall, and E. Stuart, *Marketing* (Upper Saddle River: Prentice Hall, 2008).

22. Ibid.

23. "Advertising Practices—Frequently Asked Questions," Federal Trade Commission, 2001, http://www.ftc.gov/bcp/edu/pubs/business/adv/bus35.pdf (accessed September 2, 2008).

24. "Settlement on Deceptive Drug Ads," *U.S. News & World Report*, August 18, 2008 (1180).

25. B. Janoff, "Airborne, FTC Reach Settlement," *Adweek*, August 14, 2008, http://www.adweek.com/aw/content_display/news/client/e3i1fefd617b0921810037928c6c779cb69 (accessed October 1, 2008).

26. "Statement of Ethics," American Marketing Association, 2008, http://www.marketingpower.com/AboutAMA/Pages/Statement%20of%20Ethics.aspx (accessed September 2, 2008).

27. C. Hawkes, "Regulating Food Marketing to Young People Worldwide: Trends and Policy Drivers," *American Journal of Public Health* 97, no. 11 (November 2007): 1962.

28. E. Creyer and W. Ross, Jr., "The Influence of Firm Behavior on Purchase Intention: Do Consumers Really Care about Business Ethics?" *Journal of Consumer Marketing* 14, no. 6 (Nov/Dec 1997): 421.

29. Corporate Citizenship Report, Wells Fargo Bank, 2007, https://www.wellsfargo.com/downloads/pdf/about/csr/reports/wf2007corporate_citizenship.pdf (accessed September 2, 2008).

30. M. Salzman and I. Matathia, *Next Now* (New York: Palgrave Macmillan, 2006).

31. K. Vijayraghavan and S. Vyas, "MNC Fast Food Chains Rework Menu for India," *Economic Times*, July 18, 2006, http://economictimes.indiatimes.com/articleshowarchive.cms?msid=1768877 (accessed October 1, 2008).

32. 2007 Annual Review, The Coca-Cola Company, http://www.thecoca-colacompany.com/investors/annual_review_2007.html (accessed September 2, 2008).

33. N. Pacek and D. Thorniley, *Emerging Markets* (London: Profile Books, 2007).

34. Ibid.

35. M. Corstjens and J. Merrihue, "Optimal Marketing," *Harvard Business Review* (October 2003).

36. P. Kotler and G. Armstrong, *Principles of Marketing* (Upper Saddle River: Prentice Hall, 2008).

▼ CHAPTER 5

1. Netflix Consumer Press Kit, http://www.netflix.com.

2. Roland T. Rust and Anthony J. Zahorik, "Customer Satisfaction, Customer Retention and Market Share," *Journal of Retailing* 69 (Summer: 1993) 193–215; Chris Denove and James D. Power IV. *Satisfaction: How Every Great Company Listens to the Voice of the Customer* (New York, NY: Portfolio, 2006).

3. *BusinessWeek*, March 5, 2007, 52, http://proquest.umi.com/pqdlink?index=21&did=1225142301&SrchMode=3&sid=1&Fmt=3&VInst=PROD&VType=PQD&RQT=309&VName=PQD&TS=1221580117&clientId=32427&aid=2 (accessed September 17, 2008).

4. *Sprint Hangs Up on High-Maintenance Customers*, Reuters News Service, July 9, 2007.

5. V. Kumar, J. Andrew Petersen, and Robert P. Leone, "How Valuable Is Word of Mouth?" *Harvard Business Review* (October 1, 2007).

6. Purdue University Center for Customer Driven Quality, http://www.ccdq.com (accessed October 10, 2008).

7. http://www.wheresyours.com (accessed November 2, 2008).

8. Fredrick Reichheld, *The Loyalty Effect* (Boston: Harvard Business School Press, 1996).

9. http://www.patronsocialclub.com (accessed November 2, 2008) and http://www.brandweek.com (accessed November 2, 2008).

10. Don Peppers, Martha Rogers, and Bob Dorf, "Is Your Company Ready for One-to-One Marketing?" *Harvard Business Review* (January-February 1999).

11. http://www.starbucks.com (accessed November 2, 2008).

▼ CHAPTER 6

1. http://www.marketingpower.com (accessed September 12, 2008).

2. I. Ajzen, "The Theory of Planned Behavior," *Organizational Behavior and Human Decision Processes* 50 (1991): 179–211.

3. Ibid.

4. *Takeaway Coffee*. (2002, February 22). New Zealand Press Association

5. I. Brace, L. Edwards, and C. Nancarrow, "I Hear You Knocking...Can Advertising Reach Everybody in the Target Audience?" *International Journal of Market Research* 2, no. 44 (2002): 193.

6. J. Chebat, M. Charlebois, and C. Chebat, "What Makes Open versus Closed Conclusion Advertisements More Persuasive? The Moderating Role of Prior Knowledge and Involvement," *Journal of Business Research* 53, no. 2 (2001).

7. I. Brace, L. Edwards, and C. Nancarrow, "I Hear You Knocking...Can Advertising Reach Everybody in the Target Audience?" *International Journal of Market Research* 2, no. 44 (2002): 193.

8. C. McDonald, "The Hidden Power of Advertising: How Low Involvement Processing Influences the Way in Which We Choose Brands," review of *The Hidden Power of Advertising*, by Robert Heath, *International Journal of Market Research* 1, no. 44 (2002): 121.

9. S. Youn, T. Sun, W. D. Wells, and X. Zhao, "Commercial Liking and Memory: Moderating Effects of Product Categories," *Journal of Advertising Research* 41, no. 3 (2001): 7–13.

10. Ibid.

11. Ibid.

12. J. Smith, D. Terry, A. Manstead, W. Louis, D. Kotterman, and J. Wolfs, "The Attitude-Behavior Relationship in Consumer Conduct: The Role of Norms, Past Behavior, and Self-Identity," *Journal of Social Psychology* 148, no. 3 (2008): 311–333.

13. C. S. Carver and M. F. Scheier, *Perspectives on Personality*, 4th ed. (Boston: Allyn & Bacon).

14. K. V. Henderson, R. E. Goldsmith, and L. R. Flynn, "Demographic Characteristics of Subjective Age," *Journal of Social Psychology*, 135 (1995): 447–457.

15. Zena S. Blaun, "Changes in Status and Age Identification," *American Sociological Review* 21 (April 1965): 198–203.

16. M. Levens, *Affluent Consumer Evaluation of Major Capital Goods Bundles: A Conjoint-based Segmentation Approach*, Association of Marketing Theory and Practice Proceedings (2008).

17. B. Dubois and C. Paternault, "Understanding the World of International Luxury Brands: The 'Dream Formula,'" *Journal of Advertising Research* 35, no. 4 (1995): 69–76.

18. http://www.marketingpower.com (accessed August 3, 2008).

19. D. Caracci, "The Plan Behind Plan-O-Grams," June 1, 2006, http://www.aftermarketnews.com (accessed November 2, 2008).

20. G. Cui and P. Choudhury, "Marketplace Diversity and Cost-effective Marketing Strategies," *Journal of Consumer Marketing* 19, no. 1 (2002): 54–73.

21. Ibid.

22. A. Schneider, "A Changing America Has Changing Tastes," *Kiplinger Business Forecasts* 1227 (December 23, 2002).

23. J. Hood, "Targeting a Multicultural Audience Takes More than a Dictionary: It Takes Tact, Understanding, and Relevance," *PR Week* 13 (August 18, 2003).

24. G. Cui and P. Choudhury, "Marketplace Diversity and Cost-effective Marketing Strategies," *Journal of Consumer Marketing* 19, no. 1 (2002): 54–73.

25. Ibid.

26. C. Arnold, "Coloring Outside the Lines," *Marketing News* 4 (November 25, 2002).

27. Ibid.

28. Ibid.

29. http://www.mavinfoundation.org (accessed August 20, 2008).

30. G. Khermouch, "Didja C That Kewl Ad?" *BusinessWeek*, August 26, 2002, 158.
31. YouthPulse, *Harris Interactive Preview* (2003).
32. Ibid.
33. "Diversity Is Key to Marketing to Today's Youth," *Marketing to the Emerging Majorities* 6, no. 14 (2002): 6.
34. Ibid.
35. G. Hofstede, *Culture's Consequences: Comparing Values, Behaviors, Institutions and Organizations Across Nations*, 2nd ed. (Thousand Oaks: Sage Publications, Inc).
36. D. Ackerman and G. Tellis, "Can Culture Affect Prices? A Cross-cultural Study of Shopping and Retail Prices," *Journal of Retailing* 1, no. 77 (2001): 57.
37. K. Zhou, C. Su, and Y. Bao, "A Paradox of Price-quality and Market Efficiency: A Comparative Study of the US and China Markets," *International Journal of Research in Marketing* (December 2002).
38. D. Ackerman and G. Tellis, "Can Culture Affect Prices? A Cross-cultural Study of Shopping and Retail Prices," *Journal of Retailing* 1, no. 77 (2001): 57.
39. L. Dong and M. Helms, "Brand Name Translation Model: A Case Analysis of US Brands in China," *Journal of Brand Management* 9, no. 2 (2001): 99–115.
40. http://www.hp.com/hpinfo/globalcitizenship/environment/productdesign/ecohighlights-label.html (accessed September 21, 2008).

▼ CHAPTER 7

1. http://www.merriam-webster.com (accessed August 11, 2008).
2. http://www.marketingpower.com (accessed August 10, 2008).
3. Ibid.
4. Lawrence C. Lockley, "Notes on the History of Marketing Research," *Journal of Marketing* 14, no. 5 (April 1950): 733–736.
5. http://www.aaf.org (accessed August 15, 2008).
6. http://www.merriam-webster.com (accessed August 11, 2008).
7. http://www.marketingpower.com (accessed August 10, 2008).
8. L. Oppenheim and M. Sherr, "Gathering Customer Perceptions Over the Internet," *Medical Marketing & Media* 34, no. 2 (1999), 50–58.
9. http://www.jdpower.com (accessed September 12, 2008).
10. http://www.marketingpower.com (accessed August 10, 2008).
11. http://www.onsiteresearch.com (accessed September 15, 2008).
12. D. Bradford, "Ten Years After: Online Qualitative Research Has Come a Long Way in Its First Decade," *Quirk's Marketing Research Review* 17, no. 7 (2003): 44–47.
13. N. Ray and S. Tabor, "Cybersurveys Come of Age," *Management and Applications* 15, no. 1 (2003): 33.
14. S. Rogers, and K. Sheldon, "An Improved Way to Characterize Internet Users," *Journal of Advertising Research* 5, no. 42 (2002): 85.
15. C. Maginnis, "Online Sample – Can You Trust It?" *Quirk's Marketing Research Review* 17, no. 7 (2003): 40–43.
16. http://www.e-rewards.com (accessed September 29, 2008).
17. D. Bradford, "Ten Years After: Online Qualitative Research Has Come a Long Way in Its First Decade," *Quirk's Marketing Research Review* 17, no. 7 (2003): 44–47.
18. P. Willems and P. Oosterveld, "The Best of Both Worlds; Combining Phone and Internet Research Creates More Targeted Results," *Management & Applications* 15, no. 1 (2003): 23.
19. http://www.marketingpower.com (accessed August 10, 2008).
20. Ibid.
21. Ibid.
22. Ibid.
23. Ibid.
24. Ibid.
25. P. Kotler, "A Design for the Firm's Marketing Nerve Center," in *Readings in Marketing Information Systems: A New Era in Marketing Research*, ed. S. Smith, R. Brien, and J. Stafford (Boston: Houghton-Mifflin, 1966).
26. http://www.marketingpower.com (accessed August 10, 2008).

▼ CHAPTER 8

1. H. Arnold, "Brand Aid," *Financial Management* (November 2001): 33–34.
2. P. Temporal, *Advanced Brand Management – from Vision to Valuation* (Singapore: John Wiley & Sons, 2002).
3. "Ethnic Consumers More Receptive Than Peers to Marketing, But Most Believe Messaging Lacks Relevancy, According to New Yankelovich Study," http://www.hiphoppress.com/2007/09/ethnic-consumer.html (accessed July 30, 2008).
4. Ibid.
5. "New Digital Brand Strategy for Singapore Tourism Board," http://www.asiatraveltips.com/news07/210-SingaporeTourism.shtml (accessed August 5, 2008); http://www.visitsingapore.com (accessed August 5, 2008).
6. D. Abrahams and E. Granof, "Respecting Brand Risk," *Risk Management* 4, no. 49 (2002): 40.
7. S. Broniarczyk and A. Gershoff, "The Reciprocal Effects of Brand Equity and Trivial Attributes," *Journal of Marketing Research* (May 2003): 161.
8. S. Hoeffler and K. Keller, "Building Brand Equity Through Corporate Societal Marketing," *Journal of Public Policy and Marketing* 21, no. 1 (2002): 78–89.
9. L. Williams, "What Price a Good Name?" *Business*, May 5, 2002, 23.
10. D. Abrahams and E. Granof, "Respecting Brand Risk," *Risk Management* 4, no. 49 (2002): 40.
11. Ibid.
12. http://www.interbrand.com/best_brands_2007.asp (accessed August 25, 2008).
13. A. Abela, "Additive versus Inclusive Approaches to Measuring Brand Equity: Practical and Ethical Implications," *Journal of Brand Management* 10, no. 4/5 (2003): 342.
14. A. Chaudhuri and M. Holbrook, "The Chain of Effects from Brand Trust and Brand Effect to Brand Performance: The Role of Brand Loyalty," *Journal of Marketing* 65, no. 2 (2001): 81–93.
15. S. Hoeffler and K. Keller, "Building Brand Equity Through Corporate Societal Marketing," *Journal of Public Policy and Marketing* 21, no. 1 (2002): 78–89.
16. Ibid.
17. "Interbrand 2007 Rankings," *BusinessWeek*, August 6, 2007; http://www.moet.com (accessed July 28, 2008).
18. V. Kumar, "Segmenting Global Markets: Look before You Leap," *Marketing Research* 13, no. 1 (2001): 8–13.
19. http://www.ikea.com/us/en (accessed July 30, 2008).
20. D. D'Alessandro and M. Owens, *Brand Warfare: 10 Rules for the Killer Brand* (New York: McGraw-Hill, 2002).
21. Ibid.
22. J. Mass, "Pharmaceutical Brands: Do They Really Exist?" *International Journal of Medical Marketing* 2, no. 1 (2001): 23–32.
23. NPR, "The Fall of Enron," http://www.npr.org/news/specials/enron/ (accessed August 25, 2008).
24. A. Rattray, "Measure for Measure: Brand Value May Be Relative But It Is Measurable, Either from a Company or a Consumer Point of View," *Financial Times*, July 9, 2002, 12.
25. S. Davis Brand, *Asset Management: Driving Profitable Growth Through Your Brands*, 2nd ed. (San Francisco: John Wiley & Sons, 2002).
26. http://www.traderjoes.com (accessed August 15, 2008).
27. http://www.southerncomfort.com (accessed July 17, 2008); http://www.kemps.com (accessed July 17, 2008).
28. http://www.fritolay.com (accessed July 28, 2008); http://www.kcmasterpiece.com (accessed July 28, 2008).
29. D. Arnold, *The Handbook of Brand Management* (London: Century Business, 1992).
30. http://www.crayola.com (accessed July 14, 2008).
31. M. Yadav, "How Buyers Evaluate Product Bundles: A Model of Anchoring and Adjustment," *Journal of Consumer Research* 21, no. 2 (1994): 342.
32. T. Amobi, "Disney: Mouse on the Move," *BusinessWeek*, May 7, 2007, http://www.businessweek.com/investor/content/may2007/pi20070507_602321.htm (accessed July 26, 2008).

33. T. Leopold, "Advertising Builds Character," *CNN.com*, http://www.cnn.com/2004/SHOWBIZ/08/18/eye.ent.advertising/index.html (accessed August 2, 2008).

34. http://www.starwoodhotels.com/alofthotels (accessed August 2, 2008).

35. 2007 CMO Study, http://www.spencerstuart.com (accessed July 25, 2008).

36. R. Ceniceros, "Counterfeit Crackdown: Risk Manager Role in Protecting Brand to Grow," *Business Insurance* 1 (September 10, 2001).

▼ CHAPTER 9

1. A. Bianco, "The Vanishing Mass Market," *BusinessWeek*, July 12, 2004, http://www.businessweek.com/magazine/content/04_28/b3891001_mz001.htm (accessed August 13, 2008).

2. Ibid.

3. W. DeSarbo, "Market Segmentation Practices Are Totally Inadequate," *AScribe Newsline*, June 15, 2001.

4. A. Dexter, "Egoists, Idealists, and Corporate Animals—Segmenting Business Markets," *International Journal of Market Research* 1, no. 44 (2002): 31.

5. http://www.agr.gc.ca (accessed July 16, 2008); http://www.redbull.com (accessed August 2, 2008).

6. http://www.curves.com (accessed August 3, 2008); "Fitness Club is Fastest-Growing U.S. Franchise," *Voice of America*, January 27, 2006, http://www.voanews.com/english/archive/2006-01/2006-01-27-voa18.cfm (accessed August 5, 2008).

7. http://www.moosejaw.com (accessed August 3, 2008).

8. http://www.chase.com (accessed July 21, 2008).

9. K. O'Brien, "Nokia Deal Aimed at Opening Up Mobile Software," *International Herald Tribune*, June 24, 2008, http://www.iht.com/articles/2008/06/24/business/symbian.php (accessed July 21, 2008); M. Ahmad, "Nokia Middle East and Africa Marks the Holy Month with the Launch of Ramadan Applications for Mobile Users Worldwide," *Business Intelligence Middle East*, July 13, 2008, http://www.bi-me.com/main.php?id=23493&t=1&c=129&cg=4&mset=1021 (accessed July 23, 2008).

10. S. Dibb and L. Simkin, "Market Segmentation: Diagnosing and Treating the Barriers," *International Marketing Management* 30, no. 8 (2001): 21–39.

11. D. Rowell, "All About Satellite Phone Service," *The Travel Insider*, April 22, 2008, http://www.thetravelinsider.info/phones/aboutsatellitephoneservice.htm (accessed August 21, 2008); http://www.iridium.com (accessed July 24, 2008).

12. http://www.ford.com (accessed August 22, 2008).

13. http://www.mcdonalds.com (accessed July 22, 2008).

14. http://www.movado.com (accessed July 23, 2008).

15. S. Dibb, and L. Simkin, "Market Segmentation: Diagnosing and Treating the Barriers," *International Marketing Management* 30, no. 8 (2001): 21–39.

16. http://www.apple.com (accessed July 10, 2008); D. Coursey, "The Un-Vision: What Steve Jobs Won't Do at Apple," *ZDNet*, February 7, 2002, http://review.zdnet.com/4520-6033_16-4206922.html (accessed July 24, 2008); R. Hof, "100 Million iPods Sold, but How Many Are Still in Use?" *BusinessWeek*, April 9, 2007, http://www.businessweek.com/the_thread/techbeat/archives/2007/04/100_million_ipo.html (accessed July 23, 2008).

17. "Gas-saving sedans," *Consumer Reports*, July 2008.

18. B. Calder and S. Reagan, "Brand Design," in *Kellogg on Marketing*, ed. D. Iacobucci (New York: John Wiley & Sons, 2001), 61.

19. http://www.focushope.com (accessed July 10, 2008).

▼ CHAPTER 10

1. http://www.london2012.com (accessed September 2, 2008).

2. http://www.petfinder.com (accessed September 5, 2008).

3. http://www.reuters.com/article/pressRelease/idUS126101+08-May-2008+PRN20080508 (accessed September 10, 2008).

▼ CHAPTER 11

1. U.S. Department of State's Bureau of International Information Programs, "A Service Economy," in *USA Economy in Brief*, http://usinfo.state.gov/products/pubs/economy-in-brief/page3.html (accessed August 20, 2008).

2. P. Kotler and G. Armstrong, *Principles of Marketing* (Upper Saddle River: Prentice Hall, 2008), 239–240.

3. "Amazon.com Lists Best-Selling Products," *Puget Sound Business Journal*, December 28, 2007, http://www.bizjournals.com/seattle/stories/2007/12/24/daily16.html?ana=from_rss (accessed August 22, 2008); "The Big Ideas behind Nintendo's Wii," *BusinessWeek*, November 16, 2006, http:// http://www.businessweek.com/technology/content/nov2006/tc20061116_750580.htm (accessed August 22, 2008); B. Bremner, "Will Nintendo's Wii Strategy Score?" *BusinessWeek*, September 20, 2006, http://www.businessweek.com/globalbiz/content/sep2006/gb20060920_163780.htm (accessed August 22, 2008); "Press Release: Nintendo Wii Is Market Leader in Home Console Business," VGChartz.com, August 22, 2007, http://news.vgchartz.com/news.php?id=508 (accessed October 1, 2008).

4. M. Solomon, G. Marshall, and E. Stuart, *Marketing* (Upper Saddle River: Prentice Hall, 2008), 238–241.

5. http://www.dell.com/home/laptops?~ck=mn (accessed August 21, 2008).

6. P. Kotler and G. Armstrong, *Principles of Marketing* (Upper Saddle River, New Jersey: Prentice Hall, 2008), 220–221.

7. Wrigley Company, 2007 *Annual Report*, http://library.corporateir.net/library/92/927/92701/items/278516/Wrigley2007AR.pdf (accessed August 21, 2008).

8. M. Solomon, G. Marshall, and E. Stuart, *Marketing* (Upper Saddle River: Prentice Hall, 2008), 244–245.

9. Computer Sciences Corporation (CSC), "Improving Product Success through Effective, Focused Speed to Market," http://www.csc.com/solutions/managementconsulting/knowledgelibrary/2115.shtml (accessed August 20, 2008).

10. P. Kotler and G. Armstrong, *Principles of Marketing* (Upper Saddle River: Prentice Hall, 2008), 254–263.

11. J. Quelch, *Cases in Product Management* (Richard D. Irwin, Inc., 1995), 3–42.

12. P. Fisk, *Marketing Genius* (West Sussex: Capstone, 2006), 214–215.

13. DuPont Company, Winners of the 19th DuPont awards for packaging innovation, http://www2.dupont.com/Packaging/en_US/news_events/19th_dupont_packaging_award_winners.html (accessed August 20, 2008).

14. Target Company, ClearRx, http://sites.target.com/site/en/health/page.jsp?contentId=PRD03-003977 (accessed August 21, 2008).

15. P. Kotler and G. Armstrong, *Principles of Marketing* (Upper Saddle River: Prentice Hall, 2008), 229–231.

16. The Hershey Company, *2007 Annual Report to Stockholders/Form 10-K*, February 19, 2008, 1–4.

17. J. Useem, "Internet Defense Strategy: Cannibalize Yourself," *Fortune*, September 6, 1999, http://money.cnn.com/magazines/fortune/fortune_archive/1999/09/06/265284/index.htm (accessed August 20, 2008).

18. M. Solomon, G. Marshall, and E. Stuart, *Marketing* (Upper Saddle River: Prentice Hall, 2008), 260–261.

19. K. Clancy and P. Krieg, "Product Life Cycle: A Dangerous Idea," *BrandWeek*, March 1, 2004, http://www.copernicusmarketing.com/about/product_life_cycle.shtml (accessed August 20, 2008).

▼ CHAPTER 12

1. R. Heinlein, *The Moon Is a Harsh Mistress* (G.P. Putnam's Sons, 1966).

2. http://www.apple.com (accessed November 1, 2008);
C. Sorrel, "Apple's iPod Strategy: Aggressive Prices, Overwhelming Feature," *Wired Magazine*, September 6, 2007, http://www.wired.com/gadgets/portablemusic/news/2007/09/ipod_follow (accessed September 10, 2008).
E. Hesseldahl, "Are There Problems with iPod Sales?" *BusinessWeek*, February 22, 2008, http://www.businessweek.com/technology/ByteOfTheApple/blog/archives/2008/02/is_there_troubl.html (accessed September 10, 2008).

3. Air Transport Association, *Quarterly Cost Index: U.S. Passenger Airlines*, September 9, 2008, http://www.airlines.org/economics/finance/Cost+Index.htm (accessed September 9, 2008).

4. P. Farris, N. Bendle, P. Pfeifer, and D. Reibsten, *Marketing Metrics* (Wharton School Publishing, 2006).

5. S. Maxwell, *The Price Is Wrong* (Hoboken: John Wiley & Sons, 2008), 41–44.

6. J. Manning, *Got milk? Marketing by Association* (American Society of Association Executives, July 2006).

7. M. Sodhi and N. Sodhi, *Six Sigma Pricing* (FT Press, 2007).

8. R. Baker, *Pricing on Purpose* (Hoboken: John Wiley & Sons, 2006).

9. "Hasbro Fined for Price Fixing," *CNN.com*, http://www.edition.cnn.com/2002/BUSINESS/11/29/uk.hasbro.fine/index.html (accessed September 10, 2008).

10. http://www.applebees.com (accessed November 1, 2008); http://www.danielnyc.com/dbistro (accessed November 1, 2008).

11. http://www.amazon.com (accessed September 17, 2008).

12. R. Baker, *Pricing on Purpose* (Hoboken: John Wiley & Sons, 2006).

13. J. Cooper, "Prices and Price Dispersion in Online and Offline Markets for Contact Lenses," (working paper, Bureau of Economics, April 2006).

14. I. Sinha, "Cost Transparency: The Net's Real Threat to Prices and Brands," *Harvard Business Review* (March–April 2008).

15. I. Peel, *The Rough Guide to eBay* (London: Penguin, 2006); eBay, *2007 eBay annual report*, 2008, http://www.eBay.com; http://www.shareholder.com/visitors/dynamicdoc/document.cfm?CompanyID= ebay&DocumentID=2286&PIN=&Page=4&Zoom=1x (accessed September 10, 2008).

16. S. Coomes, "The Big Cheese," *Nation's Restaurant News* 34 (January 28, 2008).

▼ CHAPTER 13

1. P. Kotler and K. Keller, *A Framework for Marketing Management*, 4th ed. (Upper Saddle River: Prentice Hall, 2008).

2. Ibid.

3. H. Italie, "Potter, At the Speed of Light," *Washington Post*, July 26, 2007, http://www.washingtonpost.com/wp-dyn/content/article/2007/07/26/AR2007072601339_pf.html (accessed August 25, 2008); J. Trachtenberg and J. De Avila, "Mischief Unmanaged," *Wall Street Journal*, July 19, 2007; D. Foust, "Harry Potter and the Logistical Nightmare," *BusinessWeek*, August 6, 2007.

4. M. Hugos and C. Thomas, *Supply Chain Management in the Retail Industry* (Hoboken: John Wiley & Sons, 2006).

5. M. Solomon, G. Marshall, and E. Stuart, *Marketing* (Upper Saddle River, New Jersey: Prentice Hall, 2008).

6. Ibid.

7. M. Hugos, *Essentials of Supply Chain Management*, 2nd ed. (Hoboken: John Wiley & Sons, 2006).

8. A. O'Connell, "Improve Your Return on Returns," *Harvard Business Review* (November 2007).

9. P. Kotler and G. Armstrong, *Principles of Marketing*, 12th ed. (Upper Saddle River, New Jersey: Prentice Hall, 2008).

10. M. Hugos and C. Thomas, *Supply Chain Management in the Retail Industry* (Hoboken: John Wiley & Sons, 2006).

11. D. Blanchard, *Supply Chain Management – Best Practices*. (Hoboken: John Wiley & Sons, 2007).

12. M. Hugos, *Essentials of Supply Chain Management*, 2nd ed. (Hoboken: John Wiley & Sons, 2006), 18–20.

13. D. Blanchard, *Supply Chain Management – Best Practices* (Hoboken: John Wiley & Sons, 2007).

14. Ibid.

15. M. Hugos and C. Thomas, *Supply Chain Management in the Retail Industry* (Hoboken: John Wiley & Sons, 2006).

16. D. Blanchard, *Supply Chain Management – Best Practices* (Hoboken: John Wiley & Sons, 2007).

17. American Marketing Association, *Resource library – Dictionary*, http://www.marketingpower.com/_layouts/Dictionary.aspx?dLetter=W (accessed September 5, 2008).

18. M. Solomon, G. Marshall, and E. Stuart, *Marketing* (Upper Saddle River: Prentice Hall, 2008).

19. D. Blanchard, *Supply Chain Management – Best Practices* (Hoboken: John Wiley & Sons, 2007).

20. Ibid.

21. Ibid.

22. U.S. Census Bureau. *Quarterly Retail E-commerce Sales – 4th Quarter 2007*; http://www.census.gov/mrts/www/data/html/07Q4.html (accessed September 9, 2008).

23. *LVMH 2007 Annual Report,* http://www.sephora.com (accessed November 1, 2008), 49–50; J. Naughton, "It's Bath Time for Sephora," *WWD*, October 19, 2007, 6; M. Prior, "Sephora Details 10-year Growth into Superstore," *WWD*, April 6, 2007, 193; M. Prior, "Specialty Chains: Rising Architects of Beauty," *WWD*, July, 7, 2006, 192.

24. Internal Revenue Service, *Retail Industry Audit Guide*, August 2005, http://www.irs.gov/pub/irs-mssp/retail_industry__102005_final.pdf (accessed September 9, 2008).

25. U.S. Census Bureau, *Statistical abstract of the United States – 2008*, http://www.census.gov/prod/2007pubs/08abstract/domtrade.pdf (statistical abstract of the United States).

26. P. Kotler and G. Armstrong, *Principles of Marketing*, (Upper Saddle River: Prentice Hall, 2008).

27. Bureau of Labor Statistics, *Wholesale Trade – Employment Statistics*, 2000, http://stats.bls.gov/oco/cg/pdf/cgs026.pdf (accessed September 9, 2008).

28. M. Solomon, G. Marshall, and E. Stuart, *Marketing* (Upper Saddle River: Prentice Hall, 2008).

▼ CHAPTER 14

1. "Dove to Introduce 'Real Beauty' Web TV Channel," *Marketing*, April 16, 2008, 3; J. Neff, "Soft Soap: In Its Campaign for Real Beauty, Dove Tells Women That They Are Beautiful As They Are," *Advertising Age*, September 24, 2007, 1; "Digital Branding: Utilising User-Generated Content," *New Media Age*, May 3, 2007.

2. P. Patton, "Looking into Harley's Heart of Darkness," *New York Times*, April 20, 2008; http://www.harley-davidson.com (accessed September 13, 2008).

3. "Heinz Names Winner of Consumer Generated Ad Contest," *Promo*, April 30, 2008, http://promomagazine.com/contests/news/heinz_names_winner_ consumer_generated_ad_contest_0430; E.A. Sullivan, "H.J. Heinz Company," *Marketing News*, February 1, 2008, 10.

4. J. Stilson, "Chinese Control of Olympics Offers Opportunities, Challenges to OOH Vendors," *MediaWeek*, July 28, 2008, http://www.mediaweek.com/mw/content_display/news/out-there/traditional/e3i0d79bda05708d38799f5a10c9f761d92.

5. C. Gibbs, "Athletic Shoe Makers Discover Mobile Advertising a Good Fit," *RCR Wireless News*, July 21, 2008; T. Lemke, "Adidas Teams Up in Ad Campaign," *Washington Times*, February 5, 2008.

6. M. Wnek, "In Praise of Modern Complexity: Forgoing Simplicity, Geico Doesn't Play to the Lowest Common Denominator," *Adweek*, March 31, 2008, 18; E. Newman, "Insurers No Longer Paying Premium for Advertising," *Brandweek*, April 21, 2008, 7.

7. K. Maddox, "Vertical Value," *B to B*, June 23, 2008, 4.

8. "Sponsorship Form: The Value of Sport to Other Kinds of Business," *Economist*, July 31, 2008, http://www.economist.com/specialreports/displaystory.cfm?story_id=11825607.

9. J. Neff, "Will P&G Use Canada as Testing Ground?" *Advertising Age*, May 19, 2008, 41.

10. A. Young, "2008 Chevy Malibu vs. Honda Accord," *Advertising Age*, August 18, 2008, http://adage.com/mediaworks/article?article_id=130319; T.A. Peter, "Automakers Put Bloggers in the Driver's Seat," *Christian Science Monitor*, January 17, 2008.

11. L. Petrecca, "Wal-Mart Takes In-Store TV to the Next Level," *USA Today*, March 28, 2007, http://www.usatoday.com/money/industries/retail/2007-03-28-walmarttv-tim-mcgraw_N.htm.

12. D. Hajewski, "Mattel Leader Aims to Keep Trust," *Milwaukee Journal Sentinel*, October 26, 2007, http://www.jsonline.com/story/index.aspx?id=679105; J. Haberkorn, "Mattel Admits Fault in Recall," *Washington Times*, September 13, 2007.

13. D. Dilworth, "Arby's Coupons Going Mobile," *DM News*, August 25, 2008, http://www.dmnews.com/Arbys-coupons-going-mobile/article/115847.

14. M. Chen, "Guidelines May Curb Drug Companies' Freebies," *Herald-Sun*, July 23, 2008; M. Healy, "Sold on Drugs: Under the Influence: Savvy Marketing Whets Our Appetite for Prescriptions," *Los Angeles Times*, August 6, 2007.

15. "Sponsorship Form: The Value of Sport to Other Kinds of Business," *Economist*, July 31, 2008, http://www.economist.com/specialreports/displaystory.cfm?story_id=11825607.
16. M. Littman, "Creating a Buzz," *Chain Leader*, April 2008, 18–19.
17. L. de Moraes, "Super Bowl's Big Score: 97.5 Million Viewers," *Washington Post*, February 5, 2008; J. Kirk, "New Deal Keeps Budweiser Name Before Eyes of Wrigley Visitors," *Chicago Tribune*, July 4, 2008.

▼ CHAPTER 15

1. *Making the Sale* (Boston, MA: Harvard Business School Press, 2008).
2. http://www.bls.gov, U.S. Department of Labor Statistics, 2007.
3. M. Solomon, G. Marshall, and E. Stuart, *Marketing: Real People, Real Choices* (Upper Saddle River: Prentice Hall, 2006).
4. A. Sacco, "Inside Pitney Bowes Choice for a Mobile CRM/ERP Solution," April 28, 2008, http://www.cio.com (accessed September 15, 2008).
5. M. Solomon, G. Marshall, and E. Stuart, *Marketing: Real People, Real Choices* (Upper Saddle River: Prentice Hall, 2006).
6. A. Barrett, "Manage Your Sales Reps Better," *BusinessWeek*, http://www.businessweek.com, June 20, 2008 (accessed September 14, 2008).
7. M. Solomon, G. Marshall, and E. Stuart, *Marketing: Real People, Real Choices* (Upper Saddle River: Prentice Hall, 2006).
8. L. Jakobson, "MetLife Rethinks Recognition," http://www.salesandmarketing.com, September 8, 2008 (accessed September 14, 2008).
9. http://www.the-dma.org (accessed September 12, 2008).
10. Ibid.
11. Internet World Stats, June 30, 2008, http://www.internetworldstats.com (accessed September 12, 2008).
12. City of Chicago, http://www.cityofchicago.org (accessed September 12, 2008).
13. "History of the Sears Catalog," http://www.searsarchives.com (accessed September 12, 2008).
14. http://www.dictionary.com (accessed September 12, 2008).
15. L. Lee, "Catalogs, Catalogs Everywhere," *BusinessWeek*, December 4, 2006, http://www.businessweek.com, (accessed September 15, 2008).
16. "Direct Mail Tries to Go Green. No, Really," *New York Times*, http://www.newyorktimes.com (accessed September 14, 2008).
17. J. Larson, "From the Inside Out," September 15, 2008, http://www.msnbc.com (accessed September 15, 2008).
18. F. Defino Jr., "Creating the Best Personalized Landing Page," September 3, 2008, http://www.salesandmarketing.com (accessed September 13, 2008).
19. http://www.the-dma.org (accessed September 12, 2008).
20. http://www.ftc.gov (accessed September 12, 2008).

▼ CHAPTER 16

1. *TNS Media Intelligence Reports U.S. Advertising Expenditures Grew 0.2 Percent in 2007*, TNS Media Intelligence, March 25, 2008, http://www.tnsglobal.com (accessed September 12, 2008).
2. S. Olehmacher, "Americans Media Use Rising," December 15, 2006, *FoxNews.com*, http://www.foxnews.com/wires/2006Dec15/0,4670,MediaUse,00.html (accessed September 13, 2008).
3. http://www.Captivate.com (accessed November 1, 2008).
4. S. Berg, "Advertising in the World of New Media," in *Kellogg on Advertising & Media*, ed. B. Calder (Hoboken: John Wiley & Sons, 2008).
5. http://www.totalmedia.co.uk/case_studies/isreal_tourism.html (accessed November 1, 2008).
6. *TNS Media Intelligence Reports U.S. Advertising Expenditures Grew 0.2 Percent in 2007*, TNS Media Intelligence, March 25, 2008, http://www.tnsglobal.com (accessed September 13, 2008).
7. P. Kotler and G. Armstrong, *Principles of Marketing* (Upper Saddle River: Prentice Hall, 2008), 436.
8. *The Nielsen Company Issues Top Ten U.S. lists for 2007*, Nielsen Media Research, December 11, 2007, http://www.nielsen.com (accessed September 14, 2008).
9. P. Farris, N. Bendle, P. Pfeifer, and D. Reibstein, *Marketing Metrics: 50+ Metrics Every Executive Should Master* (Upper Saddle River: Wharton School Publishing, 2007), 275.
10. S. Berg, "Advertising in the World of New Media," in *Kellogg on Advertising & Media*, ed. B. Calder (Hoboken: J. Wiley & Sons, 2008).
11. L. Moses, "Best Use of Print," *ADWEEK*, June 16, 2008.
12. *Key News Audiences Now Blend Online and Traditional Sources*, August 17, 2008, http://people-press.org/report/444/news-media (accessed September 15, 2008).
13. D. Oulette, "*Unfit to Print*," September 24, 2007, http://www.Mediaweek.com (accessed November 1, 2008).
14. J. Sissors and R. Baron, *Advertising Media Planning*, 6th ed. (New York: McGraw-Hill, 2002), 342–343.
15. L. Miles, "*Out of Sight*," September 24, 2007, http://www.Mediaweek.com (accessed November 1, 2008).
16. S. Berg, "Advertising in the World of New Media," in *Kellogg on Advertising & Media*, ed. B. Calder (Hoboken: John Wiley & Sons, 2008).
17. "*Future of Media Report*," July 2007, Future Exploration Network.
18. M. Shields, "*Digital Destiny*," September 24, 2007, http://www.Mediaweek.com (accessed November 1, 2008).
19. M. Shields, "*Best Use of Mobile*," *ADWEEK*, (June 16, 2008).
20. J.M. Lehu, *Branded Entertainment*, (London: Kogan, 2006), 254.
21. J.M. Lehu, *Branded Entertainment*, (London: Kogan, 2006), 142–143.
22. J. Sissors and R. Baron, *Advertising Media Planning*, 6th ed.(New York: McGraw-Hill, 2006), 215.
23. R. Lane, K. King, and J. Rusell, *Kleppner's Advertising Procedure* (Upper Saddle River: Prentice Hall, 2008), 254.
24. R. Briggs and G. Stuart, *What Sticks* (Chicago: Kaplan, 2006), 201–208.

▼ CHAPTER 17

1. N. Borden, "A Note on the Concept of the Marketing Mix," in *Managerial Marketing: Perspectives and Viewpoints*, ed. Eugene J. Kelly and William Lazer (Homewood, Illinois: Richard D. Irwin, 1958), 272–275.
2. E.J. McCarthy, *Basic Marketing: A Managerial Approach* (Homewood, IL: Irwin, 1960).
3. S. Baker, "Why Twitter Matters," May 15, 2008, http://www.businessweek.com/technology/content/may2008/tc20080514_269697.htm (accessed August 16, 2008).
4. http://www.cadillac.com (accessed August 17, 2008).
5. http://www.fiskateers.com (accessed September 10, 2008); http://www.fiskars.com (accessed September 10, 2008).
6. "Unilever's Axe Deodorant, Rheingold Beer, and Walt Disney's Buena Vista Pictures Win Business 2.0 Sweet Spot Awards(™)," *Business Wire*, May 22, 2003 (accessed September 12, 2008).
7. B. Viveiros, "Gold Standard: Godiva Revamps its Marketing Strategy to Attract a Younger Audience," http://chiefmarketer.com/cm_plus/godiva_marketing_strategy/ (accessed September 15, 2008); D. Zammit, "Chocolate Meets Fashion in New Godiva Effort," *Adweek*, September 13, 2004, http://www.godiva.com/mobile (accessed September 15, 2008).
8. R. Arnett, "The Big Picture," *Management & Applications* 14, no. 4 (2002): 33.
9. D. Wehmeyer, "Testing...Testing...1,2,3,...," *Marketing News* 36, no. 23 (2002): 14, 16.
10. D. Schwartz, "Concurrent Marketing Analysis: A Multi-agent Model for Product, Price, Place, and Promotion," *Marketing Intelligence & Planning* 18, no. 1 (2000): 24–29.
11. J. English, "The Four 'Ps' of Marketing Are Dead," *Marketing Health Services* 20, no. 2 (2000): 20–22.; N. Coviello and R. Brodie, "Contemporary Marketing Practices of Consumer and Business-to-Business Firms: How Different Are They?" *Journal of Business & Industrial Marketing* 16, no. 5 (2001): 382–400.
12. G. Runciman, "Marketing Ingredients," *Supply Management* 4, no. 20 (1999): 47.

13. B.H. Booms and M.J. Bitner, "Marketing Strategies and Organization Structures for Service Firms," ed. J.H. Donnelly and W.R. George, *Marketing of Services*, American Marketing Association, (Chicago, IL): 47–51.

14. Runciman, G. "Marketing ingredients," *Supply Management*, 1999, 4(20), 47.

15. Ibid.

16. N. Coviello, R. Brodie, and P. Danaher, "How Firms Relate to Their Markets: An Empirical Examination of Contemporary Marketing Practices," *Journal of Marketing* 66, no. 3 (2002): 33–46.

17. Ibid.

18. D. Wehmeyer, "Testing...Testing...1,2,3,...," *Marketing News* 36, no. 23 (2002): 14, 16.

19. G. Ambach, "Measuring Long-term Effects in Marketing," *Marketing Research* 12, no. 2 (2000): 20–27.

20. D. Wehmeyer, "Testing...Testing...1,2,3,...," *Marketing News* 36, no. 23 (2002): 14, 16.

21. D. Brady, "Making Marketing Measure Up," *BusinessWeek*, December 13, 2004, http://www.businessweek.com/magazine/content/04_50/b3912109.html (accessed September 14, 2008); http://www.homedept.com (accessed September 14, 2008).

22. "It's PR Time for Miller," *TelevisionWeek* 23, no. 48 (2003): 15.

Glossary

4 Cs are a classification of a marketing mix that includes customer value, cost, convenience, and communication. **(p. 213)**

4 Ps are the most common classification of a marketing mix and consist of product, price, place, and promotion. **(p. 7, 211)**

7 Ps are a classification of a marketing mix that includes product, price, place, promotion, people, physical evidence, and process. **(p. 215)**

 A

Actual product is the combination of tangible and intangible attributes that delivers the core benefits of the product. **(p. 122)**

Ad trafficking is the procedure for delivering finished ads to the correct media firms for placement. **(p. 203)**

Advertising is the paid, nonpersonal communication of a marketing message by an identified sponsor through mass media. **(p. 172)**

Advertising media (or **"media"**) is the collection of mediums (physical or electronic) used to carry marketing communications. **(p. 195)**

Antidumping laws are laws designed to prevent predatory pricing. **(p. 142)**

Antitrust law is a catchall phrase for federal legislation meant to prohibit anticompetitive actions on the part of manufacturers, wholesalers, or resellers. **(p. 140)**

Applied research attempts to answer questions related to practical problems. **(p. 70)**

Attitude is a state of readiness, based on experience that influences a response to something. **(p. 60)**

Attributes are the unique characteristics of each product, including product features and options, product design, brand name, quality, logos, identifiers, packaging, and warranty. **(p. 121)**

Auctions are markets in which buyers and sellers engage in a process of offer and counteroffer until a price acceptable to both parties is reached. **(p. 144)**

Augmented product is additional services or benefits that enhance the ownership of the actual product. **(p. 122)**

 B

Bait-and-switch pricing occurs when a firm advertises a low price on a desirable product but, in an attempt to trade customers up to more expensive items, it does not make a good faith effort to carry sufficient quantities of that product. **(p. 141)**

balanced scorecard, the is a management system that relates a business's vision and mission to individual business activities. **(p. 26)**

Banner advertising is the placement of advertisements (called banners) onto various Web sites that link to the sponsor's Web page. **(p. 199)**

Bar codes (or **barcodes**) are unique product identification codes used to monitor inventory. **(p. 158)**

Behavioral segmentation allocates consumers into groups, based on their knowledge, attitudes, uses, or responses to a product or service. **(p. 97)**

Behavioral targeting optimizes the online advertising potential for brands. **(p. 99)**

Belief is a sense of truth about something. **(p. 60)**

Benefits, realized through product attributes, define the utility (or usefulness) of a product for the customer. **(p. 121)**

Boycotts happen when consumers refuse to do business with a company or nation in order to signal their disapproval of its actions and encourage change. **(p. 35)**

Brand is a promise to deliver specific benefits associated with products or services to consumers. **(p. 3, 83)**

Brand alliance is a relationship, short of a merger, that is formed by two or more businesses to create market opportunities that would not have existed without the alliance. **(p. 88)**

Brand architecture is the naming and organizing of brands within a broader portfolio. **(p. 87)**

Brand equity is the power of a brand, through creation of a distinct image, to influence customer behavior. **(p. 84)**

Brand extension takes an existing brand into a new category. **(p. 89)**

Brand knowledge is the set of associations that consumers hold in memory regarding the brand's features, benefits, users, perceived quality, and overall attitude as a result of prior brand marketing activities. **(p. 84)**

Brand loyalty is the extent to which a consumer repeatedly purchases a given brand. **(p. 85)**

Brand management is the overall coordination of a brand's equities to create long-term brand growth through overseeing marketing mix strategies. **(p. 90)**

Brand manager is the person responsible for managing the marketing activities associated with a brand. **(p. 90)**

Brand personality consists of characteristics that make a brand unique, much like human personality. **(p. 87)**

Brand position statement is a summary of what a brand offers to the market. **(p. 102)**

Brand positioning is the location that a brand occupies in the marketplace relative to competitors. **(p. 87)**

Brand protection involves securing the brand's inherent value, including its intellectual property. **(p. 90)**

Brand strategy is the process where the offer is positioned in the consumer's mind to produce a perception of advantage. **(p. 88)**

Brand stretching is extending a brand to new products, services, or markets. **(p. 84)**

Brand valuation is the process of quantifying the financial benefit that results from owning a brand. **(p. 84)**

Branded entertainment is the integration of brands or brand messages into entertainment media, for example, films, television, novels, and songs. **(p. 201)**

Break-even point is the volume or price at which a company's revenue for a product exactly equals its fixed cost. **(p. 137)**

Breaking bulk refers to the process of reducing large product shipments into smaller ones that are more suitable for individual retailers or companies. **(p. 158)**

Broadcast media include network TV, cable TV, and radio. **(p. 197)**

Bundling refers to the practice of marketing two or more products and/or services in a single package. **(p. 89)**

Business analysis is the process of validating that the new product will meet all sales and profit objectives. **(p. 124)**

Business markets include individuals or organizations that are potential or actual buyers of goods and services that are used in, or in support of, the production of other products or services that are supplied to others. **(p. 17)**

Business mission is a statement that identifies the purpose of a business and what makes that business different from others. **(p. 24)**

Business objective is something that a business attempts to achieve in support of an overarching strategy. **(p. 24)**

Business plan is a written document that defines the operational and financial objectives of a business over a particular time and how the business plans to accomplish those objectives. **(pp. 23, 107)**

Business planning is a decision process for people and businesses to manage systems to achieve an objective. **(p. 23)**

Business-to-business, also referred to as **B2B**, involves the sales of products and services from one business to another. **(p. 17)**

Business vision is a statement in a strategic plan that identifies an idealized picture of a future state a business is aiming to achieve. **(p. 24)**

Buyclasses are major classifications of business buying situations. **(p. 17)**

 C

Cable television refers to TV broadcasts using cables or satellite dishes. **(p. 197)**

Call to action is the response that a marketer wants a consumer to take as a result of receiving a direct-mail communication. **(p. 189)**

Campaign is how a company seeks to influence its target audience over time, using a consistent communication theme and varying message creativity and delivery. **(p. 172)**

CAN-SPAM Act of 2003 (Controlling the Assault of Non-Solicited Pornography and Marketing Act) is the law that requires e-mail marketers to abide by certain requirements when e-mailing consumers. **(p. 190)**

Cannibalization is the loss of sales of an existing product within a portfolio to a new product in the same portfolio. **(p. 89)**

Carrier is the entity that physically transports goods from shipper to consignee. **(p. 157)**

Cash-and-carry wholesaler provides products for small businesses that buy at the wholesaler's location and self-transport. **(p. 161)**

Cash Cows are products or services with high market share and low growth opportunities. **(p. 25)**

Cash discount is a percentage or fixed amount off the quoted price of an item, and is given when a customer pays in cash. **(p. 146)**

Catalog is a printed direct-mail piece that showcases an assortment of products or services offered by a company. **(p. 188)**

Category management involves the management of multiple brands in a product line. **(p. 90)**

Category manager is the person responsible for managing a product line that may contain one or more brands. **(p. 90)**

Census is a survey that collects responses for each member of the population. **(p. 76)**

Channel is a system with few or many steps in which products flow from businesses to consumers while payments flow from consumers to businesses. **(p. 84)**

Channel conflict occurs when two or more channel members disagree. **(p. 154)**

Channel intermediary is a channel member between a producer and customer. **(p. 151)**

Channel leader is a firm with sufficient power over other channel members to take a leadership role in the channel. **(p. 154)**

Channel strategy describes the levels, organization, and distribution intensity of a marketing channel. **(p. 152)**

Channel switching is creating new product distribution or moving the distribution flow of products from one distribution channel to another. **(p. 84)**

Circulation is the number of published and distributed copies of a magazine. **(p. 198)**

Classified advertising is the online version of traditional classified ads. **(p. 200)**

Clickthrough fees are the amount one online entity charges another online entity for passing along a Web user who clicks an ad or link. **(p. 145)**

Close is the part of the selling process in which the salesperson asks for an order. **(p. 184)**

Closed-ended question is a question that has specific survey answer choices available to respondents. **(p. 75)**

Clutter is a qualitative assessment of the degree to which a particular media vehicle contains too many ads competing for attention. **(p. 197)**

Co-branding is the collaboration of multiple brands in the marketing of one specific product. **(p. 88)**

Coding is the numbering of the answer choices for each survey question. **(p. 75)**

Cognitive age, also referred to as subjective age, is the age that a person feels. **(p. 59)**

Cold calling is the act of contacting a prospect with whom the salesperson does not have a previous relationship, in order to identify potential customers. **(p. 183)**

Commercialization is the process of launching a new product in the marketplace. **(p. 124)**

Commission is the part of or all of a salesperson's income that is based on the amount of sales or profit delivered in a given time frame. **(p. 186)**

Commission merchant is a wholesaler who receives commissions on the sales price of products. **(p. 160)**

Competitive bidding involves suppliers in a bid process that receive identical RFQs and then return quotes in secret to the buyer. **(p. 141)**

Competitive environment includes those factors that relate to the nature, quantity, and potential actions of competitors. **(p. 15)**

Competitive intelligence involves the systematic tracking of competitive actions and plans and is a significant activity within a business. **(p. 77)**

Components are finished products companies employ to manufacture their own products, for example, microchips or engines. **(p. 123)**

Concept change is an advanced, breakthrough innovation that changes everything. **(p. 125)**

Concept development is the process of concretely defining the features and benefits of the new product. **(p. 124)**

Consignee is the receiver of goods being distributed. **(p. 157)**

Consultative selling is when salespeople focus on solving their customer's or prospect's problems, rather than focus on selling products or services. **(p. 181)**

Consumer behavior is the dynamic interaction of affect and cognition, behavior, and the environment in which human beings conduct the exchange aspects of their lives. **(p. 57)**

Consumer decision-making process is the steps that consumers take to identify and evalute choice options. **(p. 58)**

Consumer-generated media (CGM), such as blogs or video Web sites, allow ordinary people to create and send their own messages. **(p. 195)**

Consumer-influence strategies are strategies for engaging consumers and influencing how they think, feel, and act toward a brand or market offering through the use of marketing communication. **(p. 167)**

Consumer insight is perceived meanings of data collected from the study of consumer behavior. **(p. 69)**

Consumer market insight is an in-depth understanding of customer behavior that is more qualitative than quantitative. **(p. 69)**

Consumer markets include individuals and households that are potential or actual buyers of goods and services that assist in further production only indirectly or incidentally, if at all. **(p. 16)**

Consumer orientation reflects a business focus on satisfying unmet consumer needs and wants. **(p. 6)**

Consumer problem solving is how someone comes to a conclusion about a situation. This is determined by what kind of a decision a consumer is facing. **(p. 64)**

Consumer products are products that directly fulfill the desires of consumers and are not intended to assist in the manufacture of other products. **(p. 16, 124)**

Consumer sales promotion aims to get consumers (including business customers) to try a product or buy it again. **(p. 175)**

Consumer's surplus occurs when a consumer purchases a product or service at a price less than the utility of the product or service. **(p. 16)**

Consumerism is the organized efforts on the part of consumer groups or governments to improve the rights and power of buyers in relation to sellers. **(p. 35)**

Contact efficiency is the efficiency gained in terms of a reduction in the number of contacts required through the use of channel intermediaries. **(p. 151)**

Context change is when an existing product or service is taken into a new context or market. **(p. 125)**

Contract manufacturers are manufacturing firms in a foreign country that a company hires to manufacture products on its behalf. **(p. 42)**

Contribution margin is the difference between a product's price and its variable cost. **(p. 137)**

Convenience products are products that are purchased frequently with little or no shopping effort, for example, grocery staples, paper products, and candy. **(p. 122)**

Convenience store is a small store that offers convenience products and often is open 24 hours a day. **(p. 160)**

Cookies are small files containing certain personal information that are sent from Web servers to a consumer's computer to be accessed the next time a consumer visits a particular Web site. **(p. 78)**

Core benefits are the fundamental product benefits the customer receives from a product. **(p. 122)**

Corporate public relations is how management evaluates and shapes or reshapes long-term public opinion of the company. **(p. 174)**

Corporate social responsibility (CSR) is a philosophy that encourages decision makers to take into account the social consequences of their business actions. **(p. 39)**

Cosmetic change is an evolutionary change to an existing product or service. **(p. 125)**

Cost-based pricing establishes a price based on the cost to manufacture a product or deliver a service. **(p. 137)**

Cost-plus pricing adds a fixed amount to the cost of each product or service sufficient to earn a desired profit. **(p. 137)**

Cost transparency is the ability of consumers to understand a product's actual cost. **(p. 144)**

Counterfeiting is the unauthorized copying of products, packaging, or other intellectual property of a registered brand. **(p. 90)**

CPM (or cost-per-thousand) is a metric that calculates the cost for any media vehicle to deliver one thousand impressions among a group of target customers. **(p. 197)**

Creating assortments is the process of collecting an assortment of products into a single shipment to a destination. **(p. 158)**

Cross-docking is a warehousing technique that minimizes holding costs by unloading products at a warehouse or distribution center and then reloading them almost immediately for transport. **(p. 158)**

Cue is an environmental stimulus that influences a particular action. **(p. 60)**

Culture refers to the shared values, beliefs, and preferences of a particular society. **(p. 34, 62)**

Currency exchange rates are variable rates that specify the price of one currency in terms of the price of another. **(p. 142)**

Customer-based brand equity is the differential effect that brand knowledge has on the customer response to marketing efforts. **(p. 85)**

Customer lifetime value includes the projected sales revenue and profitability that a customer could provide to a firm. **(p. 4, 50)**

Customer loyalty is the degree to which a customer will select a particular brand when a purchase from that product category is being considered. **(p. 50)**

Customer relationship management (CRM) is the activities that are used to establish, develop, and maintain customer relationships. **(p. 4, 52)**

Customer relationships are created when businesses and consumers interact through a sales transaction of a product or service and continue based on ongoing interaction between the business and the consumer. **(p. 4)**

Customer retention is the degree to which a customer remains a customer once a relationship has been developed. **(p. 50)**

Customer satisfaction is the degree to which a product meets or exceeds customer expectations. **(p. 48)**

Customer value (customer perceived value) is the difference between the benefits a customer receives and the total cost incurred from acquiring, using, and disposing of a product. **(p. 47)**

 D

Data mining is the statistical analysis of large databases seeking to discover hidden pieces of information. **(p. 53)**

Deceptive pricing occurs when a price is meant to intentionally mislead or deceive customers. **(p. 141)**

Decline stage is the stage at which the demand for a product falls due to changes in customer preferences. Sales and profits eventually fall to zero. **(p. 128)**

Demand is the financial capacity to buy what one wants. **(p. 3)**

Demand curve (or **demand schedule**) charts the projected sales for a product or service for any price customers are willing to pay. **(p. 138)**

Demographic segmentation divides the market into groups, based on variables such as age, gender, family size, family life cycle, income, occupation, education, religion, ethnicity, generation, nationality, and sexual orientation. **(p. 96)**

Demographics are characteristics of human population used to identify markets. **(p. 15, 202)**

Department store is a store that offers several product lines across multiple categories. **(p. 160)**

Descriptive research is a marketing research design that is used to describe marketing variables by answering who, what, when, where, and how questions. **(p. 72)**

Differentiated marketing separates and targets several different market segments with a different product or service geared to each segment. **(p. 99)**

Diffusion of innovations is a theory concerning how populations adopt innovations over time. **(p. 129)**

Digital brand strategy is a set of marketing activities that uses digital mediums to connect consumers to brands. **(p. 83)**

Direct channel (or **zero-level channel**) is a single channel member that produces and distributes a product or service. **(p. 151)**

Direct exporting occurs when a firm establishes its own overseas sales branches to export to a foreign country. **(p. 42)**

Direct investment occurs when a firm establishes its own foreign-based manufacturing operations and businesses. **(p. 42)**

Direct mail is a printed advertisement in the form of a postcard, letter, brochure, or product sample that is sent to consumers who are on a targeted mailing list. **(p. 188)**

Direct marketing is any communication addressed to a consumer that is designed to generate a response. **(p. 187)**

Direct-response advertising is a direct marketing approach that includes a specific offer and call to action for the consumer to immediately contact the marketer to purchase or inquire about the product. **(p. 189)**

Discontinuous innovations are new product ideas that change our everyday lives in dramatic ways. **(p. 125)**

Discount store is a store focused on selling low-priced merchandise. **(p. 160)**

Distribution is the process of delivering products and services to customers. **(p. 151)**

Distribution center (DC) is a large warehouse used to store a company's products. **(p. 158)**

Distribution intensity determines the number of outlets or locations where a product will be sold. **(p. 153)**

Divesting is the process of discontinuing the production and sale of a product. **(p. 129)**

Do Not Call Registry is a list of consumers who do not want to receive phone calls from telemarketers. Consumers can contact the Federal Trade Commission to be added to the Do Not Call Registry. **(p. 189)**

Do Not Mail List is the list of consumers who do not want to receive direct mail. Consumers can contact the Direct Marketing Association to be added to the Do Not Mail List. **(p. 190)**

Dogs are products or services with low relative market share in a low growth sector. **(p. 25)**

Drive is an internal stimulus that encourages action. **(p. 60)**

Drop shipper fills retail orders for products drop-shipped from a manufacturer. **(p. 161)**

DRTV (direct-response TV) is any kind of television commercial or home shopping television show that advertises a product or service and allows the viewer to purchase it directly. **(p. 189)**

Dual distribution (or **multichannel distribution**) is the use of two or more types of distribution. **(p. 153)**

Dynamic imaging is the process of systematically populating individual e-mails with products targeted specifically to each consumer, based on specific criteria such as behavior patterns, inventory, and other criteria. **(p. 189)**

Dynamic pricing (or **"smart" pricing**) is the practice of varying prices based on marketplace conditions. **(p. 144)**

 E

Early adopters are consumers who are more socially aware than innovators and consider the prestige or social implications of being seen using a new product. **(p. 129)**

Early majority are middle-class consumers who do not want to be the first, or the last, to try a new product. They look to the early adopters for direction about product innovations. **(p. 129)**

Economic environment includes those factors that influence consumer purchase ability and buying behavior. **(p. 15)**

Elastic refers to the situation in which price elasticity is greater than one or when demand is highly responsive to a change in price. **(p. 139)**

Electronic transport is a transportation mode used for electronic media. **(p. 157)**

Environmentalism is an organized movement of citizens, businesses, and government agencies to protect and improve our living environment. **(p. 36)**

Equipment is a group of products used in the everyday operation of a business, for example, factories and copy machines. **(p. 123)**

Ethics are a system of moral principles and values, as well as moral duties or obligations. **(p. 39)**

Ethnographic research is a type of observational research where trained researchers immerse themselves in a specific consumer environment. **(p. 72)**

Exaggerated claims are extravagant statements made in advertising, either explicitly or implicitly, that have no substantiation or reasonable basis in truth. **(p. 38)**

Exchange functions are activities that promote and enable transfer of ownership. **(p. 7)**

Exclusive distribution refers to the distribution of products in only a few locations. **(p. 153)**

Experience curve is an economic model that presumes costs will decline as production volume increases. **(p. 143)**

Experiential positioning is based on characteristics of the brands that stimulate sensory or emotional connections with customers. **(p. 101)**

Explanatory research is a marketing research design used to understand the relationship between independent and dependent variables. **(p. 72)**

Exploratory research is a marketing research design used to generate ideas in a new area of inquiry. **(p. 72)**

Exporting occurs when a company produces in its home market and then transports its products to other nations for sale. **(p. 42)**

External environment of a business involves all those activities that occur outside the organizational functions of a business. **(p. 13)**

External marketing is the implementation of marketing practices directed outside the business to create value and to form productive customer relationships. **(p. 13)**

 F

Facilitating functions are activities that assist in the execution of exchange and physical functions. **(p. 7)**

Fair prices are those consumers perceive as offering good value and meeting personal and social norms. **(p. 135)**

Fair value zone is the area on a value map where customers' perceived benefits equal the customers' perceived cost. **(p. 48)**

Fixed costs (or **overhead**) are costs that are incurred regardless of any production or sales. **(p. 136)**

Focus groups are collections of a small number of individuals recruited by specific criteria with the purpose to discuss predetermined topics with qualified moderators. **(p. 72)**

Forward auction is a market in which a buyer states what he or she is seeking to purchase and sellers respond in kind with bids (or prices). **(p. 144)**

Franchising occurs when a company sells the rights to use its brand or processes in a service business. **(p. 42)**

Frequency is the number of times an individual is exposed to an advertising message by a media vehicle. **(p. 199)**

Full-line product strategy is offering a wide range of product lines within a product portfolio. **(p. 126)**

Functional positioning is based on the attributes of products or services and their corresponding benefits and is intended to communicate how customers can solve problems or fulfill needs. **(p. 101)**

Functional use is the purpose for seeking a product. **(p. 47)**

 G

Gaming includes the online and offline inclusion of advertising and brand names into games. **(p. 200)**

General benefit statement is a broad claim about the value a product or service can deliver to a prospect. **(p. 183)**

Global marketing includes all marketing activities conducted at an international level by individuals or businesses. **(p. 40)**

Globalization is the effect of an intermingling of international cultures sharing experiences, news, and commerce. **(p. 40)**

Glocal is a slang term used to describe the tension between uniform global and customized local business strategies. **(p. 41)**

Green marketing refers to marketing efforts to product more environmentally responsible products and services. **(p. 36)**

Gross Domestic Product (GDP) measures the total dollar value of goods and services a country produces within a given year. **(p. 33)**

Gross Rating Points (GRPs) are a way for planners to approximate the impact of media decisions and are the product of reach multiplied by frequency. **(p. 202)**

Growth stage is the stage at which a product is rapidly adopted in the marketplace. Sales grow rapidly and profits peak. **(p. 128)**

Guarantees are promises made by media companies that estimated audience numbers will be achieved, or part of the cost of advertising will be retuned to the advertiser. **(p. 204)**

 H

Harvesting is the process of continuing to sell a product in spite of declining sales. **(p. 129)**

Horizontal conflict occurs between channel members at the same level in a channel (e.g., two retailers). **(p. 154)**

House file is a proprietary database of customer information collected from transactions, inquiries or surveys from the company. **(p. 187)**

 I

Idea generation is the process of formulating an idea for a new product or service. **(p. 124)**

Idea screening is the process of reviewing a product idea to ensure that it meets customer wants and company goals. **(p. 124)**

Impression refers to the single delivery of an advertising message by a media vehicle. **(p. 197)**

Inbound logistics controls the flow of products or services from suppliers to manufacturers or service providers. **(p. 155)**

Income levels are average consumer earnings used to approximate national earnings. **(p. 15)**

Incremental cost is the additional cost to produce or sell one more product or service. **(p. 145)**

Independent intermediary conducts business with many different manufacturers and customers. **(p. 160)**

Indirect channel is a channel involving one or more intermediaries between producer and customer. **(p. 151)**

Indirect exporting occurs when a firm exports its products through intermediaries in a host country. **(p. 42)**

Industrial products are products sold to business customers for their direct use or as inputs to the manufacture of other products. Classifications of industrial products include equipment, MRO products, raw materials, processed materials and services, and components. **(p. 123)**

Inelastic refers to the situation in which price elasticity is less than one or when demand is relatively nonresponsive to a change in price. **(p. 139)**

Inflation is an increase in the price of a collection of goods that represent the overall economy. **(p. 15)**

Infomercial is a television show that is a combination of an information session and a commercial. **(p. 189)**

Innovators are consumers who are the most willing to adopt innovations. They tend to be younger, better educated, and more financially secure. **(p. 129)**

Inseparability, in the context of a service, recognizes that a service cannot be separated from its means or manner of production. **(p. 121)**

Inside sales are members of the sales team who reside inside the office or company location and rarely, if ever, have face-to-face contact with customers or prospects. **(p. 184)**

Insight is the act or result of apprehending the inner nature of things, or of seeing intuitively. **(p. 69)**

Intangibility, in the context of a service, recognizes that a service cannot be perceived by the five senses (sight, hearing, touch, smell, or taste) before it is produced and consumed. **(p. 121)**

Integrated marketing communication is the careful coordination of every communication contact for message consistency across all media. **(p. 172)**

Intellectual property is a collection of non-physical assets owned by an individual or company that are the result of innovation and are legally protected from being copied or used by unauthorized parties. **(p. 90)**

Intensive distribution refers to the distribution of products in a relatively large number of locations. **(p. 153)**

Interactive include electronic media such as e-mail, Web advertising, and Web sites. **(p. 197)**

Interactive media (sometimes called **digital media**) is a broad term used to refer to electronic methods of communication where users have the ability to directly shape, interact with, or respond to media. **(p. 196)**

Intermodal is a distribution strategy that uses more than one kind of transportation mode. **(p. 157)**

Internal environment of a business involves all those activities that occur within the organizational functions in a business. **(p. 13)**

Internal marketing is the implementation of marketing practices within an organization to communicate organizational policies and practices to employees and internal stakeholders. **(p. 13)**

Internet research panel is a collection of individuals who agree, for some predetermined incentive, to participate in questionnaires on a variety of topics as determined by the owner and manager of the panel. **(p. 73)**

Interval scale is a measurement in which the numbers assigned to the characteristics of the objects or groups of objects legitimately allow a comparison of the size of the differences among and between objects. **(p. 74)**

Introduction stage is the stage at which a new product is introduced to the marketplace. Sales begin to build, but profits remain low (or even negative). **(p. 128)**

Inventory is a store of goods awaiting transport or shipping. **(p. 157)**

J

Joint ownership occurs when a company joins with an investor to build its own local business. **(p. 42)**

Joint venture refers to the situation in which one company teams with another for the purposes of conducting business and marketing. **(p. 42)**

 L

Laggards are consumers who are heavily bound by tradition and are the last to adopt an innovation. **(p. 130)**

Late majority are older and conservative consumers who avoid products they consider to be too risky. They will purchase something only if they consider it to be a necessity or when they are under some form of social pressure. **(p. 129)**

Laws are rules of conduct or action prescribed by an authority, or the binding customs or practices of a community. **(p. 37)**

Lead time is the amount of preparation time a media type requires before an advertisement can be run. **(p. 198)**

Learning is knowledge that is acquired through experiences. **(p. 60)**

Legal environment includes those factors that provide rules, and penalties for violations, designed to protect society and consumers from unfair business practices and to protect businesses from unfair competitive practices. **(p. 15)**

Levels of a product comprise all products. There are three levels—core benefits, actual product, and augmented product—and each additional level has the potential to add greater value for the customer. **(p. 122)**

Licensing is the practice of a company receiving fees or royalties from partner firms for the right to use a brand, manufacturing process, or patent. **(p. 42, 88)**

Life cycle marketing is a series of targeted messages to customers and prospects based on their experience during a sequence of events that takes place during a specific stage in life. **(p. 189)**

Life stages are similar life events experienced by groups of individuals of varying chronological and cognitive ages. **(p. 59)**

Lifestyle is a way of life that individuals express through choosing how to spend their time and personal resources. **(p. 59)**

Limited-line product strategy is focusing on one or a few product lines within a product portfolio. **(p. 126)**

Limited problem solving occurs when a consumer is prepared to exert a certain amount of effort to make a purchase decision. **(p. 64)**

Line expansions are the addition of entirely new product lines to a product mix. **(p. 127)**

Line extensions are additions to an existing product line that retains the currently utilized brand name. **(p. 88, 127)**

Logistics is the coordination of all activities related to the transportation or delivery of products and services that occur within the boundaries of a single business or organization. **(p. 154)**

Logistics manager is a person responsible for coordinating the activities of all members of a company's distribution channel. **(p. 155)**

Loss-leader pricing involves the sale of items below cost to drive floor traffic. **(p. 141)**

 M

Macroenvironment includes societal forces that are essentially uncontrollable and influence the microenvironment of a business. **(p. 14)**

Mail order is the term that describes the business of selling merchandise through the mail. **(p. 188)**

Mail-order wholesaler is a catalog, mail-order, or telephone wholesaler. **(p. 161)**

Make-goods are ads given by media companies as replacements for any media that did not run as scheduled. **(p. 204)**

Manufacturer brand is a brand owned by a manufacturer. **(p. 87)**

Manufacturer-owned intermediary provides wholesaling services for a single manufacturer. **(p. 160)**

Manufacturer's agent is an independent salesperson who carries several lines of noncompeting products. **(p. 161)**

Manufacturer's showroom is a facility where a firm's products are permanently on display. **(p. 160)**

Market is a term that refers to a place, either physical or virtual, where buyers and sellers come together to exchange goods and services. **(p. 41)**

Market structure refers to the type of marketplace situation the company faces: monopoly, oligopoly, monopolistic competition, or pure competition. **(p. 136)**

Marketing is an organizational function and a collection of processes designed to plan for, create, communicate, and deliver value to customers and to build effective customer relationships in ways that benefit the organization and its stakeholders. **(p. 3)**

Marketing audit is the comprehensive review and assessment of a business's marketing environment. **(p. 27)**

Marketing channel is a network of all parties involved in moving products or services from producers to consumers or business customers. **(p. 151)**

Marketing communication process is the way a sender encodes a marketing idea and conveys it through message and medium so receivers can decode and understand it, and then respond with feedback. **(p. 168)**

Marketing concept is an organizational philosophy dedicated to understanding and fulfilling consumer needs through the creation of value. **(p. 4)**

Marketing decision support system is the software and associated infrastructure that connects the marketing activity to company databases. **(p. 77)**

Marketing environment is a set of forces, some controllable and some uncontrollable, that influence the ability of a business to create value and attract and serve customers. **(p. 13)**

Marketing ethics are rules for evaluating marketing decisions and actions based on marketers' duties or obligations to society. **(p. 39)**

Marketing functions are activities performed both by consumers and by businesses involved in value creation for specific products or services. **(p. 7)**

Marketing information system (MIS) is a series of steps that include collection, analysis, and presentation of information for use in making marketing decisions. **(p. 77)**

Marketing intelligence system is a system that gathers, processes, assesses, and makes available marketing information in a format that allows the marketing activity to function more effectively. **(p. 77)**

Marketing mix is a group of marketing variables that a business controls with the intent of implementing a marketing strategy directed at a specific target market. **(p. 27, 209)**

Marketing-mix models evaluate the contribution that each component of a marketing program makes to changes in market performance. **(p. 213)**

Marketing-mix optimization involves assigning portions of the marketing budget to each marketing-mix element so as to maximize revenues or profits. **(p. 214)**

Marketing-mix strategy is the logic that guides the selection of a particular marketing mix to achieve marketing objectives. **(p. 211)**

Marketing objective is something that a marketing function is attempting to achieve in support of a strategic business plan. **(p. 26)**

Marketing plan is a document that includes an assessment of the marketing situation, marketing objectives, marketing strategy, and marketing initiatives. **(p. 27, 108)**

Marketing planning is the part of business planning devoted to connecting a business to the environments in which that business functions in order to accomplish the business's goals. **(p. 26)**

Marketing program is a consolidated plan of all individual marketing plans. **(p. 108)**

Marketing public relations is how marketers seek to achieve specific marketing objectives by targeting consumers with product-focused messages. **(p. 174)**

Marketing research is the acquisition and analysis of information used to identify and define marketing opportunities that connect consumers to marketers. **(p. 70)**

Marketing research system is a collection of the results of marketing research studies conducted by a company. **(p. 77)**

Marketing strategy is a statement of how a business intends to achieve its marketing objectives. **(p. 27, 124)**

Markup is a percentage or fixed amount added to the cost of a product or service. **(p. 137)**

Mass marketing is communicating a product or service message to as broad a group of people as possible with the purpose of positively influencing sales. **(p. 95)**

Maturity stage is the stage at which the product has been purchased by most potential buyers and future sales are largely replacement purchases. Sales plateau and profits begin to fall. **(p. 128)**

Measurement is the process of quantifying how much of a variable's set of features or characteristics are possessed in another variable. **(p. 74)**

Media audits measure how well each selected media vehicle performs in terms of its estimated audience delivery and cost. **(p. 204)**

Media budgets specify the total amount a firm will spend on all types of advertising media. **(p. 202)**

Media buyers negotiate and purchase media properties according to the media plan. **(p. 202)**

Media buying is the negotiation and purchase of media. **(p. 202)**

Media efficiency measures how inexpensively a media vehicle is able to communicate with a particular customer segment. **(p. 197)**

Media engagement evaluates how attentively audiences read, watch, or listen to a particular media vehicle. **(p. 197)**

Media flowcharts (or **media footprints**) are visual representations of the media plan. **(p. 202)**

Media impact is a qualitative assessment as to the value of a message exposed in a particular medium. **(p. 197)**

Media mix refers to the selection of media used for an advertising campaign as well as the budget allocated to each medium. **(p. 195)**

Media objectives are clear, unambiguous statements as to what media selection and implementation will achieve. **(p. 201)**

Media optimization is the adjustment of media plans to maximize their performance. **(p. 204)**

Media planners create media plans based on their extensive knowledge about media vehicles and expertise. **(p. 202)**

Media planning involves the creation of a media plan, which is a document that describes how an advertiser plans to spend its media budget to reach its objectives. **(p. 202)**

Media plans specify the types and amounts of media to be used, the timing of media, and the geographic concentration (national, regional, or local). **(p. 202)**

Media selection refers to the process of choosing which media types to use, when, where, and for what duration in order to execute a media plan. **(p. 202)**

Media type (or **media vehicle**) refers to a form of media used for marketing communications, including types such as broadcast, print, interactive, branded entertainment, and social networks. **(p. 196)**

Merchandise broker works as broker in markets with large numbers of small buyers and sellers. **(p. 161)**

Microenvironment includes those forces close to a company, yet outside its internal environment, that influence the ability of a business to serve its customers. **(p. 14)**

Mobile advertising refers to advertisements delivered over portable communication devices. **(p. 196)**

Modeling is a tool that many large advertisers use to guide their media planning and plan optimization. **(p. 204)**

Monopolistic competition refers to a market composed of firms with somewhat differentiated products and limited pricing power sufficient to influence the price of their own products to a degree. **(p. 136)**

Monopoly refers to a market composed of a single firm with pricing power sufficient to set the marketplace price for all products or services. **(p. 136)**

Motivation is the set of conditions that creates a drive toward a particular action to fulfill a need or want. **(p. 60)**

MRO products are products used in the maintenance, repair, and operation of a business, for example, nails, oil, or paint. **(p. 123)**

Multichannel conflict refers to conflict between different types of channels. **(p. 154)**

 N

Need is a necessity to meet an urgent requirement. **(p. 3)**

Needs segmentation allocates consumers into groups, based on their product or service needs. **(p. 97)**

Negotiated price is the result of a back-and-forth discussion between a buyer and seller regarding the final price of a product or service. **(p. 141)**

Network television refers to the broadcast of programming and paid advertising through a nationwide series of affiliate TV stations. **(p. 197)**

New product development is the process of creating, planning, testing, and commercializing products. **(p. 124)**

Niche marketing is serving a small but well-defined consumer segment. **(p. 100)**

Noise is anything that might distort, block, or otherwise prevent a message from being properly encoded, sent, decoded, received, and/or comprehended. **(p. 169)**

Nominal scale is a measurement in which numbers are assigned to characteristics of objects or groups of objects solely for identifying the objects. **(p. 74)**

Nongovernmental organizations (NGOs) are groups of private individuals that monitor the behavior of marketers or governments. **(p. 33)**

Nonpersonal media refers to media that does not involve personal contact between sender and receiver. **(p. 197)**

Nonprobability sample is a procedure where each member of a population does not have an equal chance, or, in some cases, any chance, of being selected to a sample. **(p. 76)**

Nonsampling error is any bias that emerges in the study for any reason other than sampling error. **(p. 76)**

Norms are standards of behaviors imparted to members of a particular group that define membership. **(p. 63)**

North American Industrial Classification System (NAICS) classifies businesses operating in the United States, Canada, and Mexico into groups based on their activities. **(p. 17)**

 O

Odd-even pricing is a practice that sets prices at fractional numbers, instead of whole ones. **(p. 140)**

Off-price retailer is a store that offers leftover goods, overruns, or irregular merchandise at prices below normal retail. **(p. 160)**

Oligopoly refers to a market composed of a small group of firms that share pricing power sufficient to set the marketplace price for their products or services. **(p. 136)**

Online pricing is the process of setting prices for products or services sold over the Internet or through an electronic medium. **(p. 144)**

Open-ended question is a question that allows for unrestricted survey responses. **(p. 75)**

Opinion leaders are those individuals who have the greatest influence on the attitudes and behaviors of a particular group. **(p. 63)**

Ordinal scale is a measurement in which numbers are assigned to characteristics of objects or groups of objects to reflect the order of the objects. **(p. 74)**

Organic foods are foods grown naturally without the use of pesticides or synthetic fertilizers. **(p. 37)**

Out-of-Home (OOH), or display, advertising includes media types that are encountered outside the home, such as billboards, signs, and posters. **(p. 199)**

Outbound logistics controls the movement of products from points of production (factories or service delivery points) to consumers. **(p. 155)**

Outdoor boards are large ad display panels, usually near highways or other heavily trafficked locations. **(p. 199)**

Outside lists consist of consumer information compiled by an outside company and rented to a marketer. **(p. 187)**

Outside sales are salespeople who meet face-to-face with customers and prospects. **(p. 184)**

Outsourcing is procuring certain services from a third-party supplier. **(p. 84)**

 P

Paid advertising (or **media**) refers to messages delivered to an audience on behalf of a company, organization, or individual in return for payment. **(p. 197)**

Pay-for-performance compensation strategy is the compensation system in which salespeople are paid based on the amount of sales or profits they deliver to the company. **(p. 186)**

Penetration price is a price that is set low to maximize volume and market share. **(p. 143)**

Penetration strategy is the process of offering a product at a low price to maximize sales volume and market share. **(p. 129)**

Perception is a cognitive impression of incoming stimuli that influences the individual's actions and behavior. **(p. 60)**

Perceptual map defines the market, based on consumer perceptions of attributes of competing products. **(p. 102)**

Perishability in the context of a service, recognizes that services cannot be stored for later use and must be consumed upon delivery. **(p. 121)**

Personal media refers to direct, one-to-one communication between individuals. **(p. 197)**

Personal selling is when a representative of a company interacts directly with a consumer to provide information to help the consumer make a buying decision about a product or service. **(p. 181)**

Personal selling process is the practice salespeople us to identify, research, and approach potential customers to sell products and services. **(p. 181)**

Personality involves a sense of consistency, internal causality, and personal distinctiveness. **(p. 59)**

Physical distribution (or **freight transportation**) is the process of carrying goods to customers. **(p. 157)**

Physical functions are activities that enable the flow of goods from manufacturer to consumer. **(p. 7)**

Pipeline is a transportation mode used for liquids such as oil or natural gas. **(p. 157)**

Place-based advertising is advertising that reaches people outside the home, where they work, play, or shop. **(p. 174)**

Place strategy identifies where, how, and when products and services are made available to target consumers. **(p. 27)**

Placement is the implementation of the media plan via the purchased media vehicles. **(p. 202)**

Planning process is the series of steps businesses take to determine how they will achieve their goals. **(p. 23)**

Political environment includes factors that select national leadership, create laws, and provide a process for discourse on a wide range of issues. **(p. 16)**

Population is defined as the total group of individuals who meet the criteria that is being studied. **(p. 76)**

Portfolio analysis is the process a business uses to evaluate the different combinations of products and services that the business offers based its objectives. **(p. 24)**

Portfolio management comprises all of the decisions a company makes regarding its portfolio of current and future products. It involves deciding which products to add, keep, and remove from the overall product portfolio. **(p. 126)**

Positioning is the placement of a product or service offering in the minds of consumer targets. **(p. 101)**

Posters are smaller than outdoor boards and are frequently used at bus or train stops. **(p. 199)**

Predatory pricing occurs when a firm sells its products at a low price to drive competitors out of the market. **(p. 140)**

Price is the exchange value of a product or service in the marketplace. **(p. 135)**

Price bundling occurs when two or more items are priced at a single, combined price instead of individually. **(p. 140)**

Price ceiling is the price all products in a product line must be priced below. **(p. 145)**

Price discrimination occurs when a firm injures competition by charging different prices to different members of its distribution channel. **(p. 140)**

Price elasticity is the measure of a percentage change in quantity demanded for a product, relative to a percentage change in its price. **(p. 139)**

Price fixing occurs when two or more companies discuss prices in an effort to raise the market price for their products. **(p. 140)**

Price floor is the price above which all products in a product line must be priced. **(p. 145)**

Price lining (or **tiered pricing**, **versioning**) is a strategy used to create different prices for different, but related, products or services. **(p. 144)**

Price–quality ratio is the ratio between the price of a product and its perceived quality. (**p. 136**)

Price war occurs when businesses cut prices to take sales from competitors. (**p. 84**)

Pricing objectives are goals that keep marketing actions in alignment with overall business objectives. (**p. 142**)

Pricing power is the ability of a firm to establish a higher price than its competitors without losing significant market share. (**p. 136**)

Pricing practices are considerations (such as legal requirements or bidding practices) that must be taken into account when establishing a price for a product or service. (**p. 139**)

Pricing strategy identifies what a business will charge for its products and services. (**p. 27, 142**)

Primary data is information that is collected to address a current research question. (**p. 71**)

Print media include newspapers, magazines, and direct mail. (**p. 197**)

Privacy policy is a company's practice as it relates to renting customer information to other companies. (**p. 190**)

Private label brand is a brand owned by a reseller or retailer. (**pp. 87–88**)

Probability sample is a procedure where each member of a population has a known and nonzero chance of possibly being selected to a sample. (**p. 76**)

Processed materials and services are products or services used in the production of finished products or services, for example, lumber, steel, or market research. (**p. 123**)

Product design is a product's style, tactile appeal, and usability. (**p. 126**)

Product life cycle (PLC) is the model that describes the evolution of a product's sales and profits throughout its lifetime. The stages of the product life cycle are as follows: Introduction, Growth, Maturity, and Decline. (**p. 128**)

Product line is a group of closely related products. (**p. 126**)

Product mix depth is the number of versions of products within a product line. (**p. 126**)

Product mix length is the total number of products a company offers. (**p. 126**)

Product mix width is the number of product lines a company offers. (**p. 126**)

Product placement is an arrangement in which the company has its brand or product appear in a movie or another entertainment vehicle. (**p. 174**)

Product portfolio is the collection of all products and services offered by a company (also called a product mix). (**p. 126**)

Product strategy identifies the product and service portfolio, including packaging, branding, and warranty for its target market. (**p. 27**)

Product style is the visual and aesthetic appearance of a product. (**p. 126**)

Production orientation reflects a business focus on efficient production and distribution with little emphasis on any marketing strategy. (**p. 5**)

Products are items often used or consumed for personal or business use or items used to produce other items that are resold. (**p. 121**)

Profit margin is the difference between the price of a product and its total cost per unit. (**p. 136**)

Promotion strategy identifies how a business communicates product or service benefits and value to its target market. (**p. 27**)

Promotional mix is the specific combination of communication tools selected for a particular influence strategy. (**p. 168**)

Promotional pricing is the strategy of using price as a promotional tool to drive customer awareness and sales. (**p. 141**)

Prospecting is the process of researching multiple sources to find potential customers or prospects. (**p. 182**)

Psychographic segmentation assigns buyers into different groups, based on lifestyle, class, or personality characteristics. (**p. 96**)

Psychology involves the study of the mind. (**p. 57**)

Public relations is two-way communication to improve mutual understanding and positively influence relationships between the marketer and its internal and external publics. (**p. 174**)

Publicity is generating unpaid, positive media coverage about a company or its products. (**p. 174**)

Publics are the target audiences of public relations; the people inside or outside the company who have a "stake" in what it does. (**p. 174**)

Puffery refers to claims of product superiority that cannot be proven as true or false. (**p. 38**)

Pull strategy aims to have consumers ask retailers and wholesalers for a product, thus pulling it through the marketing channel. (**p. 172**)

Pure competition refers to a market composed of a large number of firms that together lack sufficient pricing power to influence the market price for their products. (**p. 136**)

Pure research attempts to expand understanding of the unknown. (**p. 70**)

Push strategy aims to have retailers and wholesalers order the product and push it through the channel to consumers. (**p. 172**)

 Q

Qualify is the process of determining whether a prospect has the potential to become a customer. (**p. 183**)

Qualitative research is a collection of techniques designed to identify and interpret information obtained through the observation of people. (**p. 72**)

Quantitative research is a process to collect a large number of responses using a standardized questionnaire where the results can be summarized into numbers for statistical analysis. (**p. 72**)

Quantity discount is a discount per item purchased that is given to customers buying a larger quantity of a product. (**p. 146**)

Question Marks are products or services with low relative market share in a sector with high growth. (**p. 25**)

Questionnaire is an organized set of questions that a researcher desires that respondents answer. (**p. 74**)

Quotas are limits on the amount of a product that can be imported into a country. (**p. 142**)

Quotation is a supplier's response to an RFQ from a potential customer. (**p. 141**)

 R

Rack jobber handles displays, inventory, and merchandise for a retailer. (**p. 161**)

Rate cards are officially published prices for different types of media. (**p. 202**)

Ratings are the percentage of the total available audience watching a TV show or tuned in to a radio program. (**p. 197**)

Ratio scale is a measurement in which the numbers assigned to the characteristics of the objects have an identifiable absolute zero. (**p. 74**)

Raw materials are unfinished products that are processed for use in the manufacture of a finished product, for example, wood, wheat, or iron ore. (**p. 123**)

Reach is a measure of the number of people who could potentially receive an ad through a particular media vehicle. (**p. 197**)

Rebate is a cash payment made back to a customer who has purchased his or her products at full price. **(p. 146)**

Reference group consists of people who directly or indirectly influence how an individual feels about a particular topic. **(p. 63)**

Regulations are rules or orders issued by an official government agency with proper authority that carries the force of law. **(p. 37)**

Reinforcement is a reduction in drive resulting from a positive response experience. **(p. 61)**

Relationship marketing is the process of developing and enhancing long-term relationships with profitable customers. **(p. 51)**

Relationship orientation reflects a business focus on creating value-added relationships with suppliers and consumers. **(p. 6)**

Reliability is the level of consistency of a measurement. **(p. 76)**

Request for quote (RFQ) is a document a buyer sends to a potential supplier that outlines the criteria for the goods or services to be purchased. **(p. 141)**

Research is the studious inquiry or examination; especially, investigation or experimentation aimed at the discovery and interpretation of facts, revision of accepted theories or laws in the light of new facts, or practical application of such new or revised theories or laws. **(p. 70)**

Research design is a framework or plan for a study that guides the collection and analysis of the data. **(p. 72)**

Research question is the question the research is designed to answer. **(p. 71)**

Response is a consumer's reaction to his or her drive and cues. **(p. 61)**

Retailing involves the sale of products or services to consumers. **(p. 158)**

Return on marketing investment (ROMI) is the impact on business performance resulting from executing specific marketing activities. **(p. 28)**

Reverse auction is a market in which a buyer states what he or she is seeking to purchase, as well as the price he or she is willing to pay. **(p. 144)**

Reverse logistics addresses the methods consumers use to send products backward through a channel for return or repair. **(p. 155)**

RFID (radio frequency identification) is an electronic chip and an antenna that can identify the precise physical location of a product. **(p. 158)**

Roles are specific actions expected from someone in a group as a member or from a particular position held. **(p. 63)**

Routine response problem solving occurs when a consumer has a well-developed process associated with fulfilling a need or want. **(p. 64)**

 S

Sales branch maintains inventory for a company in a geographic area. **(p. 160)**

Sales management is the process of planning, implementing, and controlling the personal selling function. **(p. 184)**

Sales management process is the method used by companies to plan, implement, and control the selling function. **(p. 185)**

Sales manager is the person responsible for organizing, motivating, and leading a team of salespeople and is also responsible for meeting the company's sales objectives. **(p. 184)**

Sales office provides selling services for a company in a geographic area. **(p. 160)**

Sales orientation reflects a business focus on advertising and personal selling to create demand and move product inventory. **(p. 5)**

Sales promotion is marketer-controlled communication to stimulate immediate audience response by enhancing the value of an offering for a limited time. **(p. 175)**

Sample is defined as a specific part of the population that is selected to the represent the population. **(p. 76)**

Sample error refers to any differences between the sample results and the actual results that would emerge from a census of the population. **(p. 76)**

Sample plan identifies who will be sampled, how many people will be sampled, and the procedure that will be used for sampling. **(p. 76)**

Sampling procedure involves selecting either a probability sample or a nonprobability sample as part of your sample plan. **(p. 76)**

Scatter buys are ads that are not purchased in advance via an upfront market, but are secured on a quarterly basis. **(p. 202)**

Search engine optimization is the process of enhancing Web site traffic through either organic or compensated means. **(p. 101)**

Search marketing includes techniques such as paying for inclusion in specific search results on search engines. **(p. 196)**

Secondary data is information that has been previously collected for another purpose. **(p. 71)**

Segmentation (also referred to as **market segmentation**) is the division of consumer markets into meaningful and distinct customer groups. **(p. 95)**

Segmentation base is a group of characteristics that is used to assign segment members. **(p. 96)**

Selective distribution refers to the distribution of products in relatively few locations. **(p. 153)**

Self-identity is the understanding by an individual that he or she is unique. **(p. 59)**

Selling agent handles all marketing functions for a small manufacturer. **(p. 161)**

Services are activities that deliver benefits to consumers or businesses. **(p. 121)**

Shipper is the owner of goods being distributed. **(p. 157)**

Shopping products are products that are purchased with a moderate amount of shopping effort, for example, clothing, linens, housewares. **(p. 122)**

Significant problem solving occurs when a consumer is prepared to commit considerable effort to make a purchase decision. **(p. 64)**

Skimming price is a price that is set high in order to maximize revenue or profit. **(p. 143)**

Skimming strategy is the process of offering a product at a high price to maximize return. **(p. 129)**

Social and cultural environment includes factors that relate marketing to the needs and wants of society and culture. **(p. 15)**

Social classes are characteristics that distinguish certain members of a society from others, based on a variety of factors, including wealth, vocation, education, power, place of residence, and ancestry. **(p. 63)**

Social concept asserts that marketing techniques may be employed for more than selling things and making a profit. **(p. 39)**

Social networks, such as Facebook and MySpace, connect people with common interests and those who are looking to make friends online. **(p. 200)**

Social psychology is the process to understand social phenomena and their influence on social behavior. **(p. 57)**

Social responsibility refers to a concern for how a person's (or company's) actions might affect the interests of others. **(p. 39)**

Society refers to a community, nation, or group that shares common traditions, institutions, activities, and interests. **(p. 33)**

Specialty advertising is advertising in which the marketer gives away small items bearing its name or logo to keep the audience thinking of the brand and feeling good about it. **(p. 174)**

Specialty products are products with unique characteristics that are purchased with a high degree of shopping effort, for example, luxury items, vacations, and homes. **(p. 122)**

Specialty store offers a narrow product line within a specialized category. **(p. 160)**

Specific benefit statement is a precise claim about the value a product or service can deliver to a prospect. **(p. 183)**

Spill-in occurs when ads from outside a test market "spill into" the test market area. **(p. 204)**

Spill-out happens whenever ads meant for a test market "spill out" and touch people in adjacent markets. **(p. 204)**

Sponsorship is a way of publicly associating a brand with an event or activity that the company supports financially. **(p. 176)**

Stars represent products or services with high growth and high market share. **(p. 25)**

Status is the relative position of one individual relative to others. **(p. 63)**

Sticker price or MSRP (manufacturer's suggested retail price) is the quoted or official price for a product. **(p. 141)**

Stock-keeping unit (SKU) is a unique identification number used to track and organize products. **(p. 158)**

Storefront pricing (also called **offline pricing**) refers to prices established for products or services sold through traditional sales channels like grocery stores, mass merchandisers, or other "brick and mortar" businesses. **(p. 144)**

Strategic planning determines the overall goals of the business and the steps the business will take to achieve those goals. **(p. 24)**

Strong brand occupies a distinct position in consumers' minds based on relevant benefits and creates an emotional connection between businesses and consumers. **(p. 86)**

Structured interviews are a series of discussions held between a trained interviewer and individuals, on a one-on-one basis, recruited by specific criteria, with the purpose to discuss predetermined topics. **(p. 72)**

Subcultures are groups of people, within a broader society, who share similar behaviors and values. **(p. 62)**

Subliminal perception is the processing of stimuli by a recipient who is not aware of the stimuli being received. **(p. 60)**

Supermarket is a large store that offers food and household products at low prices. **(p. 160)**

Superstore is a large store that offers a wide range of products and services, or offers a "category killer" that concentrates on a deep assortment of products within a specific category. **(p. 160)**

Supply chain management is the management of all firms or organizations, both inside and outside a company, that impact the distribution process. **(p. 155)**

Sustainability is a term used to describe practices that combine economic growth with careful stewardship of our natural resources and the environment. **(p. 39)**

SWOT analysis is a tool that helps identify business strengths, weaknesses, opportunities, and threats. **(p. 27)**

Symbolic positioning is based on characteristics of the brand that enhance the self-esteem of customers. **(p. 101)**

Syndicated research is information collected on a regular basis using standardized procedures and sold to multiple customers from a related industry. **(p. 71)**

Systems are groups of interacting related parts that perform a specific function. **(p. 23)**

 T

Tactical planning is the process of developing actions for various functions within a business to support implementing a business's strategic plan. **(p. 24)**

Target market is a group of consumers that a business determines to be the most viable for its products or services. **(p. 27)**

Targeting (also referred to as **market targeting**) is the process of evaluating and selecting the most viable market segment to enter. **(p. 98)**

Tariff is a schedule of duties (or fees) applied to goods and services from foreign countries. **(p. 142)**

Task-and-objective is an approach to media budgeting that allocates dollars sufficient to attain media objectives. **(p. 201)**

Technological environment includes factors that influence marketing, based on scientific actions and innovation. **(p. 16)**

Telemarketing is a phone call placed to a specific consumer to offer products or services for sale. **(p. 189)**

Test marketing is the process of developing prototypes of the product and using market research to evaluate customer acceptance. **(p. 125)**

Third-party logistics company (3PL) manages all or part of another company's supply chain logistics. **(p. 156)**

Time-shifting is the practice of recording a television program at one time to replay it at another. **(p. 198)**

Total cost is the sum of fixed and variable costs. **(p. 136)**

Trade-in is the cash value given to a customer when he or she offers his or her own product in trade toward a new purchase. **(p. 146)**

Trade sales promotion aims to get retail and wholesale buyers to buy an existing product, stock a new product, feature a particular product, or encourage salespeople to push a certain product. **(p. 175)**

Transit advertising appears on buses, trains, air terminals, taxis, and wherever people are being transported from one place to another. **(p. 200)**

Transportation management systems (TMS) are software programs used to automate the shipping process. **(p. 157)**

Truck jobber delivers food and tobacco items to retailers. **(p. 161)**

Turnover is the percentage of the sales force that leaves a company in one year. **(p. 181)**

 U

Undifferentiated marketing is when a company treats the market as a whole, focusing on what is common to the needs of customers rather than on what is different. **(p. 99)**

Unemployment levels are the number of unemployed persons divided by the aggregate labor force. **(p. 15)**

Unique selling proposition (USP) is an expression of the uniqueness of a brand. **(p. 101)**

United States Patent and Trademark Office (USPTO) is a federal agency responsible for assigning rights for limited times to individuals or companies to use innovations. **(p. 90)**

Universal Product Code (or **UPC**) is the standard format for retail bar codes. **(p. 158)**

Unpaid advertising (or **media**) is the delivery of messages without payment in return. **(p. 197)**

Unsought products are products that consumers do not usually search for without an immediate problem or prompting, for example, life insurance, funerals, or legal services. **(p. 122)**

Upfront markets are long-lead marketplaces where TV networks and advertisers negotiate media prices for the fourth quarter of the current year plus the first three quarters of the following year. **(p. 202)**

User-generated content such as social networks, for example, Facebook or MySpace, user blogs, and filesharing, for example, Flickr and Snapfish, are sources of word-of-mouth communications and advertising. **(p. 200)**

Utility is the satisfaction received from owning or consuming a product or service. **(p. 3)**

 V

Validity is the strength of a conclusion. **(p. 76)**

Value is the benefits that exceed the cost of products, services, or other items. **(p. 3)**

Value map is a graphical representation of the ratio between customers' perceived benefits and the perceived total cost of a product. **(p. 48)**

Values segmentation considers what customers prefer and what motivates customer response to marketing activities. **(p. 97)**

Variability, in the context of a service, recognizes that service quality may vary from experience to experience. **(p. 121)**

Variable costs are costs directly attributable to the production of a product or the delivery of a service. **(p. 136)**

Vertical conflict refers to conflict between channel members at different levels in a channel (e.g., a wholesaler and a retailer). **(p. 154)**

Vertical Marketing System (VMS) is a channel that is vertically integrated based on acquisition or formal agreement, or by a firm developing its own distribution capabilities. **(p. 153)**

Viral marketing stimulates word of mouth through activities that encourage consumers to electronically share a company's marketing message with friends. **(p. 171)**

 W

Want is a desire for something that is not essential. **(p. 3)**

Warehouse is a physical facility used primarily for the storage of goods held in anticipation of sale or transfer within the marketing channel. **(p. 157)**

Wholesaling involves the sorting, storing, and reselling of products to retailers or businesses. **(p. 158)**

Word of mouth is communication between consumers about a brand, marketing offer, or marketing message. **(p. 171)**

Index

▼ NAME INDEX

▼ SUBJECT INDEX